WETENSKAPLIKE BYDRAES OF THE PU FOR CHE
Series F: Institute for the Advancement of Calvinism

HEARTBEAT

Taking the pulse of our Christian theological and philosophical heritage

Dr. B.J. van der Walt

Potchefstroom University
Potchefstroom
1978

F.3: Collections
Number 9

PRINTED BY PRO REGE, POTCHEFSTROOM

TABLE OF CONTENTS

PREFACE

I gladly comply with the request of my friend, Dr. B.J. van der Walt, to introduce this collection of essays with a preface. There are several reasons why I look forward to the publication of these essays, written by him over the past few years, but I shall confine myself to three rather briefly.

In the first place, these essays bear witness to his wide philosophical interests, his inexhaustible zest for collecting data and his singular detective ability in searching for facts and extracting the essentials. Although this group of published and unpublished essays shows differences of purpose and quality — some being scholarly contributions to congresses or written for special occasions, and others intended more as résumés catering for the needs of the undergraduate — each in its own way contributes relevant data to a characteristic framework, which not only acquaints the interested reader with central themes in the field of study, but also orientates him concerning priorities in contemporary scholarly discussion. This collection of articles does not cover all possible subjects. It, however, contains a number of connected and relevant tangents, which indicate the contours of essential studies.

Secondly, and especially in those cases where the purpose of specific essays is not to present new facts or theories to the critical eye of the specialist, a suggestive flash of insight often compels renewed consideration. Consequently this collection becomes a useful source for further study and a critical evaluation of various approaches to the cultural and spiritual heritage of the West, thus filling part of an existing gap in Christian academic circles.

Thirdly, this collection now provides an opportunity of putting the writer's typical methods and priorities in perspective, enabling one to assess them afresh. These essays also reveal the writer's theoretic stance within the academic community of Calvinistic Philosophy, by pinpointing his basic approach and characteristic emphases. I believe that Calvinistic Philosophy has already reached such a stage of maturity that methodological and individual preferences can not only be tolerated without anxiety, but also criticized, honed to shape, and evaluated as a legitimate 'competitor' in this scientific discipline.

I hope, too, that the publication of these essays will on the one hand stimulate further research into the areas covered in this collection, as well as advance the use and development of fitting scholarly 'tools'. On the other hand I trust that this occasion may also encourage the writer to review the fruits of his pen in their new context, to scan his overall approach and handling of method, to consider both the appreciative and critical reactions of his colleagues, and finally to complement these essays with further systematic and historical studies of our Christian heritage.

Prof. N.T. van der Merwe
Department of Philosophy,
Potchefstroom University for
Christian Higher Education

INTRODUCTION

The subtitle of this volume explains its title *(Heartbeat)*. If I had to trace a recurring theme through all the essays, it would be the following. The central idea in most of the articles is the taking of the pulse of our past by means of a "cardiogram". It is intriguing to glance at paintings of great minds from our Christian past and to see what they looked like. And their life histories often make absorbing reading. But this is not sufficient. We would also very much like to know if their "hearts were in the right place", what the deepest motives of their thoughts and deeds were. It appears from Calvin's crest — a hand offering a burning heart to God with the inscription *prompte et sincère*, ready and sincere* — that he wanted to sacrifice his heart, his whole being, to the Lord.

The question posed in most of these articles is whether the various thinkers from our Christian past also succeeded in serving God in their mental labours with their *whole* heart. Did they succeed in manifesting their devoted intentions in the fruits of their intellectual endeavour? Did the Word of God attain its rightful place in their thought, or was it sometimes robbed of power because unbiblical thought patterns were given in to?

It is no luxury to busy ourselves with our theological and philosophical past. It can be of inestimable value to keep our fingers on the pulse of the past: in many areas we still wrestle with basically the same problems as our predecessors. **

Most of these essays were never written with a wide readership in mind. Many of them were engendered of necessity when I had to lecture in English for the first time at the University of Fort Hare (an institution for the Xhosa speaking Bantu of the Ciskei). Later some of the lecture notes (sometimes slightly adapted) appeared in South African periodicals. Basically, therefore, they are elementary essays, meant for undergraduate students. (A number of essays that were read as papers at conferences, or are short extracts from my M.A. and D.Phil. theses are exceptions.)

The need for publications in English, which once again became apparent from the activities of the "Clearing House" (established at the

---

* In a letter to Farel (24/10/1540) Calvin wrote: "... because I am aware of the fact that I am not my own master, I am presenting my slaughtered heart as sacrifice to the Lord" (quoniam non esse mei juris memini, cor meum velut mactatum Domino in sacrificium offero).

** This collection is to be followed by a second with the title *Horizon — surveying a route for contemporary Christian thought* (1978). The eighteen essays of *Horizon* are directed more towards the present, as the subtitle suggests.

The contents of *Horizon* appears at the end of this volume.

Potchefstroom University for Christian Higher Education after the First International Conference of Reformed Institutions for Christian Higher Education, 9-13 September 1975, at Potchefstroom), was the direct motive for the preparation of this volume. For this purpose a number of magazine articles have been translated (and sometimes slightly adapted) from Afrikaans into English. My thanks to Mr. D.N.R. Levey who has undertaken most of the translation.

Against the background of the origin of this collection, it must be understood that there will sometimes be overlapping in the content of the collected articles.

In spite of all the shortcomings I still hope that the collection — or a part thereof — may be of value to someone. I am aware of the fact that for many it will not contain anything new. However, recent international contacts have made me realize that there are still people (especially in Africa and Eastern Countries) who will be able to profit from the content. This collection has been compiled especially with such readers in mind.

In conclusion a word of thanks to my friend, Prof. N.T. van der Merwe, who was prepared to link his name to this book by way of a "Preface".

B.J. van der Walt

1. HISTORIOGRAPHY OF PHILOSOPHY
THE CONSISTENT PROBLEM-HISTORIC METHOD*

The history of Philosophy reflects a developing and continuously changing process. Philosophical movements grow and decline; they stimulate others to come into existence or they themselves are absorbed by other movements. For instance, one philosopher reacted to another: philosopher A founded a school; Pupil B modified his teacher's opinion; Pupil C rejected most of it because of the strong influence of another philosopher; and both students B and C acquired their own disciples...

To unravel this complicated philosophical process is the difficult task of the historian of philosophy.

1. CURRENT METHODS OF STUDYING THE HISTORY OF PHILO-SOPHY

In spite of the more than two thousand years of Philosophic Historiography it is not surprising that no absolutely satisfactory historiographical method has been invented. The chronological and genetic methods, the method of main currents or schools, the conceptual method, the comparative as well as the psychological-nationalistic method — to mention only a few — provided us with valuable information about the intricate history of Philosophy. Not one of them, however, proved to be comprehensive enough to untangle the complicated history of human thought. Because every historiography of Philosophy is determined by the underlying philosophical presuppositions of the personal philosophy of the historiographer, it is necessarily one-sided. It will not be difficult to illustrate this in the case of the historiographical methodologies, for instance, of K. Praechter, B. Geyer, M. Frischeisen-Köhler and W. Moog, T.K. Oesterreich[1], W. Windelband

---

* Originally published in *Tydskrif vir Christelike Wetenskap*, 9:163-184, 1973.

This essay is placed at the beginning of this volume with historical studies as it gives a brief outline of the method I have applied in some of the other essays. Cognisance of its contents will therefore facilitate a better comprehension of what follows.

1. Cf. the famous *Friedrich Ueberwegs Grundriss der Geschichte der Philosophie.*

and H. Heimsoeth[2], R. Falkenberg[3], N. Hartmann[4], R. Höningswald[5], C.B. Spruyt[6], F. Sassen[7], E. Brehier[8] and F. Copleston[9] — to name but a few of the greater works in this field.

2. VOLLENHOVEN'S CONSISTENT PROBLEM-HISTORIC METHOD

This also applies to the consistent problem-historic method, which has definite limits. As one of the most recent contemporary methods of philosophical historiography it may, however, be of great help in giving us the skeleton of a philosopher's system. Furthermore, in applying this method, we are provided with a general insight into the place of a thinker in the history of philosophy as well as his relation to others. In spite of the fact that the consistent problem-historic method provides us merely with a very general and abstract insight into the conceptual framework within which a philosopher worked, as an analytic tool at the beginning of one's enquiries, this method considerably facilitates our task and can be very illuminating as regards the complicated problem-patterns in the history of philosophy.

Together with Prof. Dr. H. Dooyeweerd Prof. Dr. D.H. Th. Vollenhoven inaugurated the "Vereniging voor Calvinistische Wijsbegeerte" in 1935 and for about 30 years Vollenhoven acted as chairman of this growing association which has members, not only from Holland, but from all over the world. In 1973 a special volume of *Philosophia Reformata* (one of the publications of the association) comprising contributions of Vollenhoven's alumni in different parts of the world was dedicated to him to commemo-

2. Cf. their wellknown *Lehrbuch der Philosophie* (15th impression, 1957).

3. Cf. his *Geschichte der Neueren Philosophie* (1902[4]).

4. Cf. his article "Zur methode der Philosophiegeschichte". *Kant Studien*, Vol. 15, p. 459-485, 1910. (Reprinted in his *Kleinere Schriften*, Vol. III, p. 1-30) as well as his study "Der philosophische Gedanke und seine Geschichte." *Abhandlungen der Preussichen Akademie der Wissenschaften*, 1936. (Reprinted in his *Kleinere Schriften*, Vol. II, p. 1-47).

5. Cf. especially the introduction to his book *Philosophie der Altertums. Problemgeschichtliche und systematische Untersuchungen* (1917).

6. Cf. his *Geschiedenis der Wijsbegeerte* (1905).

7. Cf. his five volume history of Philosophy in Dutch in many reprints. (Antwerpen, Standaard-Boekhandel).

8. Cf. *Histoire de la Philosophie*. (1947-1948) in five volumes.

9. Cf. his comprehensive *A History of Philosophy* (in many reprints).

rate his 80th anniversary.

This the second publication dedicated to Vollenhoven. In 1951 a number of his pupils contributed to the volume *Wetenschappelijke bijdragen door leerlingen van Dr. D.H. Th. Vollenhoven aangeboden ter gelegenheid van zijn 25-jarig hoogleeraarschap aan de Vrije Universiteit* (Franeker, Wever).

This essay is also meant as a tribute to one of our *philosophiae calvinianae pater*, for Christian scholars in South Africa are also greatly indebted to him.

Vollenhoven's major contribution is in the field of the Historiography of philosophy. It seemed fitting therefore to write an essay on his historiographic methodology, particularly in view of the fact that this significant contribution of Vollenhoven is not yet wellknown in South Africa. It may also be of importance outside South Africa because all the studies on this method (see Bibliography at the end) — even the one article Vollenhoven himself wrote on the method — are either demonstrations of the method in action or a discussion of the basic assumptions, theses or principles underlying the method. To my knowledge no systematic explanation, together with explanatory diagrams, is available in either Dutch or English.

This essay endeavours to contribute towards an understanding of the problem-historic method. It will, however, be impossible to go into the details of the method. This paper will merely endeavour to give a bird's eye view. In this elementary introduction it is impossible to go into the complexity, richness and circumspection of or latest developments in Vollenhoven's historiographical analysis. For more detail the interested reader is referred to the bibliography at the end of this essay — in the first place, of course, Vollenhoven's own publications.

3. REQUIREMENTS FOR A HISTORIOGRAPHICAL METHOD

To arrive at scientific knowledge the individual as knower must direct his knowing activity on the knowable. In this process of acquiring knowledge method plays an important role. The method is the road which the knower treads in his knowing activity; it is the manner whereby the knowing activity comes to a result, knowledge, about the knowable.

God calls us to serve Him in every field of life — even in our scientific endeavours. Various requirements are necessary for a Christian scientific result on the part of the *knower*, the *knowable* and the *knowing activity*.

For a Christian Science it is necessary that the knower be a Christian. His heart must be taken by God in mutual love for God, and he must strive in his knowing activity to serve and obey God.

A Christian Science presupposes further that the field of investigation (the *knowable*) shall be illuminated by the light of the Word of God. Only if the knowable, which has been obscured and has become abnormal (due to the fall into sin of the whole creation), is viewed in the light of the Bible, can it be correctly seen.

When the knower is a Christian, the *knowing* activity (which comes from the heart and is religiously determined) will also differ from that of a non-Christian scientist.

This knowing activity follows a definite method which agrees or is in accordance with the nature of the field of investigation. When this area of scientific study is viewed in the light of God's Word the method will thus also differ from instances where it it not the case. The field of study in which we are engaged is the History of Philosophy. Our field of investigation therefore is a branch of Philosophy. The method to be applied in our study of the History of Philosophy will thus be determined by this specific field under discussion. None of the current methods for the study of the History of Philosophy fulfil this first requirement, namely, that the method should be *completely* in accordance with its field of investigation.

Apart from the fact that the current methods are not doing justice to the field of investigation there is another difference in our proposed method for the study of the History of Philosophy. The people who use the abovementioned methods (cf. point 1) were either non-Christians or Christians who were proponents of so-called neutral scientific endeavour. They did not give the Bible its rightful place in their scientific methods. When we base our premises on the Bible, so as to enlighten our field of investigation, our method is also determined by it, and thus we have a Christian approach to the History of Philosophy.

4. THE TWO MAIN QUESTIONS (STREAM AND TYPE) OF THE CONSISTENT PROBLEM-HISTORIC METHOD

Our method requires that certain questions be put to every philosopher in the history of Philosophy.

The first question concerns his attitude towards Scripture and the second question is asked according to the light which Scripture sheds on the reality which every philosopher investigates.

4.1 The first question concerned: *Does the Word of God find its rightful place in the philosophy?*

Our first question stems from the query as to whether a person's heart is or is not directed towards obeying God. This religious attitude (being directed towards or against God) determines man's whole life, because from his heart comes the outflow of all his activities. The religious standpoint is thus also decisive for his philosophical conception which is the result of his philosophical activity.

In the Books of the Chronicles we have a clear example. Only certain things about a king are mentioned and for the rest the reader is referred to "The Books of the Kings of Judah and Israel" (Cf. II Chronicles 32:32). In the days of the kings "notebooks" were kept from which the writer of the Chronicles selected those deeds in which it was obvious how a certain king's heart was towards God. It was for him the most important thing in his historiography.

The place which is given to the Word of God in a certain philosophy thus reveals to us what the attitude of a philosopher was towards the God of the Word.

In the study of the philosophy of each thinker the primary question is: What happened to the Word of God in his philosophy? Concerning this question there are two possible answers: Either the revelation of God's Word received its rightful place or it did not. We will seldom find the first answer in the History of Philosophy. The second (the Word of God did not receive its appropriate place) is the dominant answer and it includes two different attitudes: either the Word of God is unrightfully and completely disregarded (pagan thought), or the Word is acknowledged but does not find its appropriate place because it was accommodated to or synthesized with the unscriptural thoughts of pagan philosophy.

Taking the period of synthetic thought as our starting point these three answers to our first question make it possible to divide the History of Western Philosophy into three great periods:

From about 700 B.C. to 40 A.D., we get the *period before synthesis* (Ancient Greek, Hellenistic and Roman thought).

From ± 40 A.D. to ± 1600 we have the *period of synthesis* (Patristic and Medieval Philosophy).

From ± 1600 to the present time we call the *anti-synthetic period* (Modern and Contemporary Philosophy).

Pre-Synthetic Thought

Before the coming of Christ the Word of God was confined more or less to Israel, the elected. The Greeks and Romans who made such a very important contribution to Philosophy knew nothing about the Bible. They were pagans in their philosophy also.

Synthetic Thought

Before the coming of Christ there already existed types of synthesis or compromise between heathendom and part of the Bible, viz., the Old Testament. (Compare, for instance, Philo of Alexandria and Mohammedanism). This synthesis, however, happened on a small scale because God limited His Word of Revelation to the patriarchs and later on to the elected nation (Israel). Christianity and paganism still developed apart from each other.

After the coming of Christ and the descent of the Holy Spirit, the Gospel was no longer restricted to the Jews only, but was preached all over Europe. Then the paths of Christianity and heathendom met and the synthesis between paganism and Christianity occurred on a considerable scale.

This synthetic thought started in the main quite innocently. If someone from the Greek or Roman world was converted to believe in God through His Word, he could not immediately reject his pagan education — no converted heathen can suddenly think and live completely as a Christian. It frequently takes ages to overcome paganism.

This is the origin of the dilemma: What is the relation between my belief, the Word of God, the service of God, etc., on the one hand and my pagan education (including the pagan philosophical edcuation) on the other? How can the two be reconciled?

Anti-Synthetic Thought

The synthesis between Christian and pagan thought could not, in the long run, endure. The paths of Christian and pagan thought separated again when it became clear that they could not co-exist. There were, however, two different motives for this anti-synthetical philosophy:

In the *anti-synthetic leftish* orientated thought we find those who, in their philosophical thought, broke with the synthetic attitude, because they wanted to distantiate themselves from the Word of God. The adherents or representatives of this direction were not necessarily unbelievers; they were perhaps Christians who did not believe that the Bible has relevance for science.

The direction of thought which may be characterized as *anti-synthetic right* wanted to break with the synthetic attitude of thought so as to give to Scripture its legitimate place in science.

Both of these anti-synthetic directions have passed through the synthetic period of thought and that is why modern (anti-synthetic left) heathendom is not the same as the heathendom of Ancient thought, and (anti-synthetic right) Christian thought is not the same as the synthetic Christianity of the Middle Ages. The so-called "post-Christian paganism" of today has to get rid of a great deal of Christian left-overs and the radical Christian philosophy has just started (from ± 1930) to discard the pagan thoughts which infected it.

It is clear that our first question in connection with every philosophy indicates the decisive meaning of the coming of Christ. His life and work is the

Diagram 1: The main streams in the history of western philosophy.

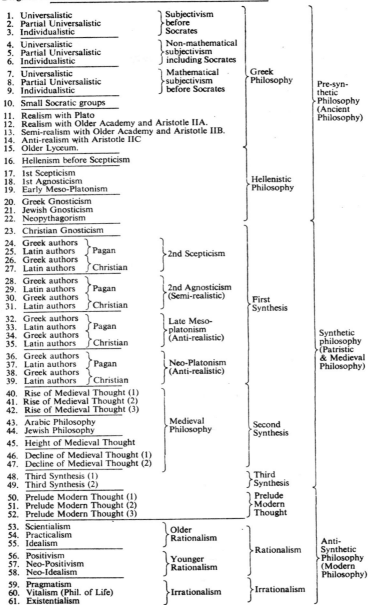

1. Universalistic 2. Partial Universalistic 3. Individualistic	Subjectivism before Socrates				
4. Universalistic 5. Partial Universalistic 6. Individualistic	Non-mathematical subjectivism including Socrates				
7. Universalistic 8. Partial Universalistic 9. Individualistic	Mathematical subjectivism before Socrates	Greek Philosophy			
10. Small Socratic groups			Pre-syn- thetic Philosophy (Ancient Philosophy)		
11. Realism with Plato 12. Realism with Older Academy and Aristotle IIA. 13. Semi-realism with Older Academy and Aristotle IIB. 14. Anti-realism with Aristotle IIC 15. Older Lyceum.					
16. Hellenism before Scepticism					
17. 1st Scepticism 18. 1st Agnosticism 19. Early Meso-Platonism		Hellenistic Philosophy			
20. Greek Gnosticism 21. Jewish Gnosticism 22. Neopythagorism					
23. Christian Gnosticism					
24. Greek authors 25. Latin authors — Pagan 26. Greek authors 27. Latin authors — Christian	2nd Scepticism				
28. Greek authors 29. Latin authors — Pagan 30. Greek authors 31. Latin authors — Christian	2nd Agnosticism (Semi-realistic)	First Synthesis			
32. Greek authors 33. Latin authors — Pagan 34. Greek authors 35. Latin authors — Christian	Late Meso- platonism (Anti-realistic)		Synthetic philosophy (Patristic & Medieval Philosophy)		
36. Greek authors 37. Latin authors — Pagan 38. Greek authors 39. Latin authors — Christian	Neo-Platonism (Anti-realistic)				
40. Rise of Medieval Thought (1) 41. Rise of Medieval Thought (2) 42. Rise of Medieval Thought (3)					
43. Arabic Philosophy 44. Jewish Philosophy	Medieval Philosophy	Second Synthesis			
45. Height of Medieval Thought					
46. Decline of Medieval Thought (1) 47. Decline of Medieval Thought (2)					
48. Third Synthesis (1) 49. Third Synthesis (2)		Third Synthesis			
50. Prelude Modern Thought (1) 51. Prelude Modern Thought (2) 52. Prelude Modern Thought (3)		Prelude Modern Thought			
53. Scientialism 54. Practicalism 55. Idealism	Older Rationalism				
56. Positivism 57. Neo-Positivism 58. Neo-Idealism	Younger Rationalism	Rationalism	Anti- Synthetic Philosophy (Modern Philosophy)		
59. Pragmatism 60. Vitalism (Phil. of Life) 61. Existentialism	Irrationalism	Irrationalism			

11

splitting point which pin-points the division in the History of Philosophy.

According to the different ideas which a philosopher accepts of the law these three main periods (pre-synthetic, synthetic and anti-synthetic) are subdivided by Vollenhoven into the 61 streams shown on page 11.

4.2 The second question: *What light does the Word of God shed on the reality which the thinkers in the History of Philosophy studied?*

This question goes further than the first question, which only asked about the religious stand-point or attitude of a philosopher (in his philosophy) towards the Word of God. In the light shed by the Word of God on reality different questions are now put to each philosopher.

Philosophy is a science embracing the whole of reality and a philosopher engages himself in his philosophical thought with everything that is in reality. The question now arises whether the various philosophers in the History of Philosophy perceived everything accurately (in other words, were their philosophies *complete*), and whether what they saw of reality was perceived *correctly*. There is a close connection between these two questions: when a philosopher's thought is incomplete the aspects of reality which he perceived become distorted.

The Bible reveals to us *what* there is and also *how* reality is. This revelation of God which we accept makes it possible for us to build up a *complete* and *correct* philosophy about reality. In the light of this Scriptural Philosophy the different philosophies in the very long history of philosophy can be judged.

In the discussion of every problem in the History of Philosophy it will firstly be ascertained what the Bible reveals concerning this definite aspect of reality. Then the specific philosophy will be examined to find out if the aspect of reality was perceived and how it was seen. The view of a philosopher regarding a specific aspect of reality will be described with precise terminology so that it is clearly distinguished from the philosophical conceptions of other philosophers. Here, too, the procedure will be first to start with the all-encompassing general questions and then gradually to take notice of the more detailed problems.

What then, is the revelation of God's Word with regard to reality?

It teaches us that *God* exists, that he created the *cosmos*, and that He gave His *law* to the cosmos. We may thus distinguish between the sovereign God, the law(s) which are binding for the creation (cosmos) and the cosmos which is subjected to the law(s). God, law and cosmos differ radically from each other and the one should not be deduced from the other or be confused with the other.

Do we find the distinction between these three radically different modes of being in the History of Philosophy? The answer is No. Most philosophers throughout the centuries did not clearly distinguish between God, law and cosmos.

Sometimes God and cosmos (His creation) are identified or confused. God is cosmologized or the cosmos is deified (idolized).

Also, God and law are confused. God is legalized or the law is deified.

With other philosophers there is no clear distinction between the law and the cosmos. The law is confused with the cosmos and so subjectified, or the cosmos with the law and thus legalized. (For instance in Plato's realism the law becomes a thing (res), it is cosmologized. In Thomas Aquinas' absolutism of law the cosmos is deduced to law.)

The Word of God does not only reveal that in reality a distinction should be made between these three radical different entities (God, law, cosmos), but it also reveals the correct relation between them and it sheds light on each of the three beings separately.

4.3 Summary. *The result of our first two questions*

The History of Philosophy must occupy itself with two problems: What constitutes the *dynamics* of the history of ideas (the *variable)*, and what constitutes the *continuity* of the history of ideas (the *constant)*. In terms of our method, question one is concerned with the former (the dynamics, the variable); it gives the different *streams*. The second question has to do with the latter (the continuity, the constant); it indicates the *type* of philosophy.

Stream

What differs in the History of Thought, if one does not commit oneself to Christ and his Word-Revelation, are the multivarious commitments that thinkers have thrown themselves on as a source of truth. The variable represents the various stances that man has taken in thought or the type of "mind" that characterizes a thinker. It is the "direction" a person takes in speaking about the structure of the cosmos. When more than one person directs himself in the same fashion, the phenomenon of "schools of thought" arises, or a community of mind results. It is this community of mind that is designated by *stream* in our method.

Type

What remains constant in the History of Thought is the recurring themes about the structure of creation. It is this which philosophy has striven to uncover and theoretically account for in the light of its conception of the law. Thus each community of mind answers to the constant problematic themes of philosophy. The result is, for instance

Mythologizing and non-mythologizing thought.
Cosmogono-cosmological and pure-cosmological thought.
Dualistic and monistic thought.
Individualistic, partial universalistic and individualistic thought, etc.

The philosophical conception composed of these themes will show us the place of thinkers and their relatedness. Together with the specific stream in which a philosopher falls, it will give us the skeleton thought of every philosopher.

H. Hart summarizes as follows:

"... Philosophers give more or less typical solutions to the problems of, e.g. cosmic structure and these typical patterns represent a number of more or less constant lines throughout the History of Philosophy.

At the same time philosophers are influenced by the spiritual climate of historic periods and movements.

These various relationships may be expressed by saying that philosophic conceptions show typical systematic kinship with past conceptions and spiritual kinship with contemporary conceptions...

The limits of the work are very definite. One can never get beyond a very abstract and simplified general insight into the conceptual structure"[10].

5. THE CONSISTENT PROBLEM-HISTORIC METHOD IN DETAIL

Scripture reveals as we have said that:
(a) *God* is there;
(b) He created the *cosmos;*
(c) He gave His *law(s)* to the cosmos.

We will first add briefly something more about (c), the law, to what we have already said about it under point 4.1 as well as in the summary point 4.3 (in connection with *stream).* Then we will briefly discuss (a) God. In this essay we will concentrate on (b) cosmos, (giving the *type of philosophy).*

5.1 Idea of Law (Stream)

What light does the Word of God shed on the law? There are three distinct usages of the word "law", namely, Structural law(s), Law of love, and Positive law. The first concerns the structures of inorganic beings,

---

10. Hart, H.: *Communal certainty and authorized truth* (1966), p. xii.

plants, animals and human beings. The second, concerns man directly. (Love towards God, his neighbour and himself). The third is the bridge between the first and the second when man positivises the commandment of love under the guidance of the different structural (or modal) laws for the different societal relationships (e.g. state, church, marriage, family, school, university, etc.).

I have warned against confusing the law with the cosmos. The problem in the History of Philosophy to search for the law *in* creation or *above* creation is thus a false problem because a spatial dimension is applied, while space is only applicable to creation and not to law or God. The only thing that can be said about the law with regard to creation is that it is valid for creation. If we find certain legalities ("wetmatighede"), in our study of the cosmos it does not mean that law and creation are to be identified. There is a difference between universal regularities ("wetmatighede") and law ("wet"). Legality belongs to creation because it is the sign that creation is subjected to the law.

What happened to the (threefold) law during the History of Philosophy?

We have already seen that throughout the History of Philosophy the Word of God has not in fact been given its rightful place. Consequently, the philosophers (for instance in the pre-synthetic period) did not know God's commandment of love. We find positive law(s), but distorted because in this case it is not the bridge between the law of love and the structural laws. The structural laws were perceived but not correctly.

For a detailed discussion of the four most important ideas about the law (Subjectivism, Objectivism, Platonic Realism and Theory Apriori) which have emerged in the history of philosophy I may refer the interested reader to the excellent work already done by H.E. Runner[11] and H. Hart[12].

5.2 The idea of God

I will be brief on this point because the idea of God, although very important in the History of Philosophy, did not occupy such an important place (as for instance the idea about the Law or the Cosmos) for the following reasons:

(a) Many philosophers of the pre-synthetic and anti-synthetic left ten-

11. Cf. Runner, H.E.: "The relation of the Bible to learning" (In: *Christian Perspectives 1960*). He starts his exposition about the law on page 127-129, on page 129-132 he concentrates on subjectivism and objectivism, on page 132-133 on Platonic Realism and on page 142-145 on the Theory Apriori.

12. Cf. Hart, H., op. cit., p. 2, 3 as well as his book *The challenge of our age* (1968), p. 42-44 for a discussion of the origin and character of the Theory Apriori.

dencies did not pay attention to God in their philosophy, because they either did not know the true God (pre-synthetic period) or preferred to ignore Him (anti-synthetic left period).

(b) To know creation to a certain degree is a definite possibility for any philosopher, even without the revelation of the Word of God, because the creation is open for scientific investigation. It is possible to know God through His revelation in creation but to know Him correctly He has to reveal Himself to us in His Word. Most philosophers did not know this Word (pre-synthetic period) or ignored it (anti-synthetic left attitude).

(c) Thus far, I have only mentioned pre-synthetic and anti-synthetic left thought about the *true* God which revealed himself in Scripture. The fact that philosophers did not know or ignored the true God does not imply that they were without any idea of god(s) in their philosophies. Nobody is a-religious; everyone serves either the true God or idols in the place of the true God. These philosophers thus also reflected on their man-made gods, although these did not always play such a significant part in their philosophies. Because their gods were absolutized aspects of the cosmos the views about their gods may just as well be discussed with their ideas about the cosmos.

(d) With regard to synthetic thought the scientific study of God was usually regarded as the task of another science, viz., Theology, and not of Philosophy, with the consequence that the idea of God is more or less excluded from their philosophies. (Except for Natural Theology — which was regarded as a branch of Philosophy).

I may add that the synthetic view of God (not only in Natural Theology but also in Supernatural Theology) was not purely scriptural because their synthesis with pagan thought also influenced their idea about God.

(e) The anti-synthetic right philosophy wants to break with the philosophical ideas of the past in so far as they were synthetical and thus did not acknowledge what God revealed in His Word about Himself. In connection with Law and Cosmos we spoke about the illuminating light of the Word of God on them. God is however unknowable. If we did not have His Word, we would still be able (if we did not suppress it) to find a small amount of knowledge about Himself from His revelation in creation but not to really know who He is. That is why Scriptural philosophy faithfully accepts what God reveals about Himself in his Word and does not speculate about God. Nothing should be added to this revelation, and nothing of what is revealed should be neglected. The idea of God, with which a Scriptural philosophy operates, is not brought about through scientific investigation but is a matter of faith.

5.3 Idea of Cosmos (type)

The following two diagrams show various possible conceptions about the cosmos:

Diagram IIA gives a survey of *mythologizing* and of *non-mythologizing cosmogonic-cosmological* thought. (p. 18).

Diagram IIB gives a survey of *non-mythologizing pure cosmological* thought. (p. 19).

5.3.1 Explanation of diagrams IIA and B

5.3.1.1 Mythologizing and non-mythologizing

Every thinker who concerns himself with the cosmos becomes necessarily confronted with the question of the *origin* of cosmic reality.

As I have said, the Word of God reveals that the cosmos was created by God.

Most of the Western philosophers did not know this revelation or rejected it as authoritative. Nevertheless, they wanted an answer to this question. Thus they drew the problem of the gods and cosmos into the field of scientific investigation. This question actually does not belong to science but is a pre-scientific problem. No person was present at the beginning of the cosmos and God is without beginning or end. Philosophers who want to say something about it are not scientific in an authentic sense but are merely speculating. It is precisely for this reason that God revealed to us that the world came into existence by His act of creation.

The fact that the origin of the world is not a scientific philosophical question is clearly illustrated by the fact that very early in the history of Western thought philosophers used different myths to explain the origin of gods and cosmos. We call this mythologizing thought. A myth is the product of pistical phantasy in a pagan milieu in connection with the origin of the cosmos and the gods. As pseudo-revelation in the place of the true Revelation of God, it can only emanate from an apostate heart.

While some philosophers used the myth as explanatory ground, others rejected it. These non-mythologizing thinkers thus had, in their own way, to answer the question of the genesis of gods and cosmos. They did not agree in this connection.

5.3.1.2 Cosmogonic-cosmological and pure cosmological attitude

In reaction against the mythologizing thought one group of non-mythologizing philosophers went so far as to reject the whole problem of

DIAGRAM II A: IDEA OF COSMOS (TYPE):
Mythologizing and cosmogono-cosmological thought

Type	Name	Sub-category		Division	Major
Individualistic / Partial Universalistic / Universalistic	Delic Appolonic	Without Dichotomy		Dualism	Mythologizing
Individualistic / Partial Universalistic / Universalistic	Delic Appolonic (Andrologic)	With Dichotomy		Dualism	Mythologizing
Individualistic / Partial Universalistic / Universalistic	Attic Appolonic (Anthropologic)	With Dichotomy		Dualism	Mythologizing
Individualistic / Partial Universalistic / Universalistic	Tracic Dionysic	Theory of Priority		Monism	Mythologizing
Individualistic / Partial Universalistic / Universalistic	Cretic Dionysic (Zoological)	Theory of Interaction		Monism	Mythologizing
Individualistic / Partial Universalistic / Universalistic	Chaldean Determinism	Parallelism		Monism	Mythologizing
Individualistic / Partial Universalistic / Universalistic	Andrologic			Dualism (Dichotomistic)	Non-Mythologizing / Cosmogono-Cosmological
Individualistic / Partial Universalistic / Universalistic	Anthropologic			Dualism (Dichotomistic)	Non-Mythologizing / Cosmogono-Cosmological
Individualistic / Partial Universalistic / Universalistic	Contradictior (Coincidentia Oppositorum)			Dualism (Dichotomistic)	Non-Mythologizing / Cosmogono-Cosmological
Individualistic / Partial Universalistic / Universalistic	Instrumentistic	With primary impetus theory	Theory of Priority	Monism	Non-Mythologizing / Cosmogono-Cosmological
Individualistic / Partial Universalistic / Universalistic	Vitalistic	With primary impetus theory	Theory of Priority	Monism	Non-Mythologizing / Cosmogono-Cosmological
Individualistic / Partial Universalistic / Universalistic	Occasionalistic	With Secondary impetus theory	Theory of Priority	Monism	Non-Mythologizing / Cosmogono-Cosmological
Individualistic / Partial Universalistic / Universalistic	Ennoetistic	With Secondary impetus theory	Theory of Priority	Monism	Non-Mythologizing / Cosmogono-Cosmological
Individualistic / Partial Universalistic / Universalistic / Phenomenological	Anthropological		Theory of Interaction	Monism	Non-Mythologizing / Cosmogono-Cosmological
Individualistic / Partial Universalistic / Universalistic / Phenomenological	Zoological		Theory of Interaction	Monism	Non-Mythologizing / Cosmogono-Cosmological
Individualistic / Partial Universalistic / Universalistic / Phenomenological	Phytological		Theory of Interaction	Monism	Non-Mythologizing / Cosmogono-Cosmological
Individualistic / Partial Universalistic / Universalistic	Limited		Parallelism	Monism	Non-Mythologizing / Cosmogono-Cosmological
Individualistic / Partial Universalistic / Universalistic	Unlimited		Parallelism	Monism	Non-Mythologizing / Cosmogono-Cosmological

DIAGRAM IIB: IDEA OF COSMOS (TYPE): *Pure cosmological thought.*

Detail	Sub-group	Group	Mode	Theory	Major theory	Class	Type	Category
Hippocratizing		Consistent	Empiristic		Hippocratic-Aristotelic (Partial Universalism without macro-microcosmos theory)	Dualism	Pure Cosmological	Non-Mythologizing
Aristotelizing		Consistent	Empiristic					
Platonizing		Consistent	Empiristic					
Hippocratizing		In-Consistent	Empiristic					
Aristotelizing		In-Consistent	Empiristic					
Platonizing		In-Consistent	Empiristic					
Hippocratizing		Semi-Mystical						
Aristotelizing		Semi-Mystical						
Platonizing		Semi-Mystical						
Not reduced	Pneumato-logical	Non-Platonizing	Intellectualistic Monarchianism					
Reduced	Pneumato-logical	Non-Platonizing	Intellectualistic Monarchianism					
Psychological		Non-Platonizing	Intellectualistic Monarchianism					
Noological		Non-Platonizing	Intellectualistic Monarchianism					
Not reduced	Pneumato-logical	Platonizing	Intellectualistic Monarchianism					
Reduced	Pneumato-logical	Platonizing	Intellectualistic Monarchianism					
Psychological		Platonizing	Intellectualistic Monarchianism					
Noological		Platonizing	Intellectualistic Monarchianism					
Without im. log. object		Non-Platonizing	Subsistence theory	Aristotle-Interpretation (P.U. without m.-m.c.t.)				
With im. log. object		Non-Platonizing	Subsistence theory					
Without im. log. object		Platonizing	Subsistence theory					
With im. log. object		Platonizing	Subsistence theory					
With im. log. object + intentionality theme		Platonizing	Subsistence theory					
Intellectualistic			Vinculum theory					
Voluntaristic			Vinculum theory					
Individualistic			Without dichotomy	Semi-Materialistic	Monism			
Partial Universalistic			Without dichotomy	Semi-Materialistic				
Universalistic			Without dichotomy	Semi-Materialistic				
Individualistic			With dichotomy	Semi-Materialistic				
Partial Universalistic			With dichotomy	Semi-Materialistic				
Universalistic			With dichotomy	Semi-Materialistic				
Individualistic				Materialistic	Monism			
Partial Universalistic				Materialistic				
Universalistic				Materialistic				

19

the genesis (origin) of the cosmos and confined themselves to the cosmos, as it exists at present. This is called the *pure cosmological* approach.

Another group did not agree with the extreme standpoint of the pure cosmological thinkers and took a position in between the mythologizing and the pure cosmological viewpoint. They rejected the myth as an explanation but did not totally ignore the problem of the origin. Their position is therefor characterized as *cosmogonic-cosmological (cosmos + genesis =* origin of cosmos and *cosmos + logos =* knowledge of cosmos as it is).

Dualism and monism

Over and above the amazement of the philosopher about the origin of the cosmos in which he lives and studies every day he is also filled with wonder about the diversity of reality, as well as the unity there is, despite its diversity. What will the scientific explanation for the wonderful state of affairs be? Is the diversity of one principle or two?

Those who answered to the former (the diversity is of one principle) are called *monists*, those who gave the second solution (that diversity is of many principles — usually two) are named *dualists*.

With regard to these problems which still exist today Scripture long ago gave the solution. It reveals that in the beginning God created a diversity; inorganic beings, plants, animals, human beings (mutually dependent upon each other). Furthermore a scriptural Philosophy distinguishes a diversity of 15 different modal aspects in the cosmos.

It is not necessary to ask the question whether there is diversity of one or more principles on account of the fact that we have this answer revealed by God Himself: unity in deversity and diversity in the unity.

Individualism, Partial Universalism and Universalism

The problem here is more or less the following:

Two trees for instance, both oaks show a certain similarity but they are also different in that they have individual characteristics which make it easy to distinguish the one from the other. You could say the same of students: a universal side giving the similarity and making it possible to speak of "students" and an individual side giving the difference, making it possible to speak of this and that specific student. This distinction of universal-individual is a fundamental one in the whole of reality and it is very important to see it correctly. It is not correct to speak of universals and individuals *(entities)* but of the universal and individual *(aspects)* because the universal and individual are not two *separate* REALMS of the cosmos, but two *inseparable* FEATURES or aspects which always and everywhere occur together, and are of equal value.

20

During the history of philosophy you find a continual struggle to understand the universal and individual in their mutual relationships:

The *universalists* saw the universal as primary, and the individual as an offshoot or outflow of the universal.

The *individualists*, on the other hand, estimate the individual as primary and the universal as of secondary importance.

Partial universalism puts the universal and the individual next to each other, and tries not to treat either one with favour over and above the other.

Here you have different possibilities.

Some partial universalists *make use of a macro-micro-cosmic* theory to explain the relation between the universal and the individual. The universal stands alongside the individual but they differ in size or extent whilst appearing similar. (The macro cosmos usually includes the large world of heaven and earth, while the micro cosmos usually include human beings, sometimes animals and plants. All that is found in the macro cosmos is found in the micro cosmos and vice versa.) The universal macro cosmos is, however, not only bigger than the individual micro cosmos but also more important because it is the *law* for the micro cosmos. (The law is incorrectly identified with the universal.)

Our standpoint (as given in the beginning) is that it is wrong to speak of *the* universal and *the* individual (because universal and particular are not *parts* or *components* of a thing) and more correct to speak of universal and individual (because they are *characteristics* or *aspects* of the same thing).

The characterizations I have given thus far are the more fundamental ontological ones. I come now to the typifying of the various anthropological conceptions amongst the ontological viewpoints, which have already been mentioned.

5.3.1.3 Further distinctions within the mythologizing thought

Without and with dichotomy

As I have said, the dualists are of the opinion that the diversity in the cosmos is derived from two original principles. The higher one of these principles is called the transcendental and the lower the non-transcendental world.

In an anthropological connotation, it is necessary to decide whether man is completely of a non-transcendental nature or whether he also possesses something transcendental.

Some philosophers believed that man is totally non-transcendental, with the consequence that there are not two different "parts" in man. This direction is called dualism *without a dichotomous* anthropology (= Delic Appolonic).

Other philosophers believe that man possesses something transcendental as for example, a part of the soul. In the structure of man there are two different "parts" (transcendental and non-transcendental) so that we qualify this viewpoint as dualism *with a dichotomy* in the anthropology concerned.

Delic Appolonic (andrologic) and Attic Appolonic (anthropological)

Amongst the mythologizing dualists with dichotomy the differentiation of sex in human being resulted in the question as to whether men only or woman also participate in the transcendental.

The *anthropological dichotomists*(Attic Appolonic) believe that both men and women participate in the transcendental.

The *andrologic dichotomists* (Delic Appolonic) assert that only men partake in the transcendental.

Theory of priority, interaction and parallelism

According to the monists the diversity is of one principle. This means that the diversity (the two species of the one principle) is secondary whereas in dualism the twoness is primary. The following anthropological question is:

How do these species relate to each other?

Some philosophers claim a priority of the higher species to the lower. This is the theory of priority (Thracic Dionysic).

Others think the two species interact: *theory of interaction.* In this case we have a special type of the theory of interaction namely the zoological (Cretic Dionysic). There are also the anthropological and phytological types. (For explanation see diagram on page 24.)

A third answer to this question is that there is no causal interaction at all between the two species of the one principle but merely a *parallelism.*

5.3.1.4 Further distinctions within the Cosmogonic-cosmological thought

Dichotomist (andrologic and anthropological) See previous explanation.

Contradictory

According to the monists the diversity is of one principle. This means that the diversity (the two species of the one principle) is secondary. The problem is now how do these species relate to each other? According to some philosophers there is a contradictory relationship between the species. Compare, for instance, Heraclitus' two species fire and water which contradict each other but fall together: *coincidentia oppositorum.* This is *contra-*

dictory monism.

Theory of priority

In connection with the above question some philosophers claimed a priority of the higher species to the lower. They are called monists with the *theory of priority.*

Amongst them there are those *with a primary and those with a secondary impetus theory.*

Impetus Theory means that the impulse from the higher species is regarded as the explanation for the movement of the lower species which do not have movement of their own.

Primary impetus theory means that the impetus or impulse is primarily from the higher species.

Secondary impetus theory means that the lower species have movement of their own.

The primary impetus theory has two possibilities:
Instrumentistic and *Vitalistic.* The first characterization indicates that the lower species is solely used as an instrument by the higher. The second indicates the organic part of the lower specie is also part of the higher species (more appreciation for the body) and not only an instrument of the higher.

Theory of Interaction

After their divergence from the unity there is an interaction between the higher and lower species.

Three types of interaction are possible; (Anthropological, Zoological, Phytological), depending on the level of the *arche* (principle of divergence) or on how many kingdoms (plants, animal, man) you get in the higher species.

The diagram on p. 24 will explain this.

Parallelism

According to this viewpoint there is no causal interaction at all between the higher and the lower. The alienation is complete. The higher and the lower develop parallel. What happens in the higher occurs in an analogical way in the lower species but without mutual influence.

Because in some cases the parallelism is more restricted we distinguish between *limited* and *unlimited* parallelism.

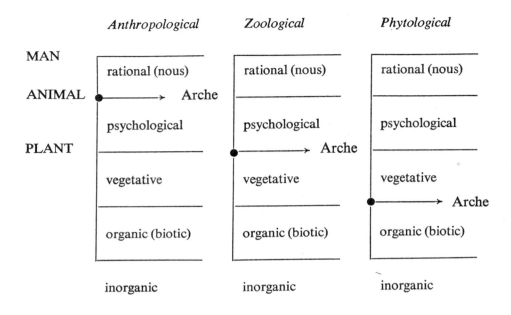

5.3.1.5 Further distinctions within the pure cosmological thought

Hippocratic-Aristotelic

As indicated in brackets this implies partial universalism without macro-micro-cosmos-theory. This partial universalism without macro-micro-cosmos-theory is qualified as Hippocratic-Aristotelic, meaning that the relation between universal and individual is viewed according to the higher-lower scheme (form-matter motive) just as Hippocrates and Aristotle did.

Amongst the Hippocratic-Aristotelic conceptions there are two possibilities: *Empiristic* and *Intellectualistic*.

Empiristic

Empirism teaches that the acquisition of knowledge is not primarily the result of human activity but of the impressions from outside which have made impacts on the passive intellect, rather like impressions made on a clear slate or wax tablet (*tabula rasa*). After these impressions have been made on the passive intellect the active intellect starts with its work.

We get two different stand-points amongst the empirists: Consistent and Inconsistent.

Consistent Empiristic

This theory regards the knowable as most important and not the knower. The impression from the knowable object must first activate the intellect (by giving its impressions on the passive intellect) before any knowledge is possible. In other words knowledge of super sensible things which cannot make impressions is impossible.

Inconsistent Empiristic

This theory is not consistent because it also regards it as possible to get knowledge of super sensible phenomena. Impressions are thus not a *sine qua non* for knowledge.

Intellectualistic

Against the empirists who are more or less philosophers of experience (as for e.g. the *bee* which takes in his nectar from various flowers), we get the intellectualistic philosophers who believe that knowledge should be derived from the intellect itself (the *spider* which spins his web out of himself).

The Semi-mystical type

Mysticism is the attitude according to which the human being should aspire to a mystical union with the transcendental (god or God). Semi-mystical is the inconsistent type of mysticism.

The Monarchianistic type

Aristotle gave birth to Monarchianism in the final dualistic phase of his philosophical development. In this conception he accepts a super individual, universal thinking spirit ("denkgees") between the transcendental godhead and non-transcendental man. Situated above all one finds the transcendental god or monarch (hence the name Monarchianism).

The non-Platonizing type

After Aristotle there was a further development of Monarchianism. Those who extend the idea further according to the viewpoint of Aristotle are called non-Platonizing.

Amongst the non-Platonizing type three varieties are possible:

Pneumatological (not reduced and reduced): The *pneuma* continues to exist after death.

Psychological: The *psyche* (soul) continues to exist after death.

Noological: The human being as totality (also *nous)* dies.

The Platonizing type

This is the group of thinkers who reconciled Monarchianism with the philosophy of Plato. Plato himself never adhered to monarchianism (it originates after Plato in the philosophy of Aristotle as I have explained above). To be able to reconcile the philosophy of Plato with monarchianism, you need an interpretation of the original Platonic thought and therefore we speak of Platonizing thinking.

Amongst Platonizing monarchianism the same three varieties as in the case of the non-Platonizing monarchianism are possible.

Pneumatological (non-reduced and reduced),

Psychological and

Noological

Aristotle-Interpretation

There is a difference between Aristotelic and Aristotelizing (or Aristotle-interpretation) thought. When one thinks in an Aristotelic manner, one accepts and follows Aristotle entirely in his whole philosophy — something which is virtually an impossibility. But when one thinks in an Aristotelizing way, one either selects certain aspects of the philosophy of Aristotle or interprets his philosophy so as to suit oneself. The result is not the original philosophy of Aristotle any more.

Subsistence Theory

The two components of the human unity (viz. body and soul) stand in the relation to each other of matter and form, forming *one* substance.

Vinculum Theory

This theory teaches that body and soul form individually a separate substance consisting of matter and form (body = matter + form and soul = matter + form). For the unity of the *two* substances (body and soul) a separate *vinculum* (tie, cord or strap) is necessary to combine them.

With the *subsistence theory* different varieties are possible:

Non-Platonizing type: the subsistence theory is not connected with the philosophy of Plato but with that of Aristotle in two forms:

Without, and;

With an immanent logical object (meaning that first the knowable was not seen in the human intellect but later on it was).

Platonizing type: the subsistence theory is connected with an interpretation of the philosophy of Plato in three forms:

Without,

With and immanent logical object, and

With an immanent logical object plus intentionality theory (intentional acts directed on the knowable placed inside the intellect and not any more outside, in reality).

With the vinculum theory there are only two possibilities:

Intellectualistic: the intellect is the primary over and above the will.

Voluntaristic: the will is the primary over and above the intellect.

Semi-materialistic and materialistic

Notice that semi-materialism is a dualistic conception, while materialism is a monistic.

Without and with dichotomy, has already been explained.

***

SUMMARY

This paper is a concise introduction to the consistent problem-historic method of the Historiography of Philosophy. The method is an attempt to gain insight into a philosophical conception by concentrating on the basic questions and answers concerning the cosmos as well as the movements or streams in the development of philosophical thought. As with every historiographical method, it has definite limits but also great advantages. Studying the history of thought by means of this method not only gives us a general insight into the conception of a philosopher and his philosophical development, but also reveals a certain philosopher's relation to the viewpoints of his predecessors, contemporaries and successors.

It is unfortunate that the significant contribution of this methodological approach is practically unknown except to a few specialists in Holland,

Canada and South Africa. The results thusfar attained by means of the consistent problem-historic method are so illuminating and promising that more historiographers should take note of it.

SELECTED BIBLIOGRAPHY

This bibliography does not include the following:
* lectures (so-called *privatissima*) given by Vollenhoven to advanced students;
* lecture notes compiled by students;
* Vollenhoven's mimeograph publications (limited circulation) such as his *Kort overzicht van de geschiedenis der Wijsbegeerte voor den Cursus Paedagogiek M.O.A.* and the accompanying *Schematische kaarten met register behorend bij "Kort overzicht van de geschiedenis der wijsbegeerte".*

K.A. Brill (Librarian, Medical Faculty, Free University of Amsterdam) has collected important unpublished material about the method in his *Tien jaar probleem-historische methode* (1971). A new edition (including material after 1971), as well as an English issue of *Schematische Kaarten* is at the moment prepared by Mr Brill.

BRILL, K.A. Tien jaar Probleem-historische-Methode. Free University of Amsterdam, Mimeograph, 1971.

HART, H. Historicale problemen. Stellingen ter bevordering van de belangstelling van de konsekwent probleem-historische methode. *Correspondentie bladen van de Vereniging voor Calvinistische Wijsbegeerte,* 28:7-10 Dec., 1965.

HART, H. De probleem-historische methode van prof. D.H. Th. Vollenhoven. *Correspondentiebladen van de Vereniging voor Calvinistische Wijsbegeerte,* 29:3-15, Nov., 1965.

KNUDSEN, R.D. Philosophical Historiography. *The Journal of the American Scientific Affiliation.* 21(3):87-89, Sept., 1960.

RUNNER, H.E. The history of ancient philosophy. Grand Rapids, Calvin College, Syllabus for Philosophy 220 (Mimeograph), 1958/'59.

SEERVELD, C.G. Biblical wisdom underneath Vollenhoven's categories for philosophical historiography. *Philosophia Reformata,* 38:127-143, 1973.

SEERVELD, C.G. The pedagogical strength of Christian methodology. Koers, 40 (4/5/6) 269-313, 1975.

TALJAARD, J.A.L. Polished Lenses. A philosophy that proclaims the sovereignty of God over creation and also over every aspect of human activity. Potchefstroom, Pro Rege Press, 1976.

VAN DER LAAN, H. De konsekwent probleem-historische methode in confrontatie met de historiografie van de moderne wijsbegeerte. *Correspondentiebladen van de Vereniging voor Calvinistische Wijsbegeerte*, 30:15-23, 1967.

VAN DER LAAN, H. The Historiography of Philosophy. *Vox Reformata* (Reformed Theological College, Geelong, Victoria, Australia), no. 29:1-31 Nov. 1977.

VAN DER WALT, B.J. Wysgerige Historiografie. *Perspektief.* (University of Potchefstroom, South Africa), 8 (2/3):70-117, June 1969; 8(4) & 9(1): 1-44, March 1970.

VAN DER WALT, B.J. Historiography of Philosophy: The consistent problem-historic method. *Tydskrif vir Christelike Wetenskap*, 9:163-184, 1973.

VAN DIJK, J. Survey of the history of Philosophy. (A mimeograph Syllabus for Philosophy 201: Perspectives in Philosophy) Department of Philosophy, Dordt College, 1969/'70.

VOLLENHOVEN, D.H. Th. De consequent probleemhistorische method. *Philosophia Reformata*, 26:1-64, 1961.

WOLTERS, A.M. An essay on the idea of Problemgeschichte. Free University of Amsterdam, Mimeograph Doctoral Essays, 1970. (Reprint 1971).

ZUIDEMAN, S.U. Vollenhoven en de reformatie der Wijsbegeerte. *Philosophia Reformata* 28:134-146, 1963.

2 ANCIENT GREEK THOUGHT: ORIGINS OF WESTERN THEOLOGY*

"Het antieke Griekeland is een merkwaardig land. Het lijkt soms, of God het in de historie heeft geplaatst, opdat alles zich eerst eens op kleine schaal, als in ontwerp, als op een architectenbestek, zou afspelen, wat later in de Westersche cultuur in het groot zich zou voltrekken. Want wij kunnen geen gedachte, geen streving, geen enkele evolutie van den menschelijken logos bedenken — afgezien van datgene, waartoe het christendom als nieuw materiaal hem in staat stelde — of het heeft zich dáár voorgedaan"[1].

Although slightly overstated, these words of A.W. Begemann are very close to the mark. Western thought begins at a high level with that of the Greeks.

A seeker after the origin of Theology will not make the long return journey of 25 centuries to Hellas in vain[2].

1 Pre-Platonic thinkers (c. 600 — 400 B.C.)

Because the source material here is exceedingly limited, historians of philosophy are still very uncertain and differ greatly among themselves.

1.1 Theology or Philosophy the first science?

Differences of opinion are immediately apparent with respect to one of the fundamental problems, i.e. the relationship of Theology and Philo-

---

* Originally published in *Philosophia Reformata* 41, 24-48, 1976 under the title "Die oorspronge van die Westerse teologie binne die antieke Griekse denke".

1. Begemann, De Logos en zijn verlossing. (*In* Gods Woord in het studentenleven, p. 111).
J. Hessen makes a similar statement: "Das Volk der Griechen war wie kein anderes philosophisch begabt. Sein Genius zeigt auf philosophischem Gebiete eine schöpferische Kraft und Fruchtbarkeit, die einzig dasteht". *Patristische und scholastische Philosophie*, p. 7.

2. "Whenever we speak of the beginnings of European philosophy we think of the Greeks; and an attempt to trace the origins of natural or philosophical theology must likewise begin with them". Jaeger, *The theology of the early Greek philosophers*, p. 1.

sophy[3].

The cause of this confusion among historiographers is the anachronistic procedure whereby later problems are read into pre-Platonic thought which then did not even exist. For this reason some consider the pre-Platonists primarily as philosophers, while others maintain that they were primarily, without exception theologians[4]. Others, again, distinguish two phases in ancient Greek thought of which the first would have been theological and the second philosophical[5]. Some are even of the opinion that Greek thought is pure Natural Theology[6].

A more accurate assessment in my opinion is that the two sciences were not so clearly distinguished at the time: "Aan het begin der wijsgerige historie zijn theologie en wijsbegeerte één. In hun eenheid handelen zij over dezelfde zaken, en de eenheid is zo innig, dat slechts vanuit de verdere evolutie der historie die de afsplitsing bracht, de tweeheid te onderscheiden valt..."[7].

Simply to assume that pre-Platonic theories about the gods were intended as Theology is incorrect[8] seeing that they did not express themselves as to this science and its field of investigation, or at least not clearly. Even the later descriptions which Plato and Aristotle, for instance, give of

---

3. There is no unanimity amongst experts on Greek thought. The matter is aggravated by the fact that even amongst the Greek thinkers themselves no unanimity existed, for every writer's philosophy determines *his* vision of the task of Philosophy and Theology!
The many meanings of the word 'theology' are apparent from amongst others the following studies: Ebeling, Theologie: Begriffgeschichtlich. (*In* Die Religion in Geschichte und Gegenwart, 6:756-770, 1962); Eisler, *Wörterbuch der philosophische Begriffe* s.v. "Theologie"; Kattenbusch, Die entstehung einer christliche Theologie. *Zeitschrift für Theologie und Kirche,* 11:161-205; 1930; Markus, The study of theology and the framework of secular disciplines. *The Downside Review,* 78:192-202, 1960 and Stiglmayr, Mannifache Bedeutung von "Theologie" und "Theologen". *Theologie und Glaube,* 11:296-309, 1939.

4. Cf. Popma, Vroeg-antieke theologieën. (*In* Wijsbegeerte en anthropologie, p. 40, 49, 85).

5. Cf.   Conford, *From religion to Philosophy,* p. 134, 135; Jaeger, op. cit. p. 5 and Peterich, *Die Theologie der Hellenen,* p. 9.

6. Cf. Weischedel, *Der Gott der Philosophen I,* p. 38, 47, 54 and elsewhere.

7. Begeman, *De relatie tussen wijsbegeerte en theologie en haar belangrijkste gestalte in de Heleense periode van het oud-Griekse denken,* p. 15.

8. Vlastos rightly observes that one is struck by the religious character of pre-Platonic thought: few words are more used among them than the word "god". But he maintains that this still does not give Jaeger the right to speak of the "theology" of the early Greek thinkers. Cf. his article Theology and Philosophy in early Greek thought. *The Philosophical Quarterly* 2(7):97 & 101, April 1952.

Theology do not qualify them or any other to be described as theologians or philosophers.

Even if their theories on the gods are accepted as giving expression to their Theology, many uncertainties still remain as to whether it examined the gods as well as the divine [9]. It might for instance be possible to label their study of the gods as their Theology and the study of the divine as their Philosophy. To be more specific, the so-called poetic theologians would study the gods and the so-called physical theologians the divine (highest) section of the cosmos. Consequently the study of the divine eventually terminates in Natural Theology (as a part of Philosophy). Later Christian thinkers build upon Physical Theology in their Natural Theology, and not on Poetic Theology, seeing that they do not accept the heathen gods.

Without going into all the hypothetical possibilities, an attempt will be made to present a general survey of developments in this regard.

1.2 Combating of mythical theology

The theologies of the earliest Greeks were expressed in their poems and theories concerning the gods [10]. Poets like Homer, Hesiod and Orpheus used a mythical form to write about the gods.

A noteworthy feature of pre-Platonic thought is the ensuing struggle against this poetic-mythic thought [11]. Premisses regarding the gods were continually further 'rationalized'. These thinkers also aimed at conquering fear of darkness, lightning, heavenly phenomena and so forth, or at least opposing the thought of a divine power operating therein [12].

1.3 Allegorical methods

The old mythic *singers* and *poets* in Greek culture were succeeded in due course by those that could be labelled *thinkers*. The thinkers or

9. "The word *theology* originally and in its true Greek sense meant the rational approach of the human mind to the 'problem' indicated by the word *gods (theoi)* and the *divine (theon)*". Jaeger, The pre-socratic philosophers as founders of philosophical theology (*In* Proceedings of the Tenth International Congree of Philosophy, Amsterdam 1948, p. 1070.)

10. Cf. Peterich, Formen und Formeln vorchristlicher Theologie. (*In* Festgabe für W. Hausenstein, p. 75).

11. Cf. Gigon, Die Theologie der Vorsokratiker. *Entretiens sur l'Antiqué Classique,* I, p. 129 also Nestle, *Vom Mythos zum Logos,* p. 6 and Solmson, *Plato's Theology,* p. 6, 38, 51.

12. Cf. Gigon, Grundprobleme der antiken Philosophie, p. 201.

philosophers took the mythic tradition (laid down in the various poems) as a basis and then proceeded very critically.

Hence in their Philosophy the philosophers also assimilated a doctrine with regard to the gods.

Their philosophical conception of God mostly disagreed with that of their religious ethos and with the myths concerning the gods. If they still wished to be "religious" — in tune with the usual custom — they had to interpret the current ideas about the gods in such a way that both concepts of god (their own, philosophical one and the current one) were in agreement. This reinterpretation frequently coincides with what we would today call "demythologizing." The myths were interpreted in an allegorical manner, for the myths express in allegorical or imaginative speech exactly what the philosophers say in more abstract and theoretical language! Myths thus mean something different from what they really say! (The word 'allegory' literally means "saying something else" than the literal text.)

In this way a bridge is being created between the mythical folk belief and the new philosophical thought-patterns. This also puts the philosophers in a position to "explain away" the "irrational" elements and contradictions in the mythical stories as well as the ignoble things which are often ascribed to the gods.

It is important to note that behind these allegorical explanations lurk apologetic motives: These people in a certain sense try to rescue the myth by showing that the new wisdom of the philosophers had already long been known to the mythic poets, but that they only dressed the facts in the beautiful garments of the myth[13].

1.4 Three theologies

It is remarkable that the mythic "theologies" of the poets were questioned but that the same was not done to the official state cult — at least not immediately. It was (initially) regarded as untouchable — to have reacted against it would have been too dangerous.

Early in Greek culture, then, there already co-existed three different kinds of theories about the gods: The mythic, the "philosophical" (in quotation marks, because the mythic was also philosophical — only in a poetic form), and the civic[14]. This is a significant fact, for it led to the

13. See on allegorical exegesis among the Greeks in general Heinisch, *Der Einfluss Philos auf die älteste christliche Exegese*, p. 5-15; Nestle, op. cit., p. 126 ff.; Pepin, *Mythe et allégorie*, p. 93 ff.; Rossouw, *Klaarheid en interpretasie*, p. 48-88 and Solmson, op. cit., p. 42.

14. Cf. Gigon, Die Theologie der Vorsokratiker. *Entretiens sur l'Antique Classique*, p. 163 and Pepin, La "theologie tripartite" de Varron. *Revue des Etudes Augustiniennes*, 2:287, 1956.

later renowned division of Theology into Mythic, Natural and Civic, in such figures as Panaetios, Scaevola, Varro, Tertullian and Augustine.

1.5 Proofs of God

It is interesting that in this era not only evidence for, but also proofs against the existence of the gods are found. The following two are taken as instances[15].

The nature of the god is not bodily, nor non-bodily. If bodily, then he would be mortal; if non-corporeal, then he would not be able to act, for we cannot exercise our perception and actions without sensible organs, i.e. without possessing corporeality. God is thus neither one nor the other and consequently does not exist.

The possession of virtues is ascribed to the gods. However, if they possess virtues, they also have those vices which are conquered by those virtues. Seeing that deity has no vice, it also has no virtue, is thus without ethical properties, and does not exist.

Kritias' stand is also familiar, viz. that the gods are creations of the rulers to lend authority to governmental laws and create a fear of transgressing them.

Xenophanes mentions the view that the gods are creations of man. This is obvious, according to him, because men believe that the gods are born, wear clothes, speak and have human natures; because the Ethiopians say their gods have flat noses and are dark of skin, while the Thracians claim that their gods have light blue eyes and red hair. If animals and horses had hands and could draw, the horses would have sketched equine gods and the other animals animal-like gods!

Gigon demonstrates that only as a result of such atheistic speculations were the proofs of God (as a counter-reaction) called into being. "Archaische Zeiten beweisen das Dasein Gottes nicht; dies wird erst in dem Augenblick notwendig, in dem es ausdrücklich geleugnet wird"[16].

Gigon detects two proofs for the existence of a deity as early already as among the Sophists[17]. The first proceeds from a historical reflection on the suggestions made about the gods which leads to the proof of the existence of god *ex consensu gentium*. A conviction (i.e. that a god exists) which is apparent among all the peoples of the earth, cannot be false. According to

---

15. Cf. Gigon, ibid., p. 143, and also *Grundprobleme der antiken Philosophie*, p. 220.

16. Id. *Grundprobleme der antiken Philosophie*, p. 221.

17. Id. Die Theologie der Vorsokratiker. *Entretiens sur l'Antiquité Classique*, I, p. 153-5.

Gigon Democritus first formulated this argument. The second is the teleological interpretation of the cosmos. Mathematical astronomy in particular gave a strong impulse to teleological thought, since a mathematically-ordered cosmos is unthinkable without a mathematical deity *(theos geometron)*.

2 Plato (427-347 B.C.)

He was the first thinker to use the word "theology"[18] and in whom this "science" showed itself more plainly. But seeing that he was no systematician, much is still unclear. Plato apparently had no desire to systematize everything he had been thinking about all his life. Aristotle was the first great analyst and systematizer; the master of distinction, grouping, and subdivision. Plato's thought could be compared to a mountain stream as contrasted with Aristotle's water in the irrigation canal.

2.1 Critical nature of his theology

Plato's theology in particular has a negative, critical function. It guards against the aberrations of the mythic poets (e.g. Hesiod and Homer). In the interests of the state, the legends of the gods are to be purified of their repulsiveness along strict lines *(tupoi)*. The criteria *(tupoi peri theologias)* for the admissibility of the sayings are, inter alia, that the gods are good and thus not the cause of evil, immutable and thus neither able to be bribed, nor liars. In his book on the laws, the state is built upon a correct religion and so the citizen must have a correct knowledge of the gods. He says, inter alia, that there are gods everywhere, that they care for mankind and that they cannot be bribed, either by prayers or by gifts[19]. The positive task of Theology is to give a description or representation of the gods on a more scholarly level.

As a result, therefore, we find in Plato, too, a conflict between mythic tradition and the more rational approach to the gods. Theoretical knowledge is set above popular folk belief.

2.2 'Pistis', 'doxa' and 'episteme'

While we are busy with the critical character of his Theology we should

---

18. Cf. inter alia his book on the Laws (10th book) and that on the State (2nd book); Jaeger, op. cit., p. 4; Caird, *The evolution of theology in the Greek philosophers I,* p. 32.

19. Vlastos, op. cit., p. 115, views Plato as one of the first founders of Theodicy.

refer to the distinction between *pistis* (belief), *doxa* (opinion) and *episteme* (true knowledge). His theology concerns itself with true (theoretical) knowledge rather than the opinions of the mythic poets. Faith *(pistis)* is not considered as being equivalent to true knowledge, but on an even lower level than opinion.

Here there is no faith - reason dilemma[20]. Pre-Christian, classical thought does not oscillate between the alternatives of worldly knowledge and other-worldly faith. Nor is there any tension yet between Philosophy and Theology. Theology is part of Philosophy — its most important part. The problem in this phase is not whether a man can know the gods rationally or has to believe first, but rather whether the gods can be better known than in the popular religion. Theology does not here oppose Philosophy, but the ephemeral religion of the *polis*. Hence the opposition in this case is not that of belief - reason, but that of *doxa - episteme*.

Although we do not come across the explicit faith and reason dilemmas of the later Christian thinkers, one does not have to look far to see a prototype of the later conflict here[21]. The idea of an autonomous science, which supposes a human autonomy alongside of and opposed to a dependence on religion, had already been conceived by the Greeks.

2.3 Conception of knowledge. Theology as knowledge of being

The Greek idea of scholarship is also of great interest for the development of later Western thought. The word "theory" means, more or less, a "showing" (a divine epiphany, for instance). The scholarly (philosophical) Theology concerns itself with a theoretical or logical showing-forth of the gods. Furthermore, the word *theoretike* is marked as a term dealing with knowledge of being. Scholarly effort is concerned with the showing of or insight into *being*. This also holds for the Philosophical Theology of the Greeks. The scientific knowledge of the gods is concerned especially with the *understanding of their being*. This accent on the ontological was a

---

20. Cf. Löwith, Wissen und Glauben. *(In* Augustinus Magister, p. 403-4).

21. Cf. Betzendörfer, *Die Lehre von der Zweifachen Wahrheit. Ihr erstmalige Auftreten im christlichen Abendland und ihre Quellen.* He traces the doctrine of the double truth, which became popular especially in late medieval thought (as a result of the faith-reason problem) back to Plato and Aristotle (p. 43-6), who tried to distil the moments of truth out of the myths of the folk religion. In Plato's and Aristotle's thought there was already a gulf between the small number of thinkers (philosophers) who wanted to possess true knowledge and the great mass of uneducated people for whom an anthropomorphic belief in god was sufficient.
Later (p. 49) he shows that there is even a link between the doctrine of the *duplex veritas* and the renowned three-fold theology. (Petrus Pomponatius for instance appeals explicitly to Q. Mucius Scaevola's three-fold Theology.)

general trait of Greek thought, in opposition to later Hellenism which had an overwhelmingly gnoseological trend[22]. Popma typified their Theology, then, as Theo-onto-logy or Being-theology. He detects this trait as early already as Hesiod who wanted to elucidate the being of the gods, wishing to understand their "being divine". This concept of theo-logy runs throughout Greek thought and is, according to Popma, also the specific feature of later Scholasticism[23].

2.4 Evidence for existence of the gods

Not until the Aristotelian writings can a whole collection of clearly recognisable proofs for the gods be found. In Plato only one such proof can be clearly discerned, viz. the teleological, which he takes over from earlier thinkers[24]. From the purposefulness and order in creation it is demonstrated that a highest architect must exist.

2.5 Ontology of law

In conclusion, of particular interest is Plato's Realism. According to him, laws do not inhere in the subjects and objects (as stated by the Subjectivists and Objectivists before him), but have to be considered (those of the true, good and beautiful) in the intelligible word. His thought, then, is especially occupied with the knowledge of these ideas (in the background) which serve as perfect, eternal examples or models for cosmic things (in the foreground).

Plato's assigning a separate existence to the law was a big step in the direction of a correct ontology. But measured against a Scriptural Ontology, three basic failings in this view of law become evident. Laws are, firstly, not "things" which exist just like cosmic things. They are laws and their onticity lies in their validity. For this reason the laws are also not simply ideal examples like Plato's ideas but they *hold* for the subjects. Lastly, Plato incorrectly saw the law as something existing by itself, not merely completely free of the reality for which it holds, but also free of the lawgiver.

Plato himself rightly distinguished these ideas from the gods. As a result of developments in neo-Platonism after his time, many synthetically-minded Christian thinkers placed the Platonic ideas (as laws) in the knowing God.

---

22. Cf. Vollenhoven, *Geschiedenis der Wijsbegeerte I,* p. 589.

23. Cf. Popma, op. cit., p. 44, 45.

24. Cf. Huonder, *Die Gottesbeweise. Geschichte und Schicksal,* p. 19-25. (Plato gives it in his *Philebos* and *Timaeos.*)

Further admixture with later speculations on the logos (originating from the Stoa, cf. 5) which entered into Christian thought via Philosophy in particular, led eventually to the idea of the law in God, which he himself also instilled into the things, from which it appears again (abstracted) in the knowing man.

3 Aristotle (384-322 B.C.)

This giant of ancient thought is of great interest and his contribution will be considered more fully.

3.1 Ontology and epistemology

In the final phase of his long development he maintains a pure cosmological dualism combined with a partial universalism which lacks a macro-microcosmic distinction. This type of philosophy implies a form-matter doctrine[25]. This means that he does not accept myths as a clarification of the origin of reality but evidently wishes to philosophize about the cosmos as he finds it. Reality is dualistically divided into a (higher) transcendent and a (lower) non-transcendent part. In the transcendent sphere he discerns the deity (or monarch) and under that the heavenly sphere, with the universal power of thought on a still lower plane. Everything in the non-transcendent sphere consists of (lower) matter, as that which is individual and potential, and also of (the higher) form as that which is universal and actual.

The Aristotelian god in the transcendent sphere is a rigid, immovable divinity who draws everything to himself like a massive magnet and causes it to move, as the Highest Cause. He is pure thought and thus pure form (in contrast to the non-transcendent world where form and matter continually co-exist). The content of his thought is himself. (It would be unworthy for the deity to think anything else.) In the knowledge and love of itself the deity finds perfect happiness. The divine thought, intellect (*nous*) and being are indentical. Thinking subject and thought about object are identical in this god.

Aristotle's concept of law differs from that of his great predecessor, Plato, in that law is no longer separated from the things but a part of them.

---

25. Cf. Spier, *Van Thales tot Sartre*, p. 49-52.

The universal form, *ousia* (being) or substance[26], which Aristotle also sees as the cause, is the law. Each thing, he maintains, consists of form (or law) — as the universal aspect — and matter, as the individual. By developing this hulemorphism Aristotle hoped to improve on Plato's doctrine of the forms. He did not accept only three ideas (truth, good, beauty) but desired each thing to have its own law in itself. His forms are thus actually a multiplication of the ideas of Plato.

This conception of law in Aristotle is of the greatest significance for what was later still to come. For this reason a few comments on developments after Plato and Aristotle are here appropriate. As we have said, Plato's ideas were located by the neo-Platonists in the divine spirit. Within Aristotelianism Plato's ideas (as we have just shown) became the forms in the things. By means of a third trend in Hellenism (the so-called a priori trend) the ideas or laws also settled in the knowing intellect of man. When these three lines finally merge, they bring us to the medieval doctrine of the *ideae ante rem* (in God himself), the *formae in rebus* (in the things) and the *normae post rem* (in the knowing intellect of man).

Measured by a Scriptural Ontology, Aristotle's conception of law is quite as unacceptable as Plato's. Where the latter separates the laws (as ideas in the intelligible world) completely from the subjects for which they are valid,

26. Cf., for the concept of substance, Berger, *Op zoek naar identiteit. Het Aristotelische substantiebegrip en de mogelijkheid van een hedendaagse metaphysiek*. In a separate chapter he deals first with the *ousia* theory of Plato and after Aristotle, the further development of the substance concept up until Thomas Aquinas. Cf. also De Vos, Het "eidos" als "eerste substantie" in de metaphysica van Aristoteles. *Tijdschrift voor filosofie*, 20:571-600, 1958; Verhoeven, Het woord substantia. *Tijdschrift voor filosofie*, 22:495-543, 1960 and Mansion, Die erste Theorie der Substanz: die Substanz nach Aristoteles. *(In* Metaphysik und Theologie des Aristoteles, p. 114 ff.) and the three contributions in the collection *Het Hulemorphisme*, viz. Kuiper, Substantiële verandering en hulemorphisme; Peters, De Plaats van het hulemorphisme in de metaphysik, and Couturier, Het hulemorphisme in de mens. Dooyeweerd gives the following short summary: "De Platonische ideeën, waarvan de empirische wereld slechts de nevelachtige afschaduwing vertoonde, verlegde Aristoteles als entelechieën in het wezen der empirische dingen zelve. Het wezen van al het bestaande werd nu volgens hem het bewegend beginsel van het potentieel (d.i. in kiem) in de stof ingeschapen doel, waarnaar de stof volgens de natuurwet als naar zijn volmaking streeft. Deze wet der entelechie ... breide hij uit tot een universeel kosmologische beginsel van beweging van de lagere naar het hogere, de stof naar den vorm, het middel naar het doel. De kroon op dit gehele teleologisch geordend wereldplan was god, de absolute, alles bewegende, maar zelve onbewogene, de eerste oorzaak en het laatste doel van alle dingen." *Calvinisme en natuurrecht*, p. 4.
Cf. also Mansion, "Die 'Philosophie der Wesen' triumphiert doch endgultig bei Aristoteles". Die Aporien der aristotelischen Metaphysik. *(In* Metaphysik und Theologie des Aristoteles, p. 221) and Moreau, "Die *ousia* ist für Aristoteles dementsprechend nicht Subject ... sondern auch Washeit und Wesen". Sein und Wesen in der Philosophie der Aristoteles. *(In* Metaphysik und Theologie des Aristoteles, p. 225.)

the former makes the mistake of not distinguishing the laws clearly enough from the cosmic subjects. The Scriptural view is that although the laws (as the will of God for the things) are to be sought "in" the things, they are definitely distinguished from the things. The thought of autonomous substances is also not appropriate to a Scriptural Ontology, which acknowledges God as Legislator.

Aristotle's Epistemology[27] deals with knowledge of the laws or forms in the things, as we have just noted. The purpose of scientific knowledge is to come to knowledge of the universal form or being, in his view. Opposite to the *episteme* which has these general and necessary aspects as its field of investigation and cannot err, we find the *doxa* which has to do with the individual and with chance and therefore can be false. However, the theoretical activity of thought abstracts the general from the particular by induction, and this knowledge concerning the general form of being is expressed in the scientific definition. But Aristotle's Epistemology is still not fully expounded hereby. The transcendent, intelligible world and the deity which belongs to it (as a dualist, Aristotle distinguishes between a transcendent and a non-transcendent world) cannot be known by means of the senses, i.e. by impressions which are made on the *tabula rasa*. Consequently Aristotle had to modify his consistent empiricism (which can only be applied to knowledge of the non-transcendent) and go over to an inconsistent empiricism, in order to be able to explain the knowledge he had of the intelligible world.

When Aristotle goes over to monarchianism we already find the idea that human thoughts are completely dependent on the suprahuman *nous* or mind (between man and deity), because man's thought have to be actualized by this supra-human *nous* before he is able to come to knowledge[28]. This activity of the suprapersonal *nous* is also directed to the intelligible world. As a result man according to Aristotle, is completely dependent on the actualizing activity of this *nous* for his knowledge of the intelligible[29].

This conception of his closely approximates the illumination theory of Plato's later years, so that there is a strong possibility that Aristotle (even before he had subscribed to monarchianism) had accepted the illumination

27. Cf. inter alia Geyser, *Die Erkenntnistheorie des Aristoteles;* Antweiler, *Der Begriff der Wissenschaft bei Aristoteles;* Zimmermann, *Ontologie oder Metaphysik?;* Merlan, *From Platonism to Neo-Platonism* (parts); Meyer, *Die Wissenschaftslehre des Thomas von Aquin* (p. 7-39) and the collection edited by Hager, *Metaphysik und Theologie des Aristoteles.*

28. Cf. Vollenhoven, *Kort overzicht van de geschiedenis der Wijsbegeerte voor den cursus Paedagogiek M.O.A.,* p. 18.

29. Cf. Vollenhoven, *'n Kort oorsig van die geskiedenis van die Wysbegeerte,* 79, 80.

theory for his knowledge of the intelligible world. A few remarks on Plato in this regard may be helpful.

In his cosmogonic years (during which he also held a partial universalism along with a macro-microcosmic theory) Plato taught that the soul of man had pre-existed in the transcendent sphere and in this way could obtain insight into the intelligible world. When this soul arrived in the body (thus becoming non-transcendent) it still had memory *(anamnêsis)* of its knowledge of the transcendent intelligible world[30].

When Plato became a monist he could no longer maintain this doctrine of *anamnêsis*.[31] seeing that the transcendent world fell away. Consequently he accepted a theory of illumination. The ideas in the intelligible world are illuminated and also men's thoughts themselves, so that the ideas are knowable. F. Sassen says of Plato's Epistemology, for instance, "De idee van de Goede speelt bij het kenproces een bijzonder rol, welke overeenkomt met die van de zon in de wereld der waarneming. Zij verleent nl. door een zekere verlichting aan de kennend zubject de kenkracht, en aan de ideën de kenbaarheid"[32].

From this it is apparant that there exists a substantial agreement between Aristotle's theory of knowledge in his dualistic phase, and that of Plato in his monistic phase[33]. In both cases the power of knowledge has to be lent to man, and the intelligible made knowable, in order for him to be able to come to knowledge.

In short: the Stagirite holds an inconsistent empirical Epistemology.

Aristotle's view that there are unprovable, self-evident principles or primeval principles, to which all knowledge returns, should also be seen in the light of the above exposition. These first principles (later called *prima*

---

30. See Ritter, *Historisches Wörterbuch der Philosophie I,* p. 263 for more particulars of Plato's *anamnêsis* doctrine. References to Plato's various writings are given and it is also shown that in his later works he either modified or rejected the doctrine. (As we saw he adopted the theory of illumination.)

31. In passing, the attention of the reader is directed to the fact that the Platonic doctrine of *anamnêsis* (as well as the illumination theory) is of great importance to Calvin and the Calvinism of the 17th Century.

32. Sassen, *Geschiedenis van de Wijsbegeerte der Grieken en Romeinen,* p. 65.

33. See Ritter, op. cit., p. 264-5, as regards this agreement. Thomas Aquinas later largely adopted Aristotle's Epistemology. It is understandable that Thomas could reconcile the Aristotelian theory with Christendom: for his knowledge of God he is also completely dependent on the Revelation of God and on a supernatural illumination. This is understandable if one remembers that Augustine had already tied the Word-revelation up with the Platonic idea of enlightenment. (It is even possible that enlightenment and revelation were already close relatives in Plato, or practically equivalent. Thomas thus merely extends a line of thought from Augustine onwards.)

principia) are none other than a reformulation of Plato's ideas, which according to Aristotle's inconsistent empiricism, can then only be known through illumination. Scientific proofs begin with these principles, in accordance with his syllogistic logic[34].

3.2 Theory of Science

The sciences are hierarchically ordered by Aristotle, in agreement with his Ontology. In the highest disciplines the highest principles are also studied and the lower sciences borrow their principles from the higher disciplines.

He has given various divisions of the sciences in different writings[35] which need not be mentioned here. Of interest to us is the division where he specifically mentions Theology.

For the sake of completeness it should first be noted that Aristotle uses the word "theology" in two senses, viz. systematic and historic. As a historian Aristotle means by *hoi theologoi* those Greek thinkers whom Vollenhoven typifies as mythologizing, but only the oldest group: Hesiod *cum suis*. According to Aristotle these theologians preceded the philosophers, of whom the first was Thales of Miletus[36]. For the present study it is especially the systematic use of the word "theology" by Aristotle — as also found in his categorization of science — that is of interest.

According to chapter 1 of the sixth book of his *Metaphysics* there are three types of thought or philosophy to be differentiated, viz. the practical-ethical, the poetic-technical and the theoretical. The last is the highest of the three. Theoretical philosophy is again subdivided into three types: the mathematical, the physical and the theological (*philosophia mathema-*

---

34. Antweiler comes to the conclusion that Aristotle discerns two possible descriptions of science: "... die Wissenschaft ist eine Annahme über die allgemeine und die notwendig seienden Dinge" and "... die Wissenschaft ist die dauernde Befähigung zu beweisen". According to him it appears as if the two exclude each other because the first is strongly "dingbezogen" and the second "denkbezogen". However he combines both Aristotle's trends of thought in the following definition: "Wissenschaft ist die Befähigung beweismässig das Allgemeine zu erkennen". Op. cit., p. 115.

35. Cf. Id., p. 81 ff. Meyer, op. cit., names three divisions of Philosophy (science): a triple one into Logic, Physics and Ethics (Platonic scheme); a twin one into theoretical and practical sciences, and a threefold one into theoretical, practical and poetic philosophy.

36. Cf. Begemann, op. cit., p. 20 and Jaeger, op. cit., p. 5.

tikè, physikè and *theologikè*)[37]. Of these three, too, the last is the highest. Physics concerns itself with that which exists separately (is independent) and moves, Mathematics with that which does not exist separately (independently) and is immovable, and Theology with that which does indeed exist separately (independently) but is immovable.

Thus, the independently existing being, which is not subject to any movement, is here assigned to Theology as its field of investigation. He also calls this discipline First Philosophy or Wisdom.

3.3 Name and field of investigation of Theological Philosophy

It is evident from his works that Aristotle had the same discipline in mind when using the names Theological Philosophy *(Philosophia theologikè)*, First Philosophy *(prote philosophia)* and Wisdom *(sophia)*. But it is not clear where the title *Metaphysics* — with which this famous work of Aristotle, later known as his Theology, is labelled — comes from, as it does not appear in the writings of Aristotle himself[38].

The problem lies however in what exactly Aristotle saw as the field of inquiry of his Theological Philosophy[39]. The main difficulty here is that it

---

37. For further details about this triple division which had already existed before Aristotle, is present throughout the Middle Ages and is even rediscovered in the eighteenth century, cf. Markus, op. cit., p. 193; Merlan, op. cit., p. 59 ff. and Strong, *Procedures in Metaphysics.*

38. Cf. for instance Reiner, Die Entstehung und ursprüngliche Bedeutung des Namens Metaphysik (*In* Metaphysik und Theologie des Aristoteles, p. 39 et seq.). Here he rejects the older theory that the name is not of such great importance because it would have "rein äusserlich als eine *bibliothekarische* Verlegenheitsbezeichnung" been "read in" (by Andronicus of Rhodos) according to the position of this work in the whole Aristotelian oeuvre. Only later did the idea develop that the title also referred to the *content* of the work. Thus Reiner advocates a "sachliche Ordnung" instead of a "bibliothekarischen Ordnung" and according to him this practical arrangement is the same as that expressed in the name "first Philosophy" (cf. p. 152). He then adds that the name "Metaphysics" very likely came about on the ground of tendencies which were present in Aristotle himself.

39. In *Das Objekt der Metaphysik bei Aristoteles* Ambühl gives the following summary of possibilities, out of various books of the Metaphysics: "In A 1-2 werden der Weisheit, die dort zur Untersuchung steht, die ersten Principien und Ursachen als Objekt zugewiesen. In Γ 1 lesen wir von einer gewissen Wissenschaft welche das Seiende als Seiendes und das ihm an sich Zukommende betrachtet. Schliesslich hat sich E 1 die 'Erste Philosophie oder Theologie' mit dem 'Unbewegen und (von der Materie) Getrennten', oder sagen wir kurz, mit dem Immateriellen, zu befassen" (p. 9).
In other words, three possibilities: the first causes or principles, being as being, and the immaterial (incorporeal) being. The question is naturally whether these three things are not (aspects of) one and the same reality, so that Aristotle assigns them all (on different occasions) to the investigative area of *one* science. See in this connection also Merlan, Metaphysik: Name und Gegenstand. (*In* Metaphysik und Theologie des Aristoteles, p. 251 ff.); Mansion, Erste Philosophie, zweite Philosophie und Metaphysik bei Aristoteles. (*In* Metaphysik und Theologie des Aristoteles, p. 299); Zimmermann: Ontologie oder Metaphysik? p. 101 ff. and also Patzig, Theologie und Ontologie in der Metaphysik des Aristoteles *Kant Studien,* 52:185-205, 1960 and Söhngen, Zum aristotelischen Metaphysikbegriff (*In:* Philosophia Perennis. Festgabe Josef Geyser I, p. 27-38).

sometimes looks as if it has being as such as its field of study, and in other instances it seems as if the highest, immovable, divine being is its subject. P. Merlan puts it like this: "Sometimes Aristotle refers to first philosophy as being theology; sometimes he refers to it as being science of being-as-such. The former seems to lead to metaphysica specialis; the latter to metaphysica generalis"[40].

Various solutions to this difficulty have been advanced by scholars like Natorp, Jaeger, Merlan, Wagner, Geiger and Patzig[41], into which we shall not go at present as this would land us in all kinds of questions of detail. Against the background of Aristotle's doctrine of being (and his form-matter doctrine) it does not seem to be an insuperable problem. Precisely as a result of his Ontology[42] there ought to be no contradiction in this fact, that he sometimes indicates the divine substance and sometimes being as such, as being the proper subjects of his Theological or First Philosophy[43].

In my opinion Patzig, Wagner, Geiger and Rompe are correct in saying that reflection on existence as such leads to the substance (form or being) as the actual being (we have seen that for Aristotle scientific knowledge deals with the universal form, being, *ousia*, or substance) and at the same time opens the way to the unmoved mover as the first, purely spiritual and unchangeable substance. For Aristotle there is thus identity between First Philosophy as knowledge of God, and Philosophy of existence as such. Elizabeth Rompe summarizes: "Man wird folglich darin, dass der Stagirite zuweilen das *on he on*, zuweilen *prote ousia* als Gegenstand der prima philosophia nennt, keine Unsicherheit darüber sehen dürfen, warum es in dieser Wissenschaft geht. Ebenso wäre es falsch anzunehmen, Aristoteles habe vielleicht zwei verschiedene Disziplinen konstituieren wollen. Die

---

40. Merlan, *From Platonism to Neo-Platonism*, p. 161. This lack of clarity in Aristotle gave rise to three different interpretations in the later medieval Philosophy (when Aristotle was newly rediscovered), according to Zimmermann, op. cit.: God is one of many subjects of Metaphysics, God only is the cause of the subject of Metaphysics, and God is part of the subject (field) of Metaphysics . Callus also refers to this great confusion: The subject-matter of Metaphysics according to some thirteenth-century Oxford Masters. (*In* Die Metaphysik im Mittelalter, p. 393).

41. For a brief summary of their various solutions cf. Rompe: *Die Trennung von Ontologie und Metaphysik. Der Ablösungsprozess und seine Motivierung bei Benedictus Pererius und anderen Denkern des 16. und 17. Jahrhunderts*, p. 19-21.

42. For this see Owens, *The doctrine of being in the Aristotelian "Metaphysics"*.

43. As a result we would like to express our agreement with Patzig when he concludes: "... für Aristoteles besteht gar nicht der anstössige Widerspruch zwischen einer 'ersten Philosophie', die allgemeine Seinswissenschaft ist, und einer 'ersten Philosophie', die als Theologie nur die Substanz Gottes erforschte". Op. cit., p. 191.

Metaphysik ist für Aristoteles... Grundwissenschaft und oberste Wissenschaft zugleich. Das bedeutet, dass für Aristoteles die Frage nach dem seienden als Seienden Zusammenfält mit der Frage nach dem sein des Göttlichen"[44].

Perhaps the difficulty becomes even clearer if it is seen in the light of what has already been said about Aristotle's Ontology under 3.1. Following his dualistic path, he distinguished between a transcendent and a non-transcendent sphere. Seeing that the transcendent sphere also contains the deity, his Theology has transcendent being and his Philosophy non-transcendent being as respective areas of study.

In the later dualistic Christian thought of Thomas Aquinas, for instance, the Biblical God takes the place of that of Aristotle in the transcendent sphere. No longer is this God known by means of illumination, as in the case of Aristotle, but by his self-revelation. (The enormous difference between the heathen idea of illumination and the Revelation of God, too, is not always clearly realized.) This makes a Supernatural Theology possible for the Christian. However, as Aristotle's Philosophy of non-transcendent existence also included proofs of God, it could easily be extended into Natural Theology within the Christian milieu.

In conclusion, it is particularly important to take note that it is Aristotle's specific ontology of law, in particular, which makes his proofs of God (as the kernel of his Theological Philosophy) possible. By means of these universal forms, entities, causes or ideas in the things, abstracted by science, the conclusion is attainable that a pure form or first cause (god) exists.

3.4 'Regina scientarum'

Aristotle does not title his Theological Philosophy *"First* Philosophy" without reason[45]. According to his *Metaphysics* (book 3, chapter 2) Theology is for him the queen of the other sciences, which must obey her like slaves without daring to contradict her. The reason for the high rank of this science is the loftiness of its field of inquiry, viz. the first (divine) being[46].

---

44. Rompe, op. cit., p. 25.

45. According to Mansion Aristotle himself only employs the expression "Second Philosophy" once (cf. op. cit., p. 336) and from a study of his works it is evident that he means by this the science of Physics (cf. op. cit., p. 342). The ranking of the three philosophical disciplines (from lower to higher) is according to Aristotle, therefore, Mathematics, Physics and Theology.

46. Cf. id., p. 314.

3.5 Proofs of God

"Erstmals in den aristotelischen Schriften finden wir Beweise für die Existenz Gottes in streng wissenschaftlichen Form. Darum darf Aristoteles als der eigentliche Schöpfer formaler Gottesbeweise bezeichnet werden"[47].

In his *Metaphysics* Aristotle gives a whole collection of proofs of god. There is a proof from the stages of being, which conclude in a most complete divine being, as a result of the increase in completeness of being *ex gradibus*[48]. In addition he also accepts the renowned teleological proof. Just as someone who sees a ship nearing the port under full sail knows that it must have a steersman on board, so does the man who views the sun and the stars in their fixed orbits look for a mighty and immortal overseer of this order in god[49]. Thirdly, Aristotle teaches the kinesiological proof, from motion. Everything which moves is moved by something else. Since the series of movements or causes of the movements cannot extend indefinitely, there must be a first mover, itself immovable, from which all the movement proceeds. The first unmoved mover is, to Aristotle, god[50]. This proof is accompanied by his doctrine of act and potentiality. (As already explained, his god, as first cause, moves the world in the way a lover behaves towards his beloved, attractingly, like a purpose which is striven for.) A fourth proof is the so-called contingency proof which reasons from chance beings to an absolute, necessary being[51].

4 Results thus far

Summarizing, we can say that among the Greeks three main strategies were followed in the conflict which broke out between the old "theologians" and the new philosophers[52].

Some tried to assimilate the old Theology into their Philosophy. Empedocles, Heraclitus and others annexed well-known divine names from the cult and myth for their Philosophy. Something similar is to be seen in Plato

---

47. Huonder, op. cit., p. 27.

48. Cf. for this Aristotle's dialogue on Philosophy, Fragment 16. (*In* Rose: Aristoteles qui ferebantur fragmenta).

49. Cf. id., fragment 11.

50. Cf. *Metaphysics*, 1073a also Huonder's (op. cit., p. 28-31) exposition in this regard.

51. Cf. for this inter alia *Metaphysics*, 1072b.

52. Cf. Gigon, op. cit., p. 215, 216.

and Aristotle (as well as in the Stoa, which is discussed below). The allegorical method was one of the ways in which this assimilation and annexation could take place.

Others, as a result of the irreconcilability of Theology (or the religious views of the time) and Philosophy, sought a solution by distinguishing between various theologies. The three types (which are later most clearly evident in the Stoa, but which must be of much earlier date[53]), have already received mention.

In the third place there are those (such as Epicurus) who openly declared that they had no place in their philosophy for the old mythical theology (or folk religion), nor for the state cult. Nevertheless most of them in practice still obeyed the state cult — apparently because they did not wish to offend or disturb others, or land in danger themselves.

Most writers[54] trace the origin of Natural Theology only as far back as the Stoa. But the results of the aforegoing investigation show that the birth of Natural Theology must be sought for much earlier in the history of Western thought. Admittedly the Greeks did not employ the term "Natural Theology". Because of its nature it can only be used within synthetic thought, where a distinction can be made between natural and supernatural. However, Philosophical Theology in the later Greek thinkers shows some of the essential features of the later Natural Theology, which is a Theological Philosophy, too. Furthermore the heart of the later Natural Theology is also those proofs in which one deduces the existence of a God or a deity from the facts of   creation. The apologetic motif of the Greeks (their struggle against Atheism) is present in Philosophical Theology too, throughout its long history. It seems reasonable to conclude, therefore, that at least the foundations of Natural Theology had already been laid in Greek thought.

5 The Stoa

The Stoic vision of Theology is of particular importance for us, as Christian thinkers of later centuries were often confronted with it.

---

53. Gigon, op. cit., p. 216, says of the three theologies "... erstens die philosophische, die nicht jedermann zugänglich ist und auch nicht jedesmann mitgeteilt werden soll, weil sie leicht missverstanden werden kann; zweitens die politische, also der Staatskult, der durch sein Alter geheiligt und wegen seines pädagogischen Nutzens unentbehrlich ist; schliesslich die Theologie der Dichter, die im Sinne eines berühmten Satzes Platons im Grunde nicht wissen, was sie tun; sie kennen die Wahrheit nicht, aber es kann sein, dass in ihren Worten, wenn der Philosoph sie deutet, eben doch Wahrheit ist".

54. So, among others, De Vos in *Nieuw Theologisch Tijdschrift*, 30:250, 1942; Ebeling in RGG, 6:755, 1962 and Kattenbusch in *Zeitschrift für Theologie und Kirche*, 11:172 1930. Hessen is one of the few who returns to Aristotle for the origins of Natural Theology. Cf. *Griechische oder biblische Theologie*, p. 29.

The following three cases underline the actuality of this philosophical current down the ages.

On one of his missionary journeys Paul met up with Stoic philosophers on the Areopagus in Athens — the cradle of Western Philosophy. Some writers declare that Paul joined the Stoic (Natural) Theology in order to bring his philosopher-audience to faith.

The powerful attraction of Stoic philosophy for early Christian thinkers is also an established fact.

During the age of the Reformation the Stoa experienced an upswing and thinkers from the Middle Stoa (e.g. Cicero) and the Late Stoa (Seneca among others) were approached very sympathetically by reformers like Calvin.

5.1 Three kinds of Theology

We have already demonstrated above that in early Greek thought three different forms of theory about the gods and the divine had already come into existence alongside each other: those of the state cult (civic), the poetic-mythic, and the more philosophic-scientific. Stoic philosophers shaped these into three kinds of theology. Augustine points them out in Varro as *theologia civilis, mythica* and *physica*[55] or *politica, fabulosa* and *naturalis*[56].

According to Tertullian[57] and Augustine[58] this tripartite division stems from Varro (116-27 B.C.), while Augustine also mentions the name of Scaevola[59]. J. Pepin, in an especially valuable article[60], has investigated Varro's sources for the triple division[61].

Scaevola indeed distinguishes between three kinds of gods *(tria genera deorum)*[62] which were introduced by the poets, philosophers and statesmen, but not *explicitly* between three theologies. Furthermore his prefer-

---

55. Cf. Augustine in *De civitate Dei,* VI, 5.

56. Id., VI, 12.

57. Cf. his *Ad nationes,* III, 8-11.

58. Cf. Augustines, op. cit., VI, 5-12.

59. Cf. ibid., IV, 27.

60. Cf. Pepin, La "theologie tripartite" de Varron. *Revue des Études Augustiniennes,* 2:265-94, 1956.

61. Cf. ibid., p. 269-71.

62. Cf. Markus, *Studia Patristica,* 6:476, 1962.

ence is evidently for the Civic (National) Theology, from which position he criticizes the Mythic and Physical (Philosophical) Theologies. The Roman Stoic priest Scaevola defends the state cult[63].

According to Pepin, though, Scaevola was only a link between Varro and the threefold theology whose history went back still further to the Stoa. He discusses Panaetios[64] and Posidonios[65] in this connection and shows that one cannot precisely determine which one of them is the source of the triple division. It is at least clear that their threefold division goes back even further — to Zeno and Chrysippus at least. In this regard Pepin also demonstrates that the soil from which the *tripartita theologia* sprang was the confrontation between the physical (philosophical) and the mythical tradition, and the allegorical interpretation of the last-mentioned by the first-mentioned[66]. However the earlier Stoic thinkers held back from judging the Mythic and Civic Theologies. Hence in this case Scaevola (who openly chose the Civic Theology) and Varro (whose sympathy was obviously with Physical Theology) went much further.

As far as Varro himself is concerned, it is significant that (according to Augustine's account) he distinguished not just between three kinds of gods and their supporters (the poets, the people and the philosophers) but also between three sorts of theology[67].

It will be interesting to refer to four other figures in whom this triple category appears and who pass it on to Varro. They all lived at the end of the first century or during the second century A.D., coming after Varro but before Tertullian or Augustine. They are Plutarch[68], Chrysostom[69],

---

63. Cf. Pohlenz, *Die Stoa*, 262, 263.
Cf. also Ueberweg, *Grundriss der Geschichte der Philosophie I*, p. 477. According to him Scaevola's objections to the theology of the poets are that it is anthropomorphic and therefore false, his objections to that of the philosophers are that it is rational and thus true but unusable, so that only the theology of the statesmen is indispensable.

64. Pohlenz, op. cit., avers (p. 197, 8) that Panaetios was the actual founder of the threefold Theology.

65. For particulars of Panaetios and Posidonios see Pepin, op. cit., p. 290-4.

66. Cf. id., p. 294.

67. Cf. for Varro, apart from Pepin, op. cit., p. 272-8, also P. Boyancé, Sur la théologie de Varron. *Revue des Etudes Anciennes*, 57:57-84, 1955; Ueberweg, op. cit., p. 471 and Henry, Frühchristliche Beziehungen zwischen Theologie und Philosophie. *Zeitschrift für katholische Theologie*, 82:429, 1960.

68. Cf. his *Amatorius*, 18, 733B.

69. Cf. his *Orationes*, XII, 39-40.

Aetius[70] and Eusebius[71].

Chrysostom's ideas (2nd century A.D.)[72] are particularly significant for our study. In the 12th book of his *Orationes* he discusses the origin of the concept of God. The fundamental source, he maintains, is the universal idea of God, the innate conception. This a priori idea forms the basis on which secondary sources can fruitfully be employed. He discerns two such sources of knowledge of God, viz. that offered by the poets and that laid down in the laws of the state. The real source of belief in the gods is, however, the unalterable *inborn idea* which is preserved in all peoples and is of a rational nature. Over against this, knowledge of god from the two secondary sources consists of acquired conceptions which can only exist by virtue of the innate idea. This acquired knowledge (in poets and legislators) does not always express itself correctly or in agreement with the first (innate) concepts. According to Pepin this inborn comprehension of God easily falls into the category of Theological Philosophy.

What we come across in Chrysostom[73] is of the utmost importance. In later centuries this distinction between inborn and acquired knowledge is extended and some thinkers speak of a *theologia naturalis insita* and *acquisita*. Especially important here is the grounding of an implanted knowledge of God upon a certain ontology of law. The a priori theme (which we shall discuss at length below when we come to the speculations of the Stoa concerning the logos) forms the basis of his Theological Philosophy. The idea (as law) no longer exists as in Plato, outside the knowing intellect of man, but rather internally. Nevertheless the concept of the innate ideas cannot be divorced from the Platonic idea of law. This immediately reminds one of Plato's doctrine of *anamnêsis* as set out above (see 3.1.).

5.2 The theology of the Stoa within the framework of the sciences

In discussing Plato's views we have already made a few remarks about the division of Philosophy into Logic, Ethics and Physics — a division also adopted by the Stoa[74]. The place assigned to Theology within this scheme

70. Cf. his *Placita*, I, 6, 2-9.

71. Cf. his *Praeparatio Evangeliae*, IV, 1, 1-5.

72. Cf. Pepin, op. cit., p. 280, 281.

73. Epicurus had already said that nature itself had impressed upon all minds the idea of the gods as a result of which every man acknowledged their existence.

74. Cf. Pohlenz, op. cit., p. 33 and Markus, The study of theology and the framework of secular disciplines. *The Downside Review*, 78:193, 194, 1960.

is a part of the *philosophia physiké*. Sometimes it is said to be a subdivision of Physics (by Cleanthes and Julian the Apostate, for instance), but in other instances it has no subdivision or any distinguishing title, so that *philosophia theologiké* is indentical with *philosophia physiké*[75]).

The study of Theology springs from a study of the cosmos (*physis*) and is, in a certain sense, identical therewith: "For the thorough going Stoic, theology was, or at least tended to be, indentical with the study of nature. The coherent, necessary and rational system of the cosmos tends to become identified with divinity, and the study devoted to it, *Philosophia physiké* with theologia"[76]).

This differs significantly from Aristotle, for example. With him Theology belonged to *Meta*physics. In the Stoa Theology is included with Physics and although they assign the highest theoretical value to Physics, insofar as it includes the doctrine of the deity, it is in fact carried out with less effort and dedication in practice than Ethics, for instance.

5.3 Doctrine of the logos and proofs of god

The Stoa's doctrine of the logos contains their law ontology wherein they admittedly build upon the previous philosophies but also offer something quite new. All previous concepts of law within Greek philosophy (Subjectivism — law is sought in the subject; Objectivism — law is objectivized; and Realism — laws are separately existing things) had agreed that the law had   to be sought outside the knowing intellect. The shift in the time of the Hellenists which (other than Greek philosophy with its overwhelmingly ontological concerns) laid great stress on epistemology, was decisive for the further development of the vision of law[77]). Here an a priori scheme came into being which transferred law into the knowing intellect. The reason for this was the wave of scepticism which unsettled all the schools with its query as to whether the law was indeed knowable, or even if it existed. By placing the law (as an a priori concept) in man's knowing intellect (logos) an attempt was made to ensure its continued safety. As the name suggests, the laws are now a priori, i.e. previous to any experience of the human spirit in the form of generally valid conceptions of good or bad (for instance), right or wrong —   or conceptions of the gods themselves.

75. Cf. Markus, op. cit., p. 194.

76. Id., p. 194.

77. For an excellent survey of the development of ideas of law from Plato via Platonism and the Stoa to Patristic and Medieval Philosophy consult Armstrong and Markus, *Christian faith and Greek Philosophy*, chapter 3.

H. Hart sketches the drastic change during Hellenistic philosophy thus: "Practical life had been robbed of its necessary certainties, its points of orientation, its criteria for judging correctly in practical affairs. This explains the predominance of moral problems and the flowering of ethical schools in this period. An important problem became: what to say about the grounds of certainty? The final answer came in the spirit of the epistemological attitude: certainty lay in the inborn pre-suppositions of the understanding, in universals preceding experience but determinative of it. The universally valid conditions for all experience were located in the universally valid logical concepts of the individual human mind or the divine mind or the universal mind. This construction of understanding with a priori laws of existence or of experience was called ratio by Cicero. Its first exponent was Chrysippos around 200 B.C. and four hundred years later it was firmly lodged in every school of philosophy"[78].

In spite of all the good intentions which must have been behind it, this a priori theme opens up no Scriptural thought. According to Scripture the law has an existence outside man, "in" the things, and not in man's reason. Only the Scriptural conception of law, which acknowledges God as legislator, can give man the necessary security for his actions. By subjectively making the law dependent on the human *nous*, law is secured only by loose screws — as was already perfectly obvious in the further development of Western thought.

In criticizing the law ontology of Hellenism in general and that of the Stoa in particular, their Theology is simultaneously being criticised, since their concept of law, as will hereafter be apparent, forms its foundation.

The Stoic thinkers conceive of the *logoi spermatikoi*[79] or germs of reason as seminal powers in the godhead or logos, immanent in creation.

---

78. Hart, *Communal certainty and authorized truth*, p. 2. He gives a more comprehensive exposition in *The challenge of our age*, p. 42-44. The a priori theme is still more thoroughly treated by Runner, The relation of the Bible to learning. (*In* Christian Perspectives 1960, p. 142-4). Cf. also the short summary of Vollenhoven, Conservatisme en progressiviteit in de wijsbegeerte. (*In* Conservatisme en progressiviteit in de wetenschap, p. 40).

79. One of the best studies of the subject is that of Holte, *Logos spermatikos. Christianity and ancient philosophy according to St. Justin's Apologies. Studia Theologica*, 12:109-68, 1958. Not only does he briefly discuss the most important research on this topic, but he also gives a short historical overview of the development of the logos in many thinkers. Of the Stoa in this connection he says (among other things): "Individual matter is regarded as part and offshoot of the Original Spirit. The effective causes of individual matter is called Logoi Spermatikoi. These, too, are only differentiations of the Original Logos and are even described as identical with him. Logos is the principle both for Man's intellectual and moral life. Logos is both natural and moral law, and the condition for all human knowledge and moral action is based upon the fact that the human reason (Logos) is an emanation of the Divine Reason (the Original Logos)." p. 120.

According to Zeno (336-279 B.C.), the father of the Stoa, the general law which exists in the reason and permeates all things is equal to the god Zeus. Hence H. Meyer maintains that the concept of the *logoi spermatikoi* is derived from Zeno[80].

It is important to note that the deity (*Logos*) manifests or reveals himself in creation by means of the law *(logoi spermatikoi)*.

Pohlenz, an expert on the Stoa, provides the following synopsis "Gottes Wesen offenbart sich uns allein in der schöpferischen Urkraft, aus der als erster Ursache alle Bewegung und alle Gestaltung des Einzelseins entspringt. Gott kann nichts anders sein als der Logos, der die vernünftige Keimkräfte füre jede künftige Entwicklung in sich trägt und die schöpferische Seite der Allsubstanz darstelt. Mit der Hyle von Ewigkeit verbunden, ist er selbst körperlich, ist Feuer, aber Zugleich Geist. Man kann ihn ebensowohl 'denkendes Feuer' wie 'feurigen Geist' nennen. Er ist mit der Physis identisch als das künstlerisch gestaltende Feuer, das auf methodischen Wegen Zum Schaffen schreitet. Gott ist Künstler, aber er steht nicht ausserhalb des Stoffes, ist nicht transzendent, sondern der Welt immanent. Er gibt allem Gestalt, wandelt sich selbst in alles, durchdringt die ganze Welt und macht sie selbst zu etwas Göttlichem. Der Kosmos umschliesst ja auch die Vernunftwesen, enthält die Keimkräfte, aus denen diese hervorgehen. Wie kan man est leugnen, dass er selbst Vernunft hat und ein vernünftiges Lebenswesen ist! Er ist das schönste und volkommenste Seiende, unendlich viel umfassender und höher als alle Einzelwesen, die ihm ihr Sein verdanken; er hat die vollendetste Gestalt"[81].

Owing to the link between the *logos* and the *logoi spermatikoi*, knowledge of the godhead can be achieved with the help of human reason. The invisible (deity) can be known by means of the signs which it has left behind

80. Cf. Meyer, H. *Geschichte der Lehre von der Keimkräften von der Stoa bis zum Ausgang der Patristik*, p. 16. According to him the Stoa conceived its doctrine of the *logoi spermatikoi* in line with the philosophy of Heraclitus. Cf. p. 7 and 16.

81. Pohlenz, op. cit., p. 95. In his contribution on the Stoa in *The Cambridge History of later Greek and early Mediaeval Philosophy* (p. 124) A.H. Armstrong provides the following accurate categorization, which aids us, too, in understanding their Physical Theology better: "The Stoic system can be interpreted in two ways. We see in it either a 'mundanization' and a materialization of the divine, or, on the contrary, a divinization and spiritualization of matter".

in the visible (including man himself)[82]. In this way a Physical or Natural Theology is possible.

In their proofs for the existence of god they begin (inter alia) with the *consensus omnium*. Cicero's observation that no people is so primitive and uncivilized that it has no conception of god is widely known. However, in Theology this natural knowledge of god is purified and illuminated.

According to K. Leese[83], however, the Stoa had already offered the three famous proofs of god which remained in force until the Enlightenment, viz. the cosmological, ontological and teleological. The cosmological begins with the existing world and concludes with the first cause. The ontological starts with the concept of the most perfect being and reasons towards his existence. The teleological begins with the beauty and purposefulness of the universe and reasons towards a primeval force which encompasses all the active powers as *logoi spermatikoi*. Panaetios even develops his own doctrine of foreknowledge in this fashion, for the beauty, order and purpose of the cosmos cannot be the work of blind chance.

The logos theories of the Stoa had a profound influence on the early Christian thinkers and also much later, when during the Reformation and Renaissance a large-scale re-awaking of Stoic thought took place. Some writers have even maintained that Paul would also have been influenced by the Stoa, and would thus also have championed a Stoic (Natural) Theology. But after the comprehensive studies of Gärtner and others[84] there should

---

82. Cf. for this R. Lorenz, Die Wissenschaftslehre Augustins. *Zeitschrift für Kirchengeschichte*, 67:230, 231, 1955/56.
"To the Stoic philosopher, man's guiding principle in this world is his reason, which is a portion of the divine *Logos*. The origin of the knowledge of God is to be sought in himself". Gärtner, *The Areopagus speech and natural revelation*, p. 105-06. Cf. also p. 110: "In Stoic philosophy ... we are dealing with a *Logos*, lodged in the cosmos, which man must fathom, and this knowledge is rendered accessible nay, more, guaranteed, by his own nature. He has a share and a kinship with this *Logos*, and this faculty enables him to achieve a true knowledge of God and the universe. Thus, the fundamental part of Stoic knowledge of God resides in the cosmos and in human reason". Ibid., p. 115.

83. Cf. Leese, *Recht und Grenzen der naturlichen Religion*, p. 20, 21. According to Gigon, *Grundprobleme der antiken Philosophie*, p. 221, by this time all the following proofs of God had however come into being: the historical argument that all people have a realization of god, god as first cause, god as final end, god as that to which the cosmic order must be ascribed, god as first mover and god as perfectly complete. Cf. also Huonder, op. cit., p. 33.

84. Cf. Gärtner, op. cit., where he carefully compares the Natural Theology of the Stoa with the Scriptural doctrine of the revelation of God in creation (Romans 1:19, 20 and Acts 17, amongst others) and convincingly demonstrates that the Bible definitely does not teach the Stoic Natural Theology nor is it influenced thereby, but rather radically rejects it. The New Testament obviously follows the Old Testament in this regard and not Hellenistic tradition.

no longer be any doubt that this was certainly not the case. The Bible's teaching on God's revelation and the natural theological speculations of the Stoic philosophers are two entirely different matters.

6 Flashback

A short review of all the different schools of thought which we have explored might be desirable at this point. Three themes in particular have been of special importance.

In the first place there was the philosophical struggle against the mythic theologies (using, amongst other devices, allegorical exegesis) and, later, even against the so-called political theologies, which gave rise to a *triplex theologiae.* Of these three the physical theology, which did not accept the existence of the gods on the authority of the myths or the state cult but wished to demonstrate it from the cosmos itself, eventually emerged as seemingly the strongest. This type of Philosophical Theology was also the forerunner of the later Natural Theology of the Christian milieu.

In the second place we cursorily followed the development of the conceptions of law from Subjectivism through Objectivism, Plato's Realism and Aristotle's Hulemorphism up to the a priori theme in the logos speculations of Hellenism. Although unscriptural, none of these ideas of law totally missed the mark. Each one caught something of the character of the law. But seeing that the pagan thinkers did not know the Word of God, in the light of which they could construct their ontologies of law, the truth was continually distorted. They did not rightly understand God's laws for the things, so that their conception of law became the basis for all kinds of theological philosophies. This happened, in particular, because they did not know, nor did they acknowledge, the radical difference between God, law and cosmos.

In the aforegoing our attention has not been focussed without reason upon the different ideas of law. This particular emphasis might create the impression that the concepts of law were over-emphasized at the cost of the other philosophical presuppositions of Philosophical Theology. However, this course was deliberately pursued because it was mainly the law which served in these schools as the ontological springboard towards a Philosophical Theology. Naturally a certain view of law goes hand in hand with a certain idea of god and of cosmos. However there was no space to give more than the essentials in this survey of many centuries.

In the third place it was apparent how all sorts of evidences for god came into being and multiplied, from apologetic motives in particular (inter alia, the struggle against Atheism). Basically all these proofs boil down to one thing, namely an argument from the cosmos as to the existence of god or gods.

***

SUMMARY

Within the limits of an article as short as this one, we could only indicate a few characteristic points. We will briefly pay attention to the pre-Platonics, Plato, Aristotle and the Stoics. A thorough discussion of these figures and developments was not possible. It is our intention merely to dig around a bit, with a view to understand the present shape of Western Theology somewhat better, and especially its so-called Natural Theology.

1. The Theology of the pre-Platonic thinkers

Scholars differ greatly about the question whether Theology or Philosophy was the first science. The cause of the confusion among historians is that a later problematics is carried into pre-Platonic thinking which did not originally occur there. For this reason the pre-Platonics are usually treated as philosophers, while others say that they were in the first place and without exception theologians. Others again distinguish two phases in ancient Greek thought, of which the first was theological and the second philosophical. Some even think that Greek thinking was purely Natural Theology.

I think that a more correct view would hold that these two sciences were not yet so clearly differentiated at that time. At the beginning of our Western history Theology and Philosophy are still one. In their unity they deal with the same matters. This unity is so close that only from a further development in history, in which we see the split of the two, can the two be distinguished.

Simply to think that the ideas of the pre-Platonics about the gods was their theology, is not correct, since they themselves did not clearly pronounce themselves about this matter. Even with the help of later descriptions of Theology given by Plato and Aristotle, we should not look for either pure Theology or pure Philosophy in pre-Platonic thought.

Even if we accept that their thinking about the gods was their Theology, there remain many difficulties, such as whether Theology dealt with divinities as well as with the divine. It could, for example, have been possible to indicate their study of the gods as their Theology and their study of the divine as Philosophy.

Already early in Greek thinking there are three different forms of thinking about the gods: a mythical type, a philosophical type (although the mythical was philosophical too which merely occurs in poetic form) and a civil type. This is very important, because it later on gave rise to Theology in mythical, natural and civil types with figures such as Panaetios, Scaevola, Varro, Tertullian and Augustine.

2. Plato (427-347 B.C.)

He was the first thinker who used the word "theology" and in whose work the science of Theology comes out a bit more clearly. But since he was not a systematician, much remains unclear here as well. He obviously did not have the need to systematise all that he thought about during his life. Aristotle was the first great analyst and systematician, the grand master of distinguishing, dividing and subdividing. (One could compare Plato's thought to a wild creek, while Aristotle's is more like a man-made irrigation.)

His Theology especially has a negative and critical function. It has the task to protect from the errors of the mythical poets such as Hesiod and Homer. In the interest of the state, and according to severe directives, the myths have to be cleansed from their offensive contents. The criteria for the admissability of myths is among other things that the gods are good and not the origin of evil, unchanging and therefore not subject to blackmail and not liars. In his book about the laws, the State is built on true religion and for that reason the citizen has to have the right knowledge of the gods.

The positive task of Theology is to give a description of the gods on a more scientific level.

We find in Plato's thought a conflict between the mythical traditions and the more rational approach to the gods. Theoretical knowledge is placed above the popular faith of the people.

3. Aristotle (384-322 B.C.)

He uses the word "theology" in two senses, namely systematically and historically.

The historian Aristotle indicates with *hoi theologoi* the Greek thinkers that Vollenhoven characterizes as mythologising. But then he means the oldest group, Hesiod *cum suis*. According to Aristotle these theologians precede the philosophers of whom Thales was the first.

Especially the systematic use of the word "theology" by Aristotle, in the way we find it also in his division of the sciences, is important.

According to the first chapter of the sixth book of the *Metaphysics* it is necessary to distinguish three types of thinking or philosophy, namely practical-ethical, poetical-technical and theoretical thought. Of these three types of philosophy the latter is the highest. Theoretical Philosophy is subdivided into three types: the mathematical, the natural and the theological *(philosophia mathematikè, physikè* and *theologikè)*. Of these three the last is the highest. In Physics, the important thing is that which exists independent by itself and is moving, while in Mathematics we investigate what does not exist independent by itself and does not move, while in Theology we investigate that which does exist by itself and is independent but does not move.

So Theology deals with independent beings which is not subject to motion. This science is also called First Philosophy or Wisdom.

Not without reason Aristotle calls Theological Philosophy *First* Philosophy. According to the second chapter of Book 3 of the *Metaphysics* Theology is the queen of the other sciences which need to obey her without daring to speak up to her. The reason for the high ranking of this science is the importance of its field of interest, namely first or divine being.

4. Results with respect to Greek thinking

In summary we can say that in the conflict between the old theologies and the new philosophy the Greeks followed three roads.

Some tried to assimilate the old Theology in Philosophy. Empedocles, Heracleitos and others annex well known gods from cult and myth for their philosophy. Something like this is found also in Plato and Aristotle and even in the Stoa who will be treated later. The allegorical method was one of the ways which allowed this assimilation and annexation.

Others, as a result of the incompatibility between Theology (or the religious view of the day) and Philosophy, looked for a solution by distinguishing different kinds of Theology. We already mentioned the three types of theology, which later on with the Stoics became much clearer, but which originate from earlier times.

In the third place there are those, like Epicuros, who openly declared that in their philosophy there was no room for old mythical theology or for civil religion and not for popular religion either. Nevertheless, most of them in practice obeyed state religion, apparently because they did not want to give offense or to let others stumble or endanger themselves.

5. The Stoics (± 300 B.C. – ± 200 A.D.)

We already indicated that early in Greek thinking there were three forms of thinking about the gods and the divine: the state-cult of civil religion, the poetic-mythical kind, and the more philosophic-scientific one. The Stoics reshape this division into three kinds of theology: *theologia civilis, mythica* and *physica* or *politica, fabulosa* and *naturalis*.

The origin of these three kinds of theology (*tripartita theologia*) is traced in this article in the work of Zeno, Chrysippos, Panaetios, Posidonios, Scaevola, Varro, Plutarchos, Chrysostom, Aetius, Eusebius, Tertullian and Augustine.

The division of Philosophy into Logic, Ethics and Physics (among others that of Plato) is taken over by the Stoics. The obvious place for Theology within this pattern is that it has to be part of the *philosophia physikè*. Sometimes this is looked upon as a subdivision of physics (for example Cleanthes and Julian the Apostate), however, sometimes without any subdivision or differentiating name, so that *philosophia theologikè* becomes identical with *philosophia physikè*.

The study of Theology resulted from a study of the cosmos *(physis)*. This is an important difference with, for example, Aristotle. In his work Theology belongs to *Meta*physics. The Stoa take Theology as part of Physics.

Special attention is also paid in the treatment of the Stoa to their views of Logos, since this makes their special view with respect to Theology more understandable.

6. Conclusion

The philosophical battle against mythical theology (among others with the use of allegorical exegesis) and also against socalled political theology, gave rise to a *triplex theologiae*. Of these three theologies the physical, which did not accept the existence of the gods on the authority of myths or of the state cultus, but which wanted to prove their existence from the cosmos itself, would finally turn out to be the strongest. This type of Philosophical Theology was the precursor of later natural theologies in Christian circles.

Most authors go back to the Stoa in dealing with the origin of Natural Theology. According to the result of our research the origin of Natural Theology must be sought much further back into the history of Western Thought. The Greeks, of course, did not use the name "Natural Theology". This could naturally first arise within synthetic thinking in which a distinction was made between a natural and a supernatural realm.

Greek and Stoic philosophical Theology show essential characteristics of later Natural Theology. The later Natural Theology also is a Theological Philosophy. In addition, the aim of later Natural Theology is also the proving of the existence of God, which leads to the conclusion of the existence of God or a divinity from out of creation. The apologetic motive of the Greeks (the battle against atheism and the resulting proofs) accompany Philosophical Theology throughout its long history.

It seems permissible to conclude that at least the foundations of later Natural Theology can already be found in Greek and Stoic thinking.

3 EISEGESIS-EXEGESIS, PARADOX AND NATURE-GRACE: METHODS OF SYNTHESIS IN MEDIEVAL PHILOSOPHY*

The aim of this article, which is dedicated to Prof. Dr. D.H. Th. Vollenhoven in celebration if his eightieth birthday, is to elaborate on his distinction between three methods of synthesis during Patristic and Medieval Philosophy**.

By way of background, a few introductory remarks concerning Vollenhoven's distinction between pre-synthetic, synthetic and anti-synthetic thought, about the causes for synthetic thought and the different solutions attempted for the problem of the relationship between the Christian and the pagan world, may be helpful.

1. Pre-synthetic, synthetic and post-synthetic thought

Vollenhoven divides the history of philosophy into three main periods. From about 700 B.C. to 40 A.D. there is the period prior to synthesis. (Ancient Greek, Hellenistic and Roman philosophy). From approximately 40 A.D. up to 1600 we have the period of synthesis (Patristic and Medieval Philosophy). From 1600 to the present time the philosophic attitude is described as anti-synthetic. (Modern and Contemporary Philosophy).

This division into three periods stems from Vollenhoven's query as to whether a philosopher's heart is or is not directed in obedience to God. The religious standpoint is decisive for every philosopher's conception. The place given to the Word of God in a philosophy clearly reveals the attitude of the philosopher towards the God of the Word. With regard to the question of how a thinker viewed Holy Scripture in his philosophy there are two possible answers: either the revelation of God's Word received its rightful place, or it did not. Seldom will we meet up with the first answer in the history of philosophy. The second possibility, viz. that the Word of God did not receive its appropriate place, is the dominant answer and it includes two different attitudes: either Holy Scripture is completely and illegitimately disregarded, or it is halfheartedly acknowledged and it does not find its rightful place because it was accommodated to or synthesized with un-

* Originally published in *Philosophia Reformata*, 38:191-210, 1973.

** The purpose of this contribution is not to present a detailed research into the methods of synthesis, but rather to offer a general introduction and survey. Specialists in the field of early Christian and Medieval Philosophy and Theology will perhaps not find anything original because it is my intention to be of assistance to both the layman and the student. This will also account for the extensive bibliographical references I have considered necessary to include in the footnotes.

scriptural ideas. Taking the period of synthetic thought as the decisive criterion enabled Vollenhoven to divide the history of philosophy into the three above-mentioned periods.

Before the coming of Christ the Word of God was confined more or less to Israel, the elect. The Greeks and Romans, who made such a very important contribution to Philosophy, knew nothing about the Bible. They were pagans in their philosophy and could not give the word of God its rightful place because it was unknown to them. Already very early there existed certain types of synthesis or compromise between heathendom and parts of the Bible, viz. the Old Testament. This synthesis, however, occurred on a small scale because God limited His Word of Revelation to the patriarchs and later on to Israel. Christianity and pagan thought developed separately. After the coming of Christ and the descent of the Holy Spirit, the Gospel was no longer restricted to the Jews but was preached all over Europe. Then the paths of Christianity and paganism converged and a synthesis between paganism and Christianity occurred on a considerable scale.

The synthesis between Christian and pagan thought could not, in the long run, endure. The paths of Christian and pagan thought again separated when it became clear that they could not co-exist in the same system. There were, however, two different motivations for this anti-synthetical philosophy which make it possible to distinguish between an anti-synthetic left and an anti-synthetic right direction. Amongst the former we find those who, in their philosophical thought, broke with the synthetic mind. The representatives of this direction were not necessarily unbelievers; they may have been Christians who did not reckon that the Bible should be accorded a positive rôle in scientific endeavour. The anti-synthetic right direction of thought on the other hand wanted to break with the synthetic attitude so as to give Scripture its legitimate place in science.

2. Focus on synthetic thought

As an introduction to the question of how synthesis became possible this article confines itself to the reasons as to *why* synthetic thought[1] developed. In other words it enquires into the methods which were applied to accomplish such a synthesis. Vollenhoven very briefly mentions three methods[2]. Further reflections on them may not only deepen our insight

1. Synthetic thought is not the same as syncretism. Cf. K.J. Popma: "Natuur en gena-de". *Philosophia Reformata*, 36:102, 1971. For a distinction between the different forms of syncretism see M.R. van den Berg: *Syncretisme als uitdaging* (1966), p. 16, 33-35.

2. Cf. *Kort overzicht van de Geschiedenis der Wijsbegeerte voor den Cursus Paedago-giek* M.O.A. Amsterdam, Theja, n.d., p. 23, 25 and 26.

into Medieval. Philosophy, but may also be relevant for our understanding of contemporary thought because, though the main tendency from about the sixteenth century onwards was anti-synthetic, the synthetic mind never completely disappeared. On the contrary, we experience a very powerful inclination towards synthetic thought within contemporary Christianity.

3. The causes for synthetic thought

The synthesis commenced in the early Christian church. The early Christians correctly realized that God had revealed the truth in His Word. They were, however, also aware of the fact that Greek philosophy had attained many moments of valuable insight. The question was what the exact relation between the Word of God and Greek philosophy should be. Different factors encouraged a synthesis between the two.

Many of the converts were philosophers. They could not immediately rid themselves of their pagan convictions and even those who enjoyed a Christian upbringing were still daily surrounded by pagan culture.

Secondly, paganism launched an attack upon the church. To make their defence understandable the Christians had to use a terminology which they borrowed from pagan philosophy. The result was that all kinds of Greek ideas crept into Christian thought[3].

Thirdly, the plague of internal heresy demanded a clearer exposition and articulation of Christian belief or dogma. In this respect Christians also borrowed the theoretical equipment for their understanding of Scriptures from pagan thought. The result was not only that the missionary type of sermon was displaced in favour of a predominantly apologetic exposition[4]

3. J. Hessen puts it as follows: "Diese (the Christians — B.J. v.d.W.) will die heidnische Welt erobern. Das kann sie aber nur, wenn sie deren Sprache redet. Aber das genügt noch nicht: sie muss auch in deren Denkformen denken. Ihr bleibt deshalb nichts anderes übrig, als dass sie den Inhalt ihrer Verkündigung in eine philosophische Form kleidet, mit den Gedankenmitteln der griechischen Philosophie zum Ausdruck bringt. Die Folge davon ist, dass aus der geoffenbarten *Botschaft* immer mehr eine geoffenbarten *Lehre wird.*" *Griechische oder biblische Theologie? Das Problem der Hellenisierung des Christentums in neuer Beleuchtung* (1956), p. 10, 11.

4. Cf. J. Quasten: *Patrology I* (1950), p. 186.

but that paganism and apostasy severely affected the Christian message5).

A fourth reason for the development of synthetic thought was the fact that for the majority of the early Christians, their conversion merely meant a change in their cultic life of worship, and they did not fully realize what the implications were for the whole of life and society. Consequently it was for them easier to decide on an attitude towards paganism in religious matters than in scientific and philosophic ones. This loss of vision of the Kingdom was of the utmost significance, because to be Christian was soon regarded as merely amounting to membership in the Christian Church. The calling and task involved in being a Christian in the all-encompassing Kingdom of God in all spheres of life was lost sight of. Because the church was not regarded as just an important facet of the Kingdom of God, but was more or less identified with it, the reforming power of the Word of God was confined to the ecclesiastical area. The world outside the church was regarded as pagan. The relationship between church and heathendom was identified with that existing between the Church and the world. In this way the false dilemma between church and/or world originated. The three different solutions given for this problem will soon be made clear.

I want to conclude my brief sketch[6] by saying that the early Christians

---

5. We meet up with various views as to the extent of pagan influence on Christianity. On the one hand we have the famous words of A. von Harnack: "Das Dogma ist in seiner Konzeption und seine Ausbau ein Werk des griechischen Geistes auf dem Boden des Evangeliums". *Lehrbuch der Dogmengeschichte I* (1900), p. 20. On the other hand the influence of pagan philosophy on Christian thought is often underestimated. Cf. for instance J. Hessen, op. cit., p. 96. In my opinion the idea that paganism merely had a "formal" and no "material" influence on Christian thought is an underestimation of the real impact of heathendom. According to proponents of this theory, Christianity, far from losing anything actually, gained by means of pagan influence. Cf. R. Seeberg: *Lehrbuch der Dogmengeschichte* (1913-1920) and W. Glawe: *Die Hellenisierung des Christentums in der Geschichte der Theologie von Luther bis auf die Gegenwart* (1912).
Interesting literature to consult in this connection is the inaugural address of J.J. Thierry: *Die Stoa van Zeno of de Zuilengang van Salomo* (1958) and H. Robbers: *Antieke wijsgerige opvattingen in het Christelijke denkleven* (1959).

6. More details will be found in the following selection of studies on this topic: R. Klein (ed.): *Das Frühe Christentum im römischen Staat* (1971); J. Speigl: *Der römische Staat und die Christen: Staat und Kirche von Domitian bis Commodus* (1970); J. Geffcken: *Das Christentum im Kampf und Ausgleich mit der griechisch-römischen Welt* (1920); O. Gigon: *Die Antike Kultur und das Christentum* (1966); W. Jaeger: *Early Christianity and Greek Paideia* (1961); A Rijswijck: "De waardering voor de klassieke bij de vroeg-christelijke schrijvers". *Hermeneus*, 20:1-5, 1948/49; G. van der Leeuw: "De botsing tusschen heidendom en christendom in de eerste vier ecuwen". *Mededelingen der Akademie van Wetenschappen. Afdeling Letterkunde*, nr. 9:53-79, 1949; W.N. Coetzee: "Die Christendom en die Klassieke". *Koers*, 22:131-150, 1954 and A Sizoo: *Het Christendom en zijn verhouding tot de antieke cultuur* (1952)
The resistence on the part of paganism is described in books such as the following: G. Bossier: *Het stervend heidendom. Een cultuurbeeld van de 4e eeuw onzer jaartelling* (1912); P. de Labriolle: *La réaction paienne, étude sur la polémique antichrétienne du Ier au VIe siècle* (1934); J. Geffcken: *Der Ausgang des griechisch-römischen Heidentums* (1963) and N.J. Hommes: "Christendom en antieke Cultuur". In: *Cultuurgeschiedenis van het Christendom* (second print 1957, I, p. 399 et seq.).

were rarely aware of the synthesis they were constructing — just as Christians today do not perhaps fully realize their adherence to unscriptural ideas. It should be remembered that it was not easy for the early Christians to maintain their identity amongst a powerful pagan culture. Because we are able to view this period from a distance and therefore more objectively, it is far easier for us to detect the pagan elements in the thought of the early Christians. We should therefore not condemn them too severely particularly when we know that up to the present day the problem of the relationship between church and world remains unsolved for many Christians. We still struggle with the age-old problem of faith (in the Word of God) and reason (modern secular science and philosophy)[7] which was already a vital issue in early Christian reflection[8].

4. Athens and Jerusalem

In the critical issue as to the relationship between the Christian (or church) and the world, we may discern three main solutions: world conformity, world flight and world compromise. All these solutions reveal a synthetic attitude and they are clearly revealed in the three methods of synthesis which Vollenhoven distinguishes. By using Tertullian's metaphor of Jersalem, i.e. the Bible, and Athens, i.e. Greek Philosophy, I can summarize as follows.

The method of *eisegesis-exegesis* revealed an attitude of *world conformity*. It claimed that Jerusalem was identical to Athens and vice versa. All that was necessary was that the pagan philosophy of Athens should obtain Biblical sanction and authority from Jerusalem by an allegorical interpretation of Scripture.

In reaction to the ideal of world conformity, but without any real solution, the method of *paradox* advocated an attitude of *world flight*. Jerusalem had nothing to do with Athens. They were directly opposed to each other and it was considered that Jerusalem (faith) should avoid Athens (reason) at every cost. Nevertheless, both had their own right of separate existence.

---

7. Illustrative of the contemporary struggle with this problem are H. Gollwitzer and W. Weischedel: *Denken und Glauben. Ein Streitgespräch* (1965); *Grensgesprekken. Evangelie en Wetenschappen* (1969); the two volumes edited by C.J. Dippel: *Geloof en Natuurwetenschap* (Vol. I, 1965 and Vol. II, 1967) and the special issue of *Annalen van het Thijmgenootschap* entitled "Leven, weten, geloven" (Vol. 56, no. 2, 1969).

8. A summary of three different solutions to the problem of faith and reason in Patristic and Medieval thought is given by the following authors: W. Betzendörfer: *Glauben und Wissen bei den Grossen Denkern des Mittelalters* (1931), p. 257; J. Finkenzeller: *Offenbarung und Theologie nach der Lehre des Johannes Scotus* (1961), p. 222-228 and E. Gilson: *Reason and revelation in the Middle Ages* (1952).

The method of nature — supernature preached *world compromise* in an attempt to avoid the extremes of both world conformity and world flight. Jerusalem, representing the Scriptures, faith, church etc. was not permitted to be merged into Athens, the secular world made up of philosophy, reason etc., nor to escape from it. Jerusalem was neither identical to Athens, nor opposed to it, but as the superior to an inferior realm, it surpassed Athens.

These solutions to the problem of the relationship between a Christian and a sinful world were of decisive importance because they shaped our Western civilization. Contemporary Western man — and especially the modern Christian — often discloses his split personality which is the result of the blending of Jerusalem and Athens nearly two thousand years ago[9].

5. The method of eisegesis-exegesis

Exegesis can never be an absolutely neutral activity of "read and listen" only. On the contrary, it can be a very risky procedure because exegesis is very often preceded by eisegesis. Vollenhoven describes this process during synthetic thought as follows: Foreign ideas clashing with biblical revelation were first read into the Bible and afterwards taken out again but now with biblical sanction[10]. Eisegesis-exegesis means the reading into and attributing unto the Scriptures what is not there or even what is in conflict with Scripture, thus making it seem as if the Bible sanctioned pagan ideas. The Word of God is used in this way to make an unbiblical way of thought and life legitimate.

In this respect allegorical exegesis was a useful device because according to this exegetical method the real meaning of a text differs from its literal

---

9. "Onze Westeuropese cultuur vertoont een merkwaardig gespletenheid, die haar oorsprong vindt in de bronnen waaruit zij is ontstaan. Twee werelden hebben samengewerkt tot het voortbrengen van de beschaving, zoals wij die heden ten dage kennen. De ene noemen wij de wereld van Athene, die andere de wereld van Jeruzalem..."
"Twee zeer onderscheiden werelden, die van Athene en die van Jeruzalem zijn dus in onze beschaving samengevloeid, maar zij zijn vaak samengevloeid zoals water en olie samenvloeien... De Europese mens is een gespleten mens". G.J. Hoenderdaal: *De mens in tweestrijd* (1965), p. 37, 41.
The following studies are worthwhile consulting for the problem of the relationship between church and world: M.C. Smit: *Cultuur en Heil* (1959); K.J. Popma: *Venster op de wereld* (1968), p. 79-83 and 92-94; R. Soedarmo: *In de wereld maar niet van de wereld. Een studie over de grondgedachten van de theologie van Friedrich Gogarten* (1957) and J.C. van der Stelt: "Church and Society (An orientation)". *International Reformed Bulletin*, 11 (34):15-36, July 1958.

10. Vollenhoven, op. cit., p. 23.

sense[11]. Strictly speaking one should not speak of allegorical *exegesis* because it is no real exegesis or explanation of the text, but merely free interpretation[12].

Allegory is a type of figurative (metaphorical) language[13] and as such nothing is wrong with it because it enriches our way of expression. The problem with allegorical interpretation, however, is that a text is assumed to be an allegory which it was never intended to be. The obvious meaning of the text is regarded as insufficient, inferior, and even offensive. The sense of the literal meaning is merely regarded to serve as a bridge or pointer to the real meaning. It is clear that in this way injustice is done to both author and text.

The vital question is *why* the allegorical exegete rejects the obvious meaning as being too poor to be conclusive. A statement of C.M. Edsman gives us an answer and reveals to us why this type of interpretation was so popular during synthetic thought: "Die allegorische Exegese oder *Allegorese* hat in allen Religionen mit heiligen Urkunden eine grosse Rolle gespielt, um den feststehenden Formulierungen einen neuen und zeitgenössischen Inhalt beizulegen und dadurch auch die Autorität kanonischer Schriften zu bewahren"[14].

These words may be applied to nearly every form of allegorical exegesis in Western thought. When a change in the view of life and world occurs, which is contrary to current religious convictions, as contained in the sacred scriptures, allegorical exegesis is applied — in order not to read what is written in the texts but to read into them what is not there. The holy book is thus used merely as a protective screen, and in reality is robbed of its authority. There are many examples of allegorical exegesis in Greek, Jewish, Arabic and Christian thought.

5.1 Allegorical exegesis among the Greeks

The allegorical type of exegesis is nearly as old as Western civilization.

---

11. ἀλληγορέω is derived from ἄλλο s (= other) + ἀγορεύω (= to speak in public) and literally means "to speak like somebody else". According to Liddel & Scott in their *Abridged Greek-English Lexicon* ἀλληγορέω means "so to speak as to imply other than what is said".

12. Cf. in this connection H.G. Stoker's article: "Uitlegging of Interpretasie." *Koers*, 2(5):26-33, April 1935, especially p. 27-28.

13. K.J. Popma discusses this in detail in his article "Philoonsche en Stoische Allegoristiek". *Vox Theologica*, 15(3):61, 1943.

14. Edsman: "Allegorie" in *Die Religion in Geschichte und Gegenwart* (3rd Print) I, p. 238.

The Greeks made use of it probably because they believed that the gods reveal themself in riddles, oracles and mysteries which could not be understood literally[15]. When the older mythological singers and poets in Greek culture were followed by the more rational philosophically inclined thinkers, allegorical exegesis became very prominent. The philosophical ideas about the gods clashed in the main, with the traditional myths about them. Because it was important for the more intellectually inclined not to be regarded as irreligious, they had to interpret the prevailing ideas about the gods in such a way as would be acceptable to both themselves and the man in the street. According to the philosophers the mythical songs and poems expressed the same ideas as those taught by them personally in a more abstract and theoretical way[16]. By these means it was possible to get a meaning from the myths other than what was actually implied.

Thus the gap was bridged and a synthesis accomplished between the mythical popular belief and the new ideas of the philosophical avant garde. Both myths and the new viewpoints were saved because the advanced notions of the philosophers merely taught in a different way what the singers and poets had contributed long ago[17].

It is clear from this brief discussion[18] that allegorical exegesis appeared at a time of fundamental change in the Greek view of life and thought and the resulting conflict between authorative tradition and critical philosophical thought.

15. Cf. Ibid.

16. "... myths could be reinterpreted, and any phrase of them that was either morally objectionable or too crude for an intellectually advanced generation could be explained away. The hidden and deeper meaning of these stories was quite different from what they superficially appeared to mean. In other words they had to be accepted not literally, but allegorically." F. Solmson: *Plato's Theology* (1942), p. 42.

17. The vital question may be asked whether philosophers still believed in the traditional myths about the gods. Was their allegorical exegesis not a useful shield to hide their secret disbelief and thus to protect themselves? We encounter a similar problem in connection with the theory of double truth. (See our discussion of the method of paradox).

18. More details about allegorical exegesis with the Greeks are provided by the following: P. Heinisch: *Der Einfluss Philos auf die älteste Christliche Exegese (Barnabas, Justin und Clemens von Alexandria.) Ein Beiträg zur Geschichte der allegorische-mytischen Schriftauslegung im christlichen Altertum* (1908), p. 5-15; H.W. Rossouw: *Klaarheid en Interpretasie. Enkele probleemhistoriese gesigspunte i.v.m. die leer van die duidelikheid van die Skrif* (1963), p. 48-83; J. Pepin: *Mythe et allegórie. Les origines grecques et les contestations judéo-chrétiennes* (1958) and W. Nestle: *Vom Mythos zum Logos* (Chapter V, p. 126 et seq.).

5.2 Allegorical exegesis among the Jews

The outstanding example here is Philo of Alexandria. Vollenhoven discusses his viewpoints briefly with an example of its eisegesis-exegesis in which the Old Testament is compromised with Greek philosophy[19]. According to L. Cohn it is impossible to explain the origin of Christian Dogmatics without reference to Philo's allegorical exegesis[20].

5.3 Allegorical exegesis among the Arabs

Averroes, to briefly mention an example,. had to show that his philosophy was not in disagreement with the Koran. He solved the problem by way of a precise definition of three levels of comprehension of the Koran, represented firstly by the great masses, who lived by imagination; secondly, the theologians, who tried to get rational justification for their belief, and thirdly, the small number of philosophers who formed the highest class. Because the philosophers were not satisfied with the so-called exterior and literal meaning of the Koran, which they considered to be proper for the uninstructed, they proceeded to the interior and hidden meaning by way of allegorical exegesis.

The simple fact of the necessity for exegesis (eisegesis) reveals that fundamentally there is no contact between the Koran (faith) and Greek Philosophy (reason). The aim of Averroes' interpretation was not to arrive at a better understanding of Koranic revelation, but on the contrary, to modify it to such a degree that it could be accommodated to Greek Philosophy[21]. Revelation and reason remained in essence foreign to each other. Only eisegesis-exegesis could relate the two, but it was rather a violation of the real literal meaning of Koranic revelation in favour of Greek philosophy[22],

19. Cf. Vollenhoven, op. cit., p. 22. Compare also the already mentioned book of P. Heinisch as well as C. Siegfried: *Philo von Alexandria als Ausleger des Alten Testaments* (1875, reprint 1970).

20. Cf. L. Cohn: *Die Werke Philos von Alexandria in deutscher Uebersetzung I* (1909), p. 7.

21. Cf. D.C. Mulder: *Openbaring en rede in de Islamitische Filosofie van Al-farabi tot Ibn Rusd* (1949), p. 167. See also his article "Openbaring en rede in de Islamitische Filosofie". *Correspondentiebladen,* 14(1):14-16, 1950.

22. According to the following statement of G. Manser: *"Der vollständige Triumph der Vernunft über die Koranautorität ist bei Averroës offenkundig.* Die philosophierende Vernunft entscheidet, was *Tradition* ist, sie bestimmt, dass, falls eine philosophische Konklusion dem Literarsinn des Korans widerspricht, eine *Interpretation gesucht werden muss;* Sie entscheidet also faktisch auch, was interpretiert soll und was endlich entscheidet sie erst recht, wie interpretiert werden muss". "Das Verhältniss von Glauben und Wissen bei Averroës". *Jahrbuch für Philosophie und spekulative Theologie,* 25:33, 1911.

than a genuine, honest explanation.

It is not surprising that the doctrine of a double truth was associated with later so-called Latin Averroism[23].

5.4 Christian allegorical exegesis in Patristic and Medieval thought

Origen may be regarded as the father of allegorical exegesis within Christianity. He introduced the distinction between three different meanings of Scripture, viz., the somatic, psychic or moral and the spiritual. He believed that it was only by way of allegorical exegesis that the essential, but hidden meaning of Holy Scripture could be grasped, and elevated to real *gnosis*. According to E. Gilson, Origen has almost continually employed an allegorical interpretation of the Bible. It enabled him to introduce a large number of ideas borrowed from outside the Bible[24] into his biblical commentaries.

We find the allegorical tradition continued throughout the Patristic and Medieval Christian Period of thought[25]. Well-known is the fourfold exegetical method of the Middle Ages: the literal, the allegorical, the moral and the anagogical. The literal interpretation acquaints the reader with the facts, the allegorical with what must be believed, the moral with what must be done and the anagogical or spiritual with what must be hoped for. It is interesting to note that, according to this scheme, one should believe the results of allegorical exegesis and not the facts of the literal meaning of the text.

5.5 Modern examples of allegorical exegesis among Christians

Christianity has never been free from allegorical exegesis. Whenever a new life and world view, and with it, a new type of philosophy, came into existence, the method of synthesis by means of eisegesis-exegesis was vigorously applied. In confrontation with new philosophies Christian Theology employed hermeneutics. By means of interpretation according to (newly) prescribed hermeneutical rules, theologians tried to show that tension between faith and science (philosophy) actually did not exist! In this way a synthesis between biblical faith and unchristian science was often effected.

Compare, for instance, the numerous efforts since the days of Darwin

---

23. The doctrine of *duplex veritas* will be discussed in my exposition of the second method of synthesis, viz. that of paradox.

24. Cf. Gilson: *History of Christian Philosophy in the Middle Ages* (1955), p. 36.

25. Cf. H. du Lubac: *Exégèse Médiévale. Les quartre sens de L'écriture.* 4 Vols. (1959-1964).

intended to reconcile the biblical doctrine of creation with the natural sciences' doctrine of evolution. Another striking example is to be found in the influence of Rationalism (in die form of Cartesianism) on Christianity[26].

It is, however, not necessary to look to the past for illustrations since at present we are confronted by the same phenomena. Christianity is challenged today by a very strong tendency towards synthetic thought. So-called Christian theologians all over the world are of the opinion that the Bible should be interpreted according to new hermeneutic rules[27] because contemporary man, with his new world and life view, cannot understand the Scriptures which reflect the ancient Eastern life and world view. In fact, Christian theologians have capitulated to a new secular, anti-biblical conception of the world. This accounts for their earnest efforts to explain the most "offending" doctrines of Scripture away in order to achieve a synthesis with contemporary thought[28]. According to them Hermeneutics alone may inform us as to which part of Scripture is merely "wrappings" and which is the hard-core essence remaining once the "wrappings" have been removed[29]. It is understandable that all that is not approved of by

---

26. Cf. E. Bizer: "Die Reformierte Orthodoxie und der Cartesianismus" *ZThK*, 55: 306-372, 1958

27. Regarding the dominating role and new form of Hermeneutics in contemporary theological thought I refer to the statements of S. U. Zuidema in "Een tweeslachtige theologische hermeneutiek". *Philosophia Reformata*, 33:56, 1968 and H.W. Rossouw in his dissertation *Klaarheid en Interpretasie* (1963), p. 11.

28. In support, I quote Zuidema: "Op zoek naar het motief, dat bedoelde theologen tot aanvaarding van juist *dit* 'denkpatroon' drijft, meen ik bij hen allen te kunnen konstateren, dat een hetzij verborgen hetzij openlijk uitgesproken apologetische beweegreden hier de hoofdrol speelt... Even als Origenes, Thomas van Aquino, Schleiermacher en Ritschl, willen ook zij het christelijk geloof akkommoderen aan 'de eisen van de tijd". "Existentie-theologische hermeneutiek" I and II *Philosophia Reformata*, 32:1-24 and 81-110, 1967.

29. I have in mind here the ideas of H.M. Kuitert. Criticism of his viewpoint is given by the following: H. van Riessen:*Mondigheid en de Machten* (1967); H.G. Geertsema: "Geloof in diskussie inzake H.M. Kuitert: De realiteit van het geloof"; *Opbouw*, 12 (11-15):85, 94, 99, 107, 115, 116, 1968. J.H. Olthuis: "Ambiguity is the key". *International Reformed Bulletin*, 12(38):6-16, 1969 and W.H. Velema: *Aangepaste Theologie* (1971).
From a Calvinistic point of view the following articles of Zuidema about Hermeneutics in general are of importance: "Hermeneutiek en contemporaine theologieën". *Algemeen Nederlands Tijdschrift voor Wijsbegeerte en Psychologie* 60(1):39-64, 1968; "De Heilige Schrift en haar sleutel" in *De Christus der Schriften en oecumenische theologie* (1965), p. 39-66; "Holy Scripture and its key". *International Reformed Bulletin*, 11 (32/33):49-60, 1968). Cf. also H.G. Geertsema: "Enkele opmerkingen in verband met hermeneutiek". *Bulletin van die S.A. Vereniging vir Calvinistiese Wysbegeerte* nr. 20:32-42, Sept. 1969.

modern secularized man (e.g. the doctrine of creation, miracles, resurrection of Christ, etc.) should be regarded as unimportant, mere wrappings. It is also clear that the essential content may be increased or dimished willy-nilly: it is impossible to determine the precise limits between "wrappings" and essence. It is obvious that even though the words "allegorical interpretation" might not be used by the proponents of these ideas, these words do in fact apply to what they are doing. Here too the Word of God is forced to say what it really does not, and not to say what it really does.

He who is aware of the dangers of allegorical exegesis may come to surprising new insights in his understanding of the Scriptures. As an example I want to mention Calvin Seerveld's exegesis of the Song of Solomon in his book *The Greatest Song in critique of Solomon*[30].

6. The method of paradox

According to Vollenhoven this is the second method (taken chronologically) applied in Christian synthetic thought, in reaction against the first. According to the adherents of the paradoxical method pagan philosophy conflicted with the Scriptures, there being no unifying ground between them.

6.1 Tertullian

The method may well be illustrated by reference to Tertullian's thought. According to Vollenhoven he accepted a pagan conception along with the Bible as did the proponents of the method of eisegesis-exegesis. He did realize, however, that Holy Scripture and Greek Philosophy were in conflict with each other on more than one point. Nevertheless he did not give up either of them. The result was the paradox: both pagan philosophy and the Bible were accepted as true, the one next to the other.

In spite of its untenable inconsistency, this viewpoint realized, at least, that pagan philosophy cannot easily and simply be accommodated to the Bible, as the supporters of the method of eisegesis-exegesis tried to sug-

---

30. Seerveld summarizes his objections against allegorical exegesis in the following words: "Allegorical exegesis assumes that the text means something different than it says, and so requires specially learned interpreters who can supply the other "real" meaning.
This procedure has two results: (1) it takes the biblical text out of the hands of the ordinary reader and gives it to the theological expert or charismatic seer who has the desired *gnosis* (inside knowledge); and (2) it prohibits any further check upon the truth of the final interpretation supplied" (p. 13).

gest[31]).

Because they have nothing in common Tertullian would not try to harmonize Christian faith and pagan thought. His famous judgment in *De praescriptione haereticorum*, 7, puts it very clearly: "What indeed has Athens to do with Jerusalem? What concord is there between the Academy and the Church? What has the heretic to do with the Christian? Our school is the porch of Solomon which taught that one should serve the Lord in simplicity of heart. Away then with all attempts to produce an intermixed Christianity of Stoic, Platonic and dialectic composition. We want no curious disputation after possessing Christ, no inquisition after enjoying the gospel. When we believe, we need nothing above our faith. That which we believe is the first..."

In the same part of *De praescriptione haereticorum* Tertullian calls Aristotle *miserum* and Socrates (declared a Christian by Justin Martyr) a *corruptor* of youth. To support his standpoint he calls upon Paul who warned us not to let anyone confuse us by means of philosophy and vain deceit (Col. 2:8).

It is no wonder that posterity attributed the celebrated phase *credo quia absurdum*, "I believe because it is absurd" to Tertullian, though it is not found in any of his works. We will find sentences such as the following: "The Son of God was crucified; I am not ashamed of it, because it is disgraceful. The Son of God died; it is by all means to be believed, because it is absurd. He was buried and rose again: the fact is certain, because it is impossible"[32]).

In this paragraph the statement *credible est, quia ineptum es* (from which the formula *credo quia absurdum est* was probably derived) is especially important. This much disputed sentence clearly reveals Tertullian's method of paradox, because, in spite of the fact that Tertullian used the word *ineptum* instead of *absurdum*, it has more or less the same meaning in this context.

Tertullian meant to say that the absurdities in Christian faith offer no obstacles to him because he did not want to bridge the gap between faith and reason but wanted to accept them both as true, mutually exclusive though they were. The contradiction between faith in the miracles of the Scriptures, and the rational truths he accepted, did not prevent Tertullian at any rate from believing in Scripture.

31. Cf. Vollenhoven, op. cit., p. 25.

32. Crucificus est dei filius; non pudet, quia pudendum est. Et mortuus est dei filius; prorsus credibile est, quia ineptum est. Et sepultus resurrexit; certum est, quia impossibile est. *De Carne Christi*, 5.

Superficially it may seem as if Tertullian's paradoxical attitude reveals an anti-synthetic approach towards pagan philosophy. On closer examination we see that Vollenhoven is correct when he calls paradox a method of synthesis. Tertullian was influenced by pagan thought in spite of his seemingly antithetic approach. In the statement of Tertullian mentioned above, the word *quia* is the crucial because it forms the link between faith and reason.

What is more: reason decides that faith is *ineptum!* Faith is again measured according to the standard of reason and philosophy in spite of the fact that it is a negative description of faith as stupid or absurd. What Tertullian intended as a defence against philosophical thought had exactly the opposite result: the Gospel, and faith in it, was transferred to a philosophical level again in the sense that it is said to be anti-philosophical!' A judgment like *Credo etsi ineptum est* (" I Believe *in spite of the fact* that it is absurd"), or "I believe *in spite of the fact that it is regarded as stupid according to pagan philosophy"*, would thus not have been so dangerous as the statement "I believe *because* it is absurd". When we study Tertullian's works in detail, we are not surprised to find a powerful influence of pagan philosophy in his system[33] in spite of the fact that he was more critical and anti-thetical in his approach than his predecessors who made use of the method of eisegesis-exegesis.

6.2 Duplex veritas

Perhaps the so-called Averroistic theory of double truth[34] should also be mentioned as an example of the method of paradox. It depends, how-

---

33. Cf. Ueberweg: *Grundriss der Geschichte der Philosophie,* II, p. 46 and B.K. Wassink: *Credo quia absurdum?* (1949). In confirmation of my own ideas I quote the statement of Wassink: "... dat het Christendom juist niet te karakteriseren is met de woorden credo quia absurdum. Weliswaar is deze karakteristiek door de theologen zelf gegeven in de strijd tegen de wijsbegeerte, maar juist in deze karakteristiek bleek toch de philosophie triompherende te zijn. Zij immers heeft wezenlijk het terrein van de strijd bepaald en de theologie terug gedrongen in een misschien wel onneembare, maar tevens volkomen geïsoleerde tegenstelling" (p. 62).

34. The following provide valuable information about this theory: W. Betzendörfer: *Die Lehre von der Zweifachen Wahrheit. Ihr erstmalige Auftreten im christlichen Abendland und ihre Quellen* (1924); Q. Breen: The twofold truth Theory in Melanchton". *(In:* Christianity and Humanism (1968), p. 69-72); E. Gilson: "Boèce de Dacie et la double vérité". *Achives d'Histoire Doctrinale et Littéraire du Moyen Age.* 22: 81-99, 1955; K. Heim: *Zur Geschichte des Satzes von der doppelten Wahrheid* (1918); A. Haufnagel: "Zur Lehre von der doppelten Wahrheit". *Tübing. theol. Quartalschirft,* 136:284-95, 1956; A. Maier: *Das Prinzip der doppelte Wahrheit* (1959); M. Maywald: *Die Lehre von der zweifachen Wahrheit* (1871); Michaud-Quantin: "La double — vérité des Averroistes. Un texte nouveau de Boèce de Dacië". *Theoria,* 22:167-184, 1956 and M. Pine: "Pomponazzi and double truth". *Journal of the history of ideas,* 29:163-176, 1968.

ever, on what precisely is meant by double truth. According to some interpreters the theory implies that the same proposition can be simultaneously true and false: true as a statement of faith (in Theology) and false as a statement of reason (in Philosophy) and vice versa. If the position indeed affirms the simultaneous truth and falsity of the same doctrines, then the theory of double truth may be regarded as an example of the paradoxical method.

It has been suggested by other interpreters, however, that the so-called *duplex veritas* was simply a sarcastic way of saying theological truth to be nonsense. It was merely a protective device which the philosophers used to protect themselves against persecution by the church. It served as a shield covering secret unbelief and faith in but one truth, viz. philosophical truth. Behind this smoke screen the philosopher could deny the basic tenets of Christian faith.

A third option seems to be that the adherents of the so-called double truth theory only tried to delimit more clearly the areas of faith and reason and that the double truth theory was not advocated by them, but imputed to them by the church dignitaries who indicted them. Siger of Brabant, John of Jandun and Boethius of Dacia, together with the other Latin Averroists, were primarily philosophers practising philosophy for its own sake rather than as *ancilla theologiae* in support and defence of Christian faith. The fact, however, that they respected reason as an autonomous instrument able to set its own course without resorting to the teaching of revelation[33] may explain why the authors of the condemnation of 1277 imputed the theory of double truth to them as a result of their ambiguous attitude: attachment to Christian faith on the one hand, but to Aristotelian philosophy in the area of science as well[36].

This doctrine of double truth, which can be traced to the 16th century in the thought of Pomponazzi[37] and even Melanchton[38], is of great relevance to the present time because, today, many Christians still take the method of paradox to be the only solution in their confrontation with contemporary secular culture.

7. The method of nature and grace

This third method of synthesis merits careful consideration. It is the final

35. Cf. A.A. Maurer: *Medieval Philosophy*, (1962), p. 201, 202.

36. Cf. F. van Steenbergen: *The philosophical movement of the thirteenth century* (1955), p. 89.

37. Cf. the bibliography in footnote 34 above.

38. Cf. the study of Q. Breen mentioned in footnote 34.

result of previous efforts in determining the relationship between Christianity and pagan philosophy so as to combine the extremes of the two methods (world conformity and world flight) already discussed. Not only is this method of great historical importance, but it is still a bone of contention in contemporary Protestant and Roman Catholic thought. Many theologians regard it as the fundamental point of difference between Protestantism and Catholicism[39].

According to Vollenhoven the relationship between pagan philosophy and Christian thought is, by the proponents of this method, considered to be like that of threshold to sanctuary, inferior to superior realm[40]. The higher sphere supersedes, or crowns, the lower. Nature is a necessary preparation for grace, and conversely, grace does not abolish nature, but perfects it — without intrinsically reforming it.

7.1 Historical background

The two-realm theory of nature and grace, already well developed during the Middle Ages, achieved its most articulate expression in the philosophy of Thomas Aquinas. It is possible, however, to trace its roots far back in history.

According to K.J. Popma the distinction between sacred and profane[41], present in Greek thought, constitutes the origin of the nature-supernature theme[42]. It forms the background of Plato's thought[43] and can also be

---

39. Cf. B. Wentsel: *Natuur en genade. Een introductie en confrontatie met de jongste ontwikkelingen in de Rooms-Katholieke theologie inzake dit thema* (1970), p. 3.

40. Cf. op. cit., p. 26.

41. "Profane" is derived from the Latin *pro + fanum* = in front of the sanctuary K.J. Popma gives many noteworthy insights about the origin and consequences of the idea of an original dualism between the profane or secular and sacred or holy in his work *Levensbeschouwing*. Vol. IV (1962), p. 57, 179-83.

42. Personally I regard the following statement of K.J. Popma as very important: "Amongst others Mircea Eliade and G. van der Leeuw made it acceptable that a dualism of a holy over against a profane 'world' belongs to the oldest traditions of human paganism. In the holy sphere gods. live their own lives and speak their own language. Man in his profane existence needs the divine message, which as such is incomprehensible to him. So he uses the intervention of a cultic functionary who is considered capable of understanding the divine language and of translating it in profane words. In his function, not in his person, this middleman was held to be divine in the same way as the god whom he represented. Sometimes his title was 'theologos', i.e. the speaker and translator of divine words; this is not only the oldest but also the original and never completely absent meaning of our word 'theologian' ". "Natuur en genade". *Philosophia Reformata*, 36:123-124, 1971.

43. Cf. Ibid., p. 110.

detected in the systems of Aristotle[44], Philo of Alexandria[45] and Tatian[46].

The implication of this very important insight is that synthetic thought in the form of the two-realm theory does not imply that the supernatural as well as the natural component has its origin in Chirstian thought alone. The *whole* dualistic scheme of nature and grace is a modification of an originally pagan dualism between the profane and the sacred. Synthetic though implies the acceptance by Christianity of the pagan idea of an original dualism between a profane and sacred realm[47].

It would be very interesting to discuss *why* such a dualism came into existence in primitive thought[48], but we will confine ourselves to the further development of the theme in Christian synthetic thought.

7.2 Clemens of Alexandria

According to Popma, Philo was the father of the idea of *praeparatio evangelica*, viz. that Hellenistic culture is a preparation for or education unto the Old Testament[49]. This idea is very clearly expressed in the thought of Clemens.

God educated the Greeks by means of their philosophy and the Jews with the Old Testament unto Christ. Greek Philosophy and the Old Testament are two rivers converging in the New Testament. Greek Philosophy is appreciated as the preparatory work or harbinger of New Testament fulfillment. In this way the revelation of God is relativized. On the one hand, Clemens accepted the Word of God as the absolute truth while on the other, he believed that the pagans had achieved truth which the Christians had

---

44. Cf. Popma: *Levensbeschouwing.* Vol. III (1961), p. 333.

45. Cf. Popma: *Philosophia Reformata,* 36:101-102, 1971.

46. Ibid.

47. In the thought of Thomas Aquinas, for instance, the theory of nature and grace does not imply a division between God (Grace) and creation (nature), but a distinction between a natural and supernatural side of God as well as in creation.

48. W. Philip has this to say of the matter: *"Religionsgeschichtlich* ist die Spannung zwischen Natur und Ubernatur allenthalben Ausdruck der Sehnsucht nacht einer seligen Oberwelt über dem düstern Weltraum, einer nahenden Heilsepoche nach blutiger Weltzeit, einer Durchdringung des todtbedrohten Menschen mit Himmelkräften". R.G.G. (3rd print) IV (1960), p. 1329.

49. Popma rejects this as an unscriptural idea. Cf. his previously mentioned article in *Philosophia Reformata.* In my opinion the idea that the pagans longed for the coming of Christ was a forerunner of the idea of *desiderium naturale* which will be discussed in detail.

only to complete and bring to perfection[50].

7.3 Origen

He also postulates the idea that the Gospel only actualized what was in potentiality present in pagan thought. Human wisdom is the pedagogue of divine wisdom. The Christians should therefore not hesitate to claim what is correct in pagan thought as their own. Just as Israel took gold and silver from the Egyptians to make utensils for the tabernacle, the conqueror (grace, faith, theology, church) may take the products of pagan culture and philosophy using it for the greater glory of God. This is regarded as legitimate because the treasures of Athens actually belonged to Jerusalem — the pagan philosophers reached moments of real truth because they plagiarised the books of Moses!

This apparently devout argument reveals a lack of radical Biblical criticism and is evidently an unobtrusive effort to evade the antithesis[51].

7.4 Augustine

E. Kinder warns that it will be incorrect and a perpetration of injustice to try to read Augustine in the light of the later Medieval two-realm theory of nature and grace[52]. Augustine does not concern himself with the two-realm theory in the form of nature-grace[53], but it has been shown suf-

---

50. The mistake many people make with regard to the so-called "moments of truth" in pagan thought is to uncritically assume a false theory of truth. The truth of a system does not consist of unconnected fragments but it forms an organic unity. Therefore ideas cannot be arbitrarily isolated from the whole of which they are   part and described as "moments of truth". They should be viewed in their context and in the light of the "spirit" of the whole book or philosophy.

51. Cf. K.J. Popma: *De oudheid en wij* (1948), p. 73.

52. Cf. his contribution "Gottesreich und Weltreich bei Augustin und bei Luther". In: H.H. Schrey (ed.): *Reich Gottes und Welt. Die Lehre Luthers von den zwei Reichen* (1969), p. 42.

53. H.H. Schrey distinguishes in his contribution "Aufhebung und Erfüllung der Geschichte? Ein Beiträg zum Verständniss der Lehre von den zwei Reichen" (in the volume mentioned in note 52 above) between three types of two-realm theories: the Manichaeistic type of Augustine, the Eusebian-Medievalı type and the Lutheran type.

ficiently that he definitely adhered to a certain type of two-realm theory[54] – possibly under the influence of Manichaeism[55]. The idea of the *desiderium naturale*, so important to the nature-grace theory, as we will soon see, can also be traced back to the neo-Platonism of Augustine[56].

7.5 Synod of Orange

The method of nature and grace received its first official sanction at the Synod of Orange (in 529 A.D.)[57] which formulated decisions against semi-Pelagianism. These canons dealt with the subject of man's state before and after the fall in such a way that it opened the door to the nature-grace theme. Before the fall man possessed a special measure of super-nature. When he fell into sin he lost the higher supernatural part (faith). Man's fall did not, however, essentially affect or change his lower natural part. It remained more or less intact. Man still possessed the natural light of reason. The human being after the fall is man minus faith, and after salvation man plus faith again. According to this view, sin or evil is only the absence of the good (faith), a lack or deprivation. According to the Bible, however, sin is a "positive", radical apostate power which leaves nothing – not even so-called natural reason – intact. .

Vollenhoven mentions two other examples in which the two-realm theory is clearly expressed. At about 1060 A.D. it was stated that the doctrine of transubstantiation could not be philosophically explained because it belonged to the area of grace. In about 1140 the theme of nature and grace facilitated another thinker's distinction between Theology (sphere of grace)

.

54. Cf. E. Teselle: "Nature and grace in Augustine's exposition of Genesis 1-5". *Recheres Augustiniennes*, 5:95-137, 1968. On page 136 he gives a description of what Augustine meant with the concept grace and nature. He also shows the connection between Augustine's two-realm theory and the doctrine of two kingdoms. In this connection see H. van der Laan: "Wezen en oorsprong van Augustinus' leer der twee rijken". *Correspondentiebladen*, 24:33-44, April 1960

K. Lorentz, in his article "Gnade und Erkenntniss bei Augustin" ZKG, 75:21-78, 1964, also proved that Augustine accepted a certain form of two-realm theory (p. 78). According to J. van Laarhoven, in his contribution "Luthers Lehre von den zwei Reichen. Notizien über ihre Herkunft" in the volume mentioned in note 52 above, Augustine should not be viewed as the spiritual father of the doctrine of the two kingdoms of Luther.

55. Cf. the contribution of A. Adam "Die manichäische Ursprung der Lehre von den zwei Reichen bei Augustin" in the volume mentioned in note 52.

56. Cf. Wentsel: *Natuur en genade* (1970), p. 446 and 448.

57. Cf. Vollenhoven, op. cit., p.26 and also *Philosophia Reformata*, 11:111, 1946. G.E. Meuleman does not agree with Vollenhoven's interpretation of the decisions of Orange. Cf. his contribution "Natuur en genade" in *Protestantse Verkenningen na Vaticanum I* (1967), p. 61.

and Philosophy (sphere of nature).

7.6 Thomas Aquinas

Undoubtedly the method of synthesis by way of the theory of nature-grace was most consistently and lucidly applied by Aquinas (1225-1274)[58]. According to him grace did not abolish nature, but perfected it. Nature, embracing the whole of reality as understood by pagan philosophy, was related to grace, i.e. the whole of life viewed in the light of the Bible, as is a threshold to a sanctuary. According to him then there are two more or less autonomous areas of life. It is impossible for the higher sphere (grace) to reform the lower (nature) because the lower enjoys a great degree of autonomy. Real Christian activity in the field of nature (for instance a radical Christian Philosophy) is neither necessary nor possible.

Problems with the idea of "desiderium naturale"

New developments within Roman Catholic thought resulted in a closer analysis of the exact relationship between nature and grace in the system of Aquinas. It is in this connection that the idea of *desiderium naturale* or natural desire was singled out for attention[59].

Thomas Aquinas emphasized the fact that God is the origin (*exitus*) and

---

58. P. Ohm summarizes Aquinas' views as follows: "Der hl. Thomas gebraucht das Wort *'Natur'* für die Wesenheit eines Dinges, speziell für die Wesenheit eines Dinges insofern es handeln und leiden kann. *'Naturlich'* ist dan für dieses die Natur mit allen, was zu ihr gehört, aus ihr folgt oder von ihr gefördert wird. Folglich ist für den Menschen 'naturlich' zunachst seine Wesenheit, dan alles was es auf Grund seiner Wesenheit hat, bezw. beanspruchen kann".
" 'Uebernatur' ist der Inbegriff alles dessen, was uns Gott ungeschuldet in freier Liebe zu den natürlichen Gaben hinzugeben hat oder geben will. Unter 'Ubernatur' verstehen wir alle Erkenntnisse, Werte und Vorzüge, Gaben und Ziele, Betätigungen und Wirkungen, welche die natürlichen Ansprüche, Bedürfnisse und Kräfte des Menschen übersteigen und von Gott aus ungeschuldeten Wohlwollen zur 'Natur' hinzu gegeben werden." *Die Stellung der Heiden zu Natur und Übernatur nach dem hl. Thomas von Aquin* (1927), p. 26, 27.

Cf. also H. Lais: *Die Gnadelehre des hl. Thomas in der Summa Contra Gentiles und der Kommentar des Franziskus Sylvestris von Ferrara* (1951). B. Wentsel discusses Aquina's viewpoint on p. 448-475 and gives a summary on p. 472-475 of his study *Natuur en Genade.*

59. Cf. B. Wentsel op. cit., as well as the following studies: P.B. Bastable: *Desire for God. Does man aspire naturally to the beautific vision? An analysis of the question and its history* (1947); J.E. O'Mahony: *The desire for God in the philosophy of St. Thomas Aquinas* (1929); F. de Raedemacker: "Het Desiderium naturale videndi Deum", *Bijdragen. Tijdschrift voor Filosofie en Theologie,* 17:56-79, 1956; J.B.J. Meyer: *De eerste levensvraag in het intellectualisme van St. Thomas van Aquino en het integraal-realisme van Maurice Blondel* (1940): Id.: "Het participatiebegrip in de Thomistische circulatieleer". In: *De Thomistische Participatieleer.* (Verslag van die Tiende Algemene Vergadering der Vereeniging voor Thomistische Wijsbegeerte), p. 55-71.

goal *(reditus)*. According to the neo-Platonic scheme everything emerges from but also aspires back to God. In this circular movement it is especially the striving to return to the Origin (God) which is important at the moment, as is Aquinas' statement *hominum insitum est desiderium naturale videndi Deum*. A detailed discussion of this doctrine is not possible here because it requires an exposition and explanation of Aquinas' whole ontology (particularly his doctrine of analogy and participation). We will confine ourselves to one main question, viz.: how is a supernatural striving in the natural sphere possible? If it is indeed possible, then there must be something supernatural in the natural sphere. Viewed from the opposite point of view we face this problem: if grace does not abolish nature, but perfects it, then there must be something natural in the supernatural sphere of grace.

In spite of its problematic character the doctrine of natural desire is of great importance in the thought of Thomas and his followers because it constitutes the liaison between the two orders (nature and grace).

Different interpretations

A glance at the history of the various interpretations may be of value for arriving at deeper insight into the whole problem.

Cajetan (died 1534) solved the problem by eliminating the natural character of the desire. He makes a supernatural desire of the *desiderium naturale* because, in his opinion, the natural human being cannot aspire to something supernatural. (He did not use the term "natural" in the concept "natural desire" in the strict sense of the word.) When man is elevated to a supernatural level he has a desire for God.

Sylvester Ferrariensis (died 1528) solved the problem by rejecting the supernatural character of the object of the desire: the natural desire is directed to the natural side of God only and not to His supernatural side.

At the end of the previous century, and also after the Second World War, quite different interpretations were advanced. According to all previous commentators on Aquinas, nature was not positively directed towards grace but constituted a more or less passive substratum. The new interpreters brought forth a great variety of possible solutions[60] but they all converged in their rejection of the idea that nature and grace existed in

60. Cf. the above-mentioned works of Meyer and Bastable.

two neatly separated worlds[61].

M. Blondel combined his dynamic view of reality with the idea of natural desire and speaks about the gap, nostalgia, defect, insufficiency and unsatisfied ontological longing of the imperfect being for the perfect (God). Blondel's problem was that by stressing the unity of nature and grace too much, the differences between them could be lost to sight. Transgression of the boundary between the two is inevitable if the natural desire reaches the supernatural destination under its own power. Another difficulty is the following: if God created such an impulse toward the supernatural in man, does it not imply that nature can lay claim to fulfilment from grace? Is God not forced to comply with nature's claim? And if this is so, is God not robbed of His sovereign freedom, and grace of its gratuitous character? This, perhaps, is the reason why Blondel in his later works avoided such expressions as 'the necessity of the supernatural' and the 'demand of nature with regard to grace'.

H. de Lubac tried to solve this interesting problem by teaching that the natural urge is not given to man as a permanent property, but that it is something which perpetually emanates from God Himself. Thus God longs towards Himself through His creation and He Himself is the answer to this longing. In this way God's freedom is saved but a new problem threatens, viz. pantheism.

A third solution that the spiritual life of man points beyond itself is suggested by K. Rahner. In a transcendental openness the inner part of man is directed towards supernatural elevation[62].

The dialectical tension resulting from the accommodation of Christian to pagan thought, in the theme of nature and grace, is clearly visible in the few interpretations mentioned. It would have been easy and simple to stress one pole of the double order of nature and grace. However, this would imply heresy: he who overemphasize grace, may be charged with pantheism, and he who overaccentuates nature, may be accused of "naturalism" or pancosmism. On the one hand, the unity between nature and grace must be

---

61. M.C. Smit summarizes the change in the following words: "Legde men in de 19e eeuw het accent op de distantie, op de gapende kloof tussen natuur en genade, in de 20e eeuw, vooral sinds 1930, zoekt men beider synthese in haar intieme verbondenheid. Tegelijkertijd echter handhaven de meeste Rooms-Katholieke denkers de distantie. Hier ligt de bron én van de polariteit én van die schier onbeperkte gevarieerdheid van hun beschouwingen". *De verhouding van Christendom en Historie in de huidige Rooms-Katholieke Geschiedbeschouwing* (1950), p. 19, 20.
See in this connection also the essay of G.E. Meuleman mentioned in note 57 above as well as the study of U. Kühn: *Natur und Gnade. Untersuchungen zur deutschen katholischen Theologie der Gegenwart.* (1961).

62. For Rahner's viewpoint see his essay "Natuur en genade volgens de leer van de Katholieke Kerk". In: *Brandpunten in de hedendaagse Theologie* (1962).

emphasized, and on the other hand, the boundary between the two must be duly observed.

It is clear that the theme of nature and grace is not only an epistemological method according to which the problem of the relationship between Christianity and pagan philosophy is solved. It can, therefore, not be qualified as either theological, or philosophical, or as a mixture of both. It is even more fundamental than the ontological level: it is basically a religious groundmotive. It reveals a synthetic religious position according to which an effort is made to serve two masters at the same time: pagan thought as well as the Word of God.

7.7 Practical consequences

Because the nature-grace theme is not a solely abstract, theoretical thought-pattern but a religious driving force and impulse, its influence in practical life is tremendous. Subject to it the whole of life is viewed as split by polar tension so that we get the following dualistic notions: secular-religious, common grace — special grace, autonomous man — sovereign God, the God of the philosophers — the God of the Bible, God the Creator — God the Redeemer, world and earthly things — heaven and heavenly things, the visible — the unseen, the body (outer life) — the soul (inner life), ordinary laymen (not in service of God) — clergymen (in special service of God), unordained — ordained, sir — the reverend, politician — priest, father —monk, mother — nun, marriage — celibacy, industry — monastery, the state and other natural institutions (marriage, family, school, university, etc.) — the church, emperor — pope, general revelation (in nature) — special revelation (in Bible), reason — faith, understanding — believing, Philosophy, natural Theology and all the other sciences (neutral) — supernatural Theology (by nature Christian), university — seminary, academy — church, classroom — chapel, secular or natural law — canon or divine (supernatural) law, natural — spiritual, autonomous — theonomous, optional — necessary, fact — value, observation — evaluation, horizontal — vertical, now — then, already — not yet, appointed by man — instituted by God, learning — praying, temporal — eternal, free will — Christian will, natural man — Christian man etc.[63].

7.8 Biblical criticism

According to this scheme the non-ecclesiastical areas of life can only have

63. Cf. the Syllabus *A survey of biblical Christianity in the Western world since the sixteenth century,* (1970), by J.C. van der Stelt, p. 6, 7, 18, 19. J.H. Olthuis gives a classification of the different types of two-realm theories in his article: "Must the church become secular?" *International Reformed Bulletin,* 10(28):14-31, 1967 which was also published in *Out of concern for the church* (1970), p. 105-125.

sense in so far as they are dominated and perfected by the church. Being a Christian is regarded as identical with belonging to the church. Religion is in this way confined to the so-called higher spheres of life. Because the lower area of so-called natural life is autonomous it cannot be christianized. In spite of the subordination of nature to the supernatural, grace floats like oil on water so that a reformation of the whole of life in the light of Scripture is out of the question.

From what has already been said it is clear that one's view about the relationship of nature and grace, and of pagan thought and the Bible, is closely related to one's conception of fall and redemption.

Thomas Aquinas advocated an ontological viewpoint, according to which fall into sin implies a loss of the supernatural and divine salvation implies the return, as a kind of *donum superadditum*, of the divine part to an unaffected human nature. Salvation actually implies a deification of man. Thomas placed the antithesis in the ontological *structure* of things (e.g. man) rather than in the *direction* of man's response to the Word of God[64]. Therefore, the viewpoint of Thomas is ignorant of the radical character of both fall and redemption. After the fall, man, by nature, is still directed to God (the *disiderium naturale*) because he is not entirely corrupted. According to Scripture, however, man is totally corrupted and cannot return to God of his own will and desire as is the case in the semi-Pelagianism of Aquinas.

Redemption is not something total and radical in Aquinas' view either, since it is confined to a certain part of the human being. His *whole* existence is not renewed. (The only difference between a Christian and a non-Christian is that the Christian has grace added). Biblically speaking redemption implies a total and radical religious change, a turn-about in direction.

The Biblical doctrine about nature and grace [65] is that grace can only be spoken of after the fall[66] so that man was not robbed of grace when he fell into sin. Further, the antithesis does not lie in the opposition between a

---

64. Cf. A Troost's critique on the two-realm theory in his article: "De openbaring Gods in de maatschappelijke orde". *Philosophia Reformata*, 34:11-12, 1969.

65. The studies of O. Noordmans: *Natuur en genade bij Rome* (1949) and A.A. van Ruler: "Natuur en genade" in his book *Theologisch Werk* Vol. I (1969), p. 121-133 does not offer radical criticism on the two-realm theory. The following are, however, worthwhile reading in this connection: D. Jacobs: *Incarnatie en genade* (1958); B. Wentsel: *Natuur en genade* (1970), cf. p. 334-352; A.D.R. Polman in *Christelijke Encyclopedie* Vol. III (1958), p. 154-155; S.G. de Graaf: "De genade Gods in de structuur der gansche schepping". *Philosophia Reformata*, I:18, 77-79, 1936. Id.: Chapter V of his work *Christus en de wereld* (1939); A.H. de Graaf: *The educational ministry of the church* (1966, reprint 1968), p. 32, 65, etc. and D.H. Th. Vollenhoven: *Het Calvinisme en de Reformatie van de Wijsbegeerte* (1933), p. 45-47.

66. Cf. Wentsel, op. cit., p. 306.

realm of grace and a realm of nature, but rather in the radical conflict between two spiritual directions: the spirit of light and the spirit of darkness, obedience to God and disobedience. The tension is not between grace and nature, but grace versus sin and the wrath of God"[67].

The final outcome of Thomas' two-realm theory in subsequent times was a progressive separation and, finally, an utter divorce between nature and grace. Secularism soon attained   dominance in the historical development of post-medieval, modern culture. Aquinas and others meant well with the two-realm theory, but the end was a secular world.

That is why my discussion of the three methods of synthetic thought cannot end but with the urgent conviction that the time for radical Christianity is now!

***

SUMMARY

The purpose of this essay is to investigate, by way of introduction, the reasons for the rise of synthetic thought in early Christianity and to elaborate on the three methods by which this synthesis was accomplished.

According to Prof. D.H. Th. Vollenhoven Christian synthetic thought manifested itself in three different religious methods which, by using Tertullian's metaphor of Athens (Greek philosophy) and Jerusalem, (the Bible), we can summarize in the following way:

The method of *eisegesis-exegesis* revealed an attitude of *world conformity*. It claimed that Jerusalem was identical with Athens and vice versa. It was only necessary that the pagan philosophy of Athens obtain biblical sanction and authority from Jerusalem by an allegorical interpretation of Scriptures.

In reaction to the ideal of world conformity, the method of *paradox* advocated an attitude of *world flight*. Jerusalem had nothing to do with Athens and vice versa. They were directly opposed to each other and Jerusalem (faith) should avoid Athens (reason) at every cost. Nevertheless, both had their own right to separate existence.

The method of *nature-grace (supernature)* preached *world compromise* in an attempt to avoid the extremes of both world conformity and world flight. Jerusalem, representing the Scriptures, faith, church, etc. was not permitted to be submerged into Athens, the secular world made up of

---

67. Cf. Wentsel, op. cit., p. 306, 430; Popma: "Natuur en genade". *Philosophia Reformata*, 36:109,1971 and Vollenhoven: *Het Calvinisme en de Reformatie der Wijsbegeerte* (1933), p. 45.

reason and philosophy, nor to escape from it. Jerusalem was neither identical to Athens, nor opposed to it, but, as the superior of two realms, it surpassed Athens.

1. In the method of *eisegesis-exegesis* allegorical exegesis was of great importance. Its historical background is traced to Greek, Jewish, Arabian and early Christian thinkers. A few examples of its actuality in modern Christian thought are given and reasons why this method is unacceptable are stated.

2. My discussion of the *method of paradox* concentrates on Tertullian's idea of *credo quia absurdum est* as well as on the theory of the so-called *duplex veritas*.

3. The historical background of the *method of nature and grace* is traced back to the distinction between the profane and the sacred among primitives. This dualism influenced Greek thought. The idea of *praeparatio Evangelica,* which was very prominent among certain early Christian apologists, was also of decisive influence in the development of the nature-grace theme. The question whether Augustine accepted a two-realm theory in the form of nature-supernature is discussed as is Vollenhoven's idea that the theme of nature and grace first appeared at the Synod of Orange. At the time of Thomas Aquinas the two-realm theory of nature and grace was well developed, but it reached its most articulate expression in his philosophy. The determination of the exact meaning of his theory of *desiderium naturale* is very important for the interpretation of his viewpoint. Some old and new interpretations to solve the problems involved are discussed in this connection. In the concluding part of the essay the unhappy consequences of the nature-grace theme are indicated. Criticism in the light of Scripture reveals something quite different about nature and grace and their relation.

4 THE PROBLEM OF THE RELATION BETWEEN FAITH AND KNOWLEDGE IN EARLY CHRISTIAN AND MEDIEVAL THOUGHT*

The question of the relationship between faith and knowledge is one of the main problems of patristic and medieval thought. Simply compare the following four pronouncements:

"Auctoritas und ratio sind die beiden Pole, zwischen denen sich das mittelalterliche Denken bewegt"[1].

"Das Verhältnis von Wissen und Glauben, von ratio und auctoritas, von Philosophie und Theologie, von Natur und Uebernatur darf seit der Patristik geradezu als das Grundproblem der christlichen Spekulation bezeichnet werden"[2].

"Die Frage nach dem Verhältnis von Glauben und Wissen gehört zu jenen wissenschaftlichen Problemen, welche sowohl auf theologischem, wie auch auf philosophischem Gebiete die Gebildeten fast aller Zeiten bis besonders auch in unsere Tage herein stark beschäftigt haben; ja, wir dürfen wohl mit Recht sagen, sie ist so alt, wie die christliche Kirche überhaupt"[3].

"Die Lehre der Scholastiker über das Verhältnis von Glauben und Wissen gehört zu den grundlegenden Problemen der mittelalterlichen Theologie"[4].

Briefly, my own stand in the matter boils down to this: the real solution is neither "faith or knowledge" nor "faith and knowledge" but "faithfilled or faith-committed knowledge" (Afrikaans: "gelowige wete"). With either of the other two viewpoints (faith or/and knowledge) a dichotomy in one's existence and a consequent secularization comes about. But "faithfilled knowledge" nips this in the bud. It is self-evident that such a faith-directed knowledge can be oriented towards the right (to the honour of the true God) or left-directed (in the service of Satan) — faith is not the Christian's monopoly.

---

* Originally published in *Tydskrif vir Christelike Wetenskap*, 12:97-117, 1976 under the title "Die probleem van die verhouding tussen geloof en wete in die vroeg-Christelike en Middeleeuse denke".

1. Betzendörfer, W.: *Glauben und Wissen bei den grossen Denkern des Mittelalters.* (1931), p.1.

2. Meyer. H.: *Die Wissenschaftslehre des Thomas von Aquin* (1934), p. 118.

3. Wendsuch, E.: *Verhältnis des Glaubens zum Wissen bei Anselm von Canterbury* (1909), p. 9.

4. Finkenzeller, J.: *Offenbarung und Theologie nach der Lehre des Johannes Duns Scotus* (1961), p. 235.

1. THE FAITH/KNOWLEDGE DILEMMA IN EARLY CHRISTIAN THOUGHT

In the epistemological arena the confrontation of Christendom with pagan thought soon led to the problem of the relationship between the Christian faith and heathen scholarship. The Christians were not always aware that this could be an false problem because, in the commerce between Christian faith and pagan philosophy, the question was not that of faith versus knowledge, but primarily that of Christian faith versus apostate faith, seeing that pagan philosophy was directed by the beliefs held by the heathens. The false dilemma gave rise to divergent standpoints. Those who tended to shun the world, for instance, emphasized the opposition, while those who aimed at world-conformity laid a greater stress on the unity of belief and knowledge.

To illustrate this, the viewpoints of a few thinkers in this period are given below:

1.1 Clement of Alexandria (d. 212 A.D.)

In Alexandria, the focal point of Hellenistic culture at the beginning of the third century, the first Christian theological school had its beginnings. Here Titus Flavius Clement, a heathen by birth, succeeded his predecessor Panaitus in about 200 A.D.

Ancient heathen philosophy plays a large part in his thought[5], especially in his view of divine revelation: God educated the Greeks with their philosophy, and the Jews with the Old Testament, towards Christ. The Old Testament and Greek philosophy are tributaries which empty into one mighty river. Both the former and the latter are, consequently, antechambers of the New Testament. Therefore Greek philosophy can be accepted and appreciated, up to a point. In Clement's own words, heathen philosophy is "the refreshing flood of revitalizing rainshowers which prepares the ground for the seed of true knowledge, the Christian Gnosis"[6].

Pagan thought prepares the way for the Christian faith because it first cleanses and purifies or instructs the soul[7]. Needless to comment that in this way the revelation of God is relativized.

Here the idea of a mutual foundation comes to the fore. Pagan philosophy forms an initial stage or ground floor on which the New Testa-

---

5. Cf. Timothy, *The early Christian apologists and Greek philosophy exemplified by Irenaeus, Tertullian and Clement of Alexandria.*

6. Clement: *Stromata*, I, 7.

7. Ibid., I. 10.

ment as fulfilment stands. It is a clear prefiguration of the later nature/ supernature scheme. K. Leese sees this clearly when he observes that the early Christian apologists and the Alexandrian theologians all, each in his own way, sought a rational foundation or antechamber to Christian belief[8].

Clement's thought is not however without some tension, since on the one hand Christendom is absolute religion but on the other heathendom saw truths which were fulfilled in Christendom[9].

At this point it will be desirable to consider these so-called "moments of truth" which are found in Clement and many other Christian thinkers after him. Several problems can be resolved by not treating all sciences exactly the same. For instance, as regards several sciences there would be no objection to a Christian taking over some of the non-Christian scholar's ideas and learning too. In sciences such as Philosophy, which are occupied with more comprehensive and fundamental problems, one would however have to proceed with great care. In Ontology, for example, which deals with the coherent diversity of God, law and cosmos, it is evident that heathen or non-Christian thinkers have perceived much, but nevertheless have distorted it. Several biased views of man could also be taken as illustration. Especially where Christian Theology is concerned, which aims at knowledge of God, it will be difficult to take over anything of non-Christian though.

A common mistake as regards the so-called moments of truth within heathendom is to isolate an idea from the context of the whole philosophical conception of which it is a part, or to isolate a work from the entire oeuvre of an author, or to detach a writer from the 'spirit' which bears him, so that statements are not seen in the light of the pagan philosophy of which they are a confession. The so-called fragments of truth or lumps of truth are wrenched out of their natural surroundings. But as soon as one sees them in context it is apparent that they can possess no truth, seeing that they are parts of a greater whole which cannot be called truth. Truth (and the lie) does not disintegrate into separate bits but forms an organic whole. This confusion in Clement and others promoted synthetic thought[10].

---

8. Cf. K. Leese, *Recht und Grenzen der natürlichen Religion* (1954), p. 30. See also De Vogel, *Wijsgerige aspecten van het vroeg-Christelijke denken*, p. 24.

9. R. Seeberg states rightly: "Das Christentum steht also im ausschliessenden Gegensatz zu allen Religionen und es ist doch auch ihr Abschluss." *Lehrbuch der Dogmengeschichte* I, (1953), p. 336.

10. For further thoughts with regard to the so-called "moments of truth" cf. Spoelstra, B. Die begrip "waarheidsmoment"... gaan dit op? *In die Skriflig*, 8(29):3-6, March 1974.

Even the argument that heathen thought can be used to oppose heathen philosophy itself (just as David beheaded the pagan Goliath with his own sword) is extremely dangerous.

This is not to imply that the heathens would only have proclaimed pure nonsense. Epistemologically, the matter can be explained thus: it is the same knowable reality which is examined by the Christian and the pagan thinker. But the results will differ as a result of the varying religious directions of the heart, which make their influence felt on the activity of knowing as well. And a second factor causing differing results of knowledge is the light of Scripture: in the case of the Christian it takes its rightful place (or ought to), in the case of the heathen it does not. Seeing that knowable reality (i.e. the created subjects and the laws to which they are subordinate) is however the same in both cases, those who have lived without the fear of the Lord and the light of his Word have nevertheless seen something of the truth.

This is quite evident from the heathen idea of law, for instance: they did indeed grasp something of God's revelation through His works. Since this is the result of left-oriented thoughts which lacked the light of Scripture, it is often distorted and falsified. Falsification does not however mean total nullification. In these views reality might emerge misshapen, but it still continued to function. The task of the Christian thinker is thus, inter alia, to examine heathen knowledge in the light of the Word — apart from his own study of reality.

Clement continually reiterates that knowledge and faith are not irreconcilable and that both are necessary. He states this in opposition to the Gnostic heretics who taught that faith and knowledge clashed. He does not, however, maintain a negative opposition, but sets his true Christian Gnosis up against the falsity of Gnosticism. He teaches that it is necessary that the Christian should not remain at the level of catechetical knowledge, but rather come to a deeper understanding of the faith, having rational insight into it. Such higher knowledge must necessarily make use of Philosophy. One should certainly be alert for the infiltration of pagan thoughts which are irreconcilable with the faith. But without Philosophy, rational penetration into the faith is not possible, yet still necessary — not simply for the exposition of Christian teaching, but also to refute heresy within the church and to confute attacks from without. Heathen Philosophy thus contributes to a strengthening of faith! In addition it is today, just as it was before the coming of Christ, still a pioneer for those who must be won over to the faith with rational proofs.

However, only within the faith-knowledge dilemma can an attempt be made to prove that Christian belief is true or reasonable. The problem is that it has already been accepted in advance that heathen scholarship is true or authoritiative to a greater or lesser degree.

In order to win the heathen over to belief with rational argument, it has to be cast in a philosophical mould which he can understand, i.e. more or less philosophized. In this way only a little may perhaps remain of the Christian message. The same holds good for the attempt to prove the truth of one's own Christian "philosophy" to the heathen by rational arguments and so win them for Christendom. Here too the victory is gained too soon, and in reality a defeat is suffered.

Clement thus distinguishes between the ordinary believer and the 'perfected' believer who has travelled from simple *pistis* to *gnosis* with the help of pagan philosophy. To explain this he employs the image of Paul in Rom. 11:17: Philosophy is like a wild olive tree which draws plenty of nourishment from the ground but bears no fruit. But a cultivated olive branch that is grafted on a wild olive can use its nourishment and produce fruit. Something similar happens if belief is grafted onto philosophical thought[11]. The Christian Gnostic, who according to Clement stands above the ordinary believer, is no other than the theologian. This view of Theology as *intellectus fidei* (Glaubenswissenschaft) was later to become very general.

1.2 Origen (182-233 A.D.)

The theological school of Alexandria reached its peak under Clement's successor, Origen, "the outstanding teacher and scholar of the early Church, a man of spotless character, encyclopaedic learning..."[12]. After everything that has already been said about Clement, there is little that is new in Origen. All the foregoing threads are largely picked up again by him.

Origen also explores the idea of heathen wisdom as a preparation for the Christian faith which provides its fulfilment[13]. The Gospel thus bring to actuality that which was already potentially present in pagan though.

Hence Philosophy is also a valuable preparative knowledge for (revealed) Theology. Human wisdom is a kind of education for the soul (cf. Clement), and divine wisdom is the eventual aim. Consequently the Christian ought not to hesitate in annexing what is good in heathen thought. Since the wisdom of the heathen thinkers was due to plagiarism of the books of Moses, the Christian can 'snatch it back' — just as the Lord commanded the Israelites on their departure from Egypt to take the treasures of the Egyptians for

---

11. Cf. Böhner, P. & Gilson, E.: *Christliche Philosophie von ihren Anfängen bis Nikolaus von Cues* (1954), p. 39 where the complete picture of Clement is given: He distinguishes between four differing modes in which the grafting can take place!

12. Qusten, J.: *Patrology* II (1953), p. 37. For a short resumé of his ideas in general see De Vogel, C.J.: *Wijsgerige aspecten van het vroeg-Christelijke denken* (1970), p. 27-35.

13. Cf. Ueberweg, F.: *Grundriss der Geschichte der Philosophie* II (1928), p. 66.

the erection of the tabernacle!

Seemingly a watertight argument, but only because of a lack of radical Biblical criticism of pagan thought. Popma rightly observes of this view of the plundering of heathen though (which later appeared in thinkers such as Augustine, Gregory of Nyssa, Cassiodorus, Alcuin and many others up till modern times): "Wanneer de apologeten op het voetspoor hunner judaïstische leermeesters de wijsheid der Grieken annexeeren voor het Christendom, dan is dit een verkapte poging om de antithese te ontgaan"[14].

The idea of this recovering of one's rightful property is not only historically inaccurate (the Greeks did not know the Bible) but also exposes an attempt to baptize or Christianize heathen views which can never lead to a Scriptural philosophy. Even had it been only an attempt at a merely 'formal' conscription of pagan thought, it would not have succeeded, for Philosophy was not content to remain a mere handmaid — and the history of early Christian thought itself is evidence for this.

According to Origen, Philosophy is actually not vital in order to come to belief or to understand the principles of revelation, but is nevertheless necessary — at any rate for those who want to rise above 'ordinary faith'. Clement's idea of two sorts of Christians thus returns with Origen. The 'exceptional believer' or theologian must acquire insight into his faith with the help of Philosophy, and refute the attacks of the heretics and heathen[15].

1.3 Tertullian (150-223 A.D.)

The two early Christian thinkers so far discussed had the common feature that their systems tended towards a relativizing of the antithesis between Christian faith and the pagan world of thought. At that time this kind of thought was the controlling tendency. Only a few Christians took a more antithetical line. Those we have so far mentioned bring about a levelling of Christendom and pagan Philosophy, whereas those who now follow more accurately perceive the opposition and irreconcilable conflict. Their representatives include among others the Syrian Tatian (a Greek author of the second century A.D.), the North African advocate Tertullian, and later still (c. 300 A.D.) Lactantius and Lucifer, bishop of Calaris, Sardinia (d. 370 A.D.). We limit our exposition to Tertullian[16]. It will become clear that — in spite of his more uncompromising attitude — he too does not offer

14. Popma, K.J.: *De oudheid en wij* (1948), p. 73.

15. Cf. Böhner, P. & Gilson, E., op. cit., p. 54.

16. For particulars of the stand taken by Tertullian, Tatian and Lucifer of Calaris cf. Popma, Patristic evaluation of culture. *Philosophia Reformata*, 38:99-113, 1974.

a satisfactory solution to the problem of the relationship between Christendom and ancient Philosophy.

He was born in Carthage in the then flourishing Roman province of North Africa, which had assimilated the Roman culture and language. He was, apart from Augustine, undoubtedly one of the most original and important church fathers. Quasten says of him, "with a profound knowledge of philosophy, law, Greek and Latin letters, Tertullian combines inexhaustible vigor, burning rhetoric, and biting satire. His attitude is uncompromising. Forever a fighter, he knew no relenting towards his enemies, whether pagans, Jews, heretics, or later on, Catholics"[17].

One of Tertullian's arch-enemies was philosophy. In this he differs from the school of Alexandria, especially from his younger contemporary, Clement. He has no desire to bring about a harmony between faith and philosophy, for they have nothing at all in common. His cry is famous: "What has Athens to do with Jerusalem? The Academy with the church? The heretic with the Christian? Our teaching comes from the hall of Solomon, who himself taught that one should serve the Lord in simplicity of heart. Away with all attempts to create a Stoic, Platonic or dialectic Christendom. We need no inquisitive discussion after we have received Christ, nor any investigation of the Gospel. When we believe, we have no need of anything more than faith. That which we believe is primary; there is nothing else which we still have to believe apart from faith"[18].

In this same section of *De praescriptione haereticorum* he speaks of the unhappy Aristotle (*miserum Aristotelem*) and cites Paul who warned in his letter to the Colossians against useless philosophy. Socrates, whom Justin had declared to be a Christian, is (elsewhere) called by Tertullian a seducer (*corruptor*) of youth.

Tertullian thus rejects any common ground between Christendom and heathen thought, any appreciation of or synthesis with philosophy, because philosophy and heresy are synonymous. He has no interest in gaining a deeper insight into faith with the aid of Philosophy — as had Clement and Origen — and thus of rising above ordinary belief. Hence he does not advocate a Theology in the sense of *intellectus fidei*.

It is understandable that the pronouncement *credo quia absurdum* (I believe because it is absurd) is ascribed to him. These specific words do not,

---

17. Quasten, op. cit., II, p. 247.

18. *De praescriptione haereticorum,* 7. For original Latin text cf. Böhner-Gilson, op. cit., p. 159. According to De Vogel (op. cit., p. 58), by such statements Tertullian strongly accentuated the supra-rational character of faith, and thereby underlined the revelatory character of Christendom, while his contemporaries all too easily trod the path from reason to Christian faith. In this connection she would even like to speak of a Protestant trait in Tertullian!

however, appear in his writings. But we do indeed find statements such as the following which tend in that direction: "Crucifixus est dei filius; non pudet quia pudendum est. Et mortuus est dei filius; prorsus credibile est, quia ineptum est. Et sepultus resurrexit; certum est, quia impossibile est"[19].

This idea rests particularly on the *credibile est, quia ineptum est,* from which the *credo quia absurdum est* is inferred. Hence Tertullian does not use the word *absurdum,* but *ineptum.* There is not, however, much difference in meaning between the two. Both can mean 'senseless', 'absurd' or 'nonsensical'.

With such statements Tertullian wishes to point out that such inconsistencies do not trouble him, seeing that it is not his purpose to build a bridge between faith and knowledge. Even the apparent conflict between the facts of redemption and reason does not prevent him from believing the former.

Nevertheless, viewed carefully, Tertullian did not succeed in disentangling himself from the faith/knowledge problem. The crux lies in that word *quia* (because), since the connection between faith and knowledge is still made there. Furthermore, faith bears the burden, for (heathen) knowledge determines that faith is *ineptum.* Once again, faith continues to be intellectualized — even though in a negative fashion which views it as nonsense or foolish. Put differently: an argument which is here meant to be against (philosophical) thought has precisely the opposite effect: it places the Gospel and faith once again on an intellectual level in such a way that they are anti-philosophical. If Tertullian had said, "Credo *etsi* ineptum est" (I belive *although* it is absurd) or "I believe although, in the view of heathen reason, to do so is foolish" his pronouncement would not have been so risky[20]. Also Christendom should not be characterized as a belief in the absurd by appealing to texts like I Cor. 1:18-25, Gal. 5:11 and Col. 2:8 so that a *sacrificium intellectus* becomes necessary[21].

It is remarkable that Tertullian's writings bear witness to the fact that — in spite of his struggle against philosophy — he was much influenced by

---

19. *De Carne Christi,* 5. Translation: "The Son of God is crucified; I am not ashamed of that, precisely because is is shameful. The Son of God died; this is completely believable, because it is nonsense. He was buried and rose; this is certain because it is impossible."

20. Cf. in this connextion also Lotz, J. Vernunft und Offenbarung bei Tertullian. *Katholik,* 1:124-40, 1913 and Schelowsky, *Der Apologet Tertullianus in seinem Verhältnis zur der griechisch-römischen Philosophie.*

21. Cf. Wassink, *Credo quia absurdum,* p. 162.

heathen thought[22]. He quite calmly quotes from diverse sayings of the philosophers to support his argument.

It must immediately be said that he does this more critically than the other figures discussed up until now. Tertullian had perceived that pagan philosophy could not simply be imported into Scripture. Although he realized that the two were in conflict at more than one point, this did not prevent him from accepting pagan philosophy as well as Scripture. But this landed him in a paradox: the one is true as well as the other, which is naturally an untenable standpoint. Nevertheless, it is important to note that this, too, is a method or form of synthetic thought[23].Tertullian, too, with his paradoxical method, views the difference between Christian and heathen thought as being relative, and causes the antithesis to fall away. This, however, is not apparent at first sight, as the appearance of opposition is maintained.

1.4 Augustine (345-430 A.D.)

The influence of Augustine, the greatest father of the church, on later Christian thought was immense. J. Hessen hardly exaggerates when he says, "Seine Ideen waren die leuchtenden Sterne am Himmel der christlichen Philosophie, die den Seefahrern im Reiche des Geistes auf Jahrhunderte hinaus zur Orientierung dienten. Die Geschichte der mittelalterlichen Philosophie ist, wie besonders die neueren Forschungen gezeigt haben, zum grossen Teil eine Geschichte des Einflusses Augustinus"[24]. This *primus inter pares* of the church fathers links the earliest Christian thought with that of the Middle Ages.

From antiquity he took over the conception of philosophy as an activity embracing everything relevant for the realization of the eventual goal of human existence. According to this usage, Christendom is also a 'philoso-

---

22. Ueberweg, op. cit., II, p. 46 and Wassink, op. cit., p. 124-6, among others refer to this. Cf. also Timothy, *The early Christian apologists and Greek philosophy exemplified by Irenaeus, Tertullian and Clement of Alexandria.*

23. Cf. Vollenhoven, D.H. Th.: *Kort overzicht van de geschiedenis der Wijsbegeerte* (1956), p. 25.
Popma here agrees with Vollenhoven. As already pointed out, he shows clearly how the tendency to solidarity with, as well as the antagonistic attitude of early-Christian thinkers towards Graeco-Roman culture, culminates in synthetic compromise. Cf. the conclusion of his article Patristic evaluation of culture. *Philosophia Reformata*, 38:112, 1974.

24. Hessen, J. *Patristische und scholastische Philosophie* (1922), p. 39.

phy'. 'Christendom' and 'true philosophy' are, for Augustine, identical[25].

But between this 'true philosophy' and the philosophy of the heathens he makes a clear distinction. The difference lies above all in the method: the Christian proceeds with belief in the authority of the Word and the heathen begins with reason.

Consequently, Augustine too has to wrestle with the question of the relationship between belief and knowledge[26]. He seizes especially upon Is. 7:9b of which the Latin translation reads: "Nisi credideritis, non intelligetis". This does not suggest, however, that Augustine proceeds one-sidedly on the basis of faith. There are other remarks where knowledge again precedes belief or where both sides are emphasized. For instance, "Intelligo ut credas, credo ut intelligas"[27]. In agreement with this Augustine is in favour of an intellectual entering-into of the truths of faith. According to M. Grabmann his striving after the *intellectus fidei* makes him the creator of the Theology of the Western World[28]. As with the earlier Christian thinkers, a polemical desire lies behind this[29]. He considers it important that reasons for belief are to be found in Scripture, such as fulfilled prophecies, revealed

25. R.A. Markus, for instance, says the following of Augustine's search for the truth: "Modern usage would not, of course, treat his inquiry as a philosophical one, but would assign it to the discipline of theology. The distinction between the two disciplines did not exist in Augustine's world, and their realms are merged in his 'Christian Philosophy' ". *The Cambridge history of later Greek and early Mediaeval Philosophy*, p. 253. See also p. 344.

26. For this, see inter alia Bezendörfer, W.: *Glauben und Wissen bei den Grossen Denkern des Mittalalters* (1931); Hähnel, J.: *Verhältnis des Glaubens zum Wissen bei Augustin* (1891): Warfield, B.: Augustin's doctrine of knowledge and authority. *PThR* 5:353 e.v., 529 e.v., 1907. Schultz, W.: Die Einfluss der Gedanken Augustin's über das Verhältnis von ratio und fides in der Theologie des 8., 9. und 11. Jahr-hundert. *Zeitschrift für Kirchengeschichte*, 34:323-59, 1913 and 35:9-39, 1914; Grabmann, M.: Augustins Lehre von Glauben und Wissen und ihr Einfluss auf das mittelalterliche Denken. (*In:* Aurelius Augustinus. Die Festschrift der Görresgesellschaft (1930), p. 87-110); Gangauf, *Verhaltnis von Glauben und Wissen nach den Prinzipen des Kirchenlehrers Augustinus;* Schwenkenbecher, *Augustinus Wort: Fides praecedit intellectum* and Weischedel, W.: *Der Gott der Philosophen I,* (1971), p. 103-6.

27. *Sermo* 43, c7. Cf. also the following pronouncements of Augustine:
"Quod intellectu capi non potest, fide teneatur, donec illucescat in cordibus ille, qui ait per Prophetam: Nisi credideritis, non intelligetis." *De Trinitate* I, 15 c.2.
"Ut ergo in quibusdam rebus ad doctrinam salutarem pertinentibus, quas ratione percipere nondum valemus, sed aliquando valebimus, fides praecedat rationem, qua cor mundetur, ut maginae rationis capiat et perferat lucem, et hoc utique rationis est et ideo rationabiliter dictum est per propbetam: Nisi credideritis, non intelligetis, ubi procul dubio discrevit haec duo deditque consilium, quo prius credamus, ut id quod credimus intelligere valeamus; proinde, ut fides praecedat, rationabiliter iussum est". *Epistola* 120 ad Consentium.

28. Cf. Grabmann, op. cit., p. 95.

29. Cf. ibid., p. 94.

miracles and the spreading of Christendom over the entire earth. Summarizing, it can however be said that in Augustine there still existed no sharp division between faith and knowledge such as later came about in the Middle Ages[30].

In this attitude towards heathen thought Augustine evidences a distinct line of development. In his earlier writings (even those after his conversion) he referred to it with much more enthusiasm than in his later works, where he was more reserved about it. Nowhere, however, does he hold the view that he wants nothing to do with the culture of classical antiquity. In his *De doctrina Christiana* (2.40) he employs the well-known figure of speech which we have already seen: just as Israel plundered the Egyptians as unlawful possessors of their treasures (Ex. 11:1,2), in order to take these along for the building of the tabernacle, even so should the truths which the heathen philosophers taught be taken and used for the right purposes, viz. the proclamation of the Gospel[31]. In the *De doctrina Christiana,* then, Augustine takes the *artes liberales*[32] and philosophy into the service of the study of Scripture. It forms a *propedeusis,* a preparation for the study of Scripture. For this reason he expresses the wish that the results of the heathen sciences, insofar as they are of interest for Biblical examination, would be collected in handbooks. Here heathen culture serves as the handmaid of Christendom[33].

According to A. Sizoo *De doctrina Christiana* should be translated not by 'On Christian Doctrine' but rather by 'On Christian Scholarship'. This work thus offers Augustine's idea of a Christian science. To a certain degree this Christian science is the counterpart of the heathen science, seeing that it uses the heathen one as foundation, but it does offer more, since it knows

---

30. Cf. Betzendörfer, op. cit., p. 8.

31. Augustine nevertheless modified this picture of Origen. He distinguished between the containers (*vasa*) which are harmless, and the dangerous wine of error *(vinum erroris)* which they contain, from which we must be liberated. The *vasa* is the mere word, rhetoric, the outward form. F.L. Battles and A.M. Hugo in their *Calvin's Commentary on Seneca's de Clementia* (1969), p. 49, justly remark, "The metaphor is hardly convincing; but it may serve as an indication of the complexity of the problem with which these men had to deal".
In my opinion this view of Augustine's is not only unconvincing but extremely dangerous. As has already been demonstrated, it is in my view not possible simply to make formal use of that which is alien, i.e. unchristian, without there being an inbuilt danger. The form and content of words and concepts cannot thus be separated.

32. Usually divided into the *trivium:* Grammar, Dialectic (Logic) and Rhetoric and the *quadrivium:* Arithmetic, Geometry, Music and Astronomy.

33. Cf. Sizzo, A.: *Augustinus: werk over de Christelijke wetenschap* (1933), especially p. 16, 17 and also his *Het oude Christendom en zijn verhouding tot de antieke cultuur* (1952), p. 46. 47.

the Scriptures too. In my opinion the Christian character of a discipline does not inhere in providing an extra or a plus above the non-Christian level. Christian scholarship must be radical, Christian (or better, Scriptural) from its very roots.

2. RETROSPECT

Individual differences apart, we have in all four of these thinkers from the early-Christian period basically the same struggle to arrive at a compromise between Biblical revelation and Graeco/Roman thought. The general trend was in the direction of synthetic thought such as is apparent, for example, from the popular but naïve conclusion that all that was good and true in Antiquity must have stemmed from the Bible. This hypothesis and others (e.g. that God prepared the heathen for the New Testament by Greek philosophy, just as he had educated the Jews towards it with the Old Testament) noticeably weakened the ciritcal perceptiveness of the early Christians and made it difficult for them to set up a principial antithesis. Instead of examining heathen philosophy in the light of the Word, the opposite was often done: the Scriptures were approached in the light of heathen philosophy and had to sanction it. This could easily have happened with the aid of the method of eisegesis and exegesis where the popular allegorical exegesis of the time came in very useful. The result was that early Christian thinkers leaned heavily on Graeco-Roman cultural ideas. Although the Christian motives of their thoughts must not be lost sight of, nor should categorical statements about all concerned be made, this baised heritage from pagan thought should not go unnoticed.

This synthetic attitude caused a philosophical schizophrenia, a dichotomy among Christian thinkers. In almost all of them a thorough study would uncover two lines, one taken from the Bible, the other betraying their Greek philosophical orientation, which is clear, for instance, in the ways in which they tackled the faith/knowledge problem. Already during the early Christian period of thought, important preparations were therefore being made for this epistemological problem to grow into the ontological division of nature and grace during the Middle Ages.

3. GROWTH AND ADULTHOOD OF THE BELIEF/KNOWLEDGE CONFLICT DURING THE MIDDLE AGES

The preceding sections of this paper showed how some thinkers stressed the unity of faith and knowledge, while others emphasized their opposition. In medieval thought the direction which stressed unity, as well as the tendency to teach an opposition between faith and knowledge, were both present. We now however find an in-between position as well, which proclaims their harmonious co-existence. Faith and knowledge are *distinguished* as separate fields, but not *separated* as opposites. Summarized: "Die mittelalterliche Scholastik hatte begonnen mit der Identifikation von wahrer Philosophie und wahrer Religion durch Johannes Scotus Eriugena, sie erreichte ihren Höhepunkt in dem Nachweis der Harmonie beider Grössen durch Thomas von Aquin und endete mit der Feststellung ihres unvereinbaren Gegensatzes durch Wilhelm von Ockham und seine Schüle einerseits, und Pietro Pomponazzi andererseits"[34].

The central question on which everything turned was whether faith and knowledge were simultaneously possible in the same person with regard to the same object[35]. We find mainly three solutions:

The first group answers in the affirmative. Here faith and understanding and also Theology and Philosophy, are not clearly differentiated. This group which belongs to the early Middle Ages, thus moves in the direction indicated by Augustine.

A second group replies negatively to the query as to whether simultaneous faith and reason are possible with respect to the same object in the same person. Faith and understanding are sharply distinguished and so too are Theology and Philosophy. Here indeed it is a problem as to whether Theology — which lies in the realm of faith — can still be *know*ledge. Even the right to existence of a Natural Theology becomes problematic, since matters of faith (such as the existence of God, for example) can only be believed and are no longer demonstrable. That which is rational vanishes from faith. This view is found mainly towards the end of the Middle Ages, e.g. in Occam and the advocates of the so-called double truth.

The third group of thinkers, which one comes across especially at the height of the Middle Ages, and of which Thomas is the clearest example, take a position in between the two extremes. Their answer to the above question is in a certain sense negative, yet also affirmative. Belief and knowledge are on the one hand clearly distinguished, so that Theology and Philosophy, as separate sciences, each has its own area of investigation. On the other hand, they also attempt to maintain the unity of and harmony

---

34. Betzendörfer, op. cit., p. 257. On p. 95 he gives a more comprehensive survey. Cf. also Finkenzeller, op. cit. p. 222-3; Weischedel, op. cit. I, p. 121-7; Armstrong, A.H. & Markus, R.A.: *Christian faith and Greek Philosophy* (1964), ch. 10 and Gilson, E.: *Reason and Revelation in the Middle Ages* (1952). Gilson deals first with those who put faith first (p. 1-34), then with those who, on the contrary, placed reason highest (p. 35-66), concluding with Thomas who "solves" the problem by accepting a harmony between reason and faith (revelation).

35. Cf. Finkenzeller, op. cit., p. 228.

between faith and reason, Theology and Philosophy. In this third movement Natural Theology receives its clearest form. As a result of the definite distinction between faith and knowledge, there are matters which can only be studied in (Supernatural) Theology and accepted in faith. (Later these kinds of questions about faith are called *articuli puri.*) Owing to the intimate connection between faith and knowledge, however, there were also matters (like the existence of God, for instance) which, apart from being accepted in faith, could also be proved by reason. (The so-called *preambula fidei* which was later known as the *articuli mixti.*) Natural Theology directs itself to the last-mentioned matters. How widely its field of inquiry is defined depends on precisely where the boundary between faith and knowledge, Theology and Philosophy, is drawn.

3.1 John Scotus Eriugena (c. 810-c. 877)

Eriugena stands very close to Augustine and Dionysius the Pseudo-Areopagite, but also makes his own contribution. He postulates the unity of faith and understanding. Just like Augustine, he gladly quotes from Is. 7: 9b: "Nisi credideritis non intelligetis". On the other hand, as again with Augustine, he also accepts the opposite. For instance, Eriugena says that Peter represents faith and John reason. When they walk to the tomb of Christ, John walks in front, because reason is quicker than faith. Nevertheless Peter arrives at the tomb first, because fulfilment is achieved only by faith[36].

To bring about agreement between philosophical speculation and the church's teaching (based on Holy Scripture), he makes use of the well-known method of allegorical exegesis. There is a double meaning in Scripture: the literal meaning and the deeper sense which is discovered by means of reason. This implies that there are also two sorts of believers: the ordinary people who cannot go deeper than the verbal sense, and the theologian-philosopher who uncovers the profounder meaning.

3.2 Anselm of Canterbury (1033-1109)

Anselm, too, exhibits agreement with Augustine, yet the differences are greater than in the case of Eriugena.

With reference to this already centuries-old problem, he also begins with faith: "For I do not seek insight in order then to believe, but I believe in

---

36. Cf. Betzendörfer, op. cit., p. 20.

order to arrive at insight. For I also believe this: if I do not come to faith, I shall not arrive at insight"[37]. Anselm also (in my opinion incorrectly) appeals to the already much-quoted Is. 7:9b, which reads: "If you do not believe — truly then you shall not be confirmed".

It would appear as if belief is primary for Anselm. Actually, though, faith is only a steppingstone, the leading-up, the initial phase or scaffolding which is to bring him to knowledge. Once faith has assisted reason into the saddle, it is left behind and pure reason remains[38]. Anselm thus only says that he "believes in order to be able to know", not that he "knows in order to believe". In this he differs from Augustine, who maintains both.

Anselm also makes the distinction already noted between two sorts of believers. There are those who, so long as they live, never pass beyond the faithful acceptance of revelation. Their faith has not yet reached the highest peak; for they do not understand what they believe. He compares them with the bat and the owl who exist in the dark, unlike the eagle which unblinkingly views the sun itself. From this it is evident that belief is handicapped as something blind or dark when compared with reason. Faith remains necessary, however, as the first phase, for reason is precisely the understanding of faith. Theology for him is *intellectus fidei* (comprehension of faith or 'Glaubenswissenschaft')[39]. With this insight into faith the Christian is put into a position to overcome his own doubt and also to defend himself against the attacks of the unbelievers. Hence the apologetic motive also plays an important role here.

3.3 Peter Abelard (1079-1142)

According to F. Ueberweg and others Abelard was the most influential

---

37. "Neque enim quaero intelligere, ut credam; sed credo ut intelligam. Nam et hoc credo, quia nisi credidero, non intelligam". *Proslogion,* ch. I, conclusion. For an exposition of Anselm's doctrine as regards faith and reason cf. Benzendörfer, op. cit., p. 30-44; Beeker, Der Satz der hl. Anselm: credo ut intelligam. *PhJGG* 19:115-27, 312-26, 1906; Grabmann, M.: *Die Geschichte der scholastische Methode,* Vol. I (1909); Haencken, E. Anselm, Glaube und Vernuft. *Zeitschrifft für Theologie und Kirche,* 48:312-41, 1951 and Wendschuch, G.: *Verhältnis des Glaubens zum Wissen bei Anselm von Canterbury* (1909).

38. Zuidema refers to this in his criticism of Barth's interpretation of Anselm's *Proslogion* in *Confrontatie met Karl Barth* (1963). So does G. Söhngen in an article "Kantz Kritiek der Gottesbeweise in religiös-theologische Sicht besonders von Anselms ontologischem Argument her" (*In:* Die Einheit in der Theologie (1952)) saying that Anselm begins only with the *credidimus* (we believe) and then carries the proofs of God *sola ratione* (with reason alone) further.

39. According to Betzendörfer, op. cit., p. 36, the original title of Anselm's *Monologion* was *Exemplum meditandi de ratione fidei* and that of his *Proslogion* was *Fides quarens intellectum.*

philosopher and theologian of the twelfth century. He is an example of a transitional figure between the overwhelmingly Augustinian tendency in the earlier Middle Ages and the movement (which ends in Thomas) in which belief and understanding, Theology and Philosophy, are more clearly distinguished. As will become evident, Abelard places even more emphasis on reason than does Anselm.

Schreiter[40] discerns three movements in the faith/knowledge debate in the time of Abelard. There was one school which gave more emphasis to faith as authoritative faith and thus did not assign such an important role to reason. The second movement (following Eriugena and Anselm) attached more importance to reason, and even tried to combat all doubt as to church doctrine with the weapons of reason. But belief remained for them strictly authoritative (grounded in the Word of God and the 'Fathers'), and they proceeded on its basis in providing rational proofs as well (cf. the *credo ut intelligam* of Anselm). The third school had no desire to begin with faith, but rather started with reason, coming to faith via the latter (more *intellego, ut credam)*. In other words: they wanted to acquire the mysteries of faith by reason. The writings of this school have practically all vanished except for those of Abelard. He, however, does not simply reverse Anselm's formula, he makes an even sharper distinction between the areas of faith and reason[41].

Abelard describes faith thus: *fide est existimatio rerum non apparantium, hoc est sensibus corporis non subjacentium.* Attention should be particularly concentrated on the *existimatio* (opinion). Faith is, according to him, an opinion. It is understandable then that he accepts as certain only that faith which is supported by rational grounds. According to Schreiter he here brought upon his own head the criticism of his contemporaries. However Abelard defended himself by saying that the fathers, after all, also sought for insights into what they believed.

Admittedly he acknowledged certain authorities, viz. the Scriptures, the writings of the Fathers and ... the works of the heathen philosophers! But he based his belief in the authority of Scripture on the fact that the Biblical writers had a very high degree of understanding, and he also often says that the Biblical writers erred, although "broadly speaking" Scripture is nevertheless true.

In his equation of the apostles and prophets with the heathen philosophers he reminds one of Justin, Clement and others. He ascribes divine inspiration not only to the writers of the Bible, but also to heathen thinkers.

---

40. Cf. Schreiter, F.: *Petrus Abälards Anschauungen über das Verhältnis vom Glauben zum Wissen* (1912), p. 1-3.

41. Cf. Ueberweg, op. cit., p. 213 and 220.

He even ascribes knowledge of the Tri-unity to the pagans. The apologetic thought that the opponent must be combated with his own weapons – just as David employed Goliath's own sword to behead him – is also evident[42].

Most authorities would rather not ascribe any Rationalism to Abelard, although they all admit that reason did play a greater and more independent role for him than had been the case up to then. This is apparent from the fact that in all cases he desired to test belief rationally or provide *rationes necessariae* before it was accepted, as also from the fact of his high regard for heathen thought.

3.4 Retrospect

The most remarkable difference between early Christian thought and the early Middle Ages is the more independent, more significant role that the reason began to play. Eriugena, Anselm and Abelard witness to this. Belief and understanding, Theology and Philosophy became continually more clearly distinguished.

4. THOMAS AQUINAS (1224/5-1274)

This *princeps scholasticorum* sharply distinguishes between the above mentioned concepts. Like his teacher, Albert the Great[43], he teaches that the same matter cannot simultaneously be an object both of faith and reason to the same person[44]. But at the same time he also maintains the

---

42. Cf. Betzendörfer, op. cit., p. 54 and Schreiter, op. cit., p. 34. Cf. what has already been said about this tendency in the thinkers of early Christianity. See also Grane, *Peter Abaelard. Philosophie und Christentum im Mittelalter.* For the influence of Abelard cf. Luscombe, D.E.: *The school of Peter Abelard. The influence of Abelard's thought in the early scholastic period* (1969).

43. In his article Glauben und Glaubenswissenschaft nach Albert dem Grossen *Zeitschrift für Katolische Theologie*, 54:1-39, 1930 Feckes has demonstrated how little Thomas differs from his master on this point. He even says: "In der Gesamtlösung und in fast allen Einzelheiten gehen die beiden grossen Aristoteliker des Mittalalters, Albert und Thomas, der Meister und der Schüler, Hand in Hand." And: "Alberts Lösung ist durch Thomas von Aquin die Lösung der Katholischen Theologie geworden. Sein grosser Schüler bringt nichts wesentlich Neues mehr hinzu, er führt nur noch konsequenter die aristotelischen Prinzipien durch..." (p. 39). Feckes shows how Albert the Great had already sharply distinguished between belief and reason, Theology and Philosophy, and how he also distinguished two theologies (a natural and a supernatural).
For Thomas's view of the relationship between faith and knowledge cf. Betzendörfer, op. cit., p. 154-84; Gilson, E.: *Reason and revelation in the Middle Ages* (1952) p. 67 et seq. and Nied, E.: *Glauben und Wissen nach Thomas von Aquin* (1928).

44. Cf. *Summa Theologiae, pars secunda secundae, quaestio 1, articulus 5.*

harmony between them. Brief attention is given here to both this distinction and the separation of faith and knowledge.

As already stated, the *knowable* or the object of knowledge is, in the case of reason, the visible creation, and is, in the case of faith, the invisible, viz. God and the content of his Revelation. Hence Thomas solves the problem by assigning a separate area or field of investigation to each of these activities of knowing. However this does not imply a watertight distinction, because there is overlapping.

Both faith and reason demand, in the second place, *activities of knowing*, functions of the intellect. However, these activities differ. As shown, reason follows the path of abstraction towards knowledge. With faith, there is illumination or supernatural enlightenment. This comes into being through the supernatural working of the grace of God. With knowledge, evidence is also brought into the picture. (The *principia* are viewed as self-evident.) With faith it is a matter of authority. (The principles are accepted on the basis of God's Word-revelation.)

In the third place there is a difference in the *result of knowing* in faith and reason. As far as certainty is concerned, faith is "objectively" concerned, more secure, for it is directed towards divine truth. "Subjectively" viewed, reason is more certain since the knower can better understand his field of inquiry. In this regard Thomas accepts the well-known distinction between opinion *(opinio)*, faith *(fides)* and knowledge *(scientia)* which has already been met with in earlier thinkers[45]. As for the degree of certainty, faith according to him adopts a position in between opinion and knowledge, more certain than mere opinion but less so than knowledge.

Thus far, then, with Thomas's threefold differentiation between faith and knowledge exists. With regard to the harmonious connection of faith and knowledge (or between the two most important disciplines which operate respectively with the faculties of faith and reason, viz. Theology and Philosophy), we shall take note first of the relationship of faith/reason and then of the reason/faith relationship.

Faith completes knowledge, exalts it.

Thomas teaches this in agreement with his two-realms doctrine, according to which, grace does not do away with nature, but uplifts it and fulfils it. This implies the following (inter alia) for the relationship between Theology and Philosophy: Supernatural Theology (which studies Scripture) helps Philosophy (in its highest aspect, viz. Natural Theology) by making known certain truths concerning God which are also knowable by reason. The reason why God reveals these truths (in spite of the fact that He is rationally knowable) is that man can then arrive more rapidly at a know-

---

45. Cf.   ibid., *pars secunda secundae, quaestio, 4, articulus 1 & 8.*

ledge of God, all men can possess it, and without aberrations too.

Apart from this orientating role of Theology with respect to Philosophy, it is also a negative criterion, for it ensures that Philosophy does not contradict Scripture.

In its turn knowledge (and Philosophy) serves faith (and Theology) in a threefold manner, viz. by preparing the way for faith *in advance*, by helping to extend the content of faith *from within*, and by defending faith *afterwards*[46]. Faith is as a result not merely encircled before and after by reason, but the latter is even permitted within the terrain of the former.

Initially reason prepares the way for faith by providing motives for the value of faith (*motiva credibilitatis* or *credentitatis*) or, as Thomas himself calls them, *praeambula fidei*. To these belong the rational conviction of God's existence, his unity, the possibility of revelation and so forth. In other words all the truths concerning God and divine things which fall within the reach of human reason — *not* the so-called mysteries of faith.

It is important to notice that according to Thomas, the Holy Scripture does not just contain supernatural truths about God, but also natural, rational truths. (Divine revelation, therefore, does not start at the point where human understanding cannot attain further knowledge and the danger of erring begins.)

In the second place reason (in the form of Philosophy) assist faith (as Theology) in the expansion of the content of faith. Reason therefore does not call a halt in front of the gates of faith. Although this might constitute trespassing on the sacredness of faith, it is as a servant who realizes that he now treads on sacred ground. Its task is not to prove the mysteries of faith, but it can nevertheless illuminate them or make them conceivable by the use of analogies. In addition it can promote a better understanding thereof through systematization and resolution of obvious contradictions.

In the third place reason or Philosophy has the apologetic task of defending the faith (as systematized in Theology)[47]. This defence is directed both

---

46. Thomas remarks in his work *Expositio super librum Boethii de Trinitate* (q. 2 a):
"In sacra doctrina philosophia possumus tripliciter uti:
"Primo ad demonstrandum ea quae sunt praeambula fidei, quae necesse est in fide scire, ut ea quae naturalibus rationibus de Deo probantur.
"Secundo ad notificandum per aliquas similitudines ea quae sunt fidei...
"Tertio ad resistendum his quae contra fidem dicuntur, sive ostendendo esse falsa sive ostendendo non esse necessaria".

47. Thomas makes a clear distinction between the first and the third employment of reason (and Philosophy) with regard to matters of belief (and Theology). Perhaps the distinction is made clearer by saying that the first use of reason with respect to faith takes place in Natural Theology, and the third use of reason with regard to faith takes place in Apologetics. Hence Natural Theology and Apologetics which was still intermingled in the thought of the Christian Apologists is, in Thomas, more clearly separated.

inwardly and outwardly[48]. It has, in the first place, a more positive task, namely to "prove" the credibility of the mysteries of faith. The second task is more negative, namely to render the counter-arguments of unbelievers powerless by demonstrating that these are neither compelling nor tenable[49].

Here something of the idea of the *fides quarens intellectum*, the search for a reasonable faith, once again rears its head[50]. The question of the rationality of faith can be stated in a two-fold sense: the (more external) question as to the credibility of Revelation and the (more internal) certainty of faith.

As regards the first, *rationes demonstrativae, manifesta indicia* or *evidentia signorum* can, according to Thomas, be adduced for the Revelation of God[51]. Here too Thomas maintains the distinction between natural and supernatural, reason and belief. Only supernatural proofs may be advanced

48. Thomas says for instance in Ch. 2 of his *Summa Contra Gentiles* (hereafter abbreviated to SCG), where he states the purpose of the SCG: "... propositum nostrae intentiones est veritatem quam fides Catholica profitetur, pro nostro modulo manifestare, errores eliminando contrarios...".

49. A particularly interesting question is how far Thomas is of the opinion that objections to faith on a rational basis can be invalidated. He deals with this, inter alia, in SCG part I, ch. 7. He concludes that all arguments brought against faith can be rebutted, seeing that there can be no clash between belief and scholarship, and arguments against faith must therefore be incorrect deductions from the self-evident principles in nature.

50. I Pet. 3:15, where it is stated that account must be given of one's faith, is often cited as scriptural proof for the necessity of this. It is interesting and amusing that the well-known distinction between two sorts of believers in the Middle Ages is often defended by an appeal to Job 1:14, where mention is made of cattle yoked to the plough and donkeys grazing beside them. Gregory the Great was the first to make use of this. He understood the *boves arantes* (ploughing cattle) to be the mature believers (priests and monks) who, because they believed also understood. By the *asinae pascentes* (grazing donkeys) he understood the immature believers who — in spite of lack of insight — nevertheless were able to profit from the spiritual labour of their brethren. (Rome also honours the doctrine of the *fides implicita*, i.e. the accepting of truths which one does not personally know!)
It is apparent here how "ordinary" faith is disqualified when contrasted with the insight of the theologian. This paved the way to the — from our point of view unacceptable — distinction between clergy and laity in Roman thought. Even today Theology and faith are often still confused, and the knowledge of the theologian is regarded as higher than that of the ordinary believer — while the difference lies rather in the *different nature* of the two types of knowledge.

51. In his attempt to provide grounds for the credibility of Christendom and its faith in the Bible, Thomas offers nothing new. This, too, stems from the time of the Christian Apologists. A. Waibel made mention of this in his book *Die naturliche Gotteserkenntnis in der apologetischen Literatur des zweiten Jahrhunderts* (1916).

for supernatural matters[52] (*in casu* the Holy Bible). Therefore for Thomas — unlike many of his predecessors — only miracles (as supernatural deeds of God) are valid as proof. Thomas in this regard distinguishes a whole number of different sorts of miracles as *motiva credibilitatis*.[53]. Apart from being called the architect of Natural Theology, he can justifiably be named as an important layer of the foundation of Roman Catholic apologetics[54].

As already noted, quite apart from the question of the credibility of Scripture, there is also the problem of the (more subjective) certainty of faith. As shown, Thomas also grapples with the problem of the security of belief (inter alia) in his distinction between opinion, faith and knowledge. This struggle also comes to the fore in the definition which he gives of faith[55]. As a result of his intellectualistic tendency (emphasizing the reason in contrast to Voluntarism, which stresses the will) he seeks certainty for faith in its reasonableness particularly[56]. A most enlightening work in this regard is that of Espenberger: *Grund und Gewisheit des übernatürlichen*

52. Cf. SCG Book III, chapter 154 where Thomas says that, since matters of belief are not evident to reason, it was necessary that the words of the preachers be confirmed in some way or another. The demonstration cannot, however, occur through rational principles because here matters which are supra-rational are in question. Therefore the oral witness is confirmed by signs (healing of the sick and other superhuman deeds) which clearly show that the words originate from God. Cf. also SCG I, 6.

53. In SCG Book I, chapter 6, Thomas mentions the healing of all sorts of diseases, the resurrection of corpses and the inspiration of the Holy Spirit so that the simple and unlearned people can immediately possess the highest wisdom and eloquence. He regards the most miraculous conversion of the world to Christendom as the clearest sign which can be given.

54. It is of the greatest importance to understand that the problem of apologetics, from the early Christian thinkers until the time of Thomas and after, continually goes hand in hand with the question of faith and knowledge. A. Lang is correct when he declares: "Die apologetische Fragestellung war in der Zeit der Scholastik ... eingegliedert in den Problemenkomplex, der unter dem Spannungsverhältnis von auctoritas und ratio, Glauben und Wissen sicht birgt; sie darf nicht losgelöst davon betrachtet werden". *Die entfaltung des apologetischen Problems in der Scholastik des Mittelalters* (1962). Cf. further in this connexion also his other study: *Die Wege der Glaubensbegründung bei den Scholastikern des 14. Jahrhunderts* (1931) in which he carries these thoughts still further. P.H. Lang deals specifically with Thomas in *Die Lehre des hl. Thomas von Aquin von der Gewisheit des übernatürlichen Glaubens* (1929).

55. Cf. inter alia *Summa Theologiae, pars secunda secundae, quaestio 1, art. 4:* "respondeo dicendum quod fides importat assensum intellectus ad id quod creditur" and *quaestio 2, art. 9:* "Ipsum autem credere est actus intellectus assentientis veritate divinae ex imperio voluntatis a Deo motae per gratiam..." Cf. also *quaestio 4, art. 1* where Thomas expounds Heb. 11:1's description of faith.

56. Thus, faith is not opposed to doubt (as Scripture teaches), but reasonable faith is the opposite of ordinary belief which is merely somewhat uncertain, blind and dim. Insight into faith, a proved faith, brings certainty. Contrast this with Scripture which teaches that faith is a *firm* trust in the things which we hope, and a *proof* of the things which we do not see (Heb. 11:1).

Glaubens in der Hoch- und Spätscholastik[57]. He deals first with the voluntaristic viewpoint which desired to link the ground of or criterion for faith with the will, then with the intellectualistic, which links it with the reason, and finally with the compromise between the two. As appears from the brief summary of Espenberger's study, the problem of the certainty of faith is not connected only with the problem of faith/reason but also with the question of faith's relationship to the will. The last-named aspect is usually treated as a *psychological* problem in contradistinction to the *epistemological* problem of faith/reason, as in the thorough study of Englhardt: *Die Entwicklung der dogmatischen Glaubenspsychologie in der mittelalterlichen Scholastik*. At its deepest, therefore, it is linked with Anthropology, viz. as to how the various capabilities of the soul (intellective, voluntative, etc.) are seen.

We need not go into all the questions in this regard here. The problems are mentioned merely to illustrate the struggles of Thomas with the faith-reason problem[58].

A more Scriptural vision of their relationship would be able to solve many of the problems. In my opinion belief and reason (even Thomas stresses their unity) cannot be separated by means of the higher-lower scheme as he does. The relationship is not "knowledge *and* belief" but "faithfilled knowledge" ("gelowige wete") *also* in the case of the so-called 'unbeliever'. Faith is not just a *donum superadditum* above reason. Berkouwer rightly remarks of such a view of faith, "Deze opvatting is in de diepste grond alleen te verklaren uit een losmaken van het geloof van de volheid en concreetheid van het menselijk leven. Men schijnt daardoor het wonder van deze gave des Geestes te meer te eren, maar doet in werkelijkheid aan deze gave te kort. Niet een nieuw orgaan word geschapen, noch is het geloof een nieuwe substantie, die ingedragen wordt in het vlak der menselijke existentie als een nieuwe, bovennatuurlijke en completerende inge-

---

57. Other studies of the problem of the certainty of belief in the Middle Ages are those of Heim, K.: *Das Gewissheitsproblem in der systematischen Theologie bis zu Schleiermacher* (1911); Lang, A.: *Die Wege der Glaubensbegründung bei den Scholastikern des 14. Jahrhunderts* (1913) and in the newer scholastic thought Schlagenhaufen, F. Die Glaubensgewissheit und ihre Begründung in der Neuscholastik. *Zeitschrift für Katholische Theologie* 56:313-74 and 530-95, 1932.
The influence of medieval views on the problems of the certainty of faith is apparent, inter alia, from the study of Dee, S.P.: *Het geloofsbegrip van Calvijn* (1918) and that of Graafland, C.: *De zekerheid van het geloof. Een onderzoek naar de geloofsbeschouwing van enige vertegenwoordigers van reformatie en nadere reformatie* (1961).

58. Heim justly comments: "Logische Evidenz und aus Autoritäts-zeugnissen erworbener Glaube sind also — mathematisch ausgedrückt — die beiden Grenzwerte, zwischen denen zich die katholische Lehrbildung über die Gewissheitsfrage hin — und herbewegen kann..." Op. cit., p. 161.

storte genade... Niet allerlei anthropologische gegevens maken samen de gave Gods uit, maar de betrokkenheid van de ganse mens vanuit het hart, vanwaar de uitgangen des levens zijn, op de onwankelbaarheid van Gods genade"59).

5. DEVELOPMENTS AFTER THOMAS

Occam (c. 1290-1350), Siger of Brabant (1234-1282), Duns Scotus (1266-1308) and Raymond of Sabunde (c. 1436) are briefly discussed. Occam[60] belongs to the second group of thinkers mentioned above: he divides faith from reason, Theology from Philosophy, and lays all the emphasis on faith so that a Natural Theology simply cannot exist, or only with great difficulty.

Siger of Brabant is a representative of the so-called dual truth theory which is found in the so-called Latin Averroists. Diverging stands are taken with regard to this doctrine of the *duplex veritas*[61]. According to some this doctrine meant the simultaneous acceptance of two (apparently contradictory) truths. Others however suggest that the doctrine was only a sarcastic manner of saying that the truth of theology or belief was pure nonsense. The proponents of the *duplex veritas* would then employ the theory merely as a shield to disguise their secret unbelief and escape from persecution on the part of the church. Behind the smokescreen of the acceptance of a double standard Philosophy and scholarship (to which the highest authority was ascribed) could deny the most fundamental Christian truths! The advocates of the doctrine were thus, in the first instance, interested in philosophy.

59. Berkouwer, G.C.: *Geloof en rechtvaardiging* (1949), p. 202.

60. Cf. for Occam's ideas the selections in Boehner, ed. *Ockham. Philosophical writings* (1967). Cf. further Guelluy, R.: *Philosophie et Théologie chez Guillaume d'Ockham* (1947); Hägglund, B.: *Theologie und Philosophie bei Luther und in der occamistischen Tradition* (1955) and Verweyen, J.M.: *Philosophie und Theologie im Mittelalter* (1911)

61. For the doctrine of the double truth see, inter alia Betzendörfer, W.: *Die Lehre von der Zweifachen Wahrheit. Ihr erstmalige Auftreten im christliche Abenland und ihre Quellen* (1924); Breen, The twofold truth Theory in Melanchton. *In:* Christianity and Humanism (1965), p. 69-72; Gilson, E. Boèce de Dacie et la double vérité. *Archives d'Histoire Doctrinale et Littéraire du Moyen-Age.* 22:81-99, 1955; Heim, K.: *Zur Geschichte des Satzes von der doppelten Wahrheit* (1918); Haufnagel, Z. Zur lehre von der doppelte Wahrheit. *Tübing. theol. Quartalschrift*, 136:284-95; Maier, *Das Prinzip der doppelte Wahrheit;* Maywald, *Die Lehre von der Zweifachen Wahrheit;* Michaud-Quantin: La double-vérité des Averroistes. Un texte nouveau de Boèce de Daci. *Theoria*, 22:167-84, 1956; Pine, M. Pompanazzi and double truth. *Journal of the history of ideas,* 29:163-76, 1968 and Van Steenberghen, F.: *Introduction à l'Etude de la Philosophie Médiévale*, p. 555-70.

Siger of Brabant, John of Jandun and Boethius of Dacia consequently also belong to the third group of thinkers mentioned previously, but differ from Occam and company in that whereas he places heaviest stress on belief and Theology, they once again accentuate reason and Philosophy. But the result, as far as it concerns Natural Theology, is just the same. The fact that they stress reason does not lead (as might perhaps be expected) to the flourishing of Natural Theology. (Another historical proof that Natural Theology is not a purely rational activity, but one inspired by faith which can only blossom within a harmonious co-existence of faith and reason!)

In Duns Scotus[62] there is still a large measure of harmony between belief and knowledge[63], so that certain truths are provable by reason and Natural Theology has a chance of existence.

However, he is greatly surpassed by Raymond of Sabunde who regarded practically everything as demonstrable[64]. In following his namesake, Raymond Lully, a missionary to Islam in Spain, the Spaniard Sabunde attempted to derive all the truths of the Christian faith from nature, in a rational manner. Of the two books in one volume which God gave us, viz. the Holy Scripture and nature, he regarded the latter as far more important for the following three reasons. In the first place it is accessible to all men, while the Bible is only accessible to the cleric. Secondly, he believes that nature, unlike Holy Scripture, cannot be distorted or falsified. In the third place, according to him, the Bible is of secondary importance, seeing that it was only given after the Fall when man could no longer read the book of nature. Nature, then, must also be studied before the Bible can be rightly understood! This is precisely the opposite of what is, in my view, the Scriptural viewpoint, viz. that nature can only be understood rightly in the light of the Word. No wonder that he was condemned by the Roman

---

62. For his thought in general cf. Gilson, E.: *Johannes Duns Scotus. Einführung in die Grundgedanken seiner Lehre* and Wolter, ed.: *Duns Scotus. Philosophical writings.*

63. Cf. Minges, P.: *Das Verhältnis zwischen Glauben und Wissen, Theologie und Philosophie nach Duns Scotus* (1908), p. 5, 9, 204; Finkenzeller, J. *Offenbarung und Theologie nach der Lehre des Johannes Duns Scotus* (1961), especially pages 231-235; Muller, Theologe und Theologie nach Johannes Duns Scotus. *Wissenschaft und Weisheit,* 1:39-51, 1934 and Betzendörfer, W. op. cit., p. 215.

64. For details of his thought cf. Huttler, *Die Religions-Philosophie des Raymundus von Sabunde* (on p. 73-6 this gives a translation of the censored prologue of Sabunde's work *Theologia Naturalis*); Makke, D.: *Die natürliche Theologie des Raymundus von Sabunde. Ein Beitrag zur Dogmengeschichte des 15. Jahrhunderts* (1846); Zöckler, O.: *Geschichte der Apologie des Christentums* (1907), p. 225-30; Id., *Theologia naturalis. Entwurf einer systematischen Naturtheologie von offenbarungsglaubige Standpunkte aus* (1860), p. 40-6; Fulton, W.: *Nature and God* (1927), p. 37-8, 55-60 and see also the literature mentioned by Stegmüller s.v. Raimund von Sabunde *In:* Die Religion in Geschichte und Gegenwart V (3rd edition), p. 771.

Church and that the prologue to his famous book, to which the name *Theologia Naturalis* was given[65], was placed on the Index.

A study of Sabunde's works reveals that he stands very close to Thomas and Duns Scotus. With Thomas particularly there are noticeable affinities which are explained by the fact that his purpose was to popularize Thomism. Sabunde is, however, clearly a transition-figure who, reacting against the so-called Supra-naturalism (which put all its emphasis on the pole of grace), emphasized the pole of nature and so became a herald of the new era.

65. This was not the original title but was preceded by many other names. Cf. Makke, op. cit., p. 3-4 for the various titles during different editions.

5 THE ENCOUNTER OF ARABIC AND CHRISTIAN CIVILIZATIONS IN MEDIEVAL PHILOSOPHY WITH PARTICULAR REFERENCE TO THE CONFLICT BETWEEN FAITH AND REASON. A COMPARISON BETWEEN THE VIEWPOINTS OF AVERROES AND THOMAS AQUINAS*

1. INTRODUCTION

Philosophy and Culture. There is a close relation between philosophy and civilization. On the one hand, every philosophy reflects a certain culture; on the other, philosophy has a profound influence on its cultural environment. Philosophy, as a discipline, is not just an interesting pastime. It exerts tremendous cultural-historical power.

Medieval Philosophy and Culture. The Middle Ages furnishes us with a panorama of man and civilizations working out their task of unfolding, developing, moulding and cultivating the cosmos. Medieval history, including its philosophy and culture, was not a stream in which people were caught up and carried along towards some undetermined destiny. It was neither a complex chain of cause and effect, nor a series of facts, dates and events bound together by some inherent law of causality. Certain decisive decisions were taken which made this period of approximately a thousand years a force which shaped our Western civilization. Far from its being an unimportant link or a barbarian interval between the ancient classical and modern culture, we will find that because there are no radical breaks, but continuity in the history of civilization, a confrontation with the Medieval era may be of the utmost significance for our way of life and thought in modern civilization. Because we encounter a variety of civilizations in Medieval Philosophy, this rich and colourful period conveys to us a message which can suggest solutions to some of the eternal problems with which mankind has to cope or which can teach us useful lessons, even if we learn only from its errors and failures.

Averroes and Thomas Aquinas. Two of the cultures which mingled in the Middle Ages were the Arabic and the Christian. This paper confines itself to two of the greatest representatives of these cultures, viz., Averroes or Ibn Rusd (1126-1198) and Thomas Aquinas (1225-1274). They were spokes-

* Paper prepared for the Fifth International Congress of Medieval Philosophy, Madrid, Gordoba and Granada: 5-12th September 1972. (Theme: The encounter of different civilizations in Medieval Philosophy).
Previously published in *Bulletin van die Suid-Afrikaanse Vereniging vir die Bevordering van Christelike Wetenskap,* no. 23:53-64, July 1972.

men for their age in a true sense because they systematized what had been in the making for many years in their respective cultures. They supplied in their systems the theoretical underpinnings of a generally accepted way of life. In this way they were real giants exerting a strong cultural, formative power by means of their philosophies.

Faith and Reason. A central problem of this period concerns the relation between faith and reason — an issue which survived the ages and is of vital importance right up to the present day.

Method of Approach. In line with the theme of this congress we are more interested in the general cultural-religious background to the problem of faith and reason. I do not intend to give an exposition of exactly *how* Averroes and Aquinas solved the matter, but rather to investigate *why* they encountered this problem. My aim is to uncover critically the basic presuppositions which gave birth to the strife between faith and reason.

Religious ground motive and cultural ideal. Religion, which must not be identified with divine worship, cultic or church life, is the all-encompassing and all-permeating throbbing power in the life of every human being. This spirit of a person denotes the characteristic dynamics of that which inspires all his acts. There is also a communal spirit, and if it prevails for a long period of time and fundamentally directs culture and the course of history, we may speak of the spirit of a specific age. Every culture reveals a certain spirit because culture gives us a picture of religion in action. In man's cultivation of the universe he is gripped by a religious ground motive which inspires every action, consciously or unconsciously. Religious motives are translated into cultural ideals or goals towards which every civilization aspires. These religious ground motives should be viewed as a driving motive power from within, whereas the cultural ideal can be likened to a guiding light which directs a civilization, mostly from without, towards a certain aim.

2. RELIGIOUS GROUND MOTIVES AND CULTURAL IDEALS IN THE ARABIC AND CHRISTIAN CULTURES AS REPRESENTED BY AVERROES AND AQUINAS

Averroes. Islamic culture is eclectic by nature. Its ground motive is orientated to:

(a) the polytheism of the early nomadic Arabs who interpreted good in terms of the possession of material goods, and evil in terms of the lack thereof;

(b) Zoroastrianism, with its two independent principles of light and darkness, together with

(c) the influence of the Jewish tradition *(inter alia* monotheism) and

(d) Christianity (with a two-realm approach).

Basically, the Islamic religious ground motive reveals a dialectical tension between the conception of God — as built on revelation, and Man — as conceived without the aid of revelation. The attempt to harmonize the Mohammedan faith with pagan Greek ideas resulted in a stress-ridden motive power. This stress-ridden motive power was translated, however, into a cultural ideal which was designed to offset the inner tension and retain the synthesis. The aim of the cultural ideal of Islam was to establish a monotheistic theocracy uniting all mankind by means of a holy war, and embracing a vision of a paradise of earthly luxury.

Thomas Aquinas. Christian synthetic thought manifested itself in three different religious methods which, by using Tertullian's metaphor of Jerusalem (i.e. the Bible) and Athens (i.e. Greek Philosophy), we can summarize in the following way:

The method of *eisegesis-exegesis* revealed an attitude of *world conformity*. It claimed that Jerusalem was identical to Athens and vice versa. It was only necessary that the pagan philosophy of Athens should obtain biblical sanction and authority from Jerusalem by an allegorical interpretation of the Scriptures.

In reaction to the ideal of world conformity, the method of *paradox* advocated an attitude of *world flight*. Jersalem had nothing to do with Athens. They were directly opposed to each other and Jerusalem (faith) should avoid Athens (reason) at all costs. Nevertheless, both had their own right to a separate existence.

The method of *nature-supernature* (grace) preached world compromise (or world colonialism), in an attempt to avoid the extremes of both world conformity and world flight. Jerusalem, representing the Scriptures, faith, church, etc. was not permitted to be submerged into Athens, the secular world made up of reason etc., nor to escape from it. Jerusalem was neither identical to Athens, nor opposed to it, but, as the superior of an inferior realm, it surpassed Athens.

At the time of Thomas Aquinas the two-realm theory of nature and grace was already well developed, but it reached the peak of its most articulate expression in his philosophy. Grace did not abolish nature, but perfected it. Nature, embracing the whole of reality viewed in the light of pagan philosophy, was related to grace, i.e. the whole of life viewed in the light of the Bible, as for example, a threshold to a sanctuary.

This approach was possible because the fall into sin was not regarded as radical. The sinner, according to his view, is a rational-moral man *minus* the supernatural, i.e. faith, and the redeemed (Christian) is the same rational-moral man *plus* faith obtained sacramentally through the institution of the church.

The Medieval world, and Thomas Aquinas as its representative, lost sight of the radical antithesis between the pagan culture and philosophy or nature, and the biblical revelation or grace, and consequently failed to recognize clearly the tension inherent in the ground motive of nature and grace. That he was aware that some form of tension was prevalent, is evident from the cultural ideal he designed to neutralize it. The cultural ideal of the *Corpus Christianum* expressed faith in the possibility of uniting nature and grace into a Christian civilization. In point of fact, however, the two historic forces, which in principle can never be synthesized because they have no point of contact, were only held together by the strength and forceful application of the *Corpus Christianum* cultural ideal. Although the Middle Ages is characterized as "Christian", it actually represents a vivid picture of the struggle between two kingdoms.

Comparison. There is a great similarity between Averroes and Aquinas because both of them formulated their philosophies from a tension-ridden synthetic religious ground motive, and both tried to merge two conflicting cultures. There is also a remarkable similarity between their cultural ideals, viz. monotheistic theocracy and *corpus christianum*.

The major difference between the two may be summed up by stating Averroes was gripped by a grace-nature religious motive, whereas Aquinas was inspired by a nature-grace religious ground motive.

Because an attempt was made to reconcile two, or even more, mutually exclusive religious ways of living and thinking by both Averroes and Thomas Aquinas, many artificial problems, or false and therefore insoluble dilemmas, were created. One of the most crucial conflicts the synthetic mind gave birth to in both Arabic and "Christian" culture was that between faith, in the sphere of the supernatural, and reason, in the realm of the natural.

3. THE RELATION BETWEEN FAITH AND REASON IN THE SYSTEMS OF AVERROES AND AQUINAS

Averroes. The relationship between faith and reason was of special interest to Islam because the Moslems came into contact with Greek-Hellenistic thought. This is illustrated by the controversy between the "mutazilite" and the "mutakalimoun" schools, of which the first was the more philosophically inclined and the latter represented the repudiation of Greek philosophy.

Averroes delimited the respective areas of faith and reason by way of an exact definition of three levels of comprehension of the Koran represented firstly by the great mass, who lived by imagination; secondly, the theologians, who tried to obtain rational justification for their belief; and thirdly, the small number of philosophers who formed the highest class. Because the philosophers were not satisfied with the exterior and literal meaning of the

Koran which they considered was meant for the uninstructed, they proceeded to the interior and hidden meaning by way of allegorical exegesis.

The simple fact of the necessity for exegesis (eisegesis-exegesis) reveals that fundamentally there is no contact between the Koran (faith) and Philosophy (reason). The aim of the interpretation by Averroes was not directed towards a better understanding of Koranic revelation, but just the opposite, viz., to modify it to such a degree that it could be accommodated in Philosophy.

Careful study reveals, however, that Averroes was not an absolute rationalist. He took into account both revelation and philosophy, although rationalism got the better of him again and again. This was in accordance with the basic motive which dominated his thought, viz. that nature is prior to grace.

Averroes exerted a powerful influence on the Christian West not only because he transmitted Aristotle's ideas, but also because he made a considerable impact on Aquinas by providing an example of how to relate the pagan philosophy of Aristotle to faith and revelation. This was a problem which was also confronting Christianity at the time, and Thomas could well have profitted from this example, even although he did not follow it.

Thomas Aquinas. At the time of Thomas the conflict between faith and reason was already age-old and a highly disputed problem. The three main solutions were considered to be those of *identification, harmony* and *opposition,* which provided three different answers to the central issue, viz. whether the same person can at the same time believe and rationally know the same object. In accordance with Aquinas' synthetic religious ground motive of grace and nature, faith and reason were both distinct and yet in harmony and complementary. His interpretation differed from Averroes in that faith has priority over reason — just as grace supersedes nature.

Thomas *distinguished* between faith and reason by means of the knower, the knowable, the act of knowing and the result, viz. knowledge. He considered that there is a *harmony* in the relation of faith-reason and reason-faith, because faith perfects, elevates and completes reason, whereas, on the other hand, reason serves faith in a threefold way:

(1) It paves the way to faith by giving the *praeambula fidei* or *prima credibilia.* In providing rational demonstration or proof that God exists, natural Theology, for instance, serves the interests of faith.

(2) Reason can help to systematize the content of faith and thus remove apparent contradictions.

(3) Reason has the task of defending faith, firstly, by illustrating the reliability of the mysteries of faith to believers, and secondly, by refuting the arguments of unbelievers against Christianity. Supernatural wonders may, for instance, serve as *motiva credibilitatis* for Scriptures.

Comparison. Let me recapitulate by saying that Averroes was more philosohically and rationally inclined by virtue of the priority he gave to nature in his system, whereas Thomas Aquinas was more of a theologian, because of the greater emphasis he placed on grace.

4. EVALUATION

In order to reach a well balanced evaluation, a brief survey of the final outcome of the faith-reason struggle in the Middle Ages is necessary. The fine balance achieved by Aquinas between faith and reason was not maintained for long. Soon we find a progressive separation, ultimately terminating in a total divorce. Two schools of thought contributed to this:

Firstly, the so-called Latin Averroists (Siger of Brabant, John of Jandun and Boetius of Dacia) who, akin to their spiritual father, were essentially philosophers. They could not adapt themselves to the harmony between faith and reason, and although it may not be true that they adhered to a *duplex veritas* theory, their separation of faith from reason, and theology from Philosophy, is an indisputable fact.

Secondly, William of Ockham, together with his followers, was determined to prove that there is no such intimate relation between faith and reason as the majority of his predecessors believed. He clearly realized the precarious situation which had arisen whereby the fusion of the areas of nature and grace could only be maintained by means of edicts and condemnations of "heresies". He drove a wedge between the twin concepts of nature and supernature, and under the hammer of his critical philosophy Scholasticism began to crumble. It is of no significance that he gave faith (and grace) top priority, depreciating, as it were, reason. The synthetic conception of faith and reason was dissolved, making room for an antithetic relationship.

The Latin Averroists and Ockham set the secular ball rolling with the result that secularism soon attained the dominant position in the historical development of post-medieval, modern culture. The cultural ideal of Averroes was a monotheistic theocracy and that of Aquinas, a *Corpus Christianum*. The result of medieval culture, however, was a secular world!

The root of the problem. The reason for the failure of both cultural ideals is to be found in the synthetic religious ground motives of both the Arabic and Christian cultures. Although I will mainly concentrate on the motive of nature-grace, my criticism is also applicable, with the necessary modifications, to the grace-nature motive which inspired Averroes. In spite of the various solutions they offered, neither Averroes nor Aquinas were able to solve the vital problem of the faith-reason conflict because, in their synthetic approach, they only emphasized one or the other side of the dilemma, and never penetrated through to the very crux of the problem.

Medieval Christian culture did not recognize sufficiently the radical difference between pagan culture and the Scriptures. The unsuccessful effort to combine concepts, which in principle could never be synthesized, resulted in a religious ground motive with a dialectical tension between the two extremes. There was no inner point of contact between nature and grace. The possibility of their separation was inherent in the two-realm theory, which was merely kept together by the strength of the *Corpus Christianum* ideal. When this cultural aim began to weaken nothing could prevent secularization.

The deliverance from the domination and control of the church over all areas of life was a cultural development on the positive side, because it is anti-normative to subject the whole of life to the authority of only one societal relationship, such as the institutionalized church. Every societal relationship, whether it be marriage, the family, the school, the university, the state, etc. is sovereign in its own sphere.

Secularism. The initial process of secularization soon developed, however, into secularism because the medieval mind likened the distinction between sacred and secular to that of ecclesiastical and non-ecclesiastical. The totality of religion had by that time been narrowly identified with the realm of grace. The church, as the representative of supernatural grace had claimed the copyright to the Bible, and thus the radical message and the total all-encompassing claim of the Gospel was stifled and curtailed in its universally reforming power. As the secularistic process unfolded and gained momentum, the Word of God was placed on the sidelines and finally its authority was completely eliminated from public affairs.

That section of life which was withdrawn from religion became greater and greater, and the area of grace smaller and smaller. Religion itself, however, was not excluded in this manner; a new religious ground motive and cultural ideal merely assumed priority to guide Western culture.

Faith and Reason. In my opinion the tension does not lie between faith (being supernatural) and reason (natural) but between obedience and disobedience to God within both activities of believing and reasoning. Faith is not something typical of the believing Christian only. To make such a claim would merely be an oversimplification, in addition to giving a distorted viewpoint. Faith, in the sense of an act of believing, is essentially human, and belongs to man's inherent nature. Thus it follows that faith is also characteristic of the so-called "unbelievers". As must now be clear, I differ radically from the viewpoint of Thomas Aquinas. When man fell into sin he did not, as Thomas thought, lose the capacity to believe. This capacity remained, but the direction of faith was diverted away from obedient service of the true God. As I view it, redemption does not mean reacceptance of the capacity to believe as a *donum superadditum*, but the redirection of faith back towards obedient service to God. The direction of man's faith will always be determined by the religious direction of his heart.

With regard to reason, in accordance with the Scripture, I reject the idea that natural reason was unaffected by man's fall into sin. His rational activities were corrupted and rechannelled away from service to the honour and glory of God. I believe that man's logical activities need redemption because his every thought and analytical activity is determined by his religious heart-commitment — whether his heart is captured by the true God or an idol in the place of God.

I trust that I have clearly proved my point as to why I do not see any conflict between faith *and* reason, and why the dilemma of "faith *or* reason" is, to me, a false one.

This conclusion implies no depreciation of the contributions made by Averroes and Aquinas. What Bernard of Chartres wrote in the twelfth century about the ancients I want to apply in this instance: We are like dwarfs seated on the shoulders of these two giants. We see more things than they and things more distant. But this is due neither to the sharpness of our own sight, nor to the greatness of our own stature, but because we are raised and borne aloft on these giants.

SELECTED BIBLIOGRAPHY

BETZENDÖRFER, W. Die Lehre von der zweifachen Wahrheit. Ihr erstmalige Auftreten im christliche Abenland und ihre Quellen. Tübingen, Oslanderi'schen Buchhandlung. 1924.

BETZENDÖRFER, W.   Glauben und Wissen bei den grossen Denkern des Mittalalters. Gotha, Leopold Klotz Verlag, 1931.

BREEN, Q. The twofold truth theory in Melanchton. (*In:* Christianity and Humanism. Studies in the history of ideas. Grand Rapids, Michigan, W.B. Eerdmans Pub. Co., 1968, p. 69-92).

BROUNTS, S.   Siger van Brabant en de wijsgerige stromingen aan de Parijsche Universiteit in de XIIIe eeuw. *Tijdschrift voor Filosofie*, 8:317-348, 1946.

FINKENZELLER, J. Offenbarung und Theologie nach der Lehre des Johannes Duns Scotus. Münster (Westf.), Aschendorffsche Verlagsbuchhandlung. 1961.

GARDET, L. Raison et foi en Islam. *RT*, 53:437-478, 1937; 45:145-167, 342-378, 1938.

GAUNTHIER, L.   La Théorie d'Ibn Rochd sur les rapports de la religion et la philosophie. Paris, 1909.

GILSON, E.   Reason and Revelation in the Middle Ages. New York, Charles Scribner's, 1952 (Also Dutch edition: De Middeleeuwsche Wijsbegeerte. Haar stromingen, haar kern en haar betekenis. (Vertaald door A. Vloemans). Den Haag, H.P. Leopolds Uitgevers Mij, 1940).

GILSON, E.   Boèce de Dacie et la double vérité. *Archives d'Histoire Doctrinale et Littéraire du Moyen-Age*, 22:81- 99, 1955.

GRABMANN, M.   Der Wissenschaftsbegriff des hl. Thomas von Aquin und des Verhältnis von Glaube und Theologie zur Philosophie und Weltlichen Wissenschaft. „Anhang" *Jahresbericht der Görresgesellschaft*. Köln, Kommissionsverlag, J.P. Bachem G.M.B.H., p. 7- 44, 1934.

GUELLUY, R.   Philosophie et Théologie chez Guillaume d'Ockham. Louvain, Paris, J. Vrin, 1947.

HÄGGLUND, B.   Theologie und Philosophie bei Luther und in der occamistischen Tradition. Luthers Stellung zur Theorie der doppelten Wahrheit. Lund, G.W.K. Gleerup, 1955.

HEIM, K.   Zur Geschichte des Satzes von der doppelten Wahrheit. Tübingen, 1918.

HÖDL, L.   Doppelte Wahrheit. *(In:* J. Ritter (ed.): Historisches Wörterbuch der Philosophie. Band II, p. 285-287. Darmstadt, Wissenschaftliche Buchgesellschaft, 1972.

HORTEN, M.   Texte zu dem Streite zwischen Glauben und Wissen im Islam. Bonn, 1913.

HAUFNAGEL, A.   Zur lehre von der doppelte Wahrheit. *Tübing. theol. Quartalschrift*, 136:284- 295, 1956.

LÖWITH, K.   Wissen und Glauben. *(In:* Augustinus Magister. Congrès International Augustinien. Paris 21-24 Septembre, Communications. Paris, Études Augustiniennes, p. 403-410, 1954).

MACDONALD, A.J.   Authority and reason in the early Middle Ages. London, Oxford Univ. Press, 1933.

MAIER, Anneliese.   Das Prinzip der doppelte Wahrheit (Studien zur Naturphilosophie der Spätscholastik, 4), Rome, 1959.

MANSER, G.M.   Das Verhältnis von Glaube und Wissen bei Averroës. *Jahrbuch für Philosophie und Spekulative Theologie,* 24:398-408, 1910, 25:3-34, 163-179, 250-277, 1911.

MAURER, A.   Boetius of Dacia and double truth. *Mediaeval Studies,* 17:233-239, 1955.

MAYWALD, M.   Die Lehre von der zweifachen Wahrheit. Ein Versuch der Trennung von Theologie und Philosophie im Mittelalter. Berlin, F. Henschel, 1871.

MEYER, H.   Die Wissenschaftslehre des Thomas von Aquin. Fulda, Fuldaer Actien Druckerei, 1934.

MICHAUD-QUANTIN.   La double-vérité des Averroistes. Un texte nouveau de Boèce de Dacie. *Theoria,* 22:167-184, 1956.

MULDER, D.C.   Openbaring en Rede in de Islamitische filosofie van Al-Farabi tot Ibn Rusd. Amsterdam, Holland Drukkerij, 1949.

MULDER, D.C.   Openbaring en rede in de Islamietische Filosofie. *Correspondentiebladen van de Vereniging voor Calvinistische Wijsbegeerte,* 14(1):14-16, 1950.

MÜLLER, J.P.   Philosophie et foi chez Siger de Brabant. La théorie de la double vérité. *Studia Anselmiana,* 7/8:35-50, 1938.

NIED, E.   Glauben und Wissen nach Thomas von Aquin. Freiburg im Breisgau, J. Waibel Universitäts-Buchhandlung, 1928.

PINE, M.   Pomponazzi and double truth. *Journal of the history of ideas,* 29:163-176, 1968.

SANTA THOMAS DE AQUINO. Summa Contra los Gentiles. I & II. (Editors: Laureano Robles Carcedo & Adolfo Robles Sierra.) Madrid, Biblioteca de Autores Christianos, 1967 & 1958.

SASSEN, F. Boëthius van Dacie en de theorie van de dubbele waarheid. *Studia Catholica,* 30:362-373, 1955.

THOMAS AQUINAS.   On the truth of the Catholic faith. *Summa Contra Gentiles.* Book One: God. (Translated by A.C. Pegis). New York, Doubleday & Co., 1955.

THOMAS AQUINAS.   On the truth of the Catholic faith. *Summa Contra Gentiles.* Book Two: Creation (Translated by J.F. Anderson). New York, Doubleday & Co., 1956.

THOMAS AQUINAS.   On the truth of the Catholic Faith. *Summa Contra Gentiles,* Book Three: Providence, Part I & II. (Translated by V.J. Bourke). New York, Doubleday & Co., 1956.

THOMAS AQUINAS.   On the truth of the Catholic faith. *Summa Contra Gentiles.* Book Four: Salvation (Translated by C.J. O'Neil). New York, Doubleday & Co., 1957.

VAN DYK, J.   A Christian approach to the study of Medieval History I & II. (Class syllabus. Dordt College.), 1971.

VAN STEENBERGHEN, F.   The philosophical movement of the thirteenth century. London, Thomas Nelson & Sons, 1955.

VERWEYEN, J.M. Philosophie und Theologie im Mittelalter. Bonn, F. Cohen, 1911.

6 IN THE STEPS OF THOMAS AQUINAS: 1274-1974 — A BIOGRAPHICAL SKETCH*

The death of the great Medieval thinker, Thomas Aquinas, seven centuries ago (7 March 1274), was remembered from 17-24 April 1974, in the form of an international Congress at Rome and Naples. Some 1500 scholars from no fewer than 60 countries in all corners of the globe attended the proceedings.

1. SIGNIFICANCE FOR CALVINISM

It is generally known that Thomas is *the* philosopher of the Roman church.

Therefore it is understandable that the Congress was attended almost exclusively by Roman scholars.

What is the point in a Calvinist attending such a congress, and is it appropriate to write about a Roman Catholic in a journal such as this? For the following five reasons this is in my opinion not at all out of place.

In the first place it should be borne in mind that the Reformation of the 16th century was still linked to Medieval thought with many bonds. The reformational movement was in a certain sense a reaction against Medieval Roman Catholic thought. It is thus possible to get a much better grip on the work of men such as Luther, Zwingli and Calvin if we know what it was that they reacted against. On the one hand one can investigate the influence of Medieval thought on them, and on the other also place the uniqueness of their labours on record.

In the second place it is a well-known fact that only a short while after the pioneering work of the reformers, Protestantism once again fell back into the Aristotelian, Scholastic thought of the Middle Ages, so that from the 17th to the 19th centuries not a unique, original, reformed Philosophy made its appearance.

Thirdly, research has shown that the revival of Thomism at the end of the previous century (partly as a result of the activities of Pope Leo XIII) had a massive influence on reformed thinkers such as H. Bavinck and A. Kuyper, among others.

* Originally published in *Koers,* 40(1):38-47, 1975 under the title: "Op die spore van Thomas van Aquino (1274-1974) : 'n biografiese skets".
This essay is included in this volume merely because it provides some biographical decor to the following essays on the philosophy of Thomas Aquinas.

In the fourth place dialogue with Roman Catholic Christians was for one or other reason always a popular subject with the advocates of the Philosophy of the Cosmonomic Idea (so-called Amsterdam Philosophy). Many Protestant theologians gain doctorates on some aspect or other of Roman Catholic thought.

Lastly, we live in an ecumenical era which would rather not hear too much of earlier divisions. Such a Congress offers an outstanding opportunity to come to grips with modern Thomistic thought, to observe how it attempts to make Thomas relevant for today in differing ways, and also to determine whether modern Roman Catholicism really has moved closer to the Bible, as is so often maintained. Is there more openness amongst them and greater readiness to test their dogmas in the light of Scripture alone?

2. THE MAN AND HIS TIME

We first want to say something on Thomas the person. Not simply because a visit to the noteworthy places in his life formed part of the Congress, but also because his philosophy and life (and also the time in which he lived) are not to be separated.

This appellation of the age in which Thomas lived as the "dark Middle Ages", does it great injustice. In the first place it was least of all a dark period and in any case it was not — as the word "middle" suggests — a mere age of transition or an unimportant intermezzo in the history of Western thought. The thousand years or so of Medieval thought form an inherent part of our history of civilization, without which we would not be able to comprehend Western civilization as it appears today. To put it in a nutshell: before the Middle Ages there was a pagan culture which did not know the Word, and afterwards modern culture, which no longer acknowledge the Word of God, came into being. What happened to Christendom during those thousand years that causes us to live in a "post-Christian" era today? This question is only intended to focus attention on the significance of the Middle Ages for us as Christians today; no answer will be given here.

3. CHRONOLOGICAL SURVEY

For convenience' sake we divide the life of this medieval philosopher into the following periods:
1224/1225-1252 years of preparation
1252-1259 first period of lecturing in Paris
1259-1268 first period of lecturing in Italy
1268-1272 second period of lecturing in Paris

1272-1274 second period of lecturing in Italy.

With this scheme as our framework we can take note of some of the finer particulars of his life.

4. BIRTH

Thomas was born in a stormy time: conflict between pope and emperor, revolutionary begging (mendicant) orders, discovery of the Aristotelian philosophy which would cause an uproar in the theological world, threats to Christendom from fanatical Islam — to mention only a few problems.

He was born at the beginning of 1224/5 in the castle of Rocca Secca, northwest of the little town of Aquino (between Rome and Naples), in what was then the kingdom of Naples — the son of Landdulphus, count of Aquino, and Theodora, a countess of Teano. Evidently of noble birth — his family was related not only to emperor Henry VI and Frederik II, but also to the kings of Aragon, Castile and France. Legend is rich in all sorts of stories of omens not only during, but even before the birth of the *doctor angelicus*-to-be.

The congress-goers arrived at Aquino late on Sunday afternoon (21 April) in order to share in the festival proceedings and to listen to eulogies in flowing Italian. After seven centuries the people at Aquino are still proud that the great saint first saw the light in their district. Thomas is pictured in the modern church of this town in superb mosaic form. The church's most treasured possession is a relic of Thomas which is protected behind gold and glass.

From Aquino we travelled among the mountains to the little place of Rocca Secca where a friendly reception awaited us from the local inhabitants. The mayor gave a speech and a Polish cardinal and a Spanish bishop made suitable replies. As a bonus a special copper medal in commemoration of the occasion was also handed out!

It had already begun to get dark — the sun hung against the evening sky like a great red ball — but we struggled up the slopes past all the ruins of forgotten ages. Halfway to the mountain stands the simple little church of Thomas which is presently being restored (actually being completely rebuilt). From here the road curves high up between the walls until eventually, right on top, the ruins of the old castle of Rocca Secca loom into view. It is a pity that at that stage it was already dark and photos were no longer possible. Thomas was a privileged child to be able to spend his earliest years here, so high in the mountains. The surrounding landscape can be seen for miles from this onetime fortress.

5. FIRST YEARS

Thomas may have been born in a naturally beautiful setting, but even more is this true of the place where he spent his early years. Thomas's father was also involved in the investiture controversy between pope and emperor, but following the peace of San Germano the five-year-old Thomas was placed by his parents into the Benedictine monastery of Monte Cassino as a "peace symbol", where, without being bound by definite vows, he shared in the simple life of the monks for nine years under the supervision of his uncle, Abbot Sinnibaldus. The isolation of this cloistered existence must have had a strong influence on the young boy. Little did his father know that Thomas would one day become a monk against his father's will!

The Italians can make first-rate wine and equally outstanding spaghetti, but they do not seem to have any particular talent for organization and still less do they run in the modern "rat race". (Rather as there is "African time" so is there, it seems to me, also something like "Italian time" — which does not differ very much.) Consequently time passed by so quickly that the planned visit to Monte Cassino had to be put off. However, no-one who has heard so much about this possibly most famous of all monasteries could stay away, and so two of us, on the way back from Naples to Rome, called there. It was worth while!

The road zigzags for 10 km from Cassino up the mountains. The panoramas from high above snatch one's breath away. The entrance was already shut, but the friendly brother was willing to let the congress-goers see something notwithstanding.

Benedictus (c. 480-547) built the first monastery here in place of a heathen temple. (Inside there are still some objects from the history of this saint and his sister Scholastica). After it was sacked round about 581 by the Longobards it was only rebuilt early in the 8th century. Shortly thereafter, in 883, it was however razed by Saracen hordes, to rise again only in the middle of the 10th century. And in 1349 it was practically levelled to the ground for a third time — not as a result of human hands this time, but because of an earthquake. It was rebuilt yet again — to be flattened on 15th February 1944 by the Allied bombardment. The massive graveyards in the valleys below are a reminder that this almost impregnable citadel cost the lives of hundreds of thousands of people in the Second World War. The motto on one of Benedictus's shields is, however, evidently also applicable to Monte Cassino: "Succisa virescit", i.e., flattened but returning to new life. In 1964 the entire complex, rebuilt like the original, was once again reopened by pope Paul VI.

6. EARLY STUDENT YEARS

From Monte Cassino to Naples: for this was the place to which Thomas fled when the war between pope and emperor broke out again in 1239 and Frederick wanted to convert the famed abbey into a fortress. This was a big step for the young Thomas to make, to go from the seclusion and protected environment of the old Benedictine monastery, with its early-medieval atmosphere which no longer suited the new age, to a great city; to the first state university in the Western World; to a university where he could make the acquaintance of Aristotle's newly discovered thought as in no other place; to a place where he would meet the first generation of the active begging orders (which propagated voluntary poverty).

Thomas studied the so-called *artes liberales* and one of his teachers, Petrus Hibernus, aided the young nobleman in getting to know Aristotle. (Thomas would later refer to this great Greek thinker as "the philosopher" because for him there was no equal to the Stagirite Aristotle!) Since the University of Naples in those days stood on the borders of the Eastern and Western world and the official Roman ban on Aristotle did not hold here, it was by far the best place to obtain knowledge of this Greek's thought.

Thomas was not only a revolutionary in studying the officially banned philosophy of Aristotle. He carried out a revolutionary act on the sacred level too, by entering the mendicant order of the Dominicans, which set voluntary poverty and study as its ideals — and this against the will and without the knowledge of his mother. In April 1244, not long after his father's death (in 1243), he received the garb of Saint Dominic in the church of S Domenico Maggiore (which can still be seen in Naples today).

7. IMPRISONMENT

His disconcerted mother Theodora rushed to Naples, but Thomas evaded her so that he would no longer be held back by her from his ideals. However, he was intercepted by his brothers Lanolfus and Arnoldus on his mother's orders while on his way from Italy to France. When he refused to listen to his mother's pleas, he was held captive in the castle. To the discomfiture of his mother Thomas persuaded one of his two sisters, who also came to plead with him, to become a nun! When his two soldier-brothers returned from their camp, Thomas was taken thoroughly in hand — even his monk's garments were torn from him. On his mother's instructions he was locked up under strong guard in the citadel of Rocca Secca. Here his uncouth brothers (still according to tradition) tried to seduce him with a loose woman, but this too was unsuccessful.

Thomas spent his captivity in studying the works of Peter Lombard and

Aristotle, amongst others. His love for the latter grew.

8. STUDENT YEARS IN PARIS AND COLOGNE

After a year (or two?) his mother realized that he was past redemption and because she feared that she might be punished, gave permission for his Dominican brothers to remove him. With the help of one of his sisters, he "escaped" in a basket after the watch had been got out of the way. In 1245 Thomas (at about the age of twenty) went from Rome to the north, to the "city of the philosophers" and the "centre of theological knowledge" — as the Paris of the time was called. Shortly after its foundation (1200) the university of Paris had become *the* university of the West.

In spite of the papal interdict the works of Aristotle were nevertheless studied at this university. And Thomas's new tutor, Albertus Magnus (1193-1280) was also a diligent student of Aristotle. This famed Dominican scholar proposed to open up the Greek (especially Aristotelian), Jewish and Arabic philosophies to the West by means of paraphrases. Albertus Magnus had a powerful influence on the growth of Thomas's thought. When Albertus moved to Cologne, Thomas followed him there and studied under him until 1252 — making seven years in all.

The story is told that Thomas was an exceedingly silent student, so much so that his fellows ascribed this to stupidity and he acquired the nickname of *bos mutus* (dumb ox). But after he brilliantly defended some topic or other under the chairmanship of Albertus, his tutor's comment was, "You call him a dumb ox but one day he's going to bellow so loudly that the whole world will hear". His fellow-students could never have dreamed of the role which his thought was still to play in the Roman Catholic Church — nor that seven centuries later an international congress would be held in his honour!

9. FIRST PERIOD OF LECTURING IN PARIS

From 1252 Thomas lectured at the same University where he was a student. Together with his colleague Bonaventura (whose death seven centuries ago was also commemorated in the form of an international congress in Rome in 1974) he had to endure a great deal as a member of the mendicant order. After a lot of conflict, however, Pope Alexander IV put an end to this persecution with a pronouncement in favour of these orders.

A magnificent anecdote about professorial wool-gathering is told at the expense of Thomas while he was engaged in a battle with the heresy of the Manicheens. At this time he was invited to dinner by Louis, the king of

France, and went along with his secretary. But during the meal he became so wrapped up in his own thoughts that to the amazement of everybody he suddenly hammered on the table with his fist and thundered out, "It is all over with the Manicheens!" and commanded his secretary, "Stand up and write!" The embarrassed secretary first had to explain to Thomas that he was not in his own house but at the royal table, and then had to request that the professor's behaviour be excused.

10. FIRST PERIOD OF LECTURING IN ITALY

From about 1259-1268 Thomas taught at various placed in Italy, such as Anagni, Viterbo and Orvieto. His residence at the court of Pope Urban IV (1261-1265) was a particular stimulus to further study of Aristotle. Urban continued the efforts of his predecessor Gregory IX to import the philosophy of Aristotle in the Christian world in such a way that the greatest profit with the least damage would accrue to Christendom. At one time (c. 1262) there were no fewer than four Aristotle-enthusiasts at the court of this pope. Apart from the pope and Thomas themselves, also Albertus Magnus and William of Moerbeke. The last-mentioned, who was a linguist, translated several commentaries on Aristotle, and also works of Aristotle himself from the Greek, or improved on existing ones. Thomas's own commentaries on Aristotle date from this period and the major part of his *Summa Contra Gentiles*, in which the massive influence of the Stagirite is evident, was also written at the court of Pope Urban.

11. SECOND PERIOD OF LECTURING IN PARIS

In 1268 Thomas was called back to Paris. As far as his literary activities are concerned, this was to be a most fruitful time. But also a difficult time, for he was involved in many conflicts. On the one hand he clashed with the conservative Augustinian faction (within the Franciscans in particular) because he advocated a more progressive Aristotelianizing trend. On the other hand he did not want to go as far as did Averroistic Aristotelianism in accepting Greek thought, so that he also found himself combating this group. Thomas's conflict with the Averroists was admittedly settled in 1270 when the Bishop of Paris officially condemned them. But the difficulties in which his synthetic thought landed him are very apparent from the fact that when the Averroists were finally condemned in 1277 (after his death) several propositions of Thomas himself suffered the same fate! His old tutor, Albertus Magnus, had to hasten from Cologne to Paris to defend his late pupil's ideas!

12. SECOND PERIOD OF LECTURING IN ITALY

In the last days of his life (1272-1274) Thomas lectured in Naples where he had received his first academic training as a student. One can still view his bedroom and study in the Chiesa San Dominico Maggiore. Outside the door hangs the bell with which the students were called to class. The most valuable item in the room is yet another relic of Thomas.

Thomas was summoned to the Council of Lyon by Pope Gregory X and undertook the long journey in January 1274. But on the way he became ill and died on 7 March 1274 in the monastery of Fossa Nova at the age of 49.

Fossa Nova (at the foot of Mount Lepini) was originally a Benedictine monastery. (The Benedictines are still today one of the many Roman orders. According to one of the Roman Catholic congress delegates, the Holy Spirit alone knows how many differring orders there are: a recent official list has about 1300!) Round about 1135 it was taken over by the Cistercians under Pope Innocent II (the Cistercians being yet another order which came into being in 1098). These monks drained the marshy surroundings by excavating a new drainage trench or *fossa nova* — whence the place's name. In a separate building alongside the cloister (apparently the guesthouse) there is an upper room which is pointed out as the place where Thomas died. The room was later converted into a chapel and above the altar the death of the saint is depicted in a superb piece of marble relief by artists of the school of Bernini.

According to tradition many miracles have occurred at Thomas's grave: a dead person was even restored to life! Because the monks were afraid that this body would be stolen, they apparently buried him elsewhere during the night, but later had to replace him in his grave. But this was not the end of the story since the Dominicans were not happy that the remains of their famed fellow-brother were in the hands of the Cistercians. With the approval of the pope, then, the body was later taken to Toulouse in France.

13. PERSONALITY AND WORK

Apart from these facts we actually know very little about Thomas. Practically nothing about himself can be deduced from his works. Whereas in the case of Augustine, for example, even in an abstract work like the *De Trinitate*, one is continually aware that this has been written by a man of flesh and blood — Thomas's works are very succinct and precise.

He must have been a highly impressive figure, tall and upright, and a tremendously big head perched on a powerful body. He was naturally humble, friendly and peace-loving and his needs were few. He devoted himself to one task only, his studies and teaching, and must have had an immense ability to concentrate, since it is claimed that he could dictate different texts to three secretaries simultaneously!

The fact that he limited himself to one task and did not dissipate his energies, together with the fact that he could proceed calmly with his work even in times of unrest and tumult, not to mention his massive powers of concentration, says something for the immense productivity of this man over a period of a little more than twenty years. In the English translation his last work, the *Summa Theologiae,* consists of twenty volumes. Altogether we possess more than sixty of his writings. According to estimates the complete critical edition of his *Opera Omnia* will consist of 75 folio volumes each of some 250 pages!

7 THOMAS AQUINAS AND THE FUNDAMENTAL PROBLEMS OF OUR TIME*

1. A GREAT OCCASION**

Scholars who are interested in the Middle Ages will long remember 1974 as an important year. Not only was Thomas Aquinas' year of death commemorated by means of an international congress in Italy, but the death of another great Medieval thinker, Bonaventura, seven centuries ago, was also recalled to mind in the international conference held in Rome from 19-26 September[1].

Thomas Aquinas and Bonaventura of Bagnorea are generally recognized as the two most important thinkers of the thirteenth century. Since the *doctor angelicus* and *doctor seraphicus* lived during the period of scholasticism's blossoming, they are also called the twin mountain peaks of the Middle Ages. They were the leaders of two of the most important Roman Catholic orders, viz. the Dominicans and the Franciscans.

1.1 Interest in Medieval thought and that of Thomas Aquinas justified

The remarkable interest exhibited in the Thomas Aquinas Congress

* Originally published in *Tydskrif vir Christelike Wetenskap*, 10:119-128, 1974 under the title: "Thomas van Aquino en die fundamentele probleme van ons tyd".

** It was the writer's privilege to attend with the generous financial support of the Human Sciences Research Council the International Congress commemorating the seven hundredth anniversary of Thomas Aquinas' death from 17-24 April 1974 at Rome and Naples.
Opinions expressed in this article and conclusions reached are those of the writer and should in no way be seen as reflecting the opinion or conclusions of the HSRC.

1. Apart from congresses the two thinkers were also commemorated by means of many publications.
Journals (such as the April-September 1974 issue of *Rivista di Filosofia Neo-Scolastica*) devoted special issues to Thomas's thought and lectures given at local commemorations in his death appeared in print (e.g. that at the University of Fribourg under the title *L'Anthrolopologie de S. Thomas.*).
A new biography under the title *San Thomasso d'Aquino*, by R. Spiazzi, has recently appeared (Rome, Idea Centro Editoriale) and similar studies in other languages are expected.
A five-part work, *S. Bonaventura 1274-1974*, has been published under the auspices of the Collegio S. Bonaventura, which deals with his iconography, life, work and teachings and also contains a complete bibliography. In 1976 the first volume of the proceedings of the Bonaventure Congress (966 pages!) was published. Title: *San Bonaventura Maestro di vita Francescana e di sapienza Christiana* (Pontificia Faculta' Theologica "San Bonaventura", Rome).

(more than 1500 participants representing 60 countries from all over the world) was fitting, for he may undoubtedly be regarded as one of the giants of Western thought.

One ought to be aware of two extremes in the evaluation of Medieval thought in general and Thomas in particular.

Many philosophers and theologians distantiates themselves today from the so-called "dark Middle Ages", not merely because this period seems so far off in the past, but also because it is regarded as too "rationalistic" and not existential, too "objective" and detached. The word "scholastic" is usually used today as an insult — often without defining precisely what it means. I feel that this attitude is mistaken, since the contribution of some-one like Thomas forms an integral part of our entire Western philosophy and culture. In addition it would be foolish to suppose that such an out-standing figure had produced nothing worthy of careful study.

On the other hand it would not be correct to maintain that nothing worth while was produced after Thomas. As far as I know Thomas himself never declared that his thought put an end to all contradictions, nor that he had said the last word. Unfortunately many of his epigones, inspired by the idea of a *philosophia perennis* or *theologia perennis,* made this mistake. Often this is the idea behind the industrios activity of past decades, devoted to the publication of the writings of Medieval scholars. Moreover, it can hardly be denied that the fact that Thomas's writings have been declared to be the official doctrine of the Roman Catholic Church has led to their over-estimation.

1.2 The central place of Thomas in Roman Catholic thought

J.B. Metz hardly exaggerates when he observes: "Noch in de oudheid, noch in de Middeleeuwen, noch in de moderne tijd is er een andere leraar in de kerk, met wie de katholieke sigzelf zo geïdentifiseerd heef... als met Thomas"[2]. Ever since 1323, the year when Thomas was canonized, practi-cally every pope has made some pronouncement about the *doctor angelicus.* In his book *St. Thomas Aquinas*[3] J. Maritain gives the pronouncements of no less than 66 people which have a direct, or indirect bearing on Thomas's thought[4]. B. Wentsel maintains that Thomas's *Summa Theologiae* was placed next to the Bible on the altar in the hall where the Council of Trent

2. Metz: *Christelijke mensbetrokkenheid,* p. 8.

3. Cf. p. 130-3.

4. These documents are available in a Dutch translation in the series *Ecclesia Docens. Pauselijke documenten voor onze tijd.*

gathered[5]). In August 1879 Thomas's philosophy was once again canonized by Pope Leo XIII as *the* philosophy of the Roman Catholic Church (in the encyclical *Aeterni Patris).* As a result of the labours of Leo XIII in particular (apart from this encyclical he issued no fewer than seven official statements on the philosophy of Thomas until 1895!), a large-scale revival of Thomism took place at the end of the previous century[6]). Some of the most renowned scholars who contributed to this revival were C. Baeumker M. de Wulf, M. Grabmann, A. Pelzer, D.O. Lottin and B. Nardi[7]). As a result the Congress of 1974 could look back on the fruits of almost a century of intensive study of Thomas.

1.3 The role of Thomas's thought in Protestant Theology

Thomas's thought is, however, not only of interest to the Roman Catholic Church, but also to Protestant churches and theology. Today it is a well-known fact that not long after the pioneering reformational labours of Luther, and Calvin in particular, Protestant Theology relapsed into Aristotelian and Thomistic patterns. It is similarly accepted that the Thomistic revival at the end of the nineteenth century (to which we have just drawn attention) had an immense influence upon the ideas of reformed theologians such as A. Kuyper and H. Bavinck. His influence on Kuyper is quite apparent from the following comment, for instance: "Alle Theologie, dien naam waard... zal dus den draad moeten voortspinnen, dien met name Thomas van Aquino ons in handen gaf"[8]).

1.4 Thomas as 'doctor communis'

The influence of Thomas is, however, not limited even to Roman Catholic and Protestant thought. He is justly called the *doctor communis*, for his ideas played a significant role not only in the area of Theology but also in the development of disciplines such as Anthropology, Psychology, Epistemology, Philosophy of Science, Ethics and Political Science. For this reason he is rightly pointed to as "one of the dozen greatest philosophers of the Western world."

5. Cf. his work *Natuur en genade,* p. 449.

6. Cf. for particulars on the "Renaissance of Medieval Philosophy" the work of F. van Steenberghen, *Introduction à l'étude de la Philosophie Médievale,* chapter V, p. 211-282.

7. Cf. ibid., p. 283-332.

8. Kuyper, *Encyclopaedie der Heilige Godgeleerdheid,* I, p. 108.

Taking everything into account, it was fitting that the work of this leader from the golden age of Medieval thought should be called to mind in an international congress.

2. ACTA OF THE CONGRESS

Four volumes of the Proceedings of the congress are already available (May 1977). The General title is *Atti del congresso internationale Tommaso d'Aquino nel suo settimo centenario* published by Edizioni Domenicane Italiane, Via Luigi Palmieri 19, 80133 Naples, Italy. Not only the 38 papers delivered at plenary sessions and the 116 lectures delivered at various symposia but also the other contributions (some 392) which could not be accommodated due to lack of time, will be included.

Some of the lectures presented during plenary sessions were already available in print during the congress in a collection entitled *Thomasso D'Aquino nel suo VII Centenario. Congresso Internazionale. Roma – Napoli, 17-24 Aprile 1974.* From the scope of this publication (535 pp) and that of the Acta in particular, which will contain about 550 papers and have about 15 volumes, the massive field which was covered in a meeting only six days long is all too apparent.

3. VISITS TO THOMAS'S PLACES OF RESIDENCE

On Sunday 21 April, during the moving of the congress from Rome to Naples, calls were made to many of the noteworthy places associated with the life of Thomas. Inter alia we saw: the castle of Rocca Secca, northwest of the little town of Aquino (also visited), where Thomas was born in 1224; the Benedictine monastery at Monte Cassino, where from his fifth to his fourteenth year he lived the simple life of a monk under the supervision of his uncle, and also the convent of Fossa Nova at Terracina where this learned man died on 7 March 1274 at the age of 49. Naples itself is closely associated with the life of Thomas, since he here received his earliest academic training (at the oldest state university in the Western World) and taught at this university towards the end of his life (1272 until the beginning of 1274). One can still see his study-bedroom in the Chiesa San Dominico Maggiore, for instance.

In all the places mentioned congress-goers were fêted during their "pilgrimage" by the local inhabitants, speeches were delivered, etc. Since a philosopher's ideas cannot be completely divorced from the circumstances of his life, this tour could be regarded as an important part of the congress. The writer was also able to track down plenty of interesting biographical marial on Thomas[9].

4. TREATMENT OF THE CENTRAL THEME

The congress was not only interested in history. It wanted to launch an investigation into the significance which Thomas's thought still has today, and for this reason as central theme "Aquinas and the fundamental problems of our time" was chosen.

This theme was examined under the following six headings, each with four subdivisions:

Aquinas in the history of thought
    The sources of Thomas's thought
    Thomas and his own time
    The development of Thomistic thought

God and the way of salvation
    The theological problem
    Our knowledge of God
    Christology
    Ecclesiology

Moral actions
    The basis of ethical norms
    Divine sovereignty and human autonomy
    Law and Gospel
    Freedom, sexuality and customs

Existence
    Metaphysics and Phenomenology
    Philosophies of Value and Philosophies of the Person
    Existential Philosophy and Linguistic Analysis
    Metaphysics and history

Man
    Anthropological problems
    Human nature and natural law
    Man and society
    Man, nature and art

9. Cf. the following, inter alia: Leccisotti, D.T.: *Tomasso d'Aquino e Montecassino* (Montecassino, 1965), Pocino, W.: *Roccasecca. Patri di san Tomasso d'Aquino.* (Roma, E. *Lazio eiri e oggi,* 1974), Pocino, W.: Le due case di S. Tomasso d'Aquino. *Lazio ieri e oggi,* 9(3) Mrt. 1973; Rossini, M.: Roccasecca. *Meta di pellegrinaggi Tomistici* (1974); Woltz, A.: *Luoghi di san Tomasso* (Roma, Herder, 1961) and Zaccaria, G.: *Vita illustrata di S. Tomasso d'Aquino* (Roma, Iter, 1974).

Scholarship and the world
   Man and his environment
   Evolution and the future
   The structure of matter, causality and finality
   Scholarship and Philosophy

5. GENERAL EVALUATION

The limited scope of this article only permits me to mention three points. Their critical character in no way implies that I have no appreciation for the immense labours of the conference organizers.

5.1 How can Thomas's philosophy be rendered relevant for today?

The theme of the congress was magnificent but also challenging: "Thomas of Aquino and the fundamental questions of our time". The key query which here raises its head is, how is it possible to relate the ideas of a thinker who lived seven centuries ago under utterly different circumstances to the last quarter of the twentieth century? A hermeneutical problem also crops up, viz. that Thomas spoke in the terms of his day while we use the language of ours — even if we do not realize it. Do we not then fall prey to an illusion in supposing that we can hold a dialogue with Thomas or that he can even communicate anything relevant to our own time? Do we not find ourselves between the sharp horns of a dilemma? Either we live in a totally different thought-world from Thomas — so that we can have absolutely nothing to say to each other —   we "translate" Thomas directly into our own "language" so that the dialogue which was intended bogs down in a monologue!

How can the cleft of time between text and reader be bridged? This is a highly relevant question for contemporary Thomists, since they wish to follow the ecclesiastically commended theories of Thomas. But how?

It was most fascinating to take note of the different trends of approach in studying Thomas. Every kind of slogan made its appearance. We reproduce some of the main ideas in speeches.

The pope made the following remarks during his address: "This congress shows that the voice of Thomas is not just an echo from the grave — as is the case with many other thinkers from the past — but that it speaks today. Thomas is and remains a living thinker because his sayings of seven centuries ago are still relevant and valid. It can still be valuable today to take one's place at the feet of the *doctor communis.*"

"Thomas is a man for all times and must now be restored to favour after the neglect of his thought by Vatican II."

"We may not draw Thomas to us and assimilate him to ourselves, but just the opposite: Thomas must be rediscovered in his originality".

"Thomas was not a Thomist. He would never have recognized himself in what they made of him in the past."

"The commemoration of Thomas's death seven centuries ago must be the start of a new life. This congress must be the sign of a return to Thomas".

Apart from such comments which advocated a relatively "literal" return to and following of Thomas (the more "conservative" trend) there were also pronouncements such as the following which suggested a freer approach to Thomas (the more "progressive" line): "Thomas does not determine our thought, but does give definitive direction thereto". "Thomas's thought must not be the *end* of ours, but rather its *beginning*". "Thomas does provide a solid basis, but has to be re-interpreted for our time". "Thomas's thought is no revelation, but merely an example which invites us to consider further". "We do not want a petrified paleo-Thomism, but an open, dynamic, progressive neo-Thomism which expresses Thomas in modern language. Paleo-Thomism, which anachronistically tries to restore the past, does Thomas no service. We must allow ourselves to be *inspired* by Thomas!" "Mere commentary on Thomas's ideas gets us nowhere". "In (open) dialogue with Thomas the accent must not be placed on the resemblance between him and ourselves — as usually happens — but on the disagreements. The result of this conversation might even be that Thomas's views are rejected."

The tension between the more conservative approach and the more liberal vision was evident. One of the former answered a question (posed to him by one of the latter) like this: "Today is the argument of those who have no argument". With just as much justification — if not more — the liberal could have replied: "The past (Thomas) is the argument of those who have no (original) argument of their own!"

Basically there were thus two main approaches (aside from smaller, relative nuances). The more orthodox group which still held fast to the idea of a *philosophia perennis* tried to render Thomas relevant for today by comparing his thought with modern theories and then (as might be expected) demonstrating the superiority of Thomism. In opposition to the conservatives the second group tried to make Thomas's thought relevant by interpreting it through one or other modern system. In the first case stress was usually placed on the fact that Thomas must be read objectively, and the aim of this was clearly to repeat more or less what Thomas had taught, in a so-called neutral manner. In the second case a translation of Thomas was attempted, using one or other form of contemporary Philosophy or Theology for this purpose. Both methods have their pros and cons. In the first instance Thomas himself was speaking (more or less), but the relevance of his ideas for today was not quite clear. In the second case the ideas expressed were undoubtedly relevant, but unfortunately not (purely) Thomas's ideas! In neither case was the main aim of the congress, viz. "Thomas and the basic questions of our time", successfully realized.

In my opinion the right approach demands knowledge of the author (Thomas) as well as of the reader himself. As far as the former is concerned, a thorough acquaintance of his background, time, milieu and life is necessary, since his writings cannot be isolated therefrom. Everyone's work is inevitably also affected by the religious direction of his heart (be it radically for or against God or somewhere in-between). Every philosopher's Ontology or Doctrine of Being (as revealed in his writings) is coloured by a pre-scientific vision of reality (or view of life), which in its turn is determined by the religious tendency of the heart. As a result the author himself must be allowed (through his writings) to tell the reader about his deepest religious convictions, since only thus can the "spirit" of the writer (in casu Thomas) be gauged.

In order to be able to arrive at a correct understanding, the reader should not only know the author, but also himself thoroughly. It is also true of the *reader* that his background, historical situation and religion in particular determine all his activities — including his exegesis of Thomas Aquinas. The reader, too, utilizes a view of reality for his interpretation of another. At its most fundamental point this view is determined by religion, and gives rise to a doctrine of reality (Philosophical Ontology). Although modern Hermeneutics often do exaggerates this aspect, it is nevertheless true that in a certain sense all understanding implies *self*-understanding! A clear, precise formulation of one's own presuppositions as exegete appears to be necessary for the right understanding of another person. Modern hermeneutic investigations have at least taught us this lesson, over against the older views which held that in order to understand rightly one first had to cut out one's own background and opinions by placing them "between brackets". It became clear that such "neutrality" is impossible since one's own "pre-understanding" of a text can not be eliminated. In itself, therefore, *pre-judgment* need not necessarily have an unfavourable connotation, as it forms an inherent part of all understanding. It is *prejudices* of which we are often not clearly aware (although they are nevertheless present) and which blind us and hold us back from a correct grasp of someone else's ideas which we should try to eliminate.

Naturally it would be very unfair to expect *every* speaker *explicitly* to consider the entire problem sketched above. For the sake of the success of a congress with such a specific purpose it could, however, have been expected that at one stage or another (preferably right at the beginning!) this absolutely basic problem should have been considered — even if the result would be that no unanimity is to be reached!

5.2 Dangers of Thomas's synthetic thought not noticed

A second point of (transcendent) criticism of the congress stems from my own view of the history of Medieval thought in general and Thomas in particular. In my opinion Thomas's thought must be characterized as synthetic, since he attempted to reconcile themes from pagan Greek thought with Biblical truth.

By typifying Thomas of Aquino as a synthetically inclined thinker, I take issue with someone like A. von Harnack who overestimates the influence of heathendom on Christendom (and so the renewing power of the Gospel too) by maintaining that Christendom in general and the Middle Ages in particular were the fruit of the Greek spirit in the soil of the Gospel.

On the other hand the influence of pagan philosophy upon Christian thought of Thomas ought not to be underestimated as in the case of E. Gilson, who has made the statement that not a single Greek philosophical image ever became a constituent element of Christian faith (theology).

Thomas was on the one hand no heathen, but on the other hand he never thought in a radical, Scriptural fashion in his philosophy and theology, but exhibited an ambiguous attitude in trying to acknowledge Aristotle (to name only the most important) as well as the Bible.

As far as the Thomas Congress is concerned, my criticism boils down to the fact that, as far as I am aware of, no speaker queried the synthetic character of Thomas's thought. Nobody apparently had any objection to Thomas's incorporation of elements of heathen Greek thought into his so-called Christian theology, nor did they realize how many insoluble dilemmas this presented to Thomas. The reason for this is possibly that their own ideas were a continuation of a synthetic attitude. A much more precise approach to Thomas might, however, have been possible had this not been the case. As far as the central theme of the Congress is concerned, the great difference between Thomas's synthesis and contemporary overwhelmingly anti-synthetic and spiritually leftish-oriented thought might have become more clearly evident.

5.3 Congress's own presuppositions not critically examined in the light of Scripture

Together with the previous point of criticism should be taken the problem Thomists have to examine (as Christians) their own and Thomas's presuppositions in the light of Scripture. The following matters which have to be regarded as erroneous in the light of the Bible are still continually regarded as dogmas.

In the first place the dualistic ontology of *one* being with a higher transcendent part (God) and a lower, non-transcendent section (the cosmos). The relationship between God and cosmos is determined according to the scheme of resemblance and difference (which in my view is only applicable to created beings), so that the doctrine of the *analogia entis* is still crucial. This doctrine makes no *radical* distinction between God and that which He has created, but only a *gradual* difference. In the hierarchical structure of being God is the higher and creation the lower section. One speaker for instance expressly declared that there is no end to the (one) being, since man could not then penetrate to God (the highest part of being) with his reason.

In the second place it was evident from several papers that the doctrine of form and matter is still a cardinal issue. This was especially obvious in the plenary session and symposium on the possibility of a Metaphysics. In this connexion it was particularly remarkable how sharply Thomists reacted against Existentialism and M. Heidegger in particular. They did not wish to accept Heidegger's accusation that Thomas forgot existence, and laid all stress only on essence. Every now and again it was emphasized that essence and existence go hand in hand and must not be separated from each other. Heidegger was accused at the Congress of neglecting essence and consequently of falling into subjective relativism.

Thirdly, it was clear from a good many speeches that the doctrine of the two realms of nature and grace, in spite of all the reflection it received in Roman Catholic thought during recent decades, is still accepted as an (unproved) a priori in the approach to practically all problems. Conceptual pairs such as the following made their appearance, for instance: revealed morals (on the level of grace) — rational morals (on the level of nature); Christian values — human values; internal law of the Spirit (freedom) — external law of nature (bondage); sacred history — profane history; Theology of history — Philosophy of history; through His birth Christ restored our nature (natural grace) — by His resurrection He took away our sins (supernatural grace).

One of the speakers even declared that the rejection of the nature-grace sheme had to be resisted at all costs, as this would lead to secularization. The realization that the doctrine of the two realms has had exactly this result (secularism) does not yet seem to have penetrated Roman Catholic thought! By dividing life into a Christian sphere of the supernatural and a neutral area of the generally-human, the sovereign rule of God has already been limited — man can now only directly serve God in the area of faith. The two realms doctrine leads to a schizophrenic existence which hinders the Christian from serving God everywhere and always and in all things. In this fashion religion is more or less confined to church activities — a result which is definitely not in accordance with the Word of God. (Modern secularistic thought has only radicalized the Thomistic standpoint in a negative sense: the realm of grace (Bible, church, sacraments and so forth) is scrapped, and so man lives *completely* without God and not merely *partly* with God, as in Thomistic thought.)

Evidently it will not be easy for Thomistic thinkers to query this a priori assumption of nature-grace (which ultimately derives from the pagan Greek distinction between profane or secular, and sacred or holy). But before this happens there is little hope that anything completely new will show up. This nature-grace scheme has given rise to certain problems which have been chewed over again and again ever since Thomas without any chance of ever being solved.

One of these problems, which often came to the fore during the Congress, was that of rational knowledge and belief (the activities of knowing in the areas of nature and grace respectively). It was emphasized that the two are not to be separated, but must work together: *fides quarens intellectum* and *intellectus quarens fidem*. Reason was strongly stressed in opposition to Irrationalism. The pope for instance emphasized that Thomas can above all teach us to think logically, and he concluded with Thomas's definition (in the *Summa Theologiae*) of what belief is: "... to believe is to think with assent." Others too showed that faith must be a rational faith and criticized the so-called Fideism (or irrationalistic idea of faith).

One of the speakers even stated that the de-Hellenization of Christendom had led to the contemporary "God is dead theology", and by this meant that Greek thought had brought a rational element into Christian belief and in so doing had made the *science* of Theology possible. I would rather make the opposite remark, namely that it was not de-Hellenization but Hellenization which was the beginning of modern secularistic Theology.

As already mentioned above, the present-day Thomist still does not perceive the danger of synthetic thought, and a miracle would have to happen for him to change his mind in this regard. There are indeed some differences amongst Thomists, but only because some lay more stress on grace (faith) and other emphasize nature (reason). As a result of the divergent interpretations of the doctrine of the two realms, the latter group would for instance be more open to modern positivistic thought and lay more stress on the rationality of faith, while the former group would more easily relapse into an irrationalistic conception of faith. Basically both groups remain trapped in the doctrine of two realms — and the Congress demonstrated this quite clearly.

Still other consequences of this teaching were apparent during the Congress: such as, for example, the major problem of the relationship between Philosophy (area of nature) and (supernatural) Theology. And in addition the age-old question as to how Theology (in the area of *faith*) can be a *science*. In contrast with the so-called "empty Lutheranism" of Karl Barth, it was pointed out that reason is essential for theological activity. Because reason is not acknowledged today, it was argued, the entire right to existence of Theology was called into question.

It is not the place here to discuss all these problems in detail, nor to show how radically Scriptural thought could bring many of them nearer to a solution. In making these few remarks I have only attempted to show that, although there were many nuances to be observed within the Thomistic camp, these scholars still basically operate within the same framework, a few exceptions — especially among the less convinced Thomists — excluded.

8 THE PHILOSOPHICAL CONCEPTION OF THOMAS AQUINAS IN HIS *SUMMA CONTRA GENTILES**

Thomas's endeavours could be compared with those of an electrical transformer . He picks up the currents of the past and in a certain sense brings the struggles and thoughts of many ages to a conclusion and a definitive result. The thought-currents of the past are collected by him and transformed into a powerful conception: so charged with energy that its impulses are still discernable. The echoes of his ideas still reverberate today — not only in the Roman Catholic Church, where his philosophy was declared the official doctrine, but also elsewhere.

1. METHODOLOGICAL PROBLEM: WAS THOMAS A THEOLOGIAN OR A PHILOSOPHER?

It is an old bone of contention as to whether Thomas was a theologian or a philosopher, or in the first place and primarily one or the other.

It is evident from his works that he was neither simply a theologian nor a pure philosopher. But the problem is as to what exactly the precise relationship between Theology and Philosophy, as presented in his works, was. Did Thomas only employ Philosophy as a means of actualizing his Theology, or did he perhaps utilize the data of Christian faith as a pretext enabling him to philosophize?

From the contents of Thomas's works, but also as a result of what he himself said about the relationship between Theology and Philosophy (to be discussed later), it can safely be accepted that he himself wanted to be a theologian in the first place. As a theologian, he aimed at interpreting, syste-

---

* Originally published in *Koers*, XLI (2):73-81, 1976 and *Koers* XLI (3/4):133-149, 1976 under the title "Die wysgerige konsepsie van Thomas van Aquino".
To save space references to the *Summa Contra Gentiles* (and also the *Summa Theologiae*) as well as to secondary sources have been left out. Full references are, however, given in chapter 2, p. 28-120 of my M.A. thesis *Die wysgerige konsepsie van Thomas van Aquino in sy "Summa Contra Gentiles" met spesiale verwysing na sy siening van Teologie* (1968, Potchefstroom University of Christian Higher Education) and in chapter 3, p. 243-338 of my doctoral thesis *Die Natuurlike Teologie met besondere aandag aan die visie daarop by Thomas van Aquino, Johannes Calvyn en die "Synopsis Parioris Theologiae". 'n Wysgerige ondersoek.* (1974, Potchefstroom University for Christian Higher Education).
We used a Spanish edition of the Summa Contra Gentiles: *Summa contra los Gentiles.* Madrid, "Biblioteca de Autores Christianos", 1967 and 1968 (2 Vols.). A cheap paperback English translation (5 Vols.) is *On the truth of the Catholic faith.* New York, Doubleday & Co., 1955-1957. (Translated by J.F. Anderson, V.J. Bourke, C.J. O'Neil and A.C. Pegis).

matizing, understanding and elucidating the Word of God in his Theology (*sacra doctrina*). The study of Philosophy, which for him was concerned with cosmic matters, was not undertaken for its own sake but was subordinated to his primary theological goal.

This state of affairs naturally makes it not quite so easy to track down the philosophical presuppositions of Thomas's thought. Most traditional Thomists (inspired by the ideal of a *philosophia perennis*), like Garrigou-Lagrange and Maritain, have begun with the presupposition that it is possible to distil a complete, purely rational Thomistic philosophy from Thomas's writings. Even someone like Gilson, who has laid more stress on the influence exerted by Christendom on Thomas's thought, believes that a complete philosophical system — although it would then be a "Christian" philosophy — could be found in Thomas. The big problem is naturally whether it is really possible to isolate the philosophical strain in Thomas's thought-system, and in so doing still to achieve an independent, vital unity in the final result. Is it not far more likely that a very artificial product would be the result?

The purpose of this examination of the ontological background to Thomas's *Summa Contra Gentiles* is not to distil a *complete* and *conclusive* system from the predominantly theological context. But since every discipline is built upon philosophical presuppositions (even in cases where this is not admitted), these can also be traced in the case of the *Summa Contra Gentiles* — especially where Thomas so clearly acknowledges that he makes use of Philosophy in his Theology, and also because his *Summa Contra Gentiles* is usually regarded as his philosophical masterpiece (whereas the *Summa Theologiae* is seen as its theological counterpart).

The conclusion may not be drawn from what has already been stated about Thomas's view of the relationship between Theology (according to him, a scientific study of the Bible) and Philosophy (a scientific study of the cosmos) that his Theology is purely Scriptural and that the Philosophy which will be extracted therefrom has a completely pagan character. The unity which Thomas, as *the* representative of the summit of synthetic thought, brought about between Biblical and Greek thought, is much more intimate, holding for Philosophy as well as Theology. A good many pagan elements crept into his theological writings as a result of this synthetic approach, while the philosophical thought-patterns which he took over from Aristotle, for instance, were themselves modified by Biblical revelation during the course of centuries.

Thomas's intention was indeed to think Biblically and Christianly in his Theology, but on account of philosophical influences the result as far as the thought context is concerned cannot be described as *radically* Biblical or Scriptural, but rather as Christian synthetic thought.

2. ONTOLOGICAL PRESUPPOSITIONS

The *Summa Contra Gentiles* represents a particular phase in Thomas's philosophical development. On some matters he held the same view in all his writings throughout his life. We could describe this very briefly by saying, for instance, he continuously maintained a synthetic, purely cosmological, dualistic and partially-universalistic conception. A careful study of his work shows, however, that there are two major periods (each with two further subdivisions) which are to be distinguished in his philosophical development.

The *Summa Contra Gentiles* falls within the second main phase of his development, in which the influence of Aristotle is more clearly evident. Whereas the first main phase can be called the Platonizing-monarchianistic period (up till about 1259), this period (1260-1274) can be characterized as a modified Aristotelianism, in which Thomas accepts the subsistence theory. Initially he maintained a Platonizing form of the subsistence theory (1260-1265), but as the influence of Aristotelianizing thought became stronger, he preferred a non-Platonizing theory of subsistence, which is characteristic of the final period of his labours (1265-1274). The *Summa Contra Gentiles* represents the second last (Platonizing) phase and the *Summa Theologiae* Thomas's last (non-Platonizing) phase.

2.1 Pure Cosmological Thought

Thomas does not resort to myths to answer the question as to where the created reality comes from; accordingly he does not mythologize. Nor does he concentrate solely on the coming into being of the cosmos, so that his view cannot be described as cosmogonic-cosmological either. He makes no attempt to explain the origin of things philosophically, but begins with the Scriptural truth about creation, of which he offers an Aristotelian-flavoured philosophical interpretation. We feel ourselves akin to Thomas' decision to philosophize on existing things and not to speculate on the question of their ultimate origin.

But his purely cosmological approach has its shady side. He admittedly makes use of the light of Scripture, but as a result of his purely cosmological point of departure this light is markedly restricted.

The word of God reveals the existence of God, that He created heaven and earth, and that He stated his laws for creation. A philosophical Ontology with Scriptural binding, therefore, has to distinguish between the coherent variety of God, law and cosmos.

The light which Scripture, according to Thomas, throws on created (cosmic) reality can be summarized in three words, viz. "creation, fall and redemption", and of these he declares that creation and redemption are the most important moments.

As the consequence of this pure cosmological approach, Thomas's Ontology is narrowed to a Cosmology (comprising creation, fall and redemption). However, since God and law are realities which cannot be denied, Thomas is forced to subsume them in one or other fashion under his Cosmology (as will shortly become apparent).

2.2 Dualism

Since Thomas's pure cosmological thought implies that he actually acknowledges only *one* being (instead of three modes of being), namely that of the cosmos, the question remains as to what effect this has on God's Being. The answer to this lies within his dualism. According to a monistic philosophy unity is primary and diversity (which comes to being out of the unity) secondary. The answer given by dualistic thinkers, on the other hand, as to the origin of reality is that diversity (usually reducible to a duality) is primary. Thomas's dualistic vision implies that one has to distinguish between a higher, transcendent, and a lower, non-transcendent, "part" within the one being. Instead of using these terms Thomas calls the two components of this Greek (and thus pagan) dualism God (Creator) and creation.

As far as terminology is concerned it seems as though Thomas takes a thoroughly Scriptural stance in differentiating Creator from creation. On closer inspection, though, he maintains an unbiblical view, by combining God and cosmos into *one* being (as the transcendent and non-transcendent parts respectively). Consequently the radical difference between God and creation becomes problematical in his Ontology.

In this "God-and-cosmos" philosophy Thomas now has to determine the relation of God and cosmos. Is God completely transcendent in relation to the cosmos, so that He has nothing at all to do with it? The Biblical revelation of God's concern with his creation forces Thomas to reject the idea. He wishes to accept the omnipresence of God. But seeing that he has already (under the influence of a dualistic Ontology) qualified God (as the transcendent) spatially "above" the cosmos, Thomas can no longer see God's omnipresence in a Scriptural manner, but only in terms of immanence, i.e. in such a fashion that God becomes part of creation. However, anyone who acknowledges the radical distinction between God and creation, and thus does not apply spatial concepts to God (for they only hold for creation), need not understand the Biblical doctrine of God's presence in such a manner that God becomes part of the universe.

From my point of view it seems inappropriate to approach the relation of God to cosmos in accordance with the category of part-to-whole. At the same time the application of concepts of similarity and difference to this relationship is unscriptural. Yet, as will become apparent below, this is exactly what Thomas does. This is most noticeable from his doctrine of the *analogia entis* where it is evident that he applies the idea of similarity-in-difference (or difference-in-similarity) to this relationship.

Before we go into that matter, we should however first consider in what sense Thomas' purely cosmological, dualistic conception affects his idea of law. Although he does not see it in a Scriptural fashion (since he admits of only one dualistically conceived being), neither did he ignore the law. On the contrary, it plays a most significant role in his entire thought.

2.3 Partial universalism without macro-microcosmic theory

Over against the extremes of universalism and individualism, which take an extreme stance on the universal and the individual aspects of cosmic reality respectively, Thomas holds a more moderate view wherein he tries to allow both a fair hearing. He considers the universal definitely the most important (from whence the classification of his view as partial *universalism*), but he allows the individual its place too. However, he does not see the two as separate entities, alongside each other, like the partial universalists which accepted the macro-microcosmic theory. According to him, both the universal and the individual (as the higher and lower components) are present in one and the same thing. This is his doctrine of form and matter or *hylemorphism*, which derives from Aristotle. The universal is the same as the higher form and the individual is identical with the lower matter. Every created thing thus consists of matter and form.

Thomas's viewpoint regarding the relation between the universal and individual facets of reality brings us to his ontology of law, since he closely relates the universal with the problematics of law.

His struggles about the place of the law eventually resulted in the idea of *universalia ante rem, in re* and *post rem:* the law exists before the cosmic things in God, is implanted by God in the things, and can be abstracted by human reason from the things again. This is Thomas's ontology of law in a nutshell, which we shall examine in much more detail in what follows.

2.4 Ontology of law

Thomas accounts for the law within the one being, which is divided into transcendent (God) and non-transcendent (creation). Law is thus confused with God as well as with the creature.

According to Thomas God is pure form or essence (law). In the creatures there is difference between form and matter, essence and existence, but in God these coincide. God is his *essentia, quidditas* or *natura.*

Hence the essence of the cosmic things also exist *in mente Dei* and are implanted by Him in the things. God's essence is the *exemplar* of all things, for in his intellect God contains the ideals or patterns (laws) of the various creatures. We must express this by saying that apart from God's own unique law, God also contains laws (*exemplares*) for each particular thing in Himself. The *exemplares* are thus not identical with the essence of God but lie pent up in the divine essence.

Schematically expressed: Of two concentric circles, the outer indicates God's existence and the inner his essence or being. Actually, Thomas puts so much stress on the essence of God that he declares that the essence and existence of God coincide. (In the light of a Scriptural Philosophy, the consequences of this are that God is subjectivized as well as "legalized". because He is seen as subject as well as law.) Between these two concentric circles lie the *exemplares*, according to which God creates the things. These archetypal examples for the created things are thus not identical with the being or essence of God, but only analogous thereto.

In accord with these forms *ante rem* in God, the forms or things are implanted *in rebus*, i.e. in the earthly things (which consist, then, out of form and matter). Thomas is fond of using the picture of the artist and his work of art to explain how the things are created by God. The artist creates according to the plan in his mind, and so does God create on the lines of the exemplares in his intellect. The forms or laws in the created things are, according to Thomas's theory of subsistence, subsisting forms, since they assist or help God in creation. These forms can be detached from their material bonds by abstraction, and can then appear *post rem* in the knowing faculty of man.

Seen more from the point of view of the creatures, these exemplars are called likenesses, representations or imitations *(similitudines)*. By means of these *similitudines* God shares his nature (being, law) with the created things. This *similitudino* or likeness to God lies in the form or law in the thing. The creatures look like God because of their forms. Thomas states plainly that since the creature owes its likeness with God to God himself (the form which God creates therein), it may only be said that the creature exhibits the likeness of God and not the reverse, namely that God bears the likeness of the creature. However, Thomas sees the likeness as being very close, and this is apparent from where he says that the things copy, imitate or represent God with regard to their forms.

In the light of the speculations about the *logos* with which one meets in the early Christian Apologists and in a different form in Augustine, it is most interesting that Thomas also speaks of the *similitudines* as *rationes*. In Augustine we come across the doctrine of the *rationes seminales, causales* or *aeternae* by which he essentially means the same as the *logoi spermatikoi* of the Christian Apologetic fathers, who in their turn took it over from the Stoa. Thomas then also calls Christ the Word or *Verbum* — the same as the Greek *Logos*. The *rationes* are words *(logoi)* of the Word *(Logos)* in the creatures.

Against this background Thomas's exegesis of Rom. 2:14-16 (where the law of God which is implanted in the hearts of the heathen is mentioned) becomes clear. The *lex aeterna* exists in God. All creatures participate, as a result of the *lex naturalis* (the forms) in them, in the *lex aeterna* in God.

Thomas speaks of the *similitudines* in the creatures as "law", however, only in the case of rational creatures, for law *(lex)* presupposes obedience and thus understanding. It accompanies the hierarchical structure which being exhibits, according to Thomas. Right at the top we find God, who is pure form, and at the very bottom *materia prima,* which is pure matter (and thus cannot actually exist). In between lies a whole series of creatures which are composed of form and matter. Thomas maintains that being is like a pyramid with differing levels of completeness. A creature's completeness depends on the measure in which it exhibits the likeness of God, in other words on how strongly the divine essence is represented therein. The clearer the *similitudino,* the higher the creature stands in the hierarchy of being, and the nearer to God it is. The further from God, the less divine is it. For this reason Thomas draws a clear distinction between man who shows the image *(imago)* of God (because, like God, he possesses intellect), and the other creatures who only bear the footprints *(vestigia)* of God.

At this point a comparison of Thomas's ontology of law with that of Plato, Neo-Platonism and Aristotle might be illuminating. When we considered Thomas's philosophical conception in the *Summa Contra Gentiles* it was mentioned that he adhered to a specific interpretation of Aristotle, classified further as a Platonizing theory of subsistence. Consequently, there are traces of Artistotle as well as of Plato to be found in the *doctor angelicus.* Plato only knew the three ideas (of the true, beautiful and good) and numbers as ideal models in the intelligible world. In his critical reflection on Plato's ideas about law Aristotle developed his hylemorphistic theory which accomodated ideas in things, so to speak.

Thomas does not advocate a pure Aristotelian idea of law, but an interpretation thereof. In order to elucidate this point we have to refer to Neo-Platonism, which thought the Platonic ideas (multiplied) to be present in the mind of God. The philosophical idea that God places the essences into the things in accordance with the *exemplares* in Himself (Thomas) is thus not a Platonic or Aristotelian point of view, but is closer to Neo-Platonism. For this reason Thomas's philosophical conception in the *Summa Contra Gentiles* is not to be described as Platonic but rather as Platonizing. In Thomas, therefore, the Platonizing inclination is especially present in his theory of subsistence: the subsisting forms of the things, proceding from the substance of God bear an assisting character.

A summary of Thomas's views on God, law and cosmos thus gives the following picture. He accepts one being which is divided into transcendent (divine) and non-transcendent (cosmic) parts. Within this one being the law exists in God as well as in the things.

Thomas further believes that reality exhibits a hierarchical character. There are various degrees of being. God is the highest, the perfection of being, and in the lower niveaus of being there is a continual departure from this completeness, in the direction of absolute absence of being. This hierarchy of being is constructed on the lines of the form-matter scheme. God is absolutely pure form or law (essence). The forms of the things are the divine laws (called *exemplar, similitudo, ratio, verbum* or *imago)* which are created therein by God. In this way God expresses his likeness in a creaturely fashion. His total perfection can only find expression in a multiplicity and variety of created things. Thomas calls God the *causa efficiens* and *causa exemplaris.* The relationship between Creator and created reality is thus that of cause and results.

As a consequence of his concept of law Thomas does not clearly distinguish between Creator and creation, since creation to him means, amongst other things, that God places something divine (law) in the things. By way of the divine law being innate in the things, there is a certain continuity between God and cosmos.

2.5 "Analogia entis"

This intimate presence of God in the things threatens to bring Thomas into conflict with God's transcendence, so that in his doctrine of the *analogia entis* he gives a closer definition of being, which is intended to express the fact that there is not only agreement between Creator and creation but also difference.

"Being", as the most comprehensive concept in the Ontology of Thomas, is not univocal *(univoce)*, not equivocal *(aequivoce)* either, but rather analogical *(analogice)*.

One speaks of univocality whenever two or more things agree with each other because they have the same sort of nature (law, form). For instance, the term "person" can be used in the same sense of Socrates, Plato and Aristotle, however different they might be. That which is expressed by the word and concept "person" is the identical nature which is found in all three.

A term is ambiguous or equivocal whenever it can be applied to several things which possess completely different natures (essences, laws, forms). Thus the word "tip" can be employed for two totally different concepts: "on the tip of my tongue" and "tip" as small fee.

Analogy stands in between univocality and equivocality. A term is analoguous if it applies to more than one thing with differing but in certain respects nevertheless identical meanings. For example, whenever it is said of God that he is Creator, and of man that he is creator.

Among other images, Aquinas uses the picture of the sun which radiates warmth into creation. There is similarity between the sun and its effects of warmth in the creation. But there is also difference, since the effects of warmth on the things are not equal to the warmth of the sun itself.

Nothing may be ascribed in a one-sided fashion to God and the things, for there is also a disparity between God and the creatures. But on the contrary, nothing may be ascribed to God and his creatures in an ambiguous way, since this would mean that the agreement between God and his creatures would fall away. Names which are used for God and creation are employed neither univocally nor equivocally, but analogically.

Seen against the background of Thomas's Ontology of law, the similarity and difference or the analogy between God and the creatures is perfectly clear. As a result of the fact that the divine being expresses itself in the creatures (via their forms), it looks like God, it exhibits a resemblance to God — just as a photo looks like the person of which it is an image. The creatures also differ from God, however — as the photo differs from the real living person of which it is a representation — because they are not identical with the divine essence.

In other words: the creatures can exhibit agreement with God, because they have received from God that which makes them look like Him, viz. the forms, *rationes* or *similitudines*. Once again, though, they differ from God, because they are not pure law (essence) like God. Although their examples lie "locked up" in God, these examples are still not identical with the divine law (essence).

Thomas's doctrine of analogy is thus the means by which he attempts to express not only the immanence of God in mortal being but also his unending transcendence of all created things. He tries to maintain continuity as well as discontinuity.

However, from my point of view the relationship between God and the cosmos cannot be approached by using the concepts agreement and difference. It is clear that the basic relation cannot simply be determined from the agreement, and just as evident that it cannot merely be determined from the difference between God and cosmos. Thomas himself was partly aware of this and for that reason he wanted to combine agreement and difference with regard to the relationship of God and cosmos. But the solution does not inhere in the simultaneous maintenance of both agreement and of difference. This could be done with respect to the relationships of cosmic things (although resemblance and disparity are not primarily measures of relationship), but it cannot be made applicable to God. Does He not declare in his Word that He cannot be compared with anything in creation? By employing the doctrine of the *analogia entis* God is brought down to the level of the cosmos — in spite of the fact that not only similarity but also disparity between God and cosmos receives attention.

2.6 Participation

Because the law is exemplar both in God and in the creatures, the latter can participate in God. Although some Thomists aver that by participation Thomas does not mean that the creatures literally partake in God (as the verb *participare* leads one to suspect), this is indeed the case.

According to the doctrine of the *analogia entis* a radical distinction between Creator and creation is not made, since they fall under one denominator, namely being (even though on two levels, degrees or niveaus of being). In the doctrine of participation it is even more obvious that the radical difference between God and that which He has created is not clearly recognized: the creation has a share in God, possesses something divine!

The difference between God and his creation is merely hierarchical, a matter of more or less being. The world does not differ from God through having something positive which He does not have, but *deficiendo*, by a lack, a want of completed divinity! It is only partly divine.

Perhaps the difference between the doctrine of participation and that of the *exemplars* could be stated thus: in the latter it is the direction from above to below that is important: God creates the *exemplars* which exist in Himself, in the creatures. In the doctrine of participation it is the direction from beneath to above which is significant: the creatures (as a result of the exemplars in themselves) have part in God. God shares himself by means of the law which he implants in the things, and the creatures have part in God as a result of the law (form) which they received from God. The law (partly) bridges the disparity between Creator and creation.

2.7 Two-realm doctrine

Until about 1255 this theme was not clearly present in Thomas's thought, gaining in importance thereafter. According to his philosophical line of development (as already briefly set out) it is thus only in his very earliest phase that the doctrine of the two domains is not present. In the *Summa Contra Gentiles*, which represents the third period of his philosophical development, the theme is already clearly developed.

Inferior nature stands to grace in the relationship of the front door to the sanctuary. Nature is not abrogated by grace but elevated and completed. Nature is thus merely an incomplete phase and does not oppose grace.

We cannot go into all the finer distinctions (inter alia his distinguishing between various types of grace) here. What is important is that Thomas's doctrine of the two realms maintains a close connection with his philosophical conception as sketched thus far. It implies a two-fold division in the area of the non-transcendent or the cosmos. Since the nature-grace theme has particular reference to man, it stands in close proximity to Thomas's distinction, as far as man is concerned, between matter and form or body and soul (which will be dealt with more fully in the following paragraph). As a result of the fact that God implants the human soul in the human body according to the *exemplar* in his own being, man has a share in divine grace. (For this reason Thomas speaks of grace already before the fall.) Grace thus has to be sought in the form or essence. The human soul is the bearer of grace. This supernatural grace allows man to share in the divine nature, it gives a certain equality with God. By means of supernatural grace God is present in the human soul, or grace is a reflection in man of God triune. Actually, therefore, the possession of grace to Thomas means that man is deified, while loss of supernatural grace boils down to loss of divinity — ideas which don't seem to be Scriptural.

2.8 Anthropology: man as the image of God

What holds for the other creatures holds also for man. God implants the *exemplar* of every man (which exists from eternity in God) in him. This does not imply the pre-existence of the soul, as it is only the *exemplar*, and not the intellective soul itself, which is present in God from eternity. For the same reason Thomas also teaches that man's intellect is not a part of the substance of God but only a likeness (*similitudo*) of God. According to Thomas the soul is not transferred with the semen (as the traducianists believed) but immediately implanted by God in every new person. He evidently honours the creationistic view.

The intellective soul which God implants as *exemplar* in man is — as with all creatures — the formal aspect. The relationship between soul and body is, according to Thomas, also that between form and matter. Since he sees form and matter as the higher and the lower components of the same thing, the relation of soul and body is also that of higher to lower. The soul, Thomas maintains, is not merely higher, but is, as the essence of man, also better and more important: the spiritual or eternal things of the soul are far more valuable than the bodily or temporary. Sin is then, according to Thomas, to be ascribed to the lower bodily urges, and salvation does not mean that the heart of man is changed by the Holy Spirit, but rather that man no longer lives physically but spiritually!

Thomas states that the intellective soul is the substantial form (*forma substantialis*) of man. This honour is not permitted to the body. As substance the soul is thus also indestructible and immortal and continues to exist untouched after death. Although the soul is not eternal (*aeternus*) like God, it is nevertheless everlasting (*perpetuum*) and thus above time.

Thomas clearly holds a substantialistic view of man. His anthropological stand can be designated thus because the *anima intellectiva* is seen as a substance or subsistent form, implanted by God in the body to assist it or make it living, and which remains living after the death of the body as individualized form or substance.

Thomas builds on ideas which were already current before him about man as the image of God. Irenaeus had already understood the Biblical expression "image and likeness' (*tselem* and *demut* in the Hebrew, *eikon* and *homoios* in the Greek and *imago* and *similitudo* in the Latin) to imply a bifurcation in man. According to him "image" referred to the rational human nature, which all men have in common, while "likeness" meant the particular supernatural gift of communion with God. While sin led to the loss of the supernatural "likeness", the natural "image" still remained, since human nature cannot be lost.

Thomas accentuates this dualism by demarcating nature and grace ever more clearly as two separate areas: the *imago (anima rationalis)* and the *similitudo (donum superadditum supernaturale)* are sharply distinguished. Actually Thomas differentiates between a tripartite image of God in man, viz. a natural image, an image of grace and one of glory. The last-mentioned is, however, only applicable to the saints in the hereafter.

What has already been said, viz. that Thomas's two-realm doctrine goes hand in glove with his Anthropology, is thus also evident from his views of man as the image of God. He says, for instance, that man is, as a result of being created after the image of God, directed towards God. The doctrine of the *desiderium naturale* (which stresses the unity of the realms of nature and grace) can thus not be viewed separately from the doctrine of the *imago Dei*. Both the natural image (*imago*) as well as the supernatural (*similitudo*) refer to a relationship of being between man and God. Even after the fall the unbeliever still bears the natural image. For Thomas the consequences are, amongst others, that man's free will has remained, that man (quite apart from grace) can do good works, that natural ethics and also a Natural Theology are possible.

Owing to the fact that the doctrine of the two realms is unacceptable from a radical Scriptural point of view, Thomas's exegesis of Gen. 1:26 and other passages in this connection must be rejected too. Thomas's idea of the image of God as something divine in man is also untenable in the light of the Biblical radical distinction between God and creature (thus including man).

However, in the light of his distinction (in one and the same being) between a transcendent God and the non-transcendent cosmos, with an analogical relation between them, his interpretation of the Biblical revelation of man as created in the image and likeness of God is understandable.

2.9 Epistemological presuppositions

Thomas's Dualism, in which *one* being is separated into a transcendent

(God) and a non-transcendent part (cosmos), has the result that he also differentiates between two types of knowledge, viz. knowledge of God and of the cosmos. The former is chiefly obtained through faith (while, as will become apparent, a natural knowledge of God through reason is also possible). As far as the knowledge of the cosmos is concerned, the intellect is the obvious faculty. The precise relationship of the two cognitive activities is discussed in the following section (2.10). This section is mainly concerned with knowledge by means of the intellect.

In the intellective soul Thomas distinguishes a speculative and a practical intellect. In the speculative intellect the reason plays the most important role and in the practical the will does so. The reason is connected with thought and the will with action. Thomas further distinguishes between the *intellectus agens* and the *intellectus possibilis* within the speculative intellect.

Through using the speculative intellect, knowledge of the sensually-perceptible things is obtained. The reason thus has the area of nature as its field of investigation.

For him, the rational knowledge possessed by the speculative intellect is concerned especially with knowledge of the *universal,* as contrasted with the practical intellect which deals with that which is *individual.* The universal is, as already shown, for Thomas the same as the *form* or *law (lex naturalis)* in the things. Knowledge of the form or being is found by abstraction from the matter which always accompanies it. Thomas here holds to an empirical epistemology, because he teaches that the form of the knowable arrives in the intellect by means of the senses (of which there are five). The direction of acquisition of knowledge is not so much from the knower to the knowable as the reverse. The form of the knowable is first impressed as *species sensibilis impressa* on the senses, and then a long process of knowing follows before one can begin to speak of the final result of knowledge.

Knowledge is thus not an awareness of facts, since facts are variable and unnecessary. Knowledge deals with the universal, constant and necessary causes. Science has to prove why something is as it is and why it cannot be anything else. In a scientific definition the knowledge of essence is laid down. From this knowledge of the essence (as set down in the definition) it is shown, for instance, that a certain property, arising from the essence, always and everywhere accrues to the given case. The agreement between Thomas Aquinas and his "philosopher", Aristotle, is here very evident.

Quite apart from this Thomas also takes over Aristotle's doctrine of the *principia.* In discussing Aristotle he mentions that he proceeds from the presupposition that there are self-evident, unprovable higher principles to which all knowledge returns. Scientific proof would follow, then, from these first principles and according to syllogistic logic. This reminds one inescapably of Plato's doctrine of the ideas and is evidently a non-empirical feature of Aristotle's epistemology. Knowledge of these highest principles can only be obtained with the aid of illumination, both of the principle and of the knower.

Thomas also declares, in following Aristotle, that scientific knowledge is inferred knowledge from *principia* or principles. These first principles are not arrived at empirically but self-evidently perceived by the intellect.

Just as Aristotle does, Thomas also maintains that not every discipline has its own principles. Some have to lean on the principles of higher disciplines. Hence Optics proceeds from the principles of Geometry, and Music from principles provided by Arithmetic. This is the "subaltern" doctrine of Thomas, viz. that some subjects are disciplines in a subordinate fashion, because they receive their principles from higher disciplines. This doctrine is of great interest inasmuch as it puts Thomas in a position to call his Supernatural Theology science as well. (Cf. section 2.11 on Philosophy and Theology).

It is important that Thomas searches for knowledge of law, essence, universals or causes. In the aforegoing we have referred to the intimate connection between the exemplar or the form in the thing, and its exemplar in God. Hence, knowledge of the universal forms of being (of the creatures) can also offer Thomas knowledge of God. And in this lies the possibility of existence for his Natural Theology.

2.10 Knowledge and belief

In the first place it can be said that the *princeps scholasticorum* very clearly distinguishes between these concepts. Just like his teacher, Albertus Magnus, he teaches that the same matter cannot simultaneously be the object both of faith and of knowledge in the same person. At the same time he also maintains the harmony between them. Brief attention will be given to both his separation and his linking of belief and knowledge.

Thomas distinguishes between the knowable, the activity of knowing and the result of knowing in rational knowledge and belief.

As already stated, in the case of rational knowledge the *knowable* or the object of knowing is the visible creation, while in the case of faith it is the invisibile, namely God and the content of his Revelation. Thomas thus solves the problem by ascribing a separate area or field of investigation to each of the activities of knowing. (This is not at all a watertight separation, because there is some overlapping.)

In the second place, both faith and rational knowledge are *activities of knowing,* functions of the intellect. They differ, however. As had been pointed out, rational knowing arrives at knowledge along the path of abstraction. In the case of faith the important factor is illumination or supernatural enlightenment; in the case of rational knowledge on the contrary one speaks of evidence. (The *principia* are seen as self-evident, while as far as faith is concerned the principles are accepted on the authority of God's Word-revelation.)

As with Aristotle, Thomas's Epistemology can be typified as inconsistent empiricism on the whole. Apart from empirical knowledge of the sensually-perceptible non-transcendent world (cosmos), he also acknowledges that cognisance of the supersensual, transcendent world (God) is possible. Thomas differs from Aristotle in ascribing to the God of the Scripture the place of the Aristotelian monarch. Moreover the enlightening power which Aristotle originally ascribed to the super-individual spirit, is now assigned to God (through his revelation, amongst other things).

In the third place there is a difference in the *result of knowing* as found in faith and rational knowledge. As far as certainty is concerned, faith, "objectively" viewed, is more certain, since it is directed towards divine truth. "Subjectively" viewed, it is rational knowledge that is more certain, because the person who knows can better understand his field of investigation. In this regard Thomas accepts the well-known distinction between opinion *(opinio)*, faith *(fides)* and knowledge *(scientia)* which struck us with earlier (Greek) thinkers. As far as the degree of certainty is concerned, he maintains that belief takes up a position in between opinion and knowledge. It is more certain than mere opinion but less secure than knowledge.

This, then, is Thomas's distinction (in threefold aspect) between belief and knowledge. With regard to the harmonious link between the two (or between the two most important disciplines which operate with the faculties of faith and rational knowledge respectively, viz. Theology and Philosophy), we shall first consider the relationship of faith to rational knowledge and then the reverse: that of knowledge to belief.

Faith completes knowledge, i.e. elevates it. Thomas maintains this in accordance with his doctrine of the two realms, whereby grace does not abolish nature but completes and exalts it. This signifies the following for the relationship between Theology and Philosophy: Supernatural Theology (which studies Scripture) helps Philosophy (in its highest part, viz. Natural Theology) by making known certain truths concerning God which are also rationally knowable. The reason why God reveals these truths (in spite of the fact that He is knowable by reason) is that man can then arrive more quickly at this knowledge of God, all men can possess it, and that without aberrations. Apart from this orientating role which Theology plays with respect to Philosophy, it also fills the part of a negative criterion as far as Philosophy is concerned, by making sure that Philosophy does not contradict the Scriptures.

In its turn knowledge (and Philosophy) serves belief (and Theology) in three ways, namely by *previously* preparing the way for faith, *therein* helping to expand the content of faith, and *afterwards* by defending faith.

Faith is thus not merely encircled before and behind by rational knowledge, but the latter is even allowed within the area of faith as a maidservant.

Knowledge starts off preparing the way for faith by providing motives for the credibility of faith *(motiva credibilitatis* or *credentitatis)* or, as Thomas himself calls them, *praeambula fidei.* To these belong the rational conviction of God's existence, his unity, the possibility of revelation and so on. In other words, all those truths about God and divine matters which are within the purview of human reason — excluding the actual mysteries of faith.

It is important to note that according to Thomas, the Holy Scriptures do not only contain supernatural truths about God and practical attitudes to life, but also natural, rational truths. Divine Revelation, therefore, does not start at the point where human understanding is not in a position to receive further knowledge and the danger of error is present.

In the second place knowledge (in the form of Philosophy) assists belief (in Theology) in the expansion of the content of faith. Hence reason does not travel all the way to the gates of faith only to stop there. It may also enter the sanctuary of faith, but only as a servant who realizes that he now walks on holy ground. Its task is not to prove the mysteries of faith but rather to elucidate it or make it conceivable by means of analogies. In addition it can promote a deeper comprehension of faith by systematization and reconciliation of apparent contradictions.

In the third place knowledge (or Philosophy) also has the apologetic task of defending faith (as systematized in Theology) both from inner and from outer attacks. Within Theology it has a more positive task, namely to "demonstrate" the truth of the mysteries of faith to the believer. Outside Theology its task is more negative, namely to render the counter-arguments of the unbelievers powerless by showing that they are neither compelling nor tenable.

Something of the *fides quaerens intellectum,* the search for a rational faith, makes its appearance here once again. The query as to the rationality of faith can be put in a double sense: the (more external) question as to the truth-value of Revelation and the (more internal) human certainty as to faith.

Concerning the first-mentioned, Thomas maintains that *rationes demonstrativae, manifesta indicia* or *evidentia signorum* can be adduced for the Revelation of God. Even here Thomas holds to the separation of natural and supernatural, knowledge and faith. Only supernatural evidence can be provided for supernatural matters *(in casu* the Holy Bible). For this reason only miracles will be accepted by Thomas as proof — unlike many of his predecessors — for they are supernatural acts of God. In this connection Thomas distinguishes between a whole variety of miracles as *motiva credibilitatis.* He is justly called not only the architect of Natural Theology but

also a significant layer of the foundation of Roman Catholic Apologetics.
We already pointed to the question of the truth-value of the Scriptures as well as to the problem of the (more subjective) certainty of faith. As shown, Thomas also struggles with the latter (amongst other things) in his distinction between opinion, faith and knowledge. This struggle is very apparent in the way he defines faith. As a result of his intellectualistic tendency (stressing reason in contrast to the voluntarists who emphasized the will) he seeks for certainty in faith in its rationality especially. A more Scriptural vision of the relation between faith and knowledge would be able to solve many of these problems. Even though Thomas stresses their unity, faith and knowledge cannot in my view be distinguished according to a higher-lower scheme. This relationship is not that of knowledge *and* faith (as an extra), but rather *faith-committed knowledge* (Afrikaans: gelowige wete) — also in the case of the so-called unbeliever. Faith is not merely a *donum superadditum.*

2.11 Philosophy and Theology

We have already said a good deal about this in our exposition of knowledge and belief.

In the first place Thomas attempts to distinguish Philosophy and Theology very clearly. The time was ripe for this, since the looser forms of education such as the monastery schools were being replaced more and more by the first universities, which brought all the various disciplines together under one roof. It is obvious that owing to organizational and other considerations an encyclopaedic grouping of the various subjects would be given. This grouping took place in four faculties: *facultas theologia, artium* (under which the famed seven *artes liberales,* consisting of the *trivium* and *quadrivium* fell), *juris canonica et civilis* and *medicinae.*

It is praiseworthy that Thomas distinguished between these two disciplines; but whether he did so correctly is another matter. It is evident that he would do so against the background of his grace-nature theory and the epistemological faith-knowledge system. Since the doctrine of the two realms, Scripturally examined, is unacceptable to us, we cannot accept the way in which Thomas distinguished between the two disciplines either. Thomas's own viewpoint was that of harmony between nature and supernature. On closer inspection, however, an inner tension is discernable between the two spheres. The tensions inherent in the nature-grace theory also appear to exist in the relationship between Theology and Philosophy as Thomas sees it. First of all there is the tension between (Supernatural) Theology as a particular discipline (*sui generis)* and Philosophy as "ordinary" science. Secondly, there is the tension between (Supernatural) Theology as self-evident and the only Christian (sacral) science, and profane Philosophy.

Thirdly there is a tension between (Supernatural) Theology as *regina* and Philosophy as *ancilla*.

In addition, it has already become clear from the exposition of Thomas's view of the relation between faith and knowledge that the boundaries separating Theology and Philosophy cannot be determined satisfactorily. Theology is not simply shut in on all sides by Philosophy, but the latter also gets the chance to offer assistance within Theology itself.

3. SUMMARY OF THE PHILOSOPHICAL PRESUPPOSITIONS OF THE "SUMMA CONTRA GENTILES"

The study of the *Summa Contra Gentiles* enables us to characterise Aquinas' philosophical conception as (1) pure cosmological, (2) dualistic, and (3) partial universalistic (without a macro-microcosmic theme). (4) In addition, it is an Ontology of law which locates the law as an entity *ante rem* in God, *in rebus* in the created things, and *post rem* in the faculty of knowing of mankind, as a result of which analogy and participation between God and the creatures is possible. (5) Furthermore it is clear that Thomas holds a dichotomistic anthropology which can be more precisely identified as a Platonizing theory of subsistence. In his view of man the idea of man as *imago Dei*, which is determined by his specific Ontology of law, plays a leading role. (6) In addition in the *Summa Contra Gentiles*, Thomas also advocates a two-realm doctrine according to which the lower sphere of nature is the first step onto the higher area of grace. (7) His epistemological position is characterized as inconsistent empiricism, since he acknowledges the importance of sensible knowledge, but also leaves room for the contribution of extra-sensory factors like faith. The first-mentioned faculty (reason) has the sphere of nature (cosmos) as its field of inquiry and the second (faith) that of grace (God). In both cases knowledge of essence or understanding of law is aimed at. In the case of rational knowledge this understanding of essence is achieved by means of sensual perception and in the case of faith via the Word-revelation of God. (8) The result of both activities of knowledge is a specific discipline. As regards faith, which obtains essential knowledge of the area of grace by means of the revelation of the Word, this discipline is Supranatural Theology. In the case of knowledge, which attains understanding of the essences in nature via sensual perception, Thomas distinguishes between two disciplines viz. Philosophy and Natural Theology. The difference between Philosophy and Natural Theology inheres in the fact that according to Thomas, Philosophy suffices in understanding

the essence of the non-transcendent, whereas Natural Theology (as the highest part of Philosophy) goes further. It studies that which is sensually perceptible insofar as it contains indications pointing to the transcendent God.

160

9 THOMAS AQUINAS' IDEA ABOUT WONDERS – A CRITICAL APPRAISAL*

"Willst du ins Unendliche Schreiten, Geh nur ins Endliche nach allen Seiten".

"Der Wunder ist das Glaubens liebstes Kind". J.F. Goethe.

"Wunder im gewöhnlichen Sinne is eine Durchbrechung des Kausalzusammenhanges der Gesetzlichkeit. Die Wissenschaft kann, da das Kausalprinzip eine ihrer obersten Stützen bildet, keinerlei Wunder annehmen". R. Eisler. *Wörterbuch der philosophischen Begriffe*, Vol. III (1910), p. 1868.

"Der Gedanke des Wunders als Mirakels ist für uns heute unmöglich geworden, weil wir das Naturgeschehen als gesetzmässiges Geschehen verstehen, also das Wunder als eine Durchbrechung des gesetzmässiges Zusammenhangs des Naturgeschehens; und dieser Gedanke ist uns heute nicht mehr vollziehbar". R. Bultmann. *Glauben und Verstehen*, Vol. I (1961), p. 214.

***

Philosophers are amazed at what most people take for granted because they see wonder in everything. The emotion of wonder is the starting-point of philosophy not only according to Plato[1] and Aristotle[2], but also Thomas Aquinas[3]. The emotion of excitement at that which surpasses experience or expectation, the encounter with the inexplicable, surprise mingled with curiosity and admiration – these constitute the beginning and the motive force behind every philosophy.

We are not surprised that the supple, encyclopedic and immensely creative mind of Aquinas, who believed *admiratio* to be the principle of wisdom or philosophy, also marvelled at the wonder or miracle itself. To commemorate the occasion of the seventh century of the *doctor communis* in a

---

* Paper read at the Seventh Century of St. Thomas Aquinas International Congress, Rome and Napels, April 17-24, 1974.
Originally published in *Bulletin van die Suid-Afrikaanse Vereniging vir die bevordering van Christelike Wetenskap*, nr. 23:39-53, September 1973 and there-after in: Atti Congresso Internazionale Tommaso d'Aquino nel suo settimo centenario. Vol. IV, p. 468-478. (Napoli, Edizione Domenicane Italiane, 1976).

1. "This emotion of wonder is very proper to a philosopher; for there is no other starting-point for a philosopher". *Theaetetus*, 155 d.

2. "For men were led to study philosophy, as indeed they are today, by wonder". *Metaphysics A* 982 b.

3. "Admiratio est principium sapientiae, quasi via ad inquirendum veritatem..." *Summa Theologiae*, Pars prima secundae, quaestio 32, articulus 8.

suitable way we should remember his interest in wonder[4].

In view of my limited space, the aim of this paper cannot be an exhaustive examination but only a general survey and initial appraisal in order to stimulate discussion.

1. DOCTRINE OF CAUSES

As with every other viewpoint about wonders or miracles, Aquinas' position is also determined by philosophical presuppositions. In the case of a picked audience of Thomas specialists it is, however, unnecessary to first treat as background the general characteristics of his philosophy.

Under nature *(ordo naturae, ordo rerum creaturam, cursus naturalium)* Thomas understands all the causes which produce their specific effects. These causes or natural laws do not exist outside God's creatures, but determine their effects from inside. God implanted the exemplars that reside within Himself in created beings as forms or essences. According to Aquinas this natural order is the same as the providence of God. Because it is planned by the divine mind it is also considered as a rational order. In the hierarchy of being, God is the first cause or *prima causa* and in the cosmos there are many secondary causes or *causae secundae.* Creation then reveals a fixed order of a plurality of causes each acting according to its own essence and capable of influencing lower causes but not superior ones. Every cause or form or law is constant in its functioning, always producing the same effect, except where it is prevented by a higher cause.

2. THE ACTIVITY OF GOD

This specific doctrine of providence gives rise to several problems. In the first place, if God rules according to a pre-fixed rational plan, is there any place for human freedom and any sense in prayer and how can evil be explained? These problems, however, fall outside the scope of this paper. I would like to investigate the following problem Aquinas encountered: Is there according to his viewpoint any possibility left for the freedom of God Himself?

The only solution is that God acts apart from *(praeter)* the order of His

---

4. We may use the words "wonder" and "miracle" as synonyms in this paper in spite of the fact that there may often be difference in meaning between the two, e.g. the word "wonder" is more or less used for the "ordinary" strange and remarkable things, while "miracle" is a marvellous event due to a really "supernatural" agency.

providence in order not to make Himself a slave of His own decree[5]. God can work apart from the definite order He implanted in creatures by producing effects without proximate intermediary causes.   God usually works indirectly, but He can also act directly and produce immediately the effects usually produced by lower causes. In His free will God sometimes does something outside the order of nature and this is called a miracle.

Aquinas however stresses the fact that, though God at times does something apart from the order implanted in things, He does nothing violent or contrary to nature[6]. The motivation is that it is God Himself who implanted the order in nature. God, the Creator and Founder of all nature, does nothing contrary to nature, for what the Source of all order in nature does, is natural to each thing. So, even though it may seem to be opposed to the proper order of a particular nature, whatever is done by God to creatures is not *contra naturam*.

3. DEFINITION OF MIRACLES

Aquinas defines miracles in the following way: "Things that are at times divinely accomplished, apart from the generally established order in things, are customarily called miracles; for we admire with some astonishment a certain event when we observe the effect but do not know its cause"[7]. Briefly stated: "These things must properly be called miraculous which are done by divine power apart from the order generally followed in things"[8].

5. Cf. *Summa Contra Gentiles* (later on referred to as S.C.G.). Book III, chapter 98, 99 and *Summa Theologiae* (later on referred to as S.T.), prima pars. quaestio 105, articulus 6.

6. Cf. S.C.G. III, 100 and S.T. I, 105, vi.

7. S.C.G. III, 101 according to V.J. Bourke's translation *On the truth of the Catholic Faith* (Image Books), Vol. III, part 2, p. 81.

8. Ibid. Bourke's translation p. 82. The Latin reads: "Illa igitur simpliciter miracula dicenda sunt quae divinitus fiunt praeter ordinem communiter servatum in rebus".
More or less the same definitions are given in S.T. I, qu. 105, art. 7. Thomas quotes from Augustine's *De utilitate credendi*: "Miraculum dicitur aliquid arduum et insolitum supra facultatem naturae et spem admirantis proveniens". In the same article he quotes Augustine from his *Contra Faustum*: "Quod cum Deus aliquid facit contra cognitum nobis cursum solitumque naturae, magnalia vel mirabilia nominantur". He concludes with the following: "Illa quae a Deo fiunt praeter causas nobis notas, miracula dicunter". In qu. 3, art.4 where Aquinas discusses the question whether angels can do wonders, he gives the same definition of miracles as *praeter ordinem naturam*.

Thomas' viewpoint then is that miracles are something super-natural[9)] because they come from the *causa supernaturalis*. A wonder implies the suspension of the natural order[10)].

It is clear that miracles for Aquinas imply the direct intervention or interference of God as the Highest Cause in which He eliminates the secondary causes while using the material substratum. God can thus suspend the activities of nature or replace them by others without destroying the creatures themselves. Though it is asserted by Aquinas that wonders are no violation of the laws of nature, the contrast between wonder and nature is evident.

It is also apparent from the preceding that miracles to the angelic doctor are the exceptional, peculiar and extraordinary. Miracles are things and occurrences that break with the natural order because they are inexplicable departures from our ordinary everyday experience.

From what has been said it is further evident that there is a close relationship between God and miracles. Actually, according to our philosopher, God alone works miracles[11)] because every creature is confined to his own order in the hierarchy of being and cannot operate above this order. Miracles, which result from the fact that an effect is produced out of context of the order in which it can naturally be accomplished, cannot be worked by the limited power of creatures.

Aquinas distinguishes between different degrees of miracles performed by God[12)]. The highest rank among wonders is held by events in which something is done by God which nature never can do. The second degree is held by those in which God does something which nature can do, but not in the same order. The third degree of miracles occurs when God does what is usually done by nature but without the operation of the principles of nature. In each of these cases Thomas gives examples.

He also distinguishes between different types of miracles: *miraculum contra naturam, miraculum praeter naturam* and *miraculum supra naturam*[13)].

9. Cf. *De Veritate*, quaestio 27, articulus 3 where he calls it a *supernaturalis effectus* and *supernaturalis operatio*. See also A. van Hove: *La doctrine du miracle chez Saint Thomas et son accord avec les principes de la recherches scientifique* (1927), p. 132. The cause of the wonder is supernatural, but its effects belong to the natural sphere.

10. "Naturalium rerum cursum mutatur divina dispensatione, aliquid nova causa suborta, ut patet in miraculis", *De Veritate*, qu. 9, art. 2.

11. Cf. S.C.G. III, 102.

12. Cf. S.C.G. III, 101, paragraph 2-4 and S.T. I, qu. 105, art. 8.

13. Cf. *2 Scriptum in 4 libros sententiarum magistri Petri Lombardi* 18.1.3 c and *Quaestiones disputatae de potentia*, 6.2 and 3. The text is given by L. Schutz in his *Thomas Lexikon* (1958), p. 486, sub voce *miraculum*.

God's purpose in the working of wonders is the manifestation of the supernatural order of grace[14]. Wonders may therefore serve as a confirmation of faith. In order to confirm those truths of faith which exceed natural, rational knowledge, wonders give visible manifestations to works that surpass the ability of all nature. This did not merely happen in the past; for in our time God does not cease to work miracles for the confirmation of faith[15].

4. TWO-REALM THEORY OF NATURE AND SUPER-NATURE

The rest of this essay will attempt to evaluate Aquinas' viewpoint within the light of my own ideas[16] about wonders.

In the background of Aquinas' theory about wonders lies the two-realm theory of nature and grace (super-nature). The relationship between the two spheres is similar to that of the threshold to the sanctuary. The higher sphere of grace supersedes or crowns the lower one of nature. Nature is an essential preparation for grace, and conversely, grace perfects nature without abolishing it. It is important to notice that the nature − supernature theme is a synthetic approach which teaches a compromise between the two antithetical poles of secular philosophy on the one hand, and Holy Scriptures on the other. By using Tertullian's well-known metaphor of Jerusalem, i.e. the Bible, and Athens, i.e. pagan philosophy, we may say that Jerusalem was neither permitted to be submerged in Athens, nor to escape from it. Jerusalem was neither identical to Athens, nor opposed to it, but, as the superior to the inferior realm, it exceeded Athens.

In spite of Aquinas' struggle to get a unity and balance between nature and grace the tension between the irreconcilable remains and is revealed

---

14. "Aliud est id propter quod miracula fiunt, scilicet ad manifestandum aliquid supernaturale". Cf. Van Hove, op. cit., p. 130.

15. Cf. S.C.G. I, cap. 6; S.C.G. III, cap. 154, paragraph 8 and 22 and S.T. pars. secunda secundae, qu. 178, art. 1.

16. For my own ideas about this most difficult problem I am much indebted to the following sources: G.C. Berkouwer: *De voorzienigheid Gods*. Kampen, Kok, 1950, Chapter 7 (also translated in English by L.B. Smedes under the title *The Providence of God* and published in 1952 by Wm. B. Eerdmans of Grand Rapids); D. Diemer: *Natuur en wonder*. Amsterdam, Buijten & Schipperheijn, 1963; W. Sikken: *Het Wonder*. Kampen, Kok, 1957; M.C. Smit: *The divine mystery in history*. Kampen, Kok, 1955; H.G. Stoker, "Wonder en wet". *Koers*, vol. 33, nr. 2, October 1955, p. 124-135; H.G. Stoker: *Beginsels en metodes in die wetenskap*. Potchefstroom, Pro Rege Pers, 1961 (chapter 25); K.H. Regensdorf: *semeion* and *teras* in Vol. 7 & 8 of *Theologisches Wörterbuch zum Neuen Testament* begründet von G. Kittel (1961-1965) and the different contributions in *Die Religion in Geschichte und Gegenwart*, vol. VI (1962), sub voce "Wunder".

in his whole philosophic system and also in his doctrine about miracles. When the "lower story" (nature) is declared (semi-) autonomous, and the sovereignty of God is confined to the "upper story" (grace), the final result is that the lower sphere begins to devour the higher so that eventually there is no place left for the supernatural. The theory of nature and grace was the beginning of secularization, viz. a gradual deliverance from supernatural or ecclesiastical bondage and finally resulted in secularism, viz. the withdrawing of life from religious commitment (since the totality of religion had been narrowly identified with the ecclesiastical sphere).

This is the reason why Thomas still accepted the possibility of miracles — in spite of the fact that it was regarded as an incidental intervention of the supernatural in an otherwise hermetically closed nature — and why most philosophers and scientists after Thomas could not accept wonders any more: the semi-autonomous natural sphere had become completely autonomous in not allowing any breakthrough from above. Examples of this last standpoint are the two quotations at the beginning of this essay. Eisler and Bultmann opposed the super-naturalism of Aquinas.

My contention is that the *whole* two-realm theory should first be rejected because it is an unbiblical construction resulting in a kind of Christian schizophrenia. It offers no solution for the relationship between Christianity and paganism, or the church and the world. We should distinguish between the *structure* of religion (man *universally* bound to God in the *totality* of his life) and the *two directions* of religion (service of either God or Satan). We encounter these two directions in the *whole* of creation — even deep in the heart of every Christian! It is impossible — as Thomas attempted to do — to *localize* these *directions* as the spiritual struggle between the kingdom of light and that of darkness. Our life in the Kingdom of God is *creationally the same* as that of the unbelievers (we do not change to a different ontological sphere or species when we become Christians), but *spiritually it is different*.

These few remarks will enable the reader to understand Aquinas' viewpoint about miracles better, and they will also facilitate comprehension of my own critique of our philosopher in the following pages.

5. SUPERNATURAL INTERVENTION OF GOD?

Behind Aquinas' viewpoint is the idea of competition between the fixed order of independent nature on the one hand and God on the other hand, or between natural law and miracle, or between the natural and the supernatural. The existence of miracles becomes problematic. Their possibility only exists in an intrusion now and then of supernatural reality into natural reality. That is why Aquinas believes that God alone can work miracles:

He is the only one who can break through the sealed-in world of ironclad natural laws. This is more or less the background of Aquinas' idea that miracles are the occasional supernatural intervention of God by means of striking events.

Because I cannot accept the philosophical presuppositions underlying our philosopher's standpoint, I do not agree with his idea about miracles.

Nature is not independent of God, or even semi-autonomous, but can only exist from moment to moment through the power of God[17]. Natural laws are essentially the servants of their Creator. Nothing withstands His will, so that it is not necessary for Him first to break through a thick reinforced concrete wall. For God there is no miracle — what we call miracle is merely His ordinary work in sustaining and governing the whole creation. I will come back to this idea that the wonder is not the exceptional but the ordinary. What I would like to stress now is the limitlessness of God's power. If we listen carefully to Scripture we do not experience Aquinas' problem that God runs the danger of becoming the slave of his own decrees. It is not necessary to limit God's activity in order to guarantee the (semi-)autonomy of nature, or, vice versa, to restrict nature's sovereignty in order to secure a small space for the intervention of God.

This last approach especially was very popular amongst certain Christians when natural scientists manifested doubts about the absoluteness of natural laws because of the crisis of the old deterministic and mechanistic worldview. Due to the relativizing of the closed natural order, there appears to be a new possibility and room for wonders again and thus for the supernatural activity of God. Natural law was no longer such a danger to the free activity of God, for by the grace of science He might start working miracles again! We fully agree with Berkouwer[18] with regard to all such apologetic attempts when he says that we can respect the good intention of these people but that in actual fact with this kind of Apologetics one has already capitulated to a non-Biblical mode of thinking.

There is nothing problematic in the activity of either God or nature. In spite of its total dependency on its Creator, creation (including man) can work without becoming the rival of its Maker. This is possible because the relationship between Creator and creation is not that of a Higher over against a lower sphere. The difference between God and nature is *more radical* than that so that no *analogia entis* (similarity in spite of difference) whatsoever is possible. The relationship between God and his creation is not an *ontological* one of more or less, higher or lower being, but a *religious*

---

17. Cf. Berkouwer: op. cit., p. 204.

18. Ibid., p. 229.

one.

Therefore God's activity is one with nature, not outside it. According to Thomas, this is pantheism, but that is not the case. What I contend is that God's activity is not contrary to nature, but natural. And his natural government and sustenance of nature is wonderful. It is not necessary that nature or natural law should first be suspended or excluded to get a wonder!

Nature, and the results of the study of the laws governing creation, are not excluded, but included in the activity of God's government. According to the Bible this is a fact even though the human mind cannot grasp it. Berkouwer gives an example: "Human power over nature is enormously increased. All sorts of things that used to appear amazing and quite impossible are now included in the observable relationships of cosmic life. But the activity of God is not excluded from these. Nor is the necessity of faith diminished. God's answer to prayer can be just as real in medical therapy as in the sudden healings of the time of Christ and the apostles. Only faith that desires special signs will fail to recognise and appreciate this relationship"[19].

It will be clear from the argumentation thus far that the distinction of Aquinas between an *indirect* government of God and a *direct* activity (when He works miracles) is unacceptable to me. For example, we should not say as we colloquially do, "it rains", and only exclaim "God gave us rain!" in exceptional circumstances (for instance after severe draught).

According to my viewpoint God works *everywhere* in the literal sense of the word because *everything is absolutely* dependent on Him and cannot exist for one single moment without Him upholding it. Therefore it is not according to Scripture to say that God only incidentally has *direct* contact with His creation. Creation is so wonderful because God works *always* and *everywhere*.

In the light of my expostulation thus far one should therefore be very careful to speak of "God's finger" in so-called "special events"[20].

6. REGULAR FUNCTIONING OF NATURE AMAZINGLY WONDERFUL

Miracles are not *contra naturam* or *praeter naturam*. There is no contrast between miracle and nature. A miracle is not an *abnormal* or unnatural occurrence presupposing an incursion into a normal nature. The situation is

19. Ibid, p. 229.

20. See M.C. Smit: *The divine mystery in history* (1955) as well as Berkouwer: op cit., chapter 6.

exactly the opposite: the wonder is the normal, and nature the abnormal because of the effects of the fall into sin! Miracles (Christ's healing of the sick etc.) evoke our surprise because we have become accustomed to the abnormality of sin which is finally punished with death! The wonder of God in his sustenance and government of the world are a redeeming reinstatement of the normality of the world. Through the government of God, which stands antithetically against the kingdom of the Devil, life can become normal again as it was at its creation by God.

This brings me to the real purpose of miracles, but before that I want to stress again that the miracle is the normal. The danger in Aquinas' viewpoint is that the "ordinary" work of God may be devalued. According to him the ordinary work of God is not wonderful — which it actually is. What is more wonderful: healing as an answer to prayer, or with medical means; a sun standing still upon Joshua's prayer, or the regular movement of the sun day after day; water transformed into wine, or ordinary wine from grapes which the vineyard in a miraculous way got from the soil in which it grows; the resurrection of the dead, or the appearance of a plant from a grain of corn which first had to die? Ordinary things like an opening flower, a ripening fruit, the birth of a baby are enormous wonders!

The ordinary things are wonderful and, vice versa, the wonderful are ordinary. This applies to the vast ocean, as well as a little drop of water, the immense universe, as well as the submicroscopic molecule[21]. It is only blindness which looks for the wonder in the extra-ordinary!

It is not the irregular but the regular functioning of nature which is amazingly wonderful. Aquinas started with the closed system of laws and then, secondly, asked whether miracles are something anti-nomic or against the law. Perhaps it would be better to take the wonder of nature as a starting point[22]. If the fact of the lawfulness of nature is wonderful, how can the wonder be against the law?

7. SIGNIFICANCE OF WONDERS

I return to a question upon which I have already touched viz. the significance of wonders. According to my view, he who approaches wonders from the standpoint of nature-grace, and therefore from the antithesis between God and nature, cannot see the deepest meaning of wonders. The purpose of wonders does not lie in their miraculousness. The intention of

21. Cf. Sikken: *Het Wonder* (1957).

22. Cf. Stoker: *Beginsels en metodes in die wetenskap* (1961), p. 235.

wonders (as related in Scripture) is not to satisfy curiosity or simply to impress. Miracles in the Bible are not extra-ordinary events, but redeeming acts. The significance of miracles is not that they are strange and unusual, but that they reveal the power of the Kingdom of God in opposition to the kingdom of Satan. The mighty acts related in the Bible are directed towards the Kingdom of God.

This is consistent with what I have stated previously, viz. that wonders are not against nature *as such*, but against *sinful* nature. (Just as a tension does not exist between the realm of grace and that of nature, but a tension does exist between grace versus sin and the wrath of God). Wonders are not against sinful nature in the sense that nature is annihilated, but only in that it is redeemed, restored to its original state. This is, of course, not the case with the wonders worked by the Devil and his followers.

The *whole* life of Christ was miraculous and not only His "signs and miracles". In the Scriptures there is, for instance, no switch-over to a supernatural tone where Christ stopped speaking to do a wonder, but it is calmly reported in the same pitch.

Christ did His wonders as a human being who (because He was without sin) still had the original power over creation. Therefore most — if not all — of Christ's wonders can be explained in a natural way[23]. To account for His deeds in this way does not imply the rejection of their wonderfulness — the natural is identical with the wonderful!

Scripture does not ascribe miracles exclusively to God — as Thomas did. Under the leading function of firm faith in the redeeming Christ and powerful prayer, certain potential powers in man and nature may be opened and the original power of man as king of the earth revealed. As every deed, these activities however, should also be directed towards the kingdom of God.

8. CONFIRMATION OF FAITH?

The purpose of wonders according to Aquinas, as we have seen, is the confirmation or proof of faith. Miracles have a special apologetic function: the Word of God and faith in it can be made worthy of belief through signs which function as persuasive witnesses. Thomas' Apologetics is based on his specific viewpoint about the relationship between faith and reason, grace and nature. We have already rejected the two-realm theory and the same applies to the false dilemma of faith and reason. Man will not be convinced, by means of miracles as proofs for the intellect, to believe.

It is clear that there is a circular movement in our philosopher's view-

---

23. Cf. Diemer: *Natuur en wonder* (1963), p. 100, 101. (Also translated in English under the title *Nature and Wonder* and published by Wedge Publishing Foundation, Toronto, 1978).

point: God works miracles, and the miracles testify to the existence of God. The problem is that you will not convince a non-believer to believe in the existence of God by drawing his attention to miracles because one can only see miracles when you already believe in their possibility. When you believe, it is not necessary to be persuaded, and if you do not believe you cannot be persuaded by miracles. The person whom you want to persuade with miracles to believe in God will easily see the *petitio principii* or circular argument: wonders refer to God, but God is the explanation of wonders.

9. SCIENCE AND WONDERS

I have already voiced my doubt about Aquinas' view about the relation between faith and knowledge or science. This will explain why I cannot accept the idea of "the more faith you have in wonders, the less scientific you are" and the converse: "the more science advances, the less place there will be for wonder."

The current contention is that as nature becomes more transparent the possibility of wonders fades. Primitive people could only explain strange phenomena by a special divine interference transcending nature, but we have no "mysterious universe" anymore. "Advanced" science today explains by means of natural causes the previously inexplicable so that the idea of miracles has become superfluous.

As far as I am concerned it is not necessary to limit science in order to rescue faith, or to restrict faith to guard the existence of science! This rival idea is false. Exactly the opposite is the case: the further science progresses, the better equipped we will be to see the amazing wonder of what we call creation! Science would long ago have completed its task if it were not for the fact that it discovers new wonders every day in this wonderful world of ours. The wonder of creation makes science possible! How can one believe then, in a tension between the two?

It is also true that only if we believe in the wonder of creation *as such*, can we be real scientists, because he who believes in wonders as super-natural intervention places all kinds of strange, abnormal events outside the field of investigation of science so that no explanation of them will ever be possible! Belief in wonders, therefore, or the recognition of God's wonders in scientific activity, is not necessarily an attribute of a primitive, unscientific, naïve, immature person. Of course belief in wonders may wrongly be used as an *asylum ignorantiae* or "a plug for the gap observed in natural causes" just as a concept of God may be used as a *deus ex machina*.

10. CONCLUSION

Perhaps someone will regard my ideas about wonders as inconsistent and self-contradictory: if *everything* is miraculous, why do I still speak of miracles? Perhaps another will accuse me of heresy in the form of pantheism because I call nature itself wonderful. I cannot reply to such objections now because I have to leave time for discussion and surprise. It is the latter, viz. surprise and amazement, which I intended to sustain in this paper: amazement at the all wonderful creation. If I have succeeded in doing that, I have also achieved to save what Aquinas regarded as the quintessence of philosophy: wonder.

* * *

SUMMARY

The question of the relationship between wonder and nature or natural law is basically determined by one's viewpoint concerning the relationship between God and the cosmos. When the correlation God — cosmos is incorrectly envisaged, the relationship wonder — nature becomes problematic. Therefore, if we survey the history of thought concerning the interrelation between wonder and nature, we encounter the following attempts at a solution: (1) an unbridgeable gap between the two; (2) nature and natural law is minimized to secure a possibility of existence for wonder; (3) wonder is underestimated in order to save natural law; and (4) an artificial and inherently contradictory compromise between the two is attempted.

In my interpretation Thomas Aquinas' thought represents the last position. After a brief exposition of the philosophical presuppositions which determine his doctrine of providence, this essay considers his idea about miracles, followed by a critical appraisal which reveals that — in spite of my great and sincere appreciation for the attempts of the *doctor communis* to solve this fascinating problem — I cannot agree with his approach. The difference in our opinions may be summarized in the following ten propositions:

1. There is no dualistic tension between the so-called fixed or sealed-in nature on the one hand, and God on the other hand, consequently no "competition" between them. As God and nature are not the rivals of one another, it is neither necessary to limit God's activity in order to guarantee the order of creation, nor to restrict nature's so-called autonomy to secure a place of freedom for God to intervene with miracles.

2. This is possible because nature, and the controlling laws of nature, are not autonomous or semi-autonomous but from moment to moment are absolutely dependent upon the sustenance of God Almighty.

3. Therefore God does not   work directly only when He works won-

ders, and otherwise merely indirectly, but in His government He is always in direct contact with His creation. Thus, to regard wonders as an occasional, incidental interference of God, in which He suspends the ordinary state of affairs, is not correct.

4. Consequently wonder is not to be viewed as something peculiar, exceptional or extraordinary, but as the ordinary. The ordinary things, to which we are used, are the most wonderful. Viewed in the light of the fall into sin, nature, which is in an abnormal state, is restored to its normal functioning by the working of wonders.

5. In accordance with the preceding the significance of wonders is not their miraculousness, because their purpose is not to impress or satisfy curiosity but they are redeeming acts revealing the power of the Kingdom of God.

6. A miracle therefore is against *sinful* nature, and not against nature *as such*.

7. It is not God alone Who works wonders, but with faith in the redeeming Christ hidden powers in man and nature may be set free.

8. Ascribing an apologetic function to wonders (viz. the visible proof and confirmation of faith in the invisible), is based on the age-old false dilemma of faith and reason.

9. To speak of the "finger of God" in the case of striking events can be very dangerous.

10. The idea of "the more faith you have, the less scientific you are", or vice versa "the more science advances, the less place there will remain for wonders" is not acceptable in the light of either the Word of God or the practical state of affairs in contemporary scientific endeavour.

10 THE RELEVANCE OF THOMAS AQUINAS' VIEW OF THEOLOGY (AS EXPRESSED IN THE *SUMMA CONTRA GENTILES*) FOR CONTEMPORARY STUDIES*

In this article I intend to summarise my critical thoughts on Thomas' view of Theology. This does not mean, however, that I have no appreciation or respect for his work in this field. In my opinion it is not until seven hundred years later that we find as profound a reflection on Theology and its relationship to Philosophy[1], viz. in the works of Karl Barth. The words of Bernard of Chartres[2] also apply here: We are like dwarfs on the shoulders of giants. If we are able to see more and further than our predecessors, it is not only due to the keenness of our sight or our height, but to the fact that we are held aloft on the shoulders of giants.

Thomas holds a distinct position in the history of Western thought. On the one hand he acts as a receiver of important insights of the past. In this respect he holds a special position, for whatever Theological thought emerged from preceding centuries, found greater clarity through him. In a certain sense he presents us with a lucid conclusion and a definite result. On the other hand — as a study of the further development of theological thought shows — there are still echoes of Thomas' vision even to this day.

The echoes can still be perceived today, not only within the Roman Catholic Church (which has proclaimed Thomism the official philosophy to be taught in Roman Catholic institutions), but also among thinkers of totally different conviction.

To do justice to this giant in the history of human thought, it should be pointed out that Thomas succeeded in a masterly fashion in gathering together thoughts of the past and so in developing a clear standpoint to meet the needs of his time as well. Furthermore, the immense influence of his standpoint throughout the centuries, would have to be mentioned. However, it would not be desirable within the scope of this study. We content ourselves with raising a few cardinal points, under the following two headings:

---

* English translation of the last chapter of my M.A. Thesis *Die wysgerige konsepsie van Thomas van Aquino in sy "Summa Contra Gentiles" met spesiale verwysing na sy siening van Teologie* (Potchefstroom University for Christian Higher Education, 1968).

1. Cf. R.A. Markus. The study of theology and the framework of secular disciplines. *The Downside review*, 78:192, 1960.

2. Quoted by E. Gilson in his work *L'Esprit de la philosophie médiévale*.

* Thomas' view of the relationship between (Supernatural) Theology and Philosophy.
* Thomas' Natural Theology as a discipline between Supernatural Theology and Philosophy.

1. THOMAS' VIEW OF THE RELATIONSHIP BETWEEN (SUPERNATURAL) THEOLOGY AND PHILOSOPHY

According to his nature-grace doctrine, Philosophy and Theology belong to two completely different spheres. The latter (in the sphere of grace) is concerned with faith and the former (in the sphere of nature) is concerned with knowledge[3]. Each of these sciences is autonomous in its own field. (On closer observation the autonomy of Philosophy is only a semi-autonomy as it falls under the final authority of Theology.)

The two-realm doctrine (nature-grace) is unbiblical[4], and the faith-knowledge problem is a false dilemma resulting in a never ending tension of having to choose between the two poles of this dilemma, and never gaining the insight that the dilemma itself should be rejected. This tension reappears in Thomas' view of the relationship of Theology and Philosophy.

We point to three facets of this tension between Theology and Philosophy in Aquinas' conception. Firstly, there is the tension between (supernatural) Theology as a science *sui generis* and Philosophy as an "ordinary" science; secondly the tension between Theology as *ipso facto* Christian and the only Christian science and Philosophy as self-evidently neutral; and thirdly the tension between Theology as *regina* and Philosophy as *ancilla*.

1.1 "Extraordinary" (religious) science versus "ordinary" (neutral) science

Thomas is confronted with the problem as to whether supernatural Theology is actually a science, since it belongs to the sphere of the supernatural (grace) and science belongs to the natural sphere of knowledge.

---

3. The fact that Thomas was able to distinguish so clearly between Theology and Philosophy constitutes a definite step forward, which is not even found in the great thinker Augustine. The problem here is whether the manner in which he differentiates between the two sciences is correct. (His acceptance of a Natural Theology has, for instance, the effect of again diminishing this distinction).

4. According to the two-realm theory the antithesis between good and bad in creation is located and seen as existing in two *spheres* into which creation is divided while in reality the antithesis lies in the *direction* (for or against God) in *all* spheres of life. Since the Fall the good-evil antithesis permeates all of creation, and it may not be localised to spheres in creation, for example: good = Church, evil = state.

His standpoint is that Theology is a science. It is not, however, an ordinary science, like other sciences in the natural sphere, but an exceptional science. Long before Thomas, Theology was described as *intellectus fidei*, science of faith. This idea reappears with him. Theology is a discipline *sui generis* because it is more than a science[5]. In short: it is something supernatural.

The result is that Theology is elevated above all criticism. Theology can have a specific critical influence on Philosophy (as happens in the Roman Catholic Church) but the reverse is not allowable[6].

A further result is that Theology has also acquired a special authority as "Glaubenswissenschaft". It not only has normal scientific authority, but also the added authority of an alliance between science and religion. Through this impermissible yoking together of science and religion, the *theology* of Thomas was canonized and became the official doctrine of the Roman Catholic *Church*.

To my mind, however, a clear distinction should be made between Theology and Church (fellowship of believers). The Church and its confession of faith is something apart from the science of Theology, even though theologians have played an important role in the history of the confession. If this were not so, the disagreeable situation might arise where a man's orthodoxy is judged, not by the confession of the Church, but by ruling theological opinion — in all probability short-lived, and easily replaced by a new theology.

Such problems are not experienced by those who reject the two-realm doctrine of Thomas and the false faith-knowledge conflict.

In the first place the problem in what sense Theology can be a science falls away: Theology too is neither more than a science, nor an exceptional science. It is just an ordinary science, structurally no more reliable than any other science, and just like other sciences dependent on presuppositions of faith.

The idea that Theology is above criticism also falls away. As an ordinary science among others it is obliged to give an account of itself and, as in

---

5. As already stated in footnote 3, we have no objection to Theology being a discipline *sui generis* in the sense that it is distinguished, for example, from Philosophy because it is different. In this sense however, Philosophy and every other science is also a discipline *sui generis*, being of its own kind and its own character. Our criticism is here directed at the fact that Theology is regarded as more than a science.

6. Philosophy according to Thomas is (semi) autonomous in its own field, so that Theology can exercise only limited criticism against it, if a Philosophy, for example, teaches doctrines which clash with faith. Conversely, when we say that according to Thomas Philosophy cannot exercise criticism against Theology, it does not exclude the possibility that Philosophy, in the sense that it has to aid Theology, has a certain critical influence. As will be pointed out later on (under 1.3) Thomas accepts Philosophical influence over Theology as self-evident.

the case of every other science, philosophical consideration of the basis of a specific theology is possible and desirable.

Investing Theology with special authority is also unacceptable. It has the same *scientific* authority as any other science.

It is its field of research, namely Holy Scripture, that makes Theology special. That which should be *presupposed* by all sciences which claim to be Christian (including Theology) also has to be *researched* by Theology. All sciences should obey the Scriptures, but Theology in addition to obeying, also has to research the Scriptures. This research can promote obedience if it is done in faith — unfortunately there are theologians who do not bow before the Word of God in obedience. A Christian theology can help the other sciences and the non-scientific world towards obedient listening. Therefore in theology we should always find an interplay of obedient research and researching obedience.

We have seen that Thomas does not differentiate clearly between Theology and Church. He is right insofar as he acknowledges a relationship between the two. The relationship is the same as that between the Holy Scriptures and Theology with which we have just dealt: like the Scriptures the Church is also a field of research for Theology. The theologian uses bifocal spectacles: in the one case the Word of God comes into focus and in the other the Church of Christ. Therefore the two focal points of Theology are: The Word and the Church.

There is an intimate relationship between these two focal points. The only true Church is the Church which listens to the Word obediently and responds to the claims of the Word in faith. In its research concerning the Church, Theology will also have to answer the question as to how in the fellowship of believers (the church) the Word of God *has* been listened to, (e.g. in Ecclesiastical History or the History of Dogma) and how it *should* be listened to (e.g. in Ecclesiology or Systematic Theology).

The difference between the two focal points come to the fore in "how it should be listened to": the Word of God and the church are not on the same level. Therefore we always mention the Scriptures first and then the Church. The Word of God bears first and final authority.

In the so-called bibliological group of theological subjects (Exegesis, Canonics, etc.) the theologian concentrates more on Scriptures; whereas in the so-called ecclesiological group of theological subjects (Church Law, Church Administration, Church History etc.) he concentrates more on the other focal point, namely the Church. Other theological subjects lie somewhere between these two focal points. For example the dogmatic group, which studies the *Church's* confession based on the *Word*.

These two focal points in the field of research of Theology are at the same time also focal points in the life of the Christian believer. Holy Scripture is the source of life to him as a believer, and the Church is the heart of the Kingdom of God of which he is a citizen[7].

Theology, as an ordinary human scientific activity, lies close to the centre. It is a privilege but also brings with it tremendous responsibility. The theologian will have to see that he remains clearly aware of the radical difference between his science and his field of research. (The Word and the Church). History often shows that it is not impossible that the theologian fails to distinguish sufficiently between his science and the Revelation of God, so that theology assumes the character of revelation. Furthermore theology can be caught up in the idea of an autonomous science and instead of performing its task with deference in a serving capacity, it acts in a dominating manner, for example assuming authority in church affairs, while it has only limited scientific authority.

Like every other science the scope of theology is limited. The rich, many-facetted life of the Christian as it unfolds outside the church in the wide area of the kingdom of God, is not a field of theological research. Here we differ radically from Thomas who identified the church with the kingdom, and so limited all Christian activity to the church, where Theology held sway[8]. The citizen listens to the Word of his King not only in the church but also in the kingdom, and responds to it in faith in politics, scientific study etc. However, it does not become a field of research for Theology merely because it is also a service *of faith*. Faith is not limited to any one aspect of life (as Thomas would have it), but is manifested in all facets of life. Theology studies only one facet, namely the church or cultic life of the believer. [9]

---

7. For the intimate connection between Church and kingdom see an article by S.C.W. Duvenage, Die verhouding van kerk en koninkryk. *In:* Die koninkryk van God, a collection of essays published in 1969 at the centenary celebration of the Theological School of the Reformed Church in S.A.. Potchefstroom, p. 113-132.

8. Except of course in so far as the principle of subsidiarity holds good.

9. In my opinion the study of the "apostate" cultic life also belongs to the field of research for Theology. The good-evil antithesis which applies to the whole of creation since the Fall, must not be ignored in the sciences either. The word "apostate" indicates the abnormality of the cultic life of those who do not believe in Christ. They do have a revelation, but it is a surrogate or pseudo revelation. They do have a cultic society but we cannot call it church — a pagan church would be a *contradictio in terminis*. Yet their activities remain apostate *cultic* expressions and not economical, ethical, judicial, etc. — even if it is a cultic expression in which economics is idolised. As such it inherently belongs to the field of research of Theology. We therefore cannot agree with A. Kuyper and others who want the study of apostate faith to be part of the faculty of arts. Paganism must also be studied in Theology which does not preclude other sciences from also studying specific facets of apostate cultic life. It is not true that Theology is merely concerned with Christianity and only so-called "Religionwissenschaft" studies paganism. Herein we see an after effect of Thomism: confrontation with paganism only takes place in Philosophy, more specifically Natural Theology. In our view these apostate cultic expressions must also be studied in the light of Scripture which is the revelation of how man's cultic life should really be conducted.

1.2 Christian Theology versus pagan Philosophy

In the preceding we have not said everything about the exceptional character given by Thomas to Supernatural Theology. His Supernatural Theology is also *sui generis* as it is the only Christian science, according to him. Furthermore it is accepted as a matter of course that Theology is Christian. This idea is very much alive to-day among many theologians so that our criticism is of current interest.

The reason why Thomas accepts this standpoint is self-evident. Supernatural Theology, according to him, belongs to the sphere of grace, and only here can Christianity be conceived of. Theology is not only a science of Christianity but the only Christian science.

Furthermore only Theology has Holy Scripture as its field for research, and can thus be pointed to as *sacra theologia* (or *sacra doctrina*). Because the field of research is holy the science studying this field is also regarded as holy.

D.H.Th. Vollenhoven says rightly: "... wat het 'uitgegaan van die waarheid' betref, daarover beslist niet de veld van onderzoek, maar de geest waarin wordt gewerkt. Want het valt niet te loochenen, dat er onder de theologen zijn die zich allerminst door de Schrift laten gezeggen en dat er onder de filosofen zijn, die dit wel doen"[10].

P.G.W. du Plessis writes: „... 'n wetenskap word nie Christelik deur sy sogenaamde voorwerp van ondersoek nie. Hoeveel Kommuniste is daar nie wat met groot toewyding en erns 'n studie maak van die Christelike geloof en daarmee seker geen Christelike wetenskap bedryf nie"[11].

In my opinion the possibility cannot be ruled out that Thomas' conception of Theology as self-evidently Christian is also based on the faulty supposition — which is still prevalent to-day — that a Christian science is a science studied by Christians. A Christian science, however, does not simply mean a science practised by Christians. Of course theologians are mostly Christians, so that it is understandable that the expectation arises that Theology should self-evidently also be Christian. Christians, however, are capable of arriving at a very unchristian result. A Christian science is not only a science practised by *Christians* (which is a necessary qualification, but still only one prerequisite) but also a *science* which is truly Christian as far as the content is concerned.

---

10. Vollenhoven. *Mededelingen van de Vereniging voor Calvinistische Wijsbegeerte,* Dec. 1965, p. 5.

11. Du Plessis. *Bulletin van die SA Vereniging vir die Bevordering van Christelike Wetenskap*, 6:120, Aug. 1966.

J.M. Spier rightly says about a Christian science: "We mogen deze niet omschrijven als de wetenschapsbeoefening van christenen, omdat er in het wetenschappelijke werk van christenen nog vaak allerlei niet-christelijke motieven kunnen voorkomen. Wetenschap, die op de naam christelijk terecht kan aanspraak maken, is die wetenschap, welker beoefenaars in alle opzichten rekening houden met het Woord van God en daarom tot resultaten komen, die met de goddelijke Woordopenbaring in overeenstemming zijn"[12].

We have to draw attention to some further fatal consequences of a viewpoint like that of Aquinas, namely that Theology is the only Christian science, and also *ipso facto* Christian.

It is understandable that Christian thinkers — especially those engaged in sciences other than Theology — would in the long run be dissatisfied with the idea that Theology alone could be Christian, and that only in this one science could one's labour be to the glory of God. A solution was accordingly found in Christianizing other sciences through Theology. The error, it seems to me, lies in the fact that the argument is still based on the two-realm doctrine held by Thomas. Theology belongs to the Christian sphere of grace and Philosophy to the neutral or in fact non-Christian sphere of nature. If a link could be established between Christian Theology, which studies the Scriptures, and non-Christian Philosophy and other neutral sciences, it might result in the natural sciences becoming Christian too. Nature is then made Christian through grace, that is, it is Chirstianised[13].

---

12. Spier. Wijsbegeerte en Kerk. *In:* Wijsbegeerte en levenspractijk, p. 30.

13. In this respect it is interesting to follow the trend within contemporary Roman Catholic thought. They are obliged to adhere to Thomas' doctrine of a neutral Philosophy but they also feel the untenability of such a position, and grapple with the question of how they can retain the grace-nature scheme, and yet provide for a Christian Philosophy.
M.C. Smit for example, points out in his Doctor's thesis, *De verhouding van Christendom en Historie in de huidige Rooms-Katholieke Geschiedbeschouwing,* how along with some Roman Catholic thinkers (like E. Bréhier and P. Mandonnet) who emphasize the duality between Philosophy and faith, and the separation between the two, there are others (like E. Gilson and J. Maritain) who maintain the duality between the two, but at the same time tend to speak of an influence on Philosophy from the sphere of faith.
Cf. for E. Gilson's point of view inter alia *The Spirit of Mediaeval Philosophy.* Chapter I especially reveals his struggle to provide for a Christian Philosophy while retaining the nature-grace theme. In chapter II he gives his solution to the problem. Cf. especially his definition of Christian Philosophy on p. 37.
M. Blondel goes still further, and despite duality, nevertheless speaks of a close connection between Philosophy and faith (Theology). The Southern African Roman Catholic philosopher E.A. Ruch, points out in his paper The problem of Christian Philosophy with special reference to the doctrine of M. Blondel (delivered at the 6th Congress of the Society for the Advancement of Philosophy in South Africa at Potchefstroom in 1961 — also published in the *Bulletin of the Department of Philosophy of Cape Town,* no. 11:83-103 Aug. 1961) how Blondel creates a "Philosophy of inadequacy", an

If an attempt is therefore made to base a Christian Philosophy, Anthropology, Sociology etc. on Theology we should immediately be on our guard: this may betray a faulty nature-grace premise.

Dooyeweerd rightly says of this standpoint (namely that Philosophy in order to be Christian should be based on the dogmatic and exegetic approach of a specific Theology): "De fundamentele misvatting van de idee ener Christelijke wijsbegeerte is ontstaan uit een gemis aan inzicht in het innerlijke aanknopingspunt tussen het wijsgerige denken en de Christelijke religie"[14].

The point of view that Theology is really the only Christian science and that other sciences can only become Christian through some sort of contact with Theology, is still common among reformed thinkers[15]. Several sup-

"open Philosophy". That is a system which acknowledges the limitation of our mind, and opens it to supernatural reality (grace) in order to be Christian. (Cf. also S.U. Zuideman "De immanentie-methode van Maurice Blondel". *Philosophia Reformata*, 26:131-160, 1961.)

In his M.A. treatise, *Rooms-Katolisisme en die Wysbegeerte van die Wetsidee met besondere verwysing na die religieuse grondmotiewe*, J.H. Smit discusses various Roman Catholic thinkers who entered into dialogue with the Philosophy of the Cosmonic Idea. Although they also seek to construct a Christian Philosophy under the influence of the Amsterdam Philosophy, they could not dispense with their basic religious motive of nature and grace.

G.C. Berkouwer also points out in his article Identiteit of conflict. *Philosophia Reformata* 21:1-44,1956 that modern Roman Catholic thinking wishes to view the relationship between nature and grace as "organic" and no longer see it from a dualistic two-realm perspective. He points this out especially in Marlet (with reference to the latter's dissertation on the Amsterdam Philosophy of the Cosmonic Idea.) Marlet's standpoint is not an isolated standpoint. "This view of Marlet does not stand isolated but finds its counterpart in Söhngen, Hans Urs von Balthasar, Van Schoonenberg, who together have drawn attention to an interpretation of the Vatican Council in which nature is no longer isolated from grace, but affected by grace, since to their minds there was no consideration in the Vatican Council of and *abstract* theologia naturalis. It is true that they do not want to do away with the relation nature-grace, but they believe that this relation must be perfected through its reverse: grace-nature" (p. 34).

For the question of a Christian Philosophy in Roman Catholisism also compare the article of the Roman Catholic J. Jansen Het vraagstuk van de Christelijke Wijsbegeerte. *Philosophia Reformata* 17:16-51, 53-76, 1952.

Further it is interesting to note that modern Roman Catholics are not only concerned with the Christian character of Philosophy, but also (like Thomas) vice versa with the scientific aspect of Theology. If the relationship between nature and grace, knowledge and faith is seen as an antithesis a Christian Philosophy is as impossible as scientific Theology. There are therefore two reasons why the unity of faith and knowledge must be emphasized by Rome at all costs!

For Thomas' viewpoint regarding neutrality in the sphere of science compare further the M.A. treatise of P.J. Heiberg, *Die neutraliteitspostulaat in die teoretiese denke by Aristoteles en Thomas*.

14. Dooyeweerd. *Philosophia Reformata*, 25:102, 1960.

15. Cf. inter alia Diepenhorst. Christelijke wetenschap en Christelijke universiteit. *In:* De Christen-academicus en de wetenschap, footnote p. 74.

porters of the Amsterdam Philosophy (Philosophy of the Cosmonomic Idea) have rightly warned against this idea[16].

In this way the Christian quality of *all* sciences is made dependent on only *one* science. Every science should be examined in the bright light of the *Word of God* and not in the feeble light of some or other Theology which is the *word of man*. This does not imply, though, that specific theological insights cannot be relevant as scientific results also in the research of other disciplines: co-operation is not identical to foundation.

We especially realise that Theology cannot offer the foundation for other Christian sciences when we keep in mind that Theology is not *ipso facto* Christian. In the past this danger was not discerned clearly enough, as is borne out by history when more than once the struggle for a Christian

---

16. To illustrate cf. J.M. Spier: "De fout in de bovenstaande redenering, dat iemand, die — hetzij in of buiten het wetenschappelijk bedrijf — zich op de Schrift zou beroepen, daarmee aan de theologie is onderworpen, ligt hierin, dat men die actie van het zich beroepen op Gods Woord niet heeft onderkend als een *geloofsacte,* maar deze als een wetenschappelijke daad meent te moeten qualificeren.
Is het een geloofsacte — hetgeen wij stellig poneren — dan heeft de theologie hierbij niet de minste bevoegdheid, omdat zij geen wet des geloofs is". *Philosophia Reformata,* 16:13, 1951.
Elsewhere: "... deze bewering vergeet, dat het Schriftgeloof en het Schriftgebruik van de man van wetenschap een *directe* band aan Gods Woord onderstelt, die niet via de theologie gaat. Als een man van wetenschap zich op de Schrift beroept, doen hij dat op dezelfde wijze, waarop iemand, die nietwetenschappelijk bezig is, zich beroepen kan op de goddelijke Woordopenbaring. Dit zich beroepen op Gods Woord is alszodanig niet een wetenschappelijke, maar vóórwetenschappelijke daad, het is niet *logisch,* maar *pistisch* gequalificeerd. En de theo-*logie* is niet primair pistisch, maar logisch bezig zijn." Wijsbegeerte en vakwetenschap. *In:* Wijsbegeerte en levenspractijk, p. 232.
Spier also signals a warning about the danger of carrying this argument through to a logical conclusion: "Wie de theologie wil inschuiven tussen de wetenschappelijke onderzoeker en de Heilige Schrift, waarop deze zich heeft te beroepen en waar deze van uit moet gaan, die moet consequent ook de stelling aandurven, dat elk christen in al z'n doen en laten de theologie niet kan missen, zodat ieder, die een goed christen wil zijn, theologie moet gestudeerd hebben. Uit deze consequentie blijkt, dat hier een bepaalde vorm van wetenschapsverheerlijking in 't spel is." *Ibid.*
We support Spier in his struggle to maintain the reformed principle that the Scriptures are not a closed book to the "ordinary" believer, and thus are not clear only to theologians. Possibly Spier is too strong in his reaction here, and forgets that Theology — as we have said before — can assist the other sciences in listening to the Scriptures. A scientist who wants to appeal to Scripture in a scientific manner will not refuse this assistance.
Of course we do not mean to propagate another current idea, namely that the other sciences should adopt doctrines ("Lehnsätze") from Theology. This idea has its roots in Thomas' doctrine of Theology as *scientia subalterna* and is bound up with his effort to prove the scientific character of Theology.

science was narrowed down to a Christian theology[17].

A theological faculty as such — however important — does not make a university Christian. According to H. van Riessen this was the mistake made by the academy founded by Calvin in Geneva, namely that Theology was regarded as pre-eminent and that a Christian Philosophy (which Calvin also thought necessary) was never developed[18].

The University of Leyden made the same mistake. By giving Theology pre-eminence the ideal of a true reformed approach to science in general consequently also failed here[19].

After all that has been done since the thirties of our century in respect of Calvinistic Philosophy in the Netherlands, South Africa, Canada and elsewhere, it seems unnecessary here to deliver a plea for a Christian scientific endeavour[20] in general and Philosophy in particular. The work of scholars like D.H. Th. Vollenhoven, H. Dooyeweerd and H.G. Stoker — to limit ourselves to the founders — has in my opinion shown convincingly that the contradistinction made by Thomas, viz. "Christian Theology — neutral Philosophy" is not acceptable to thinkers who regard the Light of the Word of God seriously in the pursuit of their scientific studies.

1.3 Queen versus handmaiden

The special or exceptional character of Theology ultimately lies in the fact that it stands as queen in relation to Philosophy and the other sciences. Thomas' motivation for this is the following. Theology is *regina scientia-*

---

17. K.J. Popma comments as follows on this: "De mening, alsof er op het terrein van de theologie géén strijd zou zijn tussen het zaad van de vrouw en het slangezaad, heeft menigeen ertoe verleid, te denken dat men aan zijn wetenschappelijke Christenplicht reeds voldaan zou hebben, wanneer men er zich toe zette om met volle ijver en alle kracht de een of andere orthodox-Christelijke theologie te beoefenen. Het is merkwaardig dat deze, in zich zelf tegenstrijdige en op alle punten onrijpe opvatting van de Christelijke theologie niet alleen onder theologen, maar ook onder beoefenaars van andere faculteiten nog veelvuldig word aangetroffen. Zo lang hierin geen verandering komt, is geheel het Christelijke wetenschappelijk leven met lamheid en onvruchtbaarheid geslagen." *Levensbeschouwing* I, p. 20.

18. Cf. Van Riessen. *The University and its basis*, p. 37.

19. Cf. id., p. 37-39.

20. I have commented on this in two articles: "Wat is Christelike Wetenskap?" *Perspektief* 4(4):3-13 and 5(1):2-13, 1966 and "Wat is die verskil tussen 'n Christelike en nie-Christelike wetenskap?" *Bulletin van die Suid-Afrikaanse Vereniging vir Christelike Wetenskap* nr. 16, Nov. 1968:266-274.

rum because of its greater certainty, the greater worthiness of its field of research (God) and the fact that in Theology the highest purpose, namely eternal blessedness, is sought.

These three points of his motivation clearly reveal an over-estimation of Theology.

The argument as to the greater certainty of Theology does not hold water. We have already pointed out that theological statements do not possess the stability, certainty and trustworthiness of the Word (as field of research for Theology). The development of theological thought also shows how theological systems become obsolete and are followed by new ones. The authority of Theology is therefore only scientific by nature and does not have the authority of Revelation.

As regards the greater worthiness of the field of research, we would not denote God as the sole field of research for Theology. Thomas might, however, well do so in his conception according to which the boundary between Creator and creation fades because of the idea of a hierarchical, step by step upward progress. He could, for instance, speculate as to how precisely God "is made up". We are, however, of the opinion that man as creature is limited to creation in his assignment. Also in scientific activity any attempt to transcend the cosmic boundary is not permitted because the result then is no longer science but speculation.

In Theology, of course, it is permitted — with due timidity and reverence — to try and summarise what God himself has revealed to us regarding Himself in his Word.

The prime concern of Theology, viz. research into   God's Word and His church (as we have argued before), accordingly also puts Dogmatics to the task of systematising what God has revealed about Himself and His relation to His creation and His Church in particular. But this is no argument for kingship.

Even the fact that Theology studies the Word is no reason why Theology should exalt itself to kingship. As we listen to and investigate Holy Scripture it behoves us to do so with reverence and humility.

Thomas' third motivation, namely that in Theology the highest end and eternal blessedness is pursued, is also unacceptable. Apart from the fact that it must be seen against the background of his acceptance of an Aristotelian teleology, Theology is here assigned a soteriological task which it cannot fulfil.

Apart from ciritcism of the reasons given by Thomas for proclaiming Theology *regina*, it should also be mentioned that his ideas should be seen in conjunction with his two-realm doctrine where grace (as the higher) reigns over nature (as the lower) . Such thinking does not fit into radical biblical thinking, where the false two-tier doctrine is rejected.

Nevertheless, we still find this viewpoint of Thomas today — not only in Roman Catholic but also in Protestant thought. Not without humour H. van Riessen remarks concerning this idea of Theology as queen: "it is too easy a victory... The queen belongs to the sphere of the state and that of chess but not to the field of science"[21].

After the queen we must now pay attention to the "handmaiden". "Handmaiden" means that Philosophy, according to Thomas, must render service to Theology. This service means that considerable influence is exerted by Philosophy on theological work. Not just "formal" influence, but the "handmaiden" determines the content and direction of Thomas' Theology in a decisive manner.

The idea of Philosophy as *ancilla theologiae* is therefore deceptive and dangerous, as it creates the impression that Supernatural Theology is elevated above the influence of the handmaiden, while the handmaiden in actual fact holds the reins!

The further development of Western thought has also clearly revealed the character of the "handmaiden": Philosophy, which according to Thomas and in the Middle Ages was the handmaiden, during the Enlightenment became the deliverer, in the nineteenth century the mistress, and is at the moment a dangerous secularised neighbour, if not an enemy, against whom Theology should be on its guard.

Ultimately Theology does not use Philosophy, but a specific Philosophy uses Theology! Thomas is a clear example of this: He thought he had brought Aristotle into the service of Christianity, but actually it was a victory for Aristotle. Aristotle gradually became a Christian to him, and in the same way Thomas read the Scriptures more and more with Aristotelian-tinted spectacles!

As a result of our study of Thomas, but also as a result of what we learned from the whole of the history of Theology, we can even assume that Theology is always bound to philosophical *presupposita*. Nobody is able to fathom a theological vision and procedure in its essence, unless the philosophical presuppositions are recognised and brought into discussion.

This assumption could be substantiated by untold concrete examples (for which this is not the proper place) and also through the research of people who through the ages have detected the defining influence of Philosophy on Theology[22].

21. Van Riessen. *Christian perspectives 1962*, p. 90.

22. We content ourselves with two quotations to illustrate this point. J. Macquarrie says in his work *An Existentialist Theology*, p. 3: "Whether for good or ill, it is a fact that throughout its history Christian Theology has fallen at various times under the influence of different secular philosophies."

It should be stated to the credit of Thomas that he (and Thomistic thinking after him) in all honesty acknowledged that Theology could not operate
without a specific philosophy. It is strange that we cannot say this about
Protestant theological thinking as such. We find either a denial of any influence or such a limiting of the influence of Philosophy on Theology that
justice is not done to the real state of affairs.

It is for instance stated that Theology makes use of Philosophy only in
a formal manner[23]. H. Dooyeweerd rightly says about this: "It is a vain
illusion to imagine that the notions borrowed from... a philosophy could be
utilised by the Theologian in a purely formal sense"[24].

Theology cannot take Philosophy into service like a slave and (if it proves
embarrassing) send it away like Sarah did to Hagar!

Others prefer to limit the influence of philosophy to certain theological
disciplines. Some acknowledge for instance that Dogmatics cannot be dis-
engaged from philosophical influence,   because it has to make use of
concepts with a strong philosophical connotation (like "nature", "being",
"person", "substance" etc.) For this reason, at present, Dogmatics is often
regarded with suspicion. Exegesis, however, is said to have the task of

A. Szekeres mentions some examples: "Om de christelijke Apologeten te kunnen verstaan is het nodig de griekse filosofie te kennen. Zonder Plato en het Neo-Platonisme is
Augustinus en zonder Aristoteles is Thomas van Aquino niet te begrijpen. Hoe wil men
zonder de kennis van de Renaissance en het Humanisme, zonder Descartes, Spinoza,
Leibniz en de Engelse empiristen de verschillende theologische concepties van deze perioden kunnen verstaan? Hij, aan wie de naam Kant of Hegel niets zegt, zal ook niet
veel zakelijks kunnen vertellen over de theologie in de XIXe eeuw. De bestudering van
Kierkegaard is de eerste vereiste om de problematiek van de dialektische theologie aan
te kunnen voelen. ,Barth zal men zeer moeilijk kunnen lezen zonder grondige wijsgerige studie. Voor het verstaan van Bultmann is het nodig om Heidegger te kennen en
men zal Brunner gemakkelijk kunnen lezen, als men op de hoogte is van de Marburgse
resp. van de moderne Ik-Gijk-filosofie". *Theologie en Wijsbegeerte*, p. 6, 7.

23. It appears that C.A. van Peursen also holds this view, which is frequently found.
He does acknowledge that Theology is fallible human work, and that it makes use of
specific forms and categories of thought, current at a specific time or in a specific culture. However, Philosophy apparently only has the function of warning Theology
against the wrong thought patterns, and of supplying the newest and the best philosophical tools for Theology (*Christelijke Encyclopedie* VI, p. 623). For this reason he
also says that Theology needs no philosophical foundation. (Id., p. 623). We find the
same ideas in his work *Filosofische Oriëntatie* in which he says among other things:
"De theologie moet de wijsbegeerte kennen, niet om er iets van over te nemen, maar
om zichzelf te leren kennen". (p. 134). Philosophy, therefore, has to assist Theology
formally with categories of thought, and for the rest see to it that Philosophy keeps
out of Theology! His words: "In ieder theologisch stelsel waart het spook der wijsbegeerte, als een vermeend gestorvene rond" (p. 134) must be understood correctly. He
condemns the fact that Philosophy has not only rendered formal service to Theology
but has also influenced it materially.!

24. Dooyeweed. *In the twilight of western thought*, p. 154. Cf. also Zuidema. *Philosophia Reformata*, 26:179, 1961.

listening to Scripture without prejudice. For this reason Exegesis should be the major subject in Theology — because it is "neutral" and the most closely related to Scripture.

C. Veenhof, however, exposes the pretensions of many exegetes that they could take a completely "blank" attitude towards Holy Scripture: "Vele predikanten zeggen b.v. dat ze zich niet met 'de philosophie' bemoeien. Ze werpen zich op 'de eenvoudige verklaring der Heilige Schrift' zonder meer. En, zeer naïef, meenen ze in oprechten gemoede, dat zich tusschen hen en de Heilige Schrift geen enkele wijsgerige constructie, geen enkel philosophisch schema of vooroordeel bevindt. Neen, ze bemoeien zich niet met 'de philosophie' — het is alleen maar jammer, dat 'de philosophie' zich zoo grondig met hen heeft bemoeid en hen stevig in haar greep houdt"[25].

History clearly reveals that the different "Christian" theologies have themselves invited non-christian philosophies into their midst. In so doing, however, they have allowed the Trojan horse within their walls. Often later theologians have realised this and desired to rectify the matter. But through their wrong actions the position was not improved: the one philosophy which had become unacceptable was cast out by another non-christian philosophy!

M.J. Arntzen says of certain modern Reformed theologians' reaction against Scholasticism that they run away from Aristotle only to fall into the hands of a much greater enemy of the Gospel. It reminds one of the man described in Amos 5:19: he fled from a lion, but went into his house and a serpent bit him![26].

Some modern Dutch and German theologians are very critical towards the philosophical background of the older theologians, but very tolerant towards various modern philosophers.

H. Dooyeweerd also points out the danger of attempting to cast out the devil by Beelzebul. In his opinion it is inconceivable that so many modern theologians claim that present Existentialism is more Scriptural than Aris-

---

25. Veenhof, *In Kuyper's lijn*, p. 12. F.H. von Meyenfeld also points to the error of the supporters of an unprejudiced exegesis: "De exegeten dachten dat ze aan geen enkel stelsel gebonden waren: ze bemoeiden zich er dan ook niet mee. Maar o wee, hun eigen opleiding aan de Universiteit had hen toch enig philosophisch venijn ingespoten! Met dit gevolg, dat ze wel degelijk philosophisch bepaald waren, echter vanwege hun niet meeleven, was hun wijsgerig colbert twee modes ten achter, zijnde een aflegger uit hun studentetijd!" *In*: Wetenschappelijke bijdragen door leerlingen van dr. D.H. Th. Vollenhoven, p. 55.

26. Cf. Arntzen. *De crisis der Gereformeerde kerken*, p. 22.

totelian Thomism[27].

Another remarkable fact is that the Philosophy with which Christian Theology operates, is very often archaic. Reformed Theology is inclined to be conservative. Several studies have revealed how the rationalism of Descartes was opposed by Voetius with the aid of Scholastic Philosophy. Naturally this conservative approach is easier, as such a Philosophy has already passed the "Sturm und Drang" period, is established and therefore more acceptable, while all the criticism is aimed at the latest vogue in Philosophy.

It is needless to point out that the wide contact and close interaction between Christian Theology with non-Christian Philosophies through the ages has been a hindrance to the progress of the Gospel.

We have to be careful, of course, not to attribute all error in Christian Theology to the corruption caused by Philosophy. Theology is not inherently pure, and Philosophy is not the source of all heresy. Such a viewpoint again betrays the Thomistic view of the relationship between Christian Theology and (Pagan) Philosophy[28].

Our conclusion regarding the relationship between Theology and Philosophy is given succinctly by Dooyeweerd in the following words: "Het dilemma voor de theologie is niet of ze al of niet wijsgerig gefundeerd moet zijn, maar of ze haar wijsgerige grondslagen in een Schriftuurlijke, dan wel in een onschriftuurlijke philosophie zal zoeken. Want zij *kan* als wetenschap niet zonder wijsgerige grondslagen bestaan"[29].

What has been said in the previous pages might create the impression that deep down in my own mind the thought prevails that some or other science has to rule over the rest. It might seem as if the writer of this article just reverses the roles: it is not Theology that rules over Philosophy, but Philosophy over Theology[30]. This, however, is not the case. We have only shown what the actual situation is, namely that Theology is decidedly determined by Philosophy.

27. Cf. Dooyeweerd, op. cit., p. 155. Cf. ook H. van der Laan, *Spanningen in de Gereformeerde kerken*, p. 46.

28. Cf. Du Plessis. *Bulletin van die Suid-Afrikaanse Vereniging vir Christelike Wetenskap*, Aug. 1966, p. 121.

29. Dooyeweerd. *Philosophia Reformata*, 23:61, 1958. Cf. also his *In the twilight of western thought*, p. 157.

30. It may also create the impression as if, in this writer's view, it is now no longer Theology which gives a Christian character to Philosophy, but Philosophy to Theology. This is not the intention by any means. The fact remains though, that seen encyclopedically, Philosophy fulfils a foundational function.

What holds good for Theology, holds good for all other sciences: "Het denken op enigerlei vakgebied kan zich wel van alle wijsbegeerte ontslagen achten, deze wijsbegeerte is niettemin overal direct aanwezig. De verbinding, welke de denker opneemt met de grond der dingen, òf zijn ontkenning dienaangaande, plaatst hem en ons midden in de *wijsbegeerte.*

"Of de mens wijsgerig wil denken dan wel zich van alle filosofie ontslagen acht, het is met wijsbegeerte dat zijn denken begint en eindigt"[31].

One can proceed consciously from a specific Philosophy or (which is mostly the case) a Philosophy can be brought into operation unconsciously. It can be a specific Philosophy, or a conglomerate of philosophies as a result of an eclectic method.

A.N. Whitehead made the telling statement that anyone who thinks he does not make use of any Philosophy in his scientific work hands himself over to a chance Philosophy[32].

The actual situation mentioned above is closely bound up with the nature of Philosophy. Our outlook on life is concerned with the pre-scientific totality vision of reality which we have. This view of life and the world also determines our view of each part or aspect of life. In the field of science, Philosophy is concerned with reality as a whole (cohesive diversity). Philosophy will therefore also be a determining factor in the different sciences, which only study aspects of the whole. The different sciences firstly study the *diversity.* They should, however, not be content with that. They must secondly also pay attention to the *cohesiveness* of the diversity. It is precisely in this respect that the sciences are determined by Philosophy, which directs its attention to the mutual cohesiveness in the rich diversity of the creation of God[33].

If we further consider that Philosophy above all busies itself scientifically with the pre-scientific view of life, and that this view of life also has a determining influence on our scientific study, it becomes clear why Philosophy has such great influence on Theology and other sciences.

It is very important in the further development of a really reformed Theology to notice and not to ignore this nature and intrinsic character of

31. Mekkes. *Scheppingsopenbaring en Wijsbegeerte,* p. 52.

32. Cf. Van Riessen. *Mens en werk,* p. 118.

33. J.P.A. Mekkes puts it this way: "In elk (vak)wetenschap, die een bepaald aspect of enkele aspecten van het bestaande als eigen theoretisch veld betreedt, doet zich dus wijsbegeerte gelden, want men kan een aspect niet geordend bestuderen indien men zich er geen rekenschap van geeft wat het als 'aspect' van het geheel, temidden van den samenhang van alle aspecten, beteekent, welke rol het daar speelt, welke invloeden het vandaar ondergaat en daarop uitoefent". De wijsgerige vraag over de Theologie. *Bulletin van die Suid-Afrikaanse Vereniging vir Christelike Wetenskap,* nr. 19, June 1969, p. 6.

Philosophy. It is inconceivable that the majority of Theologies have beeen unable to see their relationship with Philosophy clearly, while today, more than ever, they reveal their dependence on Philosophy[34].

While there is great diversity in creation, it is also intimately cohesive. If the sciences studying this creation in its diversity will stand together, this can be of great value in our endeavour to achieve a united Christian approach in science[35].

In spite of the fact that Thomas Aquinas attempted to achieve harmonious co-existence for Theology and Philosophy with the aid of his two-realm doctrine, he did not succeed in excluding tension between Theology and Philosophy. In the second main section of this article light is shed on Natural Theology in this tension between Supernatural Theology and Philosophy.

2. THOMAS' NATURAL THEOLOGY AS A DISCIPLINE BETWEEN SUPERNATURAL THEOLOGY AND PHILOSOPHY

2.1 Actuality

Thomas is undoubtedly the architect of Natural Theology. The idea existed before him, and the specific title *theologia naturalis* followed later (by Raymundus of Sabunde, died 1432) but the honour of being called the father of Natural Theology is Thomas'.

The greater part of the *Summa Contra Gentiles* (3 of the 4 books) is of the nature of a Natural Theology. Further, we are confronted in the *Summa Contra Gentiles* not with *a* but with *the* Natural Theology of the Middle

---

34. K. Runia mentions in an article "Some features of contemporary liberal Theology" *International Reformed Bulletin* 9(24/25) 1-2, 1966, where he deals with the most important features of contemporary Theology, that one of the features is the fact that current Theology more clearly than ever has a Philosophical foundation. He goes so far as to speak of the *dependence* of modern Theology on fashionable philosophies: "A second rather common feature is the *dependence on some philosophical system or method*. On purpose we use the term 'dependence' and not, for example, 'interaction'. The latter would be too weak as an indication of the relationship between these modern theologians and philosophy. The philosophical system or method is for them not a subordinate auxiliary used for the clarification of certain concepts, but it constitutes an integral and material part of their theology" (p. 3, 4). (Cf. also his contribu tion Calvinism and present day theological tendencies. *In:* Die atoomeeu – "in U lig", p. 67).

35. In view of the subject of this article, we are here only concerned with the relationship between Theology and Philosophy, and our plea is for the co-operation and mutual assistance of these sciences. This however applies to *all* sciences, that there should be support for each another in their common service in the kingdom of God.

Ages. C.J.J. Webb calls the *Summa Contra Gentiles* "... the central work of the Middle Ages on Natural Theology". In the light of the subsequent history of the development of Natural Theology, we may say, without the danger of exaggeration, that the *Summa Contra Gentiles* may be called the prototype of all Natural Theology. This applies not only to Roman Catholic but also to Protestant thinking[36].

After A. Kuyper, who still cautiously made use of it, there follows a period during which Natural Theology was apparently forgotten in Reformed circles. This was not the case outside these circles. We need only refer to the great polemic in Lutheran circles in Germany (beginning with K. Barth and E. Brunner) from the thirties onward. Natural Theology is no dead species, and reflection on it therefore no fossil study. K. Runia, for instance, states that the renewed interest in Natural Theology is one of the most important characteristics of contemporary Theology[37].

Therefore, just as our confrontation with his Super-natural Theology was of contemporary significance, so also is our discussion of Aquinas' Natural Theology. In any case it is a good starting point, as it was he who first gave form to this very interesting science, and made a clear distinction between it and Supernatural Theology.

2.2 Decisive role of an apologetic aim

The birth-place of Natural Theology should be sought centuries before

36. O. Zöckler says in his *Geschichte der Apologie des Christentums*, p. 223, 224: "Die Summe wider die Heiden ist das klassische Hauptzeugnis der abendländlisch-apologetischen Lehrtätigkeit aus ihrer scholastischen Epoche. Der tiefgreifende und nachhaltige Eirfluss, den sie als Vorbild für spätere Apologien geübt hat, ist nicht auf das Mittelalter beschränkt geblieben. Auch die protestantische Orthodoxie beider Reformationskirchen, der lutherischen wie der reformierten, hat da, wo sie das kirchliche System unter apologetischem Gesichtpunkte zur Darstellung brachte, dem thomistischen Lehrverfahren in der *Summa contra gentiles* mehr oder weniger bewusste Nachfolge geleistet. Namentlich in der Unterscheidung zwischen den natürlichen, der Vernunft zugänglichen, und den übernatürlichen, der Vernunft überragenden Wahrheiten stehen auch die protestantischen Dogmatiker und Apologeten des 16. bis 18. Jahrhunderts mehr oder weniger alle als Nachahmer des Aquinaten da. Dies selbstverständlich nicht ohne dass bei ihnen die evangelische Lehr- und Erkenntnisgrundlage das Hervortreten mancher wichtiger Abweichungen von dem mittelalterlichen Vorbild bewirkte."

37. Cf. article by Runia quoted under footnote 34. Obviously Natural Theology has changed its complexion, and is not precisely the same since Thomas. Runia says of the newer types: "The new attempts may be critical of the older deistic form of natural theology, which assumed that God can be discovered like a fact of nature. The new liberals virtually all maintain that knowledge of God is possible only when He himself *gives* knowledge of Himself. Yet they do agree with the older natural theology that the knowledge of God may not be narrowed to the biblical or Christian revelation. *John Macquarrie*, for instance, says that the traditional natural theology 'was correct and justified in claiming a wider and indeed universal possibility for knowing God'." Calvinism and present day theological tendencies. *In*: Die atoomeeu — "in U lig", p. 65.

Thomas. She carries on her forehead a mark of Greek origin. It is so deeply ingrained that it will not wear off — no matter how wrinkled the forehead. Even this early Natural Theology (or what was later to become Natural Theology) already had an apologetic tendency. The Christian Apologists as it were, officiated at the birth of Natural Theology, and here the apologetic tendency shows even more clearly.

We find the same in the *Summa Contra Gentiles* as Thomas expounds his Natural Theology. The inducement to write the *Summa Contra Gentiles* was a request from missionaries confronted by Islam to a philosopher (Thomas) to write a (philosophical) work by means of which Islam could be convinced of the truth of the Christian *faith* by *reasonable* arguments. The *Summa Contra Gentiles* is therefore clearly an apologetic work, and according to M. Grabmann, an eminent authority on the Middle Ages "... das bedeutendste apologetische Werk der Scholastik"[38].

Natural Theology continues to show this apologetic trait also in its later history[39]. This also applies to Natural Theology within Protestant Orthodoxy of the seventeenth and eighteenth centuries[40].

The apologetic motive is the motivation behind Natural Theology. In addition to this there is still a further consideration.

2.3 Two-realm doctrine essential

An apologetic aim need not necessarily result in Natural Theology. An Apologetics which is not of the nature of Natural Theology is possible. History proves, however, that it is mostly the case that an apologetic aim gives rise to Natural Theology, when the method of approach is a two-realm doctrine.

The reason for this is obvious. Christianity, which is limited to the sphere of grace, must be brought into contact with heathendom, which is limited to the sphere of knowledge as reason belongs to the Christian and the heathen jointly. The ultimate purpose is not, however, to remain in this communal sphere, because the heathen must be elevated to a position of

---

38. Grabmann: Augustins Lehre von Glauben und Wissen. *In:* Aurelius Augustinus. Die Festschrift der Görres-Gesellschaft zum 1500. Todestage des Heiligen Augustinus (Köln, J.P. Bachem, G.M.B.H., 1930), p. 97. Cf. also the statement of O. Zöckler in footnote 36 above.

39. Cf. inter alia A. Lang. *Die Entfaltung des apologetischen Problems in der Scholastik des Mittelalters.*

40. Cf. P. Swagerman. *Ratio en Revelatio: Een theologisch critisch onderzoek naar het Godsbewijs en de Godsleer uit de menslijke ratio en de verhouding van de natuurlijke theologie tot de geopenbaarde theologie bij enige Nederlandsche hoogleraren in de theologie of in de filosofie van 1650 tot 1750,* p. 189.

faith.

That there is a "point of contact" is closely bound up with Thomas' view of nature as basically good except for something (faith) which was lost at the Fall (and which through redemption can be received back as a *donum superadditum*). Through the aid of reason heathendom can also progress considerably so that only in the end does God intervene by granting faith in His Revelation[41].

In addition to this there is Thomas' doctrine of the natural desire *(desiderium naturale)* of man (including the unbeliever) for the supernatural (God)[42], which again is bound up with his view of a hierarchical structure in creation. An important question here is how the *homo naturalis* (being purely natural) is to arrive at a supernatural idea, namely this perfecting through grace. Indeed, Aristotle did not arrive at this opinion! The *desirium naturale* is therefore not as natural as Thomas maintains — it already contains a spark of the supernatural.

2.4 No real proofs offered

It appears that Thomas' Natural Theology is not purely natural either. We may illustrate this from his proofs of God's existence which lie at the heart of his Natural Theology. He maintains that he can conclude from creation that God exists, when actually he already believed in God. H. Dooyeweerd noticed this when he said, it is suggested in Natural Theology that theoretical thinking in purely scientific argument ascends towards an idea of the Origin — while from the outset the latter is accepted[43]. Thomas' Natural theoretical must therefore be typified as a dogmatic pseudo science. Not because it is determined by religious preconceptions, but because it proclaims religious presuppositions to be purely theoretical axioms, and actually does nothing more than explain its a prioristic idea of the

---

41. It is important to remember that Thomas' Natural Theology — unlike reformed orthodoxy of a later period — was not based on a so-called "general revelation". With him revelation is allowable only in the sphere of grace.

42. Cf. inter alia P.B. Bastable: *Desire for God. Does man aspire naturally to the beatific vision? An analysis of this question and its history* (1947); J.B.J. Meijer: *De eerste levensvraag in het intellektualisme van St. Thomas van Aquino en het integraal-realisme van Maurice Blondel* (1940) en J.E. O'Mahony: *The desire for God in the philosophy of St. Thomas Aquinas* (1929).

43. Cf. Dooyeweerd *Philosophia Reformata,* 17:167, 1952.

Origin by means of logical "proofs"[44].

Proof is even offered for the negative: people who believe that God does not exist, succeed in proving His non-existence from creation too. We find such anti-god proofs (or negative theologies) as far back as the pre-Platonic thinkers — and their arguments are no less logical and convincing! As the bee and the poisonous insect, while drinking the same nectar, produce honey in the one case, and poison in the other, so it seems possible, proceeding from the same creation, to either prove the existence of God or to deny it. This engenders doubt about the legitimate character of Thomas' so-called "proofs" of God.

Thomas possibly forgets — understandably so, as a result of his two-realm doctrine — that acceptance of the existence of God is not a rational matter. From my point of view man will never succeed in proving from creation by way of reason that God exists or that he does not exist. It is just as fruitless as trying to prove through all sorts of arguments that the Bible is the Word of God[45].

For those who honour the radical difference between Creator and creation, such "proofs" are not possible. We express our unqualified agreement with the words of G.E. Meuleman: "... wie al redenerend van gevolg naar oorzaak nadenkt over de samenhang der dingen kan nooit de grenzen overschrijden van de geschapen werkelijkheid, waarvan hij in zijn bewijsvoering uitging".

"In de oorzaak moet dan immers steeds weer iets liggen van het gevolg, waarbij men de redenering aanving. Een stap naar iets absoluut anders kan men niet doen, juist krachtens de aard der redenering. Gevolg en oorzaak moeten daarin steeds iets gemeenschappelijks hebben, moeten zich op de een of andere wijze 'onder één noemer' laten brengen. Als dat gemeenschappelijke moment fungeert in de R.K. natuurlijke theologie het 'zijn', dat niet alleen God eigen is, maar waarin ook het schepsel deelt. Wie echter op deze

---

44. Cf. Id., p. 180. P. Swageren (op. cit., p. 212, 213) offers the same criticism against the Natural Theology of Protestant Orthodoxy, in the form of a striking example: "De conclusie is onontkoombaar, dat de auteurs als kenners van de bijzondere openbaring hier bewust naar Bijbelse noties of posita uit de christelijke dogmatiek toewerken en met alle reverentie voor de 'goede' bedoelingen van hun opzet worden we gedrongen hen, mede door de zelfverzekerdheid van hun betoogtrant en door de indruk, die zij (willen) wekken, dat hun conclusies met een vanzelfsprekende 'gladheid' getrokken worden, te vergelijken met goochelaars, die met een zekere triomfantelijkheid een konijn uit een hoge hoed toveren, waarvan zij weten, dat ze het er eerst ingestopt hebben."

45. In an article How do we know that the Bible is the Word of God? Bulletin van die Suid-Afrikaanse Vereniging vir Christelike Wetenskap no. 15, Sept. 1968:215-224 we offered some remarks on this. It was no doubt exaggerated in certain areas — as H.G. Stoker pointed out in the following issue of the same paper — but it did reveal some of the problems involved.

wijze redeneert kan er niet aan ontkomen, óf het geschapene enigermate te vergoddelijken, óf God iets creatuurlijks toe te kennen"[46].

2.5 Without meaning for Salvation

It is hardly necessary to point out that knowledge of God, outside of Christ, according to Holy Scripture, is not possible. Nobody comes to the Father but through Him, and whoever has seen Him has seen the Father[47].

It is remarkable that rational argumentation in order to persuade to belief was regarded of such importance in the time of Aquinas. Such arguments may, of course, be of some assistance (e.g. in the removal of misapprehensions about Christianity) to pave the way towards a better comprehension about Christian faith. The approach should, however, not be overemphasised: it may occur that the heathen who is able to see through the weakness of some of the arguments, will rather be driven away from God! The final decision in these matters is taken on a deep religious level and not solely on rational considerations. Thomas must have realized this, because his Natural Theology, according to him, only has *some* significance for the sinner and is therefore supplemented by his Supernatural Theology.

A serious problem, however, is that with his two theologies Thomas creates two ideas about God, which are not reconcilable. On closer inspection it becomes clear that there is also a dualism in God himself[48].

2.6 No need for a Natural Theology in a radically Christian science

Thomas' Natural Theology is indissolubly connected with his two-realm doctrine. It follows naturally that it also shares in the tension which exists between the two.

Stimulated by apologetic motives, his Supernatural Theology seeks a

---

46. Meuleman. *De Encycliek "Humani Generis"*, p. 35. Meuleman adds on the following page: "De grondfout van de R.K. 'natuurlijke theologie' is dus deze dat ze de afstand tussen Schepper en schepsel niet tot zijn recht doet komen. De relatie van de mens tot God is in haar aard een *religieuze* en niet een *zijns*relatie. God wordt aan de mens alleen bekend, wanneer deze Gods openbaring in het geloof aanvaardt. De R.K. 'natuurlijke theologie' miskent, dat Paulus in Rom. 1 spreekt van kennis, die het resultaat is van Goddelijke *openbaring*, die als zodanig een *religieus* karakter draagt en alleen dus kan worden aanvaardt door een instemming van religieus karakter. De mens kan niet door redenering opklimmen tot God."

47. Cf. Berkouwer. *De algemene Openbaring*, p. 58.

48. Cf. Proposition IV in a dissertation by M.C. Smit: *De verhouding van Christendom en historie in de huidige Rooms-Katolieke geschiedbeschouwing*: "Het Rooms-Katholieke thema van natuur en genade impliceert een dualisme tussen het natuurlijke en het bovennatuurlijke in de leer omtrent God."

platform from which her persuasive voice can be heard in the profane sphere of nature. Philosophic or Natural Theology was born out of this urge. Actually a miracle takes place here: the queen drops the draw-bridge from her castle across the deep moat separating her from nature. In this manner a science is created out of and between two opposing sciences.

As the tension is greatest in the stone at the apex where the two pillars of a trimphal arch meet, so the tension is most observable in Natural Theology which has to act as the apex of Supernatural Theology and Philosophy. In Natural Theology, Supernatural Theology has to use the language of the pagan or unbeliever in order to persuade him rationally about the truth of the Bible. Supernatural truths have to be translated into natural language. There is the risk that the true meaning is lost in this translation. Supernatural Theology is faced with the impossible choice of either keeping quiet (and continuing in a supernatural "secret language" which the natural man does not grasp) or of translating the "message" at the risk of the message not getting through because translation gives it a new shade of meaning, or blurs its meaning completely.

So, it not only once again becomes clear how Natural Theology derives its existence from a dialectic tension between two poles of the false two-realm doctrine and is therefore unacceptable, but it also appears that we cannot be content with criticism of Natural Theology alone, while favouring Supernatural Theology — as is unfortunately often the case.

The fact that we do not find Thomas' Natural Theology acceptable within Christian philosophy, neither — in reaction to it — a Supernatural Theology, does not mean that we are blind to the problems involved. The problems on which this false solution, as I see it, is based, do exist and are not imaginary. We have great admiration that the *doctor angelicus* grappled with these difficulties in great earnestness.

11 MAN, THE TENSION-RIDDEN BRIDGE BETWEEN THE TRANSCENDENT AND THE NON-TRANSCENDENT WORLD IN THE THOUGHT OF BONAVENTURE OF BAGNOREA*

> "Why is its history a necessary introduction to philosophy? Because philosophy is actually a continuous chain of philosophers who have conducted in the West, for twenty-five centuries, a sort of conversation on the ultimate problems the human mind can ask... And what better way is there to learn to philosophize than to observe the great philosophers of the past?"
>
> Gilson: *Introduction to Medieval Philosophy.*

1. INTRODUCTION

Seven centuries have passed since the death of Thomas Aquinas and Bonaventure, and we are privileged to commemorate this year, by way of international congresses[1] and various publications[2], these twin peaks of Medieval thought.

Sextus V likened them to two olive trees and two candlesticks giving light in the house of God. It was by the divine providence of God that they emerged simultaneously in the 13th century as two stars from two of the most famous orders[3]. The *doctor angelicus* and the *doctor seraphicus* not only represent the epitome of Scholasticism, but also rank amongst the giants of the entire history of Western thought.

I am opposed to the delineation of Medieval Philosophy in general, and the thought of Aquinas and Bonaventure in particular, as intellectual ob-

---

* Paper written for the International Congress held at the Seventh Century Commemotation of the death of Bonaventure, Sept. 19-26, 1974. Previously published in *Philosophia Reformata*, 39:156-169, 1974.

1. The Seventh Centenary of St. Thomas Aquinas International Congress at Rome and Naples from April 17-24, 1974 and the Seventh Centenary of St. Bonaventure of Bagnorea International Congress at Rome from September 19-26, 1974.

2. Cf. in the case of St. Bonaventure the Centenary Volume *S. Bonaventura* (1274-1974) in 5 parts of the Quaracchi editors by order of the Collegio S. Bonaventura. It contains contributions in the principal European languages. The first part is devoted to the iconography of Bonaventure, three parts to his life, work and teachings, whilst the fifth part consists of a complete bibliography with elaborate indices and tables.

3. "Hi enim sunt olivae et duo candelabra (Apoc. XI, 4) in domo Dei luculentia, qui et caritatis pinguedine et scientiae luce totam ecclesiam collustrant; hi singulari Dei providentia eodem tempore tamquam duae stellae exorientes ex duabus clarissimis regularium Ordinum familiis prodierunt, quae sanctae Ecclesiae ad catholicam religionem propugnandam maxime utiles et ad omnes labores et pericula pro orthodoxa fide subeunda paratae semper existunt..." ex Bulla Triumphantis Jerusalem, par. 13, *Opera Omnia S. Bonaventurae*, ed. Ad Claras Aquas I (1882), p, L.

scurantism, because their thinking took place so many centuries ago. Their philosophizings form an integral part of the history of European philosophy and therefore merit close scrutiny. Amongst their contemporaries they were men of outstanding ability, and they have enriched us in a most significant and powerful way. I find it quite impossible to accept even the suggestion that the intense theological-philosophical thought of two such great men produced nothing worth while.

At the other end of the scale, however, I cannot agree with those people who consider that nothing of value has been said since Aquinas and Bonaventure. To my knowledge neither of them ever claimed their thought to be the last word, and the final truth, and in this essay, therefore, I shall try to avoid the danger of either overrating or underrating the work of Bonaventure. Because far less acumen is required to refute a philosophy than to understand it, I shall first give a brief exposition of Bonaventure's philosophical conception.

2. REFLECTION ON MAN

Three themes control the history of Western thought: God, man and the world. Of these three, man occupies a central place. The question then arises: Who or what is man and what is his relation and orientation towards God, and towards the world? We shall see that in the case of the *doctor seraphicus*, man actually functions as the link between God (the transcendent) and the world (non-transcendent). This is also the reason for man's ambivalent existence, as will be indicated in this paper.

My aim is not to paint an extensive and comprehensive picture of Bonaventure's ideas in this respect; I would require a far larger canvas than I have at my disposal to accomplish that. A brief survey, followed by my own critical appraisal, might be more stimulating for a selected panel of Bonaventure specialists.

Bonaventure — theologian, philosopher, mystic, preacher, and leader of the Franciscan order — rendered us a great service in dealing with such a crucial issue, and his writings warrant careful study to enable us to reach a biblically more correct viewpoint about man. Such a stimulating confronta-

---

4. I have mainly consulted two of his most important works viz. his *Commentarius in quatuor libros sententiarum cum textu authentico ipsius Petri Lombardi.* (Tomi I-IV in the 10 volume critical edition of the Franciscans of the Collegium S. Bonaventura at Quarrachi edited between 1882 and 1902) and his *Intinerarium mentis in Deum* (Tomus V, p. 293-316 of the above mentioned Quarrachi edition). An English translation of the *Intinerarium* under the title *The mind's road to God* by G. Boas (Bobbs Merrill publishers of New York) is available. For other translations (also of the *Commentary on the Sentences*) see A.A. Maurer: *Mediaeval philosophy*, (1962), p. 401.

tion with the *doctor seraphicus* will, to my mind, be a fitting way to commemorate the centenary of this coryphee of the golden age of Scholastic thought.

3. SYNTHETIC THINKING

From the outset we should bear in mind that Bonaventure was a synthetic thinker. By way of the doctrine of nature and grace (supernature) he achieved a compromise between the Bible and Greek philosophy. The synthetic way of thinking characterized the entire patristic and medieval period. This compromise between pagan and biblical ideas became possible for Bonaventure because he distinguished between four meanings of the biblical text: the *sensus litteralis, allegoriae, topologiae et anagogiae*[5]) and accordingly applied two principles in his exegesis of the Bible. According to the *sensus litteralis* we should accept the literal meaning of the Word of God. But according to the three other senses the real meaning of the biblical text differs from its literal sense.

Allegory is a metaphorical figure of speech — a means of speaking otherwise than one seems to speak — and as such, enriches our means of expression. The fault with the allegorical interpretation of Bonaventure, however, is that the text of the Bible, which was never so intended, is assumed to be an allegory. The obvious meaning of the Bible is regarded as inadequate, even inferior and offensive, and the literal text is regarded merely as a bridge or reference to the real, deeper meaning. This constitutes a serious injustice to the Bible.

It is clear, however, why Bonaventure rejected the obvious meaning of the Bible as being far too inadequate to be conclusive: allegorical exegesis provided him with the instrument by means of which the Bible could be consulted (eisegesis) and then interpreted (exegesis) according to his own judgement, viz. the foreign pagan philosophical ideas which he had inherited from his predecessors.

It is not merely a matter of expressing the religious truths of Christianity in Greek philosophical language. By means of allegorical exegesis a text can be forced to say on the one hand what it does not intend and on the other not to say what it actually means. Thus this procedure results in removing the biblical text from the lay reader, passing it on to the theological expert. As only interpreters of considerable acumen are able to supply the so-called "real" meaning, any further check on the truth of the supposed "deeper

---

5. This distinction used by Bonaventure is not something new he invented. Cf. De Lubac, H.: *Exégèse Médiévale. Les quatre sens de L'écriture*, 4 vols. (1959-1964).

meaning" of the theological interpretation is prohibited[6].

According to Bonaventure, one should as a Christian thinker, neither totally avoid Greek philosophy nor strive towards complete conformity but rather towards a compromise or adaptation. The Bible should not be permitted to be submerged into pagan thought, but it should also not be permitted to escape from it. By using Tertullian's metaphor of Jerusalem, i.e. the biblical truth, and Athens, i.e. Ancient philosophy, we may say that, according to Bonaventure, Jerusalem is neither identical with nor opposed to Athens, but as the superior to the inferior realm, it surpasses Athens. The relationship between pagan philosophy and Christian thought is considered to be that of the threshold to the sanctuary. The higher sphere (grace) supersedes or crowns the lower (nature). Nature is a necessary preparation for grace, and conversely grace does not abolish nature, but perfects it — without radically reforming it.

According to the two-realm theory of nature and grace, Bonaventure also appreciated the task which confronted the fields of philosophy and theology. From this division between philosophy (sphere of nature) and theology (the supernatural sphere) we should not conclude that Bonaventure's theology — he was first and foremost a theologian[7] — was not influenced by pagan philosophy. As is the case with any theologial system, his had a definite philosophical background or basis which clearly revealed the influence of both biblical and non-biblical ideas. It is exactly these unscriptural ideas which caused difficulty in his concept of man and on which we shall therefore now focus our attention.

4. TRANSCENDENTAL AND NON-TRANSCENDENTAL WORLDS

Bonaventure's most basic assumption is that of two worlds: a transcendent and a non-transcendent. The transcendent world includes God, the angels and the human soul, while the non-transcendent world consists of the animal-somatic-psychical nature, the *vegetabilia, mineralia, natura caelistis* and *natura elementaris*.

God, as one of the most important parts of the transcendent world, is the

---

6. For further details about and critique on allegorical exegesis amongst Greek, Jewish, Arabian and Christian thinkers cf. my articles: "Eisegesis exegesis, paradox and nature-grace: methods of synthesis in Mediaeval philosophy". *Philosophia Reformata,* vol. 38, p. 191-210, 1973.

7. Cf. Maurer, A.A.: *Medieval Philosophy* (1962), 138; Gilson, E.: *History of Christian philosophy in the Middle Ages* (1955), p. 331 and Van Steenberghen, F.: *The philosophical movement of the thirteenth century* (1955), p. 58.

Creator. Out of nothing He created three different types of being: *substantia spiritualis, substantia corporalis* and *substantia ex utrisque composita.* Whilst God himself is eternal and the corporeal world temporal, the spiritual world has a position in between which is described as *aevum* or *aeternitas creata.* The spiritual creatures are those nearest to God, the corporeal creatures are those nearer to the void, and man, who is the union of these two, has a position in between God and nothingness (*nihil*). Man, the mixture of the spiritual and corporeal world, is a citizen of two worlds,

The created world then comprises the area between God as the highest being (*ens*) and the void (*non-esse*). The created universe has a double origin: God and non-existence. Bonaventure tried to neutralize this dualistic tension with his idea of man as the link between God (the transcendent, the absolute spiritual) and the non-transcendent or corporeal world. As a dichotomistic creature, consisting of both *spiritus* and *corpus,* man is capable of uniting the two opposed worlds. The two worlds are brought together in this way but the tension existing between the two worlds also influenced Bonaventure's anthropology: man has by nature an ambivalent existence.

Had Bonaventure not interpreted Biblical revelation of creation in terms of the pagan Greek dualism of a transcendent over against a non-transcendent world, his anthropology would not be such a tension-ridden one. According to the Bible, God does not stand as the transcendent above a non-transcendent sphere. The Bible merely reveals that God created the cosmos in the beginning and He created it *totally* different from Himself — which does not deny a relation between God and that which has been created by Him. One should not view God and the created universe as the transcendent and the non-transcendent parts of *one* being such as a circle divided in the middle to give a higher and a lower part.

Superficially it may seem that in accepting the biblical revelation of a *radical* difference between God and what He has created, one will get a tension between God and creation. Far from being so, the exact opposite is the case viz.: tension arises when a philosopher does not accept the radical difference between God and creation according to Scripture.

Bonaventure's dualistic starting-point forced him, for instance, to teach on the one hand the transcendence of God above creation, and on the other hand the immanence of God in creation. According to him, God cannot be totality transcendent because He will then have no contact with creation. On the other hand, God cannot be absolutely immanent in creation because He will then no longer be God. In the light of the Word of God we should reject the whole false dilemma of God's transcendence and immanence. It is not necessary for God to be part of His creation to be able to rule and govern it. Only when one has first separated God and His creation according to pagan dualism, is it necessary to try to re-unite them by way of the idea of

God's immanence.

Furthermore, Bonaventure's basic philosophical assumptions forced him to describe the relationship between God and the cosmos — as two parts of one being — in terms of similarity and difference or part and whole. That this is indeed the case in the thought of Bonaventure is apparent from the fact that he described the relationship between God and cosmos as analogous, thus implying similarity and difference at the same time! The idea of analogy is an idea bristling with inner tension. Evidence that Bonaventure also applied the scheme of part-whole to the relationship between God and cosmos is given in the fact that he believed in the participation of man in the divine being. Man is not wholly divine (otherwise he would not be man), but he participates in that which is divine.

We should, however, first take a brief look at the transcendent and the non-transcendent worlds separately.

5. BONAVENTURE'S COSMOLOGY

In the non-transcendent world (including *materia signata, elementa, mineralia, vegetabilia* and *sensibilia)* there is nothing divine. The transcendent world in its totality, however, is not divine as it includes, in addition to God, two types of creatures, viz. the angels and the *anima rationalis* of human beings. As far as the divine part is concerned, Bonaventure regards God as the highest being *(ens)*, who is identical to the highest good. There can be nothing higher and better than God. God is the *prima causa*, pure form and immutable. In His creative act He produced first the *substantia spiritualis* (nearest to Himself, still part of the transcendental world), thereafter the *substantia corporalis* (at a great distance from God) and lastly man, the combination of spiritual and corporeal nature (in a middle position between God and non-being).

In the created world everything consists of form and matter. Form (the principles of actuality) is related more intimately to God (as pure act), while matter (the principle of potentiality) gives contact with the void. Form and matter thus again remind us of the dual origin of created reality: *Deus et nihil.* The distinctive feature of Bonaventure's hylemorphism is that it is a universal hylemorphism: everything consists of matter and form. Spiritual beings are not pure form but they consist of both form and matter. Whereas Aristotle and Thomas Aquinas regarded the lower (individual) matter as the *principium individuationis*, which individualizes the universal (higher) form, Bonaventure taught that individualization requires the combination of both form and matter.

A further characteristic of the created world is its hierarchical structure. The *natura elementaris, vegetabilia, sensibilia, natura humana* and *natura angelica* do not have a position adjacent to each other, as different kingdoms, but stand one above the other. From God as the absolute being and absolute good, being and goodness diminish step by step to the ultimate point of *non-esse* or the void, from which God originally brought forth everything. Conversely creation displays a gradual ascending line from the lowest creature towards God as the most complete *ens* and *bonum*. In the two directions the ladder or chain of created reality leads towards its dual origin: either God, the *ens perfectum* or the non-existent void, *defectus entis*. The whole created reality bears the mark of the original tension (before creation) between God and "non-God" *(nihil)*. No matter at what point in the scale of the hierarchy, every created being is at the same time divine and not divine.

This will become clearer when we keep in mind Bonaventure's teaching that created reality is the shadow *(umbra)*, trace *(vestigium)* and image *(imago)* of the divine trinity. Especially in its form the created being is an expression of God as God created it according to the eternal forms or ideas contained in the Word, the second Person of the Trinity. Creatures are the "Abbild" (copy) of the "Urbild" (model) or ideal exemplar in the divine mind. According to Bonaventure's exemplarism then, the world is likened to a book of the Trinity because it bears the stamp of its Creator. He who looks at creation recognizes the Creator. The higher one ascends in the hierarchy of being, the clearer it becomes: the lower things show merely the shadow and traces of God, but man is the real image of God. In the highest part of his soul, man is the *expressa similitudo Dei*. According to Bonaventure the human soul is *capax Dei*, God is present in the (rational) human soul, in the human soul one encounters God, soul refers to God. Everything comes from and through God, but it is also directed back towards God again. God is the *causa efficiens, exemplaris et finalis*. Bonaventure's exemplarism gives the philosophical basis for the itinerary of the soul towards God and makes it possible, as will be explained at a later stage, for the sensible world to be a road which leads to God.

In agreement with the above Bonaventure believes in the participation of creation (especially the human soul) in God. This participation is based on the analogical relationship which Bonaventure conceived of as existing between Creator and creation. Because he did not accept the revelation of God with regard to the *radical* difference between Creator and creation, he had to assume some similarity as ontological point of departure. As he could not identify God and creation, however, he had, at the same time, to stress the difference. Analogy — similarity in spite of difference and difference in spite of similarity — may perhaps be applied in the comparison of different beings in created reality, but definitely not in the case of Creator and creation. The Bible clearly reveals that God cannot and should in no way be compared with creation! Once again I draw attention to anthropological consequences of the unbiblical concepts of participation and analogy (which have their backgrounds in the ontic dualism of Bonaventure's thought — God and creation the transcendent and non-trancendent parts of *one* being), namely that man is torn asunder to an ambivalent existence. Man is not fully man because he also has a divine part, and vice versa, man is not fully divine because he is also human.

6. MAN IN HIS FOURFOLD STATUS

We now have enough background to take a closer look at the anthropology of the *doctor seraphicus*[8]. Bonaventure distinguishes between a fourfold status: *status innocentiae sive integritatis, peccati, redemptionis sive viae* and *gloriae sive patriae*. We will follow his conception of man in each of these stages.

Man, according to Bonaventure, was created as the bridge between, a mixture of, spiritual and corporeal nature. In his *anima* man is linked to the spiritual world and in his *corpus* he is connected to the corporeal world.

Bonaventure held a psycho-creationistic point of view regarding the soul: the individual soul does not exist before the body, but God creates every human soul in the body of a new human being, the bodily part having its origin in both parents. The human soul, as the form of the body, is the actualization over and against the potentiality of the body. He distinguished between three potencies in the soul: *vegetativa, sensitiva* and *intellectiva* by which the soul not only gives existence to the body but also life, feeling and understanding. In its highest part (intellectual or rational), the soul is the image of God. While Christ is *imago conaturalis Dei* the human soul is *imago naturalis Dei*. In accordance with the two-realm theory of nature and grace Bonaventure distinguished further between a double image of God in man: *imago creationis* and *imago recreationis*. In the first image (natural) the cognitive potency includes *memoria* and *intelligentia* and the effective potency *voluntas*. In the second image (supernatural) the cognitive includes one virtue (*fides*) and the affective two (*spes et caritas*). In this theory of the double *imago Dei* (natural and supernatural) the synthetic mind of Bonaventure is once again exposed. He inherited his ideas of *imago creationis* from Greek anthropology and his conception of *imago recreationis* came from the Biblical revelation of faith, hope and love. As man is the

8. Cf. the following secondary sources about his anthropology. Gilson, E.: *The philosophy of St. Bonaventure* (1938); O'Learly, C.J.: *The substantial composition of man according to St. Bonaventure* (1931), Pegis A.C.: *St. Bonaventure and the problem of the soul as substance* (1934). I want to mention separately the brilliant dissertation of Van der Laan, H.: *De wijsgerige grondslag van Bonaventura's denken* (1968).

head of woman, Bonaventure assumed further that the image of God in man is more excellent in the male than in the female.

Because Bonaventure believed that God created the individual soul and the soul is the image of its Creator he also postulates its immortality. At death the soul, leaving the body behind, will return to God.

In this life the soul can be united to God. He adheres to the idea of a mystical religion. Bonaventure's view of religion is not the biblical one, viz. that we should serve God with our whole being in the world we live in. In this life we should serve God by obeying his commandments. Bonaventure, however, regarded created reality as merely an instrument for the soul to ascend to God and be united with Him. Man's journey to God is from the external to the internal and from the temporal to the eternal. Because of the traces of God in the soul we can climb the ladder until we finally come to an *excessus mentalis et mysticus*. In this state man does not only transcend the *mundus sensibilis*, but also himself, thus to become one with God. Bonaventure's mysticism is a semi-mysticism: only the soul, not the whole of man, becomes one with God. His religion is an asomatic religion because the body has no place in it. It is also acosmic in character because man has to leave the world behind to be able to approach God.

After this brief sketch of the soul in the *status integritatis*, little is left to say about Bonaventure's ideas of the body. The human *corpus* inherited from both parents and consisting of four elements (water, earth, fire and light), is not the image of God, not immortal and exists merely for the service of the soul. It will be resurrected one day for the sake of the soul but it is not so important because the immortal soul can exist without it. We have already noted that the body does not play any significant role in the service of God.

According to the final conception of Thomas Aquinas, the two components of the human unity, viz. body and soul, stand in the relation of matter and form, and constitute one substance. Bonaventure did not agree with Aquinas' subsistence theory. In accordance with his universal hylemorphism he was an exponent of the *vinculum* theory, which teaches that body and soul form separate individual substances each consisting of matter and form. For the unity of the two substances, viz. body and soul, a *vinculum*, i.e. a tie, cord or strap, is necessary in order to combine them into a third substance, viz. man.

7. THE "STATUS PECCATI"

The *status peccati* depicts man in his sinful state. Bonaventure's idea of the fall into sin was again determined by his whole synthetic ontology and anthropology. He considered that sin is not primarily disobedience to the laws of God, but merely a change of direction. We have already seen that true religion according to him is the means by which man is directed towards God so as to become more spiritual, more divine, the apex of this religion being the mystical union with God. The region of sin, however, lies in the exact opposite direction and towards that of the lower beings. Therefore Bonaventure could say that sin exists when the body (the lower) governs the soul (the higher) the ideal being just the reverse. This is also the reason why Bonaventure defines sin as *privatio boni*. As being *(ens)* and the good are so closely related in his thought, Bonaventure could also state that sin is the defect of being. When the human being directs his attention towards the lower part of creation, he moves in the direction of non-being. By sin man loses his *imago creationis*. This idea of sin being the failure of man to be like God, is absolutely unbiblical. The Bible teaches exactly the opposite: sin originated from the desire of man to be like God! The negative view of evil namely that it is the absence of good, a lack, a privation, cannot be accepted in the light of Scripture which reveals that sin is a "positive" apostate power. It is a privation merely in the sense that it constitutes alienation from God. However, this is not what Bonaventure had in mind.

Because of his synthetic thought, Bonaventure failed to realize the severity of God's punishment for sin in the death of man. God said *man* would die when he does not obey God. Bonaventure, in terms of his dichotomistic anthropology, taught that only the body would die, but not the immortal soul. Death is nothing serious because the *vinculum,* which keeps body and soul together, is simply loosened and the soul escapes death to return to God and the body goes back to whence it came!

As a result of Bonaventure's distinction between a double image of God in man, it is easy to explain what happened in the *status redemptionis:* in addition to his *imago creationis*, God gave back to man his *imago recreationis*.

Because of his whole synthetic ontology Bonaventure did not clearly realize that in the *status gloriae* this renewed earth will be the abode of man and not the heavens.

8. A MORE BIBLICAL VIEW OF MAN

My cursory remarks on Bonaventure's anthropology might perhaps become more explicit as I proceed to discuss briefly what I consider to be a more Biblical view of man.

Man is a unity of extreme complexity. But even to say that man is a unity implies two or more parts forming a whole. The unity of man is not a secondary fact, i.e. man is not a unity only after two or more basic parts or elements have been put together. Man is not a unity as the result of a union.

What follows now is actually a summary of the results of various studies concerning the different anthropological concepts used in the Bible and so it may give the impression of monotonous repetition: soul, body, spirit, flesh and heart all indicate the whole man. The aim of my enquiry is, however, not to enter into the *differences* between these anthropological concepts in the Word of God, but to draw attention to the fact that each of them does not denote something *in* man, but man as a whole from a specific viewpoint.

According to the Bible man as man, as such, is soul[9], and the soul is not a part of man. Man in his totality is soul. Man is in every degree soul, and soul is in every degree man. The word "soul" denotes the concrete, earthly personality for whom breathing and circulation of blood, emotional life etc. are most important.

Soul means quite simply a living being (man, animal or plant), an individual personality, a human being. It is also often used to indicate the seat of emotions, desires and needs. That is why the Bible speaks about a soul that eats, about the souls of animals, about a dead soul (and not of an immortal one), a soul of flesh (and not a spiritual one). According to the Bible the soul dies. Sometimes it may be said that the soul departs when man dies. (Gen. 35:18). Similarly it is said that the soul returns when it is revived (I Kings 17:21-22). Such expressions do not imply that death results in the departure of the soul from the body, leaving the soul untouched by death because it merely goes elsewhere. It simply means that *life* departs or that life returns once more.

Also "body" in the Bible[10] does not indicate a separate (lower) part of man. It denotes the *whole, concrete man.* In some instances it has more or less the same meaning as flesh and indicates *man* (again not a part of man) as fragile, weak and sinful.

The spirit[11] of man is also not a separate (higher) substance in man. Spirit is man himself, man himself is spirit. Man in his totality is spirit. Spirit may also be viewed as the seat of different emotions or a constant

9. Cf. the following works of Janse, A.: Om *"de levende ziel"* (n.d.), *De mensch als "levende ziel"* (1936), *Van idolen en schepselen* (1938); Von Meyenfeldt, F.H.: *The meaning of ethos* (1964), p. 54-56 and Ridderbos, H.: *Paulus. Ontwerp van zijn Theologie* (1966), p. 127, 128.

10. Cf. Ridderbos, H.: *op. cit.,* p. 123 and Kuitert, H.M.: "Mens en lichaam in de Heilige Schrift". *Vox Theologica,* 34(2):37-50, 1963.

11. Cf. in this connection Crump, F.J.: *Pneuma in the Gospels* (1954), Scheepers, J.H.: *Die Gees van God en die gees van die mens in die Ou Testament* (1960) and Waaning, N.A.: *Onderzoek naar het gebruik van "pneuma" bij Paulus* (1939).

power which causes vitality, an inner, concentrated motive force. The spirit of a person denotes the dynamic characteristics which inspire and motivates his actions.

The Biblical word "flesh"[12] signifies the *whole* man and all earthly creatures and characterizes man in a certain way, viz. as fragile, weak, frail and perishable, in contrast to God who is strong and eternal. There is no antithesis between flesh and soul. According to the Bible the soul of man is flesh and the flesh is soul. There is nothing wrong with flesh as such; flesh is not an inferior or sinful part of man.

In the Bible we sometimes find a close relationship between flesh and sin. Then flesh does not indicate a lower *part* of man as sinful, but the *whole* unregenerated sinful man.

In the same sense we will have to use the word "carnal" and its opposite, "spiritual". To be carnal means to rely on oneself, to live in disobedience to the law of God and to hate God and fellowmen. Therefore, "works of the flesh" are not only adultery and sexual sins but also hatred, wrath, strife, heresies, idolatry, witchcraft etc. (Gal. 6:19, 20). To be spiritual means to be guided by the Holy Spirit in everything we do — including our corporal life.

Our preliminary conclusion is that the Biblical words "soul", "body", "spirit" and "flesh" do not analyse man into his component *parts*. These concepts always denote the *total* man from a certain viewpoint. They are four different facets of the one diamond and four colours of the same prism.

As far as the word "heart"[13] in the Bible is concerned, we do not have in mind here heart in its biotic sense, as the beating organ in our breast. We imply the meaning of heart as the innermost "part", the central point, the most important constituent, the nucleus of man.

Because of this "heart" has a representative use. It is the genuine, the essential, the authentic in which something is completely represented. It represents the *whole* person. This implies a differentiation between the heart and its owner, because the representative and the represented can be differentiated. But it does not imply an independent existence of the heart. The representative may be *distinguished* but it cannot be *separated* from the

12. Cf. Lindijer, C.H.: *Het begrip sarx bij Paulus* (1952).

13. Cf. the following studies: Becker, J.H.: "Het begrip 'hart' in het Oude Testament". *Gereformeerd Theologisch Tijdschrift*, 50:10-16, 1950; Von Meyenfeldt, F.H.: *Het hart (leb, lebab) in het Oude Testament* (1950) and his contribution entitled "Enige algemene beschouwingen gegrond op de betekenis van het hart in het Oude Testament." In: *Wetenschappelijke bijdragen door leerlingen van Vollenhoven* (1951), p. 52-67. Cf. also his already mentioned work *The meaning of ethos* (1964), p. 49-54 and Ridderbos, H.: op. cit., p. 126, 127.

whole man. It is the "part" of the totality in which it finds its concentration point. "Heart" does not denote the traditional "spiritual part" of man. The heart of man is not his double or "second half" and does not imply a dichotomy in man. "Heart" implies no reduction of man to an essence from which the covering or bark — the body — may be easily stripped off.

Because "heart" has the meaning of a concentration point or nucleus in which the whole man is represented, it has a predominantly religious significance. It is the one centre in man which is turned towards God (or a god), in which religious life (man's relationship to God) is rooted. Any form of activity starts from the heart. The *whole* of life is religion because man's whole life is an outflow from his heart. Primarily the heart — and not the body — is responsible for sin. In other words in the heart of man the course of his life is determined.

It should be clear now that it is not possible to operate with sharply defined dimensions when we discuss the structure or nature of man in the light of the Bible. It is, for instance, wrong to imagine the relation between body and soul as two circles which either do not touch at all or overlap slightly. Man is not a composition of different *parts* but an indivisible whole of extreme complexity in which one may discern different *facets*. The difficulty is that one usually tries to make independent *substances* of the *facets* one has abstracted.

9. CRITICAL EVALUATION OF BONAVENTURE'S ANTHROPOLOGY

Equipped with the light of the Word of God — which should be the final authority for a Christian — let us now look again at Bonaventure's ideas about man. According to him, God created Adam by putting a separate spiritual substance — the immortal soul — into a material (clay) statue. The soul is of divine origin, because He breathed it into the statue (body).

This however, is not what Scripture reveals. When in the story of the creation it is told that God breathed the spirit of life into a man of clay he had moulded, it must not be understood that the clay is the body and the spirit of God the soul, which is seated and acts within the body. J. Pedersen says in this connection: "The base of its (man's) essence was the fragile corporeal substance, but by the breath of God it was transformed and *became a nephesh*, a soul. It is not said that man was *supplied with* a *nephesh*, and so the relation between body and soul is quite different from what it is to us. Such as he is, man, in his total essence, is a soul ... man as such is soul"[14].

---

14. Pederson, J.: *Israel. Its life and culture* (1959), p. 99. (Italics of "became" and "supplied with" by B.J. van der Walt).

The word "dust" (Hebrew *aphar*) in Gen. 2:7 ("And the Lord formed man of the dust of the ground, and breathed into his nostrils the breath of life; and man became a living soul") does not denote merely one part of man. The being dust of man denotes the *whole* man. (Nota bene: "The Lord formed *man* of dust..." and not the *body!*) Just as with *basar* (or the Greek *sarx)*, *aphar* indicates the total man in his fragility and weakness as was previously indicated.

Bonaventure regarded the (higher) soul as the image of God in man. Holy Scripture, however, does not tell us that the image of God is somewhere in man, but that the *whole* man *is* the image of God[15].

According to Bonaventure, man becomes a human being only when God has created a soul in the more or less animal body. *When* does this happen? At conception, after a few months, or at birth? If it only happens after a few months or at birth, then abortion cannot be regarded as a sin. Further: Is this view in accordance with the doctrine of original sin, as the implication is that God created sinful souls? Is this view in accordance with Gen. 2: 2 where Scripture reveals that God *completed* his creation in six days?

What is meant by the soul being *in* the body, if the soul does not occupy any space? It is a contradiction to say that the soul is *in* the body and at the same time to assert that it cannot be shown *where* in the body. If the soul is a part of *created* reality it must have a geometrical aspect (space). The simplest creatures, viz. the inorganic beings, appear in at least four modalities: the arithmetical, geometrical, kinematic and physical. (Usually the soul is regarded as a much higher substance). Even if souls are the lowest "creatures" they should at least have geometrical and physical aspects. In other words, if souls exist they should be measurable and weighable!

Bonaventure's view of the soul therefore does not fit in the Biblical view of the created cosmos. In his thinking it is something transcendental like God. We cannot accept something divine in the cosmos, because God Himself revealed the radical difference between Creator and the creatures, including man as a whole.

The Biblical view of the structure of man is also the reason why I have to reject Bonaventure's idea of immortality. The Bible speaks only of the resurrection of man and nowhere of an immortal soul escaping death.

.

---

15. For the Biblical meaning of man as the image of God cf. Berkouwer, G.D.: *De mens het beeld Gods* (1957), which has also been translated in English *Man: The image of God* (1962); Kruyswijk, A.: *"Geen gesneden beeld"* (1962) and Schrotenboer, P.G.: "Man in God's World". *International Reformed Bulletin,* 10(31):11-30, Oct. 1967. We have learned much from the works of K.J. Popma to reach a genuine radical biblical view about man. Brilliant criticism of the traditional Scholastic Christian anthropology can be found at various places in the seven columes of his major work *Levensbeschouwing* (1958-1965).

Immortality is used merely in connection with *man* (N.B. not the soul) *after* resurrection.

A dichotomistic anthropology is not a harmless theoretical idea, but it has fatal consequences in practical life. For instance, the higher so-called spiritual things are quite wrongly deemed more important than the so-called lower bodily activities. The aim of the proclamation of the Gospel to unbelivers is narrowed down to the salvation of souls and not the salvation of living human beings in their everyday life. Furthermore the clergy are regarded as the only men who are privileged to serve God in spiritual matters. Bonaventure stressed the life hereafter, when the soul will be freed from the body and united with God and not the life here on earth, when we, I submit, must serve God.

10. CONCLUSION

By way of conclusion I return to my starting-point namely that Bonaventure was a synthetic thinker, and also to my proposition that it was his compromise between the Biblical and pagan philosophical ideas which caused the tensions in his view about man.

On the one hand I cannot agree with Adolf von Harnack that Christianity in general and Medieval thought in particular are a construction of Greek inspiration erected upon the soil of the Gospel[16]. On the other hand I also reject E. Gilson's viewpoint that in Medieval philosophy "not a single Greek philosophical notion... has ever been a constitutive element of Christian faith as such"[17]. It is a rather easy solution, but I think the truth lies between these two extreme viewpoints.

I therefore neither want to overrate nor to minimize the part played by unbiblical philosophy in Bonaventure's view about man. His anthropology was not infected or contaminated to such a degree by paganism that we have the right to describe it as virtually pagan. At the same time we cannot qualify his anthropology as "Christian" — at least if we accept Christian thought to be fundamentally biblical, anti-synthetic thinking. My unwillingness to regard the anthropology of Bonaventure as distinctly Christian accordingly, does not originate from an effort to blame or condemn a fellow Christian.

We may, however, benefit if we regard the *doctor seraphicus'* anthropology as the result of his synthetic mind because his anthropology clearly

16. Cf. Von Harnack, A.: *Das wesen des Christentums* (1900).

17. Gilson, E.: *op. cit.,* p. 5.

shows the impossibility of fusing heterogeneous, foreign elements. His effort in this respect was indeed ingenuous, but fails to stand up to close scrutiny. The finished product contains a series of cracks from top to bottom. Because he tried to reconcile the irreconcilable, it reveals an inner tension.

What we need in the place of the type of anthropology Bonaventure advocated, is one embracing an unqualified loyalty to Scripture; this alone will give cohesion and truth to our doctrine about man, and guard it against inner conflict.

***

SUMMARY

The death on the 15th July 1274, of Bonaventure, one of the greatest scholastic philosophers of the Middle Ages, was commemorated by way of an international Congress in Rome from September 19-26 1974. In this article one aspect of his theology, viz. his anthropology, is discussed from a fundamental Biblical viewpoint. The intention of this critical approach is not to decry or refute, but to strive to obtain a more Biblically directed viewpoint about man.

Firstly it is indicated that Bonaventura was a synthetic thinker who combined in his theology non-scriptural, pagan philosophical conceptions with Biblical themes. He applied allegorical exegesis to blend Greek philosophy and the Bible in the relation of nature and supernature (grace). This synthetic spirit of the theology of the *doctor seraphicus* is the most basic reason for the inner tensions in his anthropology.

As a further *vitium originis* for the ambivalent character of his anthropology Bonaventure's ontic dualism between a transcendent and a non-transcendent world is discussed. Attention is focused in particular on his ideas relating to created reality — hierarchy, exemplarism, participation and analogy — as the background to a more extensive study of his anthropology.

In the discussion of his view about man special attention is paid to the following: man as the combination of or bridge between the spiritual and the corporeal world, the creation of the soul as a spiritual substance by God, man as the *imago Dei*, his immortality, the *vinculum*-theory, semi-mysticism, and sin as *privatio boni*.

The brief exposition of the real meaning of Biblical anthropological concepts such as "soul", "body", "flesh", "spirit" and "heart" is followed by an appreciation of Bonaventure's anthropological conception in the light of what the Bible reveals about man. The final conclusion is that the tension-ridden character of the anthropological concepts of this coryphee of the Golden Age of Scholasticism is a clear proof of the unacceptability of synthetic thinking. Only unqualified loyalty to Scripture will give cohesion and truth to our doctrine concerning man.

212

12 REGNUM HOMINIS ET REGNUM DEI. HISTORICAL-CIRITCAL DISCUSSION OF THE RELATIONSHIP BETWEEN NATURE AND SUPERNATURE ACCORDING TO DUNS SCOTUS*

Contemporary scholars of mediaeval studies may consider themselves privileged. Within the last four years (1972-1976) no less than five international medieval congresses have heralded a new interest in an often neglected period in the history of Western thought. From 5-12 September 1972, the Fifth International Congress of Medieval Philosophy was held in Spain (Madrid, Cordoba, Granada)[1]. The Seventh Centenary of St. Thomas Aquinas International Congress at Rome and Naples followed from 19-24 April 1974[2]. In the same year (19-26 September) the Seventh Centenary of St. Bonaventure of Bagnorea was also commemorated by way of an international congress[3]. This year (1976) we will have the first Congress of the International Society of Catholic Philosophy from 8-15 September at Genoa and Barcelona closely followed by the Fourth International Scotist Congress to be held at Padua from 24 to 29 September.

Indeed a very rich fare especially if one considers the voluminous proceedings and other publications accompanying all the events!

1. INTRODUCTION

At all the above-mentioned congresses a very important question was and will be as to the relevance of medieval thought in our present situation. The promoters of the 1976 Scotist Congress also aim to establish a constructive dialogue between Scotist thought and contemporary culture.

To attain this end they correctly realize that it will not be feasible simply

---

* Paper prepared for the Fourth International Scotus Congress, Padua, 24-29 September 1976. Previously published in *Bulletin van die Suid-Afrikaanse Vereniging vir die Bevordering van Christelike Wetenskap*, no. 50/51:21-39, Sept/Dec. 1976.

1. The proceedings of this congress are — as far as I know — still unpublished.

2. First few volumes of the proceedings already published by Edizione Domenicane Italiane, Naples, under the title *Atti del congresso internationale Tomasso d'Aquino nel suo settimo centenario.*

3. The first volume of the *Atti del congresso internazionale par il VII centenario di san Bonaventura da Bagnoregio* has already been published by Pontificia Facolta' Teologia "San Bonaventura" of Rome, 1976. Reprinted as the first essay in this volume.

to repeat the message of Scotus today. Our *doctor subtilis* had a powerful, vigorous, original and highly critical mind which enabled him to cut through many a jungle of inherited concepts and terms. His dialectical skill, patient and careful thought combined with audaciousness is characteristic of great intelligence. This critical and fearless attitude of Scotus towards the fashionable doctrines of his predecessors and contemporaries should also characterize our own approach towards history (including Scotus himself) as well as present-day philosophies and theologies.

Though Scotus was impregnated with tradition, his thought really belongs to the closing epoch of so-called dogmatic philosophy (thirteenth century) heralding the new movement of the fourteenth century. The *doctor subtilis* stands at the juncture of two ages. We may see in his system a bridge between two centuries, between the age of the great speculative systems (of which Aquinas is an outstanding example) and the age of radical criticism (which was to characterize the Ockhamist movement). Aware of the transitional character of Scotus' philosophy, the promoters of the recent Paduan Congress emphasized especially those aspects of his thought in which he was critical about the doctrines of his time and more open towards that which we nowadays consider as "permanent values of modern though".

The dialogue between Scotist and contemporary thought, according to the organizers of the Congress, should also be sought at the level of basic principles and not at the level of superficial convergencies[4]. To attain this aim it is necessary first to view such principles in their historical context in order to be able, in the second place, to free them from their cultural-historical circumstances and then to apply them to contemporary problems that are not identical to those of the Middle Ages.

In so far as the organizers of this Congress do not have the intention of regarding Scotus' thought as a *philosophia* or *theologia perennis* I am in full agreement. I do not want to overrate Scotus' contribution to the history of Western thought but at the same time one should not underrate it. Many philosophical and theological problems discussed by Scotus are still relevant today.

---

4. According to the terminology of the consistent problem-historic method the philosophical conception of Scotus can be described in the following way: purely cosmological, dualistic, Aristotle-interpretation (partial universalism, without a theory of macro-microcosmos, in other words accepting the form-matter motive), vinculum theory (in his anthropology) and voluntarism. An explanation of the consistent problem-historic method and the terminology above is given in my article "Historiography of philosophy: The consistent problem-historic method", *Tydskrif vir Christelike Wetenskap*, 9:163-184, 1973 (A brief summary of this method appeared under the title "The consistent problem-historic method" in *Perspektief*, 12(4):16-25, September 1973).

This paper will elaborate on one such problem, viz. that of the relationship between nature and supernature or the so-called two-realm theory. In the light of the motto of the Congress, *Regnum homines et regnum Dei,* I consider it an appropriate contribution.

At the same time it is one of the most basic principles or presuppositions in the thought of Scotus. It is not simply a theoretical (e.g. philosophical or theological) but a deep-seated religious vantage point and motive force determining all his thought and action.

Personally I regard this theme as of the greatest importance not only for our present situation but also for the entire history of Christianity. It was and is an issue in nearly all Christian denominations, e.g. Roman Catholic, Calvinist and Lutheran[5]. I am fully convinced that I do not in the least make an overstatement when propounding the thesis that it is the two-realm theory, which haunted Christianity for nearly two thousand years, weakening its reformational power in every field of activity.

Unfortunately this theme can not be considered as one in which Scotus belonged to the *avant garde.* While he was a critical scholar in the sense that he investigated critically the positions of other philosophers and theologians, he did not conduct a fundamental investigation of his own presuppositions on this point. His criticism was a criticism *within* the framework of the dualism of nature and supernature.

Of course I am fully aware of the fact that to be critical of one's own presuppositions certainly is one of the most difficult assignments. I assume, none the less, that it will not be against either the spirit of Scotus himself or the present Congress to stress the necessity of reconsidering one of the *doctor subtilis'* most basic assumptions.

In an historical-critical approach my essay will cover the following three main points. First a brief survey of the origin, historical background and development of the two-realm theory up to Scotus. Secondly Scotus' own viewpoint, and thirdly my own critical comments.

2. ORIGIN AND DEVELOPMENT OF THE TWO-REALM THEORY OF NATURE AND SUPERNATURE

The dualism of a profane world against a holy world belongs to the oldest traditions of ancient thought. Our word "profane" is derived from

---

5. I traced its influence in some detail in my dissertation *Die Natuurlike Teologie met besondere aandag aan die visie daarop by Thomas van Aquino, Johannes Calvyn en die "Synopsis Purioris Theologiae" — 'n Wysgerige ondersoek.* Potchefstroom University for Christian Higher Education, 1974.

the Latin *pro + fanum* literally meaning "in front of the sanctuary". "Sacred" comes from the Latin *sacer* which means both "holy" and "accursed". The holy as well as the accursed are in the hands of the god(s) — either under his (their) care or wrath — and therefore withheld from common use. In the idea of taboo (still encountered amongst so-called primitive cultures today) we get the same combination of the sacred (possession by a god) and accursed (also dedicated to the god but in this case to his vengeance).

When Christianity conquered the Western World its encounter with pagan thought resulted in a synthesis. One of the most popular ways in which this synthesis between Christianity and ancient Greek and Roman philosophy was accomplished, was by means of the scheme of nature-supernature. This dualism of nature-supernature was merely a modification of the age-old original pagan dualism of profane-sacred.

Studying the attitude of Christianity from the Apologists and Patristic thinkers we discern a gradual development in which this idea of a *duplex ordo* becomes clearer until it reaches its most articulate expression in e.g. Thomas Aquinas, Duns Scotus and other Medieval thinkers. A brief sketch tracing this development will be sufficient[6].

The idea of the *praeparatio evangelica*, of which *Clemens of Alexandria* was a clear exponent had already prepared the way for the two-realm idea.

God educated the Greeks by means of their philosophy and the Jews with the Old Testament unto Christ. Greek Philosophy and the Old Testament are two rivers converging in the New Testament. Greek Philosophy is appreciated as the preparatory work or harbinger of New Testament fulfilment. In this way the revelation of God is relativized. On the one hand, Clemens accepts the Word of God as the absolute truth while on the other, he believes that the pagans had achieved truth which the Christians only had to complete and bring to perfection.

Origen also postulates the idea that the Gospel only actualized what was in potentiality present in pagan thought. Human wisdom is the pedagogue of divine wisdom. The Christians would therefore not hesitate to claim what is correct in pagan thought as their own. Just as Israel took gold and silver from the Egyptians to make utensils for the tabernacle, the conqueror (grace, faith, theology, church) may take the products of pagan culture and philosophy using them for the greater glory of God. This is regarded as legitimate because the treasures of Athens actually belonged to Jerusalem — the pagan philosophers approached moments of real truth because they plagiarised the books of Moses!

This apprently devout argument reveals a lack of radical criticism from

6. Cf. dissertation mentioned in footnote 5 above, p. 137-206 and p. 261-270.

a Biblical point of view and is evidently an unobtrusive effort to evade the antithesis.

It will be incorrect and a perpetration of injustice to try to read *Augustine* in the light of the later Medieval two-realm theory of nature and grace. Augustine does not concern himself with the two-realm theory in the form of nature-grace, but it has been adequately demonstrated that he definitely adhered to a certain type of two-realm theory — possibly under influence of Manicheism. The idea of the *desiderium naturale*, so important to the nature-grace theory, can also be traced to the neo-Platonism of Augustine.

The method of nature and grace received its first official sanction at the *Synod of Orange* (in 529 A.D.) which formulated decisions against Pelagianism. These canons dealt with the subject of man's state before and after the fall in such a way that they opened the door to the nature-grace theme. Before the fall man possessed a special measure of super-nature. When he fell into sin he lost the higher supernatural part (faith). Man's fall, however, did not essentially affect or change his lower natural part. It remained more or less intact. Man still possessed the natural light of reason. The human being after the fall is man minus faith, and after salvation man plus faith again. According to this view, sin or evil is only the absence of the good (faith), a lack or deprivation. According to the Bible, however, sin is a "positive", radical apostate power which leaves nothing — not even so-called natural reason — intact.

Two other examples in which the two-realm theory is clearly expressed: at about 1060 A.D. it was stated that the doctrine of transubstantiation could not be philosophically explained because it belonged to the area of grace. In about 1140 the theme of nature and grace facilitated a distinction between Theology (sphere of grace) and Philosophy (sphere of nature).

Undoubtedly the method of synthesis by way of the theory of naturegrace was most consistently and lucidly applied by *Aquinas*. According to him grace did not abolish nature, but perfected it. Nature, embracing all of reality as understood by pagan philosophy, was related to grace, i.e. the whole of life viewed in the light of the Bible, as is a threshold to a sanctuary. According to him then there are two more or less autonomous areas of life. It is impossible for the higher sphere (grace) to reform the lower (nature) because the lower enjoys a great degree of autonomy. Real Christian activity in the field of nature (for instance a radical Christian Philosophy) was neither necessary nor possible.

3. DUNS SCOTUS' TWO-REALM THEORY

Like many of his contemporaries he tried to solve the problem of the relationship between Christian faith and non-Christian culture within the framework of the basic religious motive of nature and supernature. We confine ourselves to the prologue of his *Ordinatio* (later known as his *Oxford Commentary on the Sentences of Peter Lombard*).

In his case too the problem is discussed in a gnoseological context. In his theory of knowledge he puts the question about the necessity of supernatural inspiration in the case of a doctrine in which the human being in this life cannot acquire knowledge by the natural light of his intellect because of the structural deficiency of the intellect after the fall into sin.

The philosophers, according to Scotus, usually deny the consequences of original sin and defend the perfection of nature while the theologians realize the defectiveness of natural reason and consequently the necessity of supernatural revelation. Reality as a natural reality, according to the Christian theologian, is not perfect but in need of supernatural perfection. Reality in its fullness therefore is both natural and supernatural.

Scotus fully realizes that it is impossible to demonstrate to natural man with the arguments of natural reason that there ought to be something supernatural. The only way to achieve this is to use theological arguments based on faith and supernatural revelation. In the case of a selected panel of Scotist specialists it is not necessary that I should discuss the five *rationes principales* which Scotus advanced to convince the philosophers about the necessity of a supernatural knowledge of the *telos* or final end of the human being[7]. His contention is that, although we possess a natural desire for God, we can only supernaturally reach Him, not naturally. He stresses the lack of certainty, the errors, doubt and ignorance in the thoughts of the philosophers on the teleological structure of our knowledge.

In this context then he characterizes the supernatural nature of revealed knowledge through the agent intellect and sense perception. The knowable object, according to its nature, impresses a form on the receptive faculty of the intellect. This is the natural way of attaining knowledge. But if the relation between agent and the receptive faculty of the human intellect is not a relation of natural impression, then we have something supernatural. In this case the agent being does not bring about knowledge according to the natural usual structure. Supernatural knowledge therefore is not necessary according to the general laws of the occasion of knowledge. It is possible for God to cause a special supernatural knowledge by way of revelation. Supernatural knowledge comprises such phenomena as for instance: the defectiveness of nature, separated substances, the final end of mankind as well as God triune.

The controversial discussion between philosophers and theologians, by means of which Scotus develops his idea of nature and supernature in the

---

7. Cf. H. van der Laan: Nature and supernature according to Duns Scotus, *Philosophia Reformata*, 38:67 et seq., 1973.

prologue to his *Ordinatio*, gives us in summary the following picture. The philosophers suppose nature to be perfect. Man therefore has no other destination than his natural end. They are unaware of the fact that man needs divine grace in order to attain a second, higher, viz. supernatural end. Natural man reaches his natural end by means of his (theoretical and practical) reason because it provides him with valid, necessary knowledge. Over against the philosophers, the theologians profess to possess knowledge of man's supernatural end, his beatitude, the vision and fruition of God. This is because, as theologians, they have the supernatural inspiration of God's special revelation in his Word.

In spite of a certain discontinuity between the natural and supernatural, and his disengaging of what belongs to theology from what is accessible to philosophical reason, Scotus (like Aquinas) adheres to the idea of *desiderium naturale*. Man possesses a natural desire to attain the supernatural end — although he does not know this end and cannot reach it in his natural state. It may be that the doctrine of the natural desire constitutes the liaison between the two orders (nature and supernature). Two problems, however, immediately arise. In the first place: how is it conceivable to have a natural desire towards a supernatural end without at least a slight knowledge about this supernatural goal? Secondly: can a striving towards the supernatural in the natural sphere be possible? If it is indeed possible as Scotus contends, then there must be something supernatural in the natural sphere. Viewed from the opposite side we face this problem: if grace does not abolish nature, but perfects it (in the supernatural end), then something natural is mixed with the supernatural sphere of grace. Is this in agreement with Scotus' intention to help clarify boundaries between the natural and supernatural?

It should be noted in conclusion that Scotus' criticism of the philosophers is one within a previously accepted framework, viz. that of the *duplex ordo* of nature and supernature. As mentioned in our introduction we do not find in Scotus' *Ordinatio* a critical questioning of this assumption. He did not query his solution to the problem of the relationship between Christian faith and non-Christian thought. According to his two-realm theory a compromise has been made: the lower position is assigned to pagan philosophy (nature) and the higher to Christian theology (supernature). As in the case of the *doctor angelicus* the relationship between the two is that of a threshold (the profane) to the sanctuary (the sacred). Supernatural grace does not abolish nature, but perfects it.

It should be noted that pagan thinking in this compromise was not hermetically sealed off from Christian theology. Its influence on theology was real and could easily be indicated, in Scotus' theology too. Scotus regards it, however, as compatible with Christian theology.

This two-realm theory of Duns Scotus was conceived after the condemnation at Paris and Oxford in 1277. Hence the tendency, clearly felt in Scotus' thought, to rely upon revelation and faith more than upon philosophical reasoning in order to ascertain truth in theology. His predecessors before the condemnation (like Thomas Aquinas) had more confidence in the value of philosophy. The long honeymoon of theology and philosophy was however slowly coming to an end. One can discern in his thought the faint beginnings of the retreat, of a discrepancy between reason and faith instead of a harmony as was the case in Aquinas. His system begins to upset the precarious balance between reason and faith, nature and supernature. Although he had the opposite intention, his critical ideas breached their previous unity too far for others following him not to widen the gap.

4. CRITICAL APPRAISAL

Because of the disintegration of Scholastic synthetic thought from the fourteenth century onwards Scotus' viewpoint of nature *and* supernature, the kingdom of man *and* the kingdom of God was changed to the adage, we may say, of *either* the kingdom of man *or* the kingdom of God.

The image medieval man had of himself was centred on the final end, God — as we clearly saw in Scotus. He knew that he was called to live on earth as a pilgrim en route to eternal happiness.

Diametrically opposed to this theocentric attitude is the contemporary cosmocentric outlook. The aspirations of man today (because the extraordinary progress of science, technology and organization provides him with nearly unlimited powers to dominate nature) is centred, above all, on man himself. He considers his happiness as bound to the conquest of the universe which he endeavours to subordinate to himself. Hence the unknown powers of modern man are extolled today as giving significance to life. The ultimate goal is a paradise on earth, the kingdom of man — *Regnum hominis* — without the least thought about God or His kingdom. Secularization (the becoming independent of the sphere of nature at the close of the Middle Ages) went over into secularism (the dechristianization of life). When the church lost its power, God also died in the mind of modern man. We may also say: the sphere of supernatural grace was totally devoured by the new independent sphere of nature.

Certainly we cannot agree with the contemporary secularistic approach in which a Christian is supposed to choose between the kingdom of God and that of man. At the same time, however, I do not think the solution is to be found in a return to the Scotist idea of the kingdom of God and that of man as two juxtaposed spheres of human life.

It is true that Scotus, like other Medieval thinkers, saw a unity between nature and supernature. Even when he distinguished, perhaps more clearly than his predecessors, between these domains it was not with the intention of dividing or separating them. The *vitium originis* according to my mind is to be found in the fact that Scotus *cum suis* accepted two spheres in creation: a more or less neutral, profane, natural realm common to all human beings *(Regnum hominis)* and a holy or sacred realm in which all attention was focussed on the contemplation and service of God *(Regnum Dei)*. Western history has already clearly revealed that such a synthesis could not withstand the assault of the age from the fourteenth century onwards. The final outcome of the Medieval two-realm theory was the progressive separation of and, finally, a total divorce between, nature and supernature. Secularism soon attained dominance in the historical development of post-medieval, modern culture. Scotus and others meant well with their double-storey, two-dimensional thinking, but the end was a one-dimensional, purely secular world.

This tragic outcome, of which the germs were already present in the *regnum hominis — regnum Dei* distinction, should have been foreseen if Scotus and others had adhered more closely to Biblical revelation. Scripture clearly reveals that man is called to the service of God not merely (to use Scotus' terminology) in the spiritual, supernatural sphere, but also in the natural, ordinary everyday-life. Man's service of God encompasses his *whole* life, *all* his activities, *every* day of the week. That is the Biblical revelation about the Kingdom of God. *Regnum Dei* is not confined to a so-called upper compartment. The Bible does not sustain   compartmentalized Christianity.

What I am advocating is a third alternative. Medieval synthesis (Scotus) proclaims *Regnum Hominis ET regnum Dei*. Contemporary antithesis adheres to *regnum hominis VEL regnum Dei* — usually resulting in a *regnum hominis solius*. The Biblical thesis (formulated in the same terms as the two other viewpoints) is *regnum hominus IN regno Dei*, more precisely stated as *regnum Dei solius* (the kingdom of God alone).

According to Holy Scripture there should be no independent, autonomous kingdom of man over against the Kingdom of God. Such a kingdom can only exist as the *regnum Satanis*, the kingdom of the evil. Because man finds his fulfilment and happiness in the Kingdom of God, in His service (here on earth and in the end on a new, reborn earth) there is no place in the Word of God for two kingdoms next to each other: the one of man and the other of God.

This Kingdom of the Sovereign God includes not merely the church and all kinds of ecclesiastical affairs. After the redemptive work of Christ and after the gift of His Spirit that has been bestowed upon the faithful, there are no longer separate holy people, places and specially sacred times. Everybody, everywhere, always, should live a holy life unto God.

A man serving in two kingdoms is divided in himself. According to the dual order of nature-supernature man leads a schizophrenic existence.

Because the nature-grace theme is not a solely abstract, theoretical thought-pattern but also a religious driving force and impulse, its influence in practical life is tremendous. Subject to it the whole of life is viewed as split by a polar tension so that we get the following dualistic notions: secular — religious; common grace — special grace; autonomous man — sovereign God; the God of the philosophers — the God of the Bible; God the Creator — God the Redeemer; world and earhtly things — heaven and heavenly things; the visible — the unseen; the body (outer life) — the soul (inner life); ordinary laymen (not in service of God) — clergymen (in special service of God); unordained — ordained, sir — the reverend; politician — priest; father — monk; mother — nun; marriage — celebacy; industry — monastery; the state and other natural institutions (marriage, family, school, university, free associations etc.) — the church; emperor —pope; general revelation (in nature) — special revelation (in Bible); reason — faith; understanding — believing; Philosophy, natural Theology and all the other sciences (neutral) — supernatural Theology (by nature Christian); university — seminary; academy — church; classroom — chapel; secular or natural law — canon or divine (supernatural) law; natural — spiritual; autonomous — theonomous; optional — necessary; fact — value; observation — evaluation; horizontal — vertical; now — then; already — not yet; appointed by man — instituted by God; learning — praying; temporal — eternal; free will — Christian will; natural man — Christian man, etc.

God *or* man, the church *or* the state, faith *or* reason... Because this is actually what happens in practice (especially apparent today) in spite of the fact that Scotus cum suis desired harmony between God and man, church and state, faith and reason etc.

The consequences of the viewpoint I am advocating are not that man is annihilated or rendered of no importance. On the contrary! The genuine Biblical vision, however, enables man in his totality, in every human activity, to give himself — not merely a part of his life — to the service of God Almighty, Sovereign over every domain of His creation. According to this new perspective man is, for instance, no longer a Christian, *and* also an artist, engineer, teacher, scientist (Scotus). It is also not a question of *either* a Christian *or* scientist etc. (the current idea). Many people still think that if you are a Christian you cannot be intellectually respectable and if you are intellectual, your Christian confession is somehow suspect. The Biblical perspective makes it possible to be a Christian artist, engineer, teacher, scientist and much more. The scholarly activities of the Christian scientist are directed and guided and practised in the light of the Word of God. His motto is neither "faith *and* science" (Scotus), nor "faith *or* science" (the slogan of many contemporary thinkers), but "faith-committed science". In other words a science in which religious commitment is openly confessed and not disguised because it is considered a handicap instead of a privilege.

It will be clear now why I am in total disagreement with a well-known medievalist who concludes one of his books on the history of Medieval philosophy in the following way: "it would sound absurd to speak of 'Christian biology' or 'Christian mathematics': a biologist or a mathematician can be a Christian, but not his biology or his mathematics. Similarly, it might be said, a philosopher can be a Christian, but not his philosophy. His philosophy may be true and compatible with Christianity; but one does not call a scientific statement Christian simply because it is true and compatible with Christianity. Just as mathematics can be neither pagan nor Moslem nor Christian, though mathematicians can be pagans or Moslems or Christians, so philosophy can be neither pagan nor Moslem nor Christian, though philosophers can be pagans or Moslems or Christians.

"The most that the phrase 'Christian philosophy' can legitimately means is a philosophy compatible with Christianity; if it means more than that, one is speaking of a philosophy which is not simply philosophy, but which, partly at least, is theology."

A very decisive mistake of Scotus was that he did not fully realize the consequences of original sin — in spite of the fact that he emphasized the fact in his controversy with the philosophers. He interpreted it wrongly because of his acceptance of a *duplex ordo* of nature and supernature. The *religious antithesis* existing in creation after the fall into sin and redemption in Christ is *localized in an ontological way* in certain spheres of life. The religious antithesis between life in accordance with the Word and Spirit of God on the one hand, and life in disobedience on the other hand, cannot be localized in the way Scotus attempted in his two-realm theory. The result of this theory is that we get two different lives in the same human being instead of two conflicting spiritual directions. One part of human life (the so-called natural) is withdrawn from the kingship and rule of God. In this way the Kingdom of God becomes more or less identified with the Church.

It is true that the Bible clearly informs us about two separate kingdoms, viz. that of God and Satan, the kingdom of light and that of darkness. But nowhere does it teach that those kingdoms could or should be localized as two separate parts or worlds in creation: the one in which man should live as man and the other in which he should live as a Christian. According to this scheme the non-ecclesiastical areas of life can only have sense in so far as they are dominated and perfected by the church. Being a Christian is regarded as identical with belonging to church. Religion is in this way confined to the so-called higher spheres of life. Because the lower area of so-called natural life is autonomous it cannot be christianized. In spite of the subordination of nature to the supernatural, grace floats like oil on water so that a reformation of the whole of life in the light of Scripture is out of the question.

Scotus' incorrect interpretation of Biblical revelation about the fall into sin is clearly seen in the way he viewed its anthropological consequences. He advocated an ontological viewpoint, according to which fall into sin implies a loss of the supernatural and divine salvation implies the return, as a kind of *donum superadditum*, of the divine part to an unaffected human nature. (Salvation actually implies a deification of man.) Scotus placed the antithesis in the ontological *structure* of things (e.g. man) rather than in the *direction* of man's response to the Word of God. Therefore, the viewpoint of Scotus is ignorant of the radical character of both fall and redemption. After the fall, man, by nature, is still directed to God (the *desiderium naturale*) because he is not entirely corrupted. According to Scripture, however, man is totally corrupted and cannot return to God of his own will and desire as is the case in Scotus.

Redemption is not something total and radical in Scotus' view either, since it is confined to a certain part of the human being. His *whole* existence is not renewed. (The only difference between a Christian and a non-Christian is that the Christian has grace added). Biblically speaking redemption implies a total and radical religious change, a turn-about in direction.

The Biblical doctrine about nature and grace is that grace can only be spoken of after the fall so that man was not robbed of grace when he fell into sin. Furthermore, the antithesis does not lie in the opposition between a realm of grace and a realm of nature, but rather in the radical conflict between two spiritual directions: the spirit of light and the spirit of darkness, obedience to God and disobedience. The tension is not between grace and nature, but grace versus sin and the wrath of God.

We are living today in an age of radical thinking and doing. Halfheartedness is no longer the spirit of the leaders in our contemporary secularized world. The kingdom of man *and* the Kingdom of God? The answer will be an emphatic "No." No longer a halt between two positions: the kingdom of man alone.

I cannot end this paper but with the urgent conviction that the time for radical Christianity is now: *sola Scriptura, soli Dei gloria, solum regnum Dei!*

BIBLIOGRAPHY

BARLIC, C.: The life and works of John Duns Scotus. *In:* John Duns Scotus 1265-1965. (Ryan, J.K. & Bonänsea, B.M. e.d.), Washington D.C., 1965, p. 1-27.

BARLIC, C, EPPING, A., EMMER, A. & KöRVEN, B.: Doctor Subtilis. Vier studien over Johannes Duns Scotus. 's-Hertogenbosch, Teulings' Uitgeversmaatschappij ., 1946.

BéRUBé, C.: L'année scotiste et le septième centenaire de la naissance de J. Duns Scot. *Collectanea Franciscana*, 37:154-185, 1967.

BETTONI, E.: Duns Scotus. The basic principles of his philosophy. (Trans. and ed. by B. Bonansea), Washington, D.C. Catholic Univ. of America, 1961.

BETZENDöRFER, W.: Glauben und Wissen bei den grossen Denkern des Mittelalters. Gotha, Leopold Klotz Verlag, 1931 (p. 215 et seq. on Scotus).

BRéHIER, E.: Histoire de la Philosophie. Tome premier: L'antiquité et le moyen age. Paris, Presses Universitaires de France, 1947.

COPLESTON, F.C.: Medieval Philosophy. London, Methuen & Co., 1952.

COPLESTON, F.: A history of philosophy Vol. II: Augustine to Scotus. London, Burns Oates & Washbourne, 1954.

DE DOCTRINA J. DUNS SCOTI: Acta Congressus Scotistici internationalis, Oxonii et Edinburgi, 11-17 Sept. 1966. (Studia Scholastico-Scotistica, Vol. I-IV). Vol. I: Documenta et studia in Duns Scotum introductio. Rome, 1968. Vol. II: Problema Philosophica. Rome, 1968. Vol. III: Problema Theologica. Rome, 1968. Vol. IV: Scotismus de cursa saeculorum. Rome, 1968.

DEUS ET HOMO AD MENTEM, J. DUNS SCOTI. Acta tertii congressus scotistici internationalis, Videbonae, 28 Sept. - 2 Oct. 1970. (Studia Scholastico-Scotistica, Vol. V.) Rome, 1972.

DE SAINT-MAURICE, B.: John Scotus, A teacher for our times. (Trans. by D. Duffy) St. Bonaventure, NY, Franciscan Institute, 1955.

Doctorus subtilis et mariani Ioannis Duns Scoti, Opera Omnia, iussu et auctoritate Rmi. P. Pacifici M. Perantoni, studio et cura commissionis scotisticae, ad fidem codicum edita praeside P. Carolo Balic. Civitas Vaticana, 1950.

FINKENZELLER, J.: Offenbarung und Theologie nach der Lehre des Johannes Duns Scotus. Eine historische und systematische Untersuchung. Münster (Westfalen), Aschendorffsche Verlagsbuchhandlung, 1961.

225

GIEBEN, S.: Bibliographica scotistica recentior. *Lautianum*, 6:1-31, 1965.

GIEBEN, S., GROSSETESTE, S., BACON, R., OLIVI, P.J.: J. Duns Scotus (Series: Subsidia Scientifica Franciscalis, 6). Rome, Institutio Storico dei Cappucini, 1977.

GILSON, E.: Jean Duns Scot. Introduction à ses positions fondamentales. Paris, J. Vrin, 1952. (German edition: Johannes Duns Scotus. Einführung in die Grundgedanken seiner Lehre. Düsseldorf, 1959).

GILSON, E.: History of Christian Philosophy in the Middle Ages. London, Sheed and Ward, 1955.

GRAJEWSKI, M.: Scotistic bibliography of the last decade. *Franciscan Studies*, I & II, 1941-1942.

HARRIS, C.R.S.: Duns Scotus. Vol. I & II. Oxford, Clarendon Press, 1927.

HOERES, W.: La volonta come perfezione para in Duns Scoto. Padua, Ed. Liviana, 1976.

KLUXEN, W.: Johannes Duns Scotus. Abhandlung über das erste Prinzip. (Latin with German translation). Darmstadt, Wissenschaftliche Buchgesellschaft, 1974. (See p. xx-xxii for bibliography).

LEFF, G.: Medieval Thought. Harmondsworth, Penguin, 1968.

MARCEL, P. Ch.: La conception de la loi chez Duns Scot. *Philosophia Reformata*, 2:224-49, 1937.

MAURER, A.A.: Medieval Philosophy. New York, Random House, 1962.

MESSNER, R.: Schauendes und begriffliche Erkennen nach Duns Scotus mit kritische Gegenüberstellung zur Erkenntnislehre von Kant und Aristoteles. Freiburg, 1942.

MICKLEM, N.: Reason and revelation. A question from Duns Scotus. Edinburgh, Thomas Nelson and Sons, 1953.

MINGES, P.: Das Verhältnis zwischen Glauben und Wissen, Theologie und Philosophie nach Duns Scotus. Paderborn, Ferdinand Schöningh, 1908.

MINGES, P.: Joannis Duns Scotus doctrina philosophica et theologica. Vol. I & II, Quaracchi, 1908 (reprint 1930).

226

MüLLER, M.: Theologe und Theologie nach Johannes Duns Scotus. *Wissenschaft und Weisheit,* 1:39-51, 1934.

POLMAN, A.D.R.: Duns Scotus, Johannes. *In:* Christelijke Encyclopedie I, p. 519-20. Kampen, Kok, 1957.

RYAN, J.K. & BONANSEA, B.M. (ed.): John Duns Scotus 1265-1965. (Philosophy and the History of Philosophy, Vol. 3). Washington, 1965.

SASSEN, F.: Geschiedenis der Patristische en Middeleeuwse Wijsbegeerte. Antwerpen, Standaard-Boekhandel, 1950.

SASSEN, F.: Wijsgerig denken in de Middeleeuwen. Haarlem, De Erven F. Bohn, 1965.

SCHAEFER, O.: Bibliographia de vita, operibus et doctrina J. Duns Scoti ac Marioni Saecolorum xix-xx. Rome, Herder, 1955.

SCHAEFER, O.: Conspectus brevis bibliographiae scotisticae recentioris. *Acta Fratrum Minorum* 85:471-591, 1966.

SCHAEFER, O.: Resenha abreviada de bibliografia escotista mais recente. *Revista Portuguesa de Filosofia,* 23:338-368, 1967.

SHARP, D.E.: Franciscan philosophy at Oxford in the thirteenth century. Oxford, University Press, 1930.

SCHMIDT, A.M.: Literatur zu J. Duns Scotus (Zeit 1935). *Theologische Rundschau,* 34:1-41, 1969.

SEEBERG, R.: Die Theologie des Duns Scotus. Eine dogmengeschichtliche Untersuchung. Leipzig, Dieterich'sche Verlags-Buchhandlung, 1900.

TODISCO, D.: Lo spirito christiano della filosofia di Giovanni Duns Scoto. Rome, Ed. Abete, 1975.

UEBERWEG, F.: Grundriss der Geschichte der Philosophie. Vol. II: Die patristische und scholastische Philosophie (herausgegeben von B. Geyer.) Berlin, E.S. Mittler & Sohn, 1928.

VAN DER LAAN, H: Nature and supernature according to Duns Scotus. *Philosophia Reformata,* 38:62-76, 1973.

VIGNAUX, P.: Justification et prédestination au XIVe siècle. Duns Scot, Pierre d'Auriole, Guillaume d'Occam, Grégoire de Rimini. Paris, Librairie Ernest Leroux, 1934.

WOLTER, A.B.: The "theologism" of Duns Scotus. *Franziscanische Studien*, 7:257-73, 367-98, 1947.

WOLTER, A.B.: Duns Scotus and the necessity of revealed knowledge. Prologue to the *Ordinatio* of John Duns Scotus. *Franciscan Studies*, 11(3/4): 231-72, 1951.

WOLTER, A.: Duns Scotus. Philosophical writings. (Latin with English translation). Edinburgh, Thomas Nelson and Sons, 1962.

ZAMORA, G.: Dos anos de filosofia escotista (1965-1966). *Naturaleza y Gracia*, 14:385-96, 1967.

ZAMORE, G. & DE SOTIELLO, G.: Dos anos de filosofia escotista (1965-1966). *Naturaleza y Gracia*, 15:75-116, 1968.

13 BIBLICAL AND UNBIBLICAL TRAITS IN CALVIN'S VIEW OF MAN*

"The Catholic who thinks criticism of the *Summa* calls the gospel into question would be as wrong as the Calvinist who equates criticism of the *Institutes* with doubt about faith". Q. Breen: "St. Thomas and Calvin as theologians: A Comparison". *In:* The Heritage of John Calvin. Grand Rapids, W.B. Eerdmans, 1973, p. 24.

It is indeed the case that even today some Calvinists equate Calvin's doctrines with the Word of God. Quite recently I happened to hear that Calvin was not to be "tampered with".

H.A. Oberman defines this type of interpretation of Calvin as follows: "... not unlike the German phenomenon in the field of theology when a reference to Scripture is replaced by a quotation from Martin Luther, the classical school interprets Calvin with the pretence of presenting the Word of God itself. Valid theology is the reiteration of the positions described — and hence prescribed! — by Calvin"[1].

These types of Calvinists apparently regard Calvin as a super-historical figure who could interpret Scripture infallibly. With all the appreciation we should have for the pioneer work of the Reformer of Geneva in making the Word of God more explicit, we must never forget that he was a contemporary of his own times. Like any other thinker he was also exposed to various spiritual trends — including the secular ones — of his times. An unhistorical approach would be an injustice to Calvin. He can only be rightly understood — and valued — when his thinking is studied against the background of the climate of thought of the 16th century[2].

In this contribution only a preliminary reconnaissance in respect of one

* Abstract — apart from introduction and conclusion — from my dissertation *Die Natuurlike Teologie met besondere aandag aan die visie daarop by Thomas van Aquino, Johannes Calvyn en die "Synopsis Purioris Theologiae"*. 2 Vol.s, 900 pages (1974), p. 398-418. This abstract has been published (in Afrikaans) in *Tydskrif vir Christelike Wetenskap*, vol. 13:172-189, 1977.

1. H.A. Oberman: Calvin's critique of Calvinism. *In: Christian Higher Education. The contemporary Challenge*. Potchefstroom, IAC, 1976, p. 373.

2. For the various philosophical tendencies at the time of the Reformation cf. my thesis: *Die Natuurlike Teologie met besondere aandag aan die visie daarop by Thomas van Aquino, Johannes Calvyn en die "Synopsis Purioris Theologiae"*. (1974), p. 343-353 and p. 380-389.

facet of Calvin's thinking, viz. his Anthropology, is being attempted[2a].
The question arises as to what extent he could make the revelation of
Scripture manifest in his views about man and in what degree he was influenced by earlier and contemporary trends that would not be able to withstand the test of Scripture.

1. MAN AS A RELIGIOUS BEING

The deep religious character of the Reformation in a positively Christian
sense is also revealed in Calvin's view of man. Religion[3] is not regarded by
him as a subjective, introvert piety but is taken in the sense that man in the
core of his being is aligned to God and that this religious alignment controls
and determines his whole being. In this religious relationship man does not
occupy the foremost position but God, who has placed man in a covenant-

---

2.a. Apart from the secondary literature on Calvin's view of man supplied in the footnotes hereunder, the following literature can also be consulted on the subject:

G. Bockwoldt: Das Menschenbild Calvins. *Neue Zeitschrift für systematische Theologie
und Religionsphilosophie,* 19(2):170-198, 1968; H.H. Esser: Zur Anthropologie Calvins. Menschenwürde — imago Dei zwischen humanistischen und theologischem
Ansatz. (Paper delivered at Calvin Congress,   10-11 August 1977 in Pretoria);

J. Faber: Imago Dei — Calvijns leer over de mens als beeld God krachtens de schepping.
Lucerna, 1:5-32, 1960;

B. Hall: Calvin and Biblical humanism. *Huguenot Society of London.* Proceedings,
20:1959-2009, 1961;

Ph. Liard: *L'Anthropologie de Calvin. Recherche des thèmes, de leurs sources et essai
de critique.* (Montpellier, 1963);

R. McAlpine: *The Anthropology of Calvin and Brunner. A comparison* (Thesis, Union
Theological Seminary, Richmond, 1940);

R. Prins: The image of God in Adam and the restoration of man in Jesus Christ. A study in Calvin. *Scottish Journal of Theology,* 25:32-44, 1972 and

J.L. Schmidt: *A comparative study of the doctrine of man in Sigmund Freud and John
Calvin* (Thesis, Xenia Theological Seminary, Pittsburg, 1959).

Of great importance for the influence of Classical Philosophy (e.g. Plato, Aristotle,
Epicureans and Stoics) on Calvin's thought in general and his anthropology in particular is the recent study of C. Partee *Calvin and Classical Philosophy* (Leiden, Brill, 1977)
Unfortunately I received it at a stage when it was not possible any more to incorporate
important results from Partee's study in this article.

3. Calvin not only uses the concept *religio* (cf. the Latin title of his *Institutes*) but also
the word *cultus Dei.* A comparison of how Calvin uses these concepts reveals that they
are used as synonyms. Furthermore, with these two terms Calvin does not have in mind
private worship or church worship only, but rather the service of God in all areas of
life. (I recommend, therefore, that Calvin's concept *religio* should be translated in
Afrikaans and Dutch as "religie" and not "godsdiens".)

relationship to Himself, does[4].

2. SELF-KNOWLEDGE DEPENDENT ON KNOWLEDGE OF GOD

Already in the opening words of the *Institutionis Christianae Religionis* (in future abbreviated to ICR)[4a] it is evident how much importance Calvin attaches to the religious relationship between God and man especially in the knowledge of the self. "Nearly all the wisdom we possess, that is to say, true and sound wisdom, consists of two parts: the knowledge of God and of ourselves. But, while joined by many bonds, which one precedes and brings forth the other is not easy to discern. In the first place, no one can look upon himself without immediately turning his thoughts to the contemplation of God, in whom he 'lives and moves'. For, quite clearly, the mighty gifts with which we are endowed are hardly from ourselves; indeed, our very being is nothing but subsistence in the God"[5].

4. Cf. especially Schroten, De anthropologie van Calvijn. *In:* Waarheid, Wysheid en leven, p. 48:
„Wordt Calvijns anthropologie bepaald door de Schrift, dan volgt daaruit ook, dat zij zuiver religieus van aard is... Hem interesseert niet in de eerste plaats de mens-in-dekosmos, maar de-mens-voor-God.
„Wat is nu... het meest-typerend van Calvijns Anthropologie? Dat is onmiskenbaar dit: dat Calvijn voortdurend, zonder rechts of links te zien, de mens ziet *in zijn verhouding tot God"* (p. 58).

4.a. References to the *ICR* (we used the *Opera Selecta,* Vol. III-V edited by P. Barth and G. Niesel) are indicated in the following way: II, 15, 3 of which the Roman figure indicates the book (in this example Book II), the second figure the chapter (in this case chapter 15) and the last figure the paragraph (e.g. third paragraph).
In the case of translation from the *ICR* we made use of Calvin: *Institutes of the Christian Religion* edited by J.T. McNeill and translated by F.L. Battles (Vol. XX and XXI in "The Library of Christian Classics". Philadelphia, The Westminster Press, 1977[8]).

5. "Total fere sapientiae nostra summa, quae vera demum ac solida sapientia censeri debeat, duabus partibus constat, Dei cognitione et nostri. Caeterum quum multis inter se vinculis connexae sint, utra tamen alteram praecedat, et ex se pariat, non facile est discernere. Nam primo, se nemo aspicere potest quin ad Dei in quo vivit et movetur, intuitum sensus suos protinus convertat: quia minime obscurum est, dotes quibus pollemus, nequaquam a nobis esse; imo ne id quidem ipsum quod sumus, aliud esse quam in uno Deo subsistentiam." *ICR,* I, 1, 1. In *ICR* I, 15, 1, Calvin even makes the statement that "... God can not be clearly and thoroughly known to us unless knowledge of one's self accompanies this." ("... non potest liquido et solide cognosci Deus a nobis nisi accedat mutua nostri cognitio.").

The beginning of the second paragraph presents the opposite side of the picture: "Again, it is certain that man never achieves a clear knowledge of himself unless he has first looked upon God's face, and then descends from contemplating Him to scrutinize himself"[6].

Before going into the problems that are latent in these statements allow me first to make a more positive remark. In my opinion a clear proof is found in these quotations that Calvin's thinking is not purely cosmological[7]. Because he does not narrow down Ontology to Cosmology, he can begin immediately with God[8]. He does not need at a later stage to deduce the existence of God via creation. He does not make the knowledge of God dependent on the knowledge of creation but states emphatically that self-knowledge is not possible without knowledge of God. The visible does not determine the invisible but vice versa.

The problem in these statements of Calvin is, however, seated in the fact that he also maintains that self-knowledge can lead to knowledge of God. This standpoint of Calvin has already led to violent controversy. That selfknowledge would lead to knowledge of God is doubtful: "Calvijn zag schijnbaar voorbij, dat de kennis van onze ellendige toestand ons alleen tot God doet vlieden, wanneer de kennis van God reeds aanwezig is; men kan toch niet beweren, dat de kennis van onszelven als zodanig reeds leid tot de kennis van God"[9].

Others have seen in this the clear influence of St. Augustine on Calvin, considering that St. Augustine also saw the gist of wisdom in both self-

---

6. "Rursum, hominem in puram sui notitiam nonquam pervenire constat nisi prius Dei faciem sit contemplatus, atque ex illius intuitu ad sepsum inspiciendum descendat." *ICR*, I, 1, 2.

7. In typifying Calvin's thinking I apply D.H.Th. Vollenhoven's consistent problem-historical method. For a short exposition of this and an explanation of the terminology of the method see my articles: Wysgerige histioriografie. *Perspektief*, 8(2/3):70-117, June, 1969; 8(4):1-44, March 1970 and The Consistent problem-historic method. *Tydskrif vir Christelike Wetenskap*, 9:163-184, 1973.(This article is published as the first essay in this volume)

8. Matthews sees the importance of this point of departure of Calvin's when he affirms: "This conception of the infinite and sovereign God is the foundation-stone of Calvin's religion... Catholicism is essentially a doctrine of the church. Calvinism is essentially a doctrine of God". John Calvin. *In:* Hernshaw, ed., The Social and political ideas of some great thinkers of the Renaissance and the Reformation, p. 199.

9. Talma. *De anthropologie van Calvijn*, p. 25.

knowledge and knowledge of God[10]. On this point Calvin would then show the clear influence of Neo-Platonism. According to Battenhouse there can be no doubt about this: "The Neoplatonists regard intuition, the interior apprehension of the divine within the self and of the self in the light of the divine, as knowledge. They would advise man to begin with a study of himself, since in coming to know himself he must come to know God. If man will but survey his own talents, says Calvin in the opening paragraph of the *Institutes*, he will see that they are 'as it were so many streams conducting us to the fountainhead', God. The metaphor clearly suggests the Neoplatonic concept of emanation"[11].

In the author's opinion care must be taken that we are not led to over-hasty conclusions by the mere sound of words. Polman is probably nearer the truth. He shows that Luther, just as in the case of Calvin, accentuates the close relationship between self knowledge and the knowledge of God and that in this particular respect a stand is made against the neo-Platonic Augustinian conception: "Naar de klank der woorden beoordeeld schijnt hier een treffende overeenkomst te zijn tussen Augustinus' uitspraak en de beide door ons gegeven citaten van Luther en Calvijn. In werkelijkheid is het onderscheid radicaal. De Reformatoren gaat het om kennis in Bijbelse zin. Augustinus gaan het om kennis in Griekse zin..."[12].

In the writer's opinion what has already been formulated in connection with the religious character of Calvin's anthropology offers a solution here. In this respect it is profitable to refer to Schroten who says the following about Calvin: "Zijn leer aangaande de mens is geen psychologie, geen socio-logie, geen filosofie... Het gaat hem er niet in de eerste plaats om, de ver-houding van lichaam en ziel te doorgronden, noch om de mens te zien in zijn verhouding tot zijn medemens, of in zijn verhouding tot al wat maar ob-ject van zijn kennen kan zijn: hij richt zich op de verhouding van de mens tot zijn God, en van God tot de mens. Zijn anthropologie is een integre-rend deel van zijn 'onderwijzing in de christelijke godsdienst'.

10. Cf. inter alia St. Augustine's well-known statements in *Solioquia*, I, 7 and 11 4: "Deum et animam scire cupio. Nihilne plus? Nihil omnino", "Deus semper idem, no-verim me, noverim te."
The influence of St. Augustine on Calvin was indeed great. Cf. in this connection the register of writers used in the *ICR* as given by A. Sizoo in the Vol. III, p. 619-31 of his Dutch Translation of the *Institutes*. According to this Calvin makes roughly 260 refer-ences to St. Augustine! Cf. especially L. Smits *Saint Augustine dans L'oevre de Jean Calvin* (2 Vols.)

11. Battenhouse. The doctrine of man in Calvin and in Renaissance Platonism. *Journal of the history of ideas*, 9:453, 1948.

12. Polman: Calvijn en Luther. *In:* Vier redevoeringen over Calvijn (1959), p. 45.

"Calvijn ziet de mens steeds en vóór alles *in zijn relatie tot God.* Hij zoekt niet de zelfkennis op de weg der filosofen (vgl. I, 15, 6), die de mens op zichzelf zien, als een zelfstandig, autonoom wezen, met een eigen waardigheid en voortreffelijkheid, afgedacht van God. De mens is voor hem in geen opzicht te denken, zonder dat hem meteen Gód in gedachten komt"[13].

If we therefore interpret Calvin correctly, his statement does not mean that we must first get to know ourselves before we can know God. The introductory words of the ICR state emphatically that knowledge of self and knowledge of God take place as it were simultaneously and that the one cannot take place without the other. Viewed in the light of the religious relationship between God and man, as defined in Holy Scripture, this is correct, for only he who knows and acknowledges God and His Word, will know himself; and only he who (in the light of the Word) knows himself as a child of God, will acknowledge his Father.

The second citation quoted above reveals something more about Calvin's philosophy. In this citation his dualistic Ontology is faintly apparent when he says that man *descends* from his view of God to himself. From God as the transcendent man descends to the lower niveau of being, viz. man as part of the non-transcendent world.

3. MAN AS SOUL AND BODY

If uncertainty should still exist as to whether Calvin actually accepted a dualistic Ontology, this does become apparent in his anthropological views. Calvin's doctrine of a heavenly soul (because it originates from a transcendent God) and an eartly (i.e. non-transcedent) body reveals that he links up with an age old tradition.

As far back as his first writing after his conversion to Protestantism he treats of the structure of man, viz. consisting of body and soul. The *Psychopannychia* (1534) combats the idea of the soul in a sleep of death, in the case of deceased who have been believers[14]. A comparison of this work with what Calvin later formulated in ICR, I, 15 shows that he remained faithful to his earliest views. Consequently the ICR is mainly followed in our exposition and the *Psychopannychia* is only referred to when it provides

13. Schroten, op. cit., p. 56.

14. According to his "Foreword" the inventors of the theory are certain Arabs — evidently Averroes especially who taught that souls had no individual existence after death as they returned to the super-individual spirit.

more detail[15].

According to Calvin it remains undoubtedly a fact that man consists of two parts, viz. a heavenly soul and an earthly body[16]. He is also assured that the body is the incarceration *(ergastulum)* of the soul[17]. The body is the lower part of man, the less important, so that Calvin does not devote further attention to it but gives all his attention to the soul as the noblest part of man. The soul is the real man, the body happens to be incidental and, according to Calvin, practically a fortuitous evil. Calvin already implies this when he calls the body a prison or jail. It is even clearer when he states in ICR I, 15, 6 that man has undoubtedly been created for the purpose of contemplating heavenly life, but especially in chapters 9 & 10 of Book III where he treats of the contemplation of future life and the utilisation of this earthly life. Here the consequences of his dichotomistic view of man become apparent in a contempt for earthly corporal life. He says for example: "For this we must believe: that the mind is never seriously aroused to desire and ponder the life to come unless it be previously imbued with contempt for the present life"[18].

"Indeed, there is no middle ground between these two: either the world must become worthless to us or hold us bound by intemperate love of it. Accordingly, if we have any concern for eternity, we must strive diligently to strike off these evil fetters"[19].

Such statements may, of course, be interpreted that Calvin merely follows Biblical revelation. In the Bible we also encounter the tension

---

15. Of the *Psychopannychia* (in future abbreviated to *Ps.*) a Dutch translation in the series *Stemmen uit Geneve,* part VIII no. 8, July 1969 has been consulted. References occur according to the pages of this translation.

16. Cf. the opening words of *ICR* I, 15, 2: "Porro hominem constare anima et corpore, extra controversiam esse debet". Cf. also *Ps.,* p. 14 where it is propounded that man is divided into two parts of which the body has been taken from the earth, and the soul displays the image of God. Also p. 35 where he propounds that the heavenly soul must be distinguished from the earthly body.

17. Cf. e.g. *ICR* I, 15, 2 where it is expressed twice that the soul is released from the imprisonment *(ergastulum)* of the body and *ICR* III, 9, 4 where the liberation of the body as if from a prison is discussed. Cf. further *Ps.* p. 5 (The soul, as the best part of man is held fast by his earthly dwelling); p. 30 (The soul, as the better part is kept confined by the bonds of flesh and released by death); p. 34 (The body is a prison and foot-shackles for the soul) and p. 42 (The body is a burden to the soul).

18. *ICR* III, 9, 1.

19. *ICR* III, 9, 2.

between sinful present life and reborn future life. In the next paragraph (3) Calvin correctly states that contempt of life is not synonymous with hating life and showing ingratitude to God[20].

In the following paragraph (4) it is, however, evident that Calvin says more than Scripture permits. It becomes clear from this paragraph that un-biblical influences are responsible for an overstatement. His anthropological views are responsible for his contempt of life in this world. He states that present life compared to future life must be completely despised. For if heaven is our fatherland, what is the earth other than a resort of exile? If passing from this world is synonomous with entrance to life, what is the world then other than a grave? And what is living in the world other than lying in death? If release from the body entails being brought into complete freedom, what is the body then other than a prison?

In my opinion these ideas of Calvin are definitely not in accordance with Holy Scripture. His views in this connection are, however, understandable when seen against the background of his dualistic Ontology of a transcen-dent (heavenly) and a non-transcendent (earthly) sphere. Holy Scripture reveals that man as a creature of God is an inherent part of this (earthly) creation and – in spite of his fall – is domiciled here. For this reason the Bible speaks of a new *earth* which shall be man's fatherland.

Calvin's dichotomic Anthropology in which the soul is kept imprisoned by the body, necessitates an unscriptural longing for death, for through death the soul is freed from the body. According to him[21] there should be a longing for and no fear of death, for then we get rid of the "unstable, crumbling, corruptible, dilapidated, transitory tabernacle of our body" and the soul is recalled to its actual heavenly fatherland. He even suggests that no one has made good progress in the school of Christ if he does not await the day of his death with joy. As the result of his dichotomic Anthropology Calvin no longer espies anything terrifying in death. Death is actually a friend, as it releases us from the body and it does not affect the immortal soul – which is the actual human being.

It is true that Calvin uses well-known Biblical concepts and expressions (e.g. "tabernacle"). At the same time, however, it is also clear that his use of Biblical revelation is coloured by a specific anthropological conception.

---

20. This point of view in Calvin is classified by Weber & Troeltsch as "innerweltliche Askese". Cf. for more particulars, Duvenage: *Beroepsarbeid in die lig van die gerefor-meerde Etiek,* p. 41, foot-note 1. Runia, *Calvijn's betekenis voor onze tijd,* p. 38, 39 also uses this term in order to describe Calvin's attitude to life, shows exactly what he means by it and also that it need not necessarily be in conflict with Holy Scripture.

21. Cf. *ICR* III, 9, 5.

Stellingwerff's finding regarding Calvin's view of man is correct: "Deze dualistische mensopvatting van Calvijn doet geen recht aan de eenheid van de mens, strijdt met wat Gods Woord over de mens zegt, leidt tot valse problemen en tot verachting van de schepping. De leer dat de mens uit twee delen bestaat, een onsterfelijke ziel die in een lichamelijke kerker woont, is van griekse en niet Bijbelse afkomst. Die onsterfelijkheid van de ziel poogt Calvijn te bewijzen uit de heilige Schrift door te verwijzen naar plaatsen waar Paulus spreekt over de onsterfelijkheid die de gehele mens in de opstanding zal ontvangen. Wat in de herschepping aan de gehele mens geschonken wordt, kent Calvijn aan de ziel toe vanaf de schepping, zodat de opstanding des vleses voor Calvijn een bijkomende zaak wordt"[22].

Battenhouse also points to the unscriptural origin of Calvin's view of man when he says: "But one point, I think, is clear: that both the Neoplatonists and Calvin base their thinking about man on the premise of a dualism between soul and body. The soul is associated to the body yet ideally detached; the world is but a vestibule to heaven... The other-worldliness of Calvin, it seems quite clear, is more Greek than Hebrew. A fundamental dichotomy is set up between the inner man, who is concerned for eternal life, and man's external conduct, which concerns civil justice"[23].

Calvin's dualistic Anthropology also becomes apparent from the fact that he describes the soul as an incorporal being which has been placed in the body in which it lives as if in a house which it manages[24]. A variation on the image of the house (body) and its occupant (soul) is that of the body as a tabernacle.

Calvin defines the soul as follows: "I understand by the term 'soul' an

22. Stellingwerff: *Oorsprong en toekomst van de creatieve mens*, p. 20.

23. Battenhouse, op. cit., p. 468.
From the mere fact that Calvin adheres to a dichotomic Anthropology, it cannot be deduced that he is a neo-Platonic thinker. There are many types of dichotomic anthropologies!

24. Cf. *ICR* I, 15, 6. His problems with regard to dualism come to the fore in these words: "... now we must add that, although properly it (the soul) is not spatially limited, still, set in a body, it dwells there as in a house..."
According to the latest developments in Calvinistic philosophy everything in creation — also man as a whole — is spatially bound. Therefore the soul cannot be *in* the body and at the same time not spatially qualified. It would, however, be unfair to labour this point, because Calvin did not have the philosophical insights at his disposal which we have today.

immortal yet created essence, which is his nobler part"[25].

He adds that soul is equivalent to spirit (*spiritus*). However, if the words "soul" and "spirit" are used concomitantly, they have different meanings[26]. Apart from the question as to the correctness of this point of view it is very important that he uses *anima* and *spiritus* (mostly) as synonyms. As will become apparent later, his Anthropology is characterized as spiritualistic on these grounds.

Calvin also stresses (as was also apparent from former citations) that the soul or spirit is the "master" which directs the body[27].

In the light of Holy Scripture these anthropological views of Calvin cannot be accepted. Man, according to Holy Scripture, is not a combination of two different parts viz. soul and body but an indivisible unity of extraordinary complexity. To go into all Calvin's proofs from Scripture[28], is impossible at the moment as it would be within the compass of a new treatise. For this reason reference is only made to the most important contemporary literature on Biblical concepts like "soul"[29], "body"[30], "spirit"[31],

---

25. "... atque animae nomine essentiam immortalem, creatam tamen intelligo, quae nobilior eius pars est." *ICR*, 1, 15, 2.

26. A remarkable argument which only reveals Calvin's embarrassment when he tries to fit the different anthropological concepts of Holy Scripture (and the philosophers) into the dichotomic Anthropology, in which there is room for only *two* components in man!

27. Cf. especially *Ps.*, p. 31. (The soul, as the life of the body is such a mighty power that it maintains the material substance of the body, keeps it in motion and propels it); p. 41 (The soul gives man motion, feeling, the ability to reason, intellect and will) and p. 42 (The soul sets the body in motion and maintains it).

28. Calvin still sometimes relapses in this respect into allegorical exegesis. Cf. *Ps.* p. 29 for a superb example.

29. Cf. Becker: *Het begrip nefesh in het Oude Testament;* Id., Ziel, Bijbelsche gegevens *In:* Christelijke Encyclopaedie VI:693-5; Janse, *Om "de levende ziel";* Id. *De mensch als "levende ziel";* Id. *Van idolen en schepselen;* Von Meyenfeldt: *The meaning of ethos,* p. 54-6 and Ridderbos, *Paulus. Ontwerp van zijn Theologie,* p. 127, 128.

30. Cf. Ridderbos, op. cit., p. 123 and Kuitert, Mens en lichaam in de Heilige Schrift. *Vox Theologica,* 34(2):37-50, 1963.

31. Cf. Crump, *Pneuma in the Gospels;* Scheepers, *Die Gees van God en die gees van die mens in die Ou Testament* en Waaning, *Onderzoek naar het gebruik van "pneuma" bij Paulus.*

"flesh"[32] and "heart"[33], which in the opinion of the writer reveals an interpretation more in accordance with Holy Scripture than that of Calvin.

A. Janse, who has undertaken such pioneer work to develop an Anthropology more in accordance with the teachings of Holy Scripture, finds it a pity that Calvin did not dispute the Greek conception of the soul more profoundly and replace this with a conception based on the teachings of Holy Scripture[34]. I keep in mind the possibility that I may err, but the reading of the ICR often gives the impression that Calvin (as the result of an inadequate historical notion, mainly as regards the history of philosophy) in his rejection of certain standpoints derived from Greek or synthetic thought often delivers criticism more of the *implications* thereof, than of the *basic points of departure* and presuppositions. This may be one of the reasons why he (sometimes too easily?) makes use of the fruits of pagan thought.

4. IMMORTALITY OF THE SOUL

Attention must particularly be directed to the fact that the soul is an immortal being (*essentia immortalis*). Calvin lays great stress on the fact that man has an essence (*essentia*)[35], viz. the soul, as well as the fact that this is an immortal essence. It is, however, difficult to reach definite conclusions on the ground of these statements of Calvin, such as that he (like Aristotle and Thomas Aquinas) would think in a hylemorphistic manner or would accept a subsistence theory. Although he calls the soul itself the essence of man, he says later again that the divine seed is engraved in the soul. (Interesting research may await the person who would endeavour to trace

32. Cf. Lindijer, *Het begrip sarx bij Paulus.*

33. Cf. Becker, Het begrip ,,hart" in het Oude Testament. *Geref. Theol. Tijdschrift.* 50:10-16, 1950; Von Meyenfeldt, *Het hart (leb, lebab) in het Oude Testament;* Id. Enige algemene beschouwingen gegrond op de betekenis van het hart in het Oude Testament. *In:* Wetenschappelijke bijdragen door leerlingen van Vollenhoven, p. 52-67; Id. *The meaning of ethos,* p. 49-54 and Ridderbos, op. cit., p. 126, 127. The study of Popma's *Levensbeschouwing* in seven parts is worth while reading for a real Biblically orientated Anthropology.

34. Cf. Janse, *De factoren die geleid hebben tot de inzinking van het Calvinisme in ons land in de 17e en 18e eeuw,* p. 18.

35. Cf. *ICR* I, 15, 2 where attention is often (seven times) drawn to the fact that the soul is something "essential". From other statements it appears that "essence" and ,,substance" are used by him as synonymous.

the influences of Stoicism on Calvin's thought in this respect).

Calvin produces various proofs that the soul is an *immortal* essence. Such is the conscience, which can distinguish between good and bad, an indisputable proof of an immortal spirit. Furthermore the fact that the soul can have knowledge of God proves that it is immortal. All the excellent gifts of the soul, the mobility with which it can examine heaven and earth as well as the fact that intelligence can comprehend the invisible, like God and the angels, are also used as proofs. According to Calvin something must lie hidden in the body which is differentiated from it, for even in sleep, which seemingly renders man unconscious and deprives him of life, man can have thoughts of present and future matters.

After these reasonable proofs Calvin further tries to confirm his belief in an immortal soul with proofs from Holy Scripture[36]. Holy Scripture, according to him, also teaches that at death we depart from the tabernacle of the flesh, the corruptible body. The soul has originated from another world and is not quite at home in this world. It ascends above this world: "The very knowledge of God sufficiently proves that souls, which transcend the world, are immortal"[37].

It therefore looks as if the soul is something transcosmic which tarries only temporarily in the cosmos (human body). In any case it is clear that the background of Calvin's dichotomistic thought that the soul originates "from another world" and transcends this world to a certain extent, is seated in his dualistic Ontology: the soul is either a part of the transcendent world (to which God also belongs) or something from the transcendent sphere in the non-transcendent world.

Calvin expressly also says that "something divine is engraved" in the soul[38].

The difficulty here — as throughout this whole essay — is *how serious* such statements of Calvin should be taken. Does he simply utilise the common language of his day to say something about man, or should such statements be regarded as a deliberate effort towards a theological (or philosophical) explication of his anthropology. To put it differently: was Calvin fully aware of the fact that he uses expressions with a long tradition and

---

36. Cf. chiefly the *Psychopannychia* in which Calvin substantiates with many "proofs" from the Bible the immortality of the soul after death, in opposition to the propopents of the soul in a death sleep.

37. "iam ipsa Dei cognitio satis coarguit, animas quae mundum transcendunt, esse immortales..." *ICR* I, 15, 2.

38. Cf. *ICR* I, 15, 2.

often dangerous philosophical background?

Calvin will, however, be misunderstood if he should be accused that he has not distinguished between God and man. He actually criticises those (like the Manichees and Servetus) who think that the soul is a shoot from the divine being as if a part of the infinite godhead should have flowed into man: "All these things one must attribute to God's nature, if we understand the soul to be from God's essence, or to be a secret inflowing of divinity. Who would not shudder at this monstrous thing? Indeed, Paul truly quotes Aratus that we are God's offspring, but in quality, not in essence, inasmuch as he, indeed, adorned us with divine gifts"[39]. He subsequently refutes, in a reasonable way, the idea that man would be an effusion from the being of God. The being of God certainly cannot be torn apart so that each creature possesses a part!

As will be evident later, Calvin wishes to call man the image of God although not implying by this an equality of being between God and man. Man can be a mirrored reflection of God, owing to the fact that he is "divine" on a small scale.

In spite of Calvin's above-mentioned criticism of the idea of a relativity of being between God and man, his thought is not entirely free from speculations about the essence of being. His creationistic viewpoint concerning the origin of the soul clearly shows that the soul is something divine in man[40].

According to Schroten Calvin simply means the continued existence after death when he speaks of the immortality of the soul, for Holy Scripture proclaims eternal death (i.e. the God-forsakenness) of the unbelievers and it would not be possible if the souls ceased to exist after the death of the body. The soul that sins will die, because life can only exist in communion with God. "Immortality", according to Calvin, thus primarily means

---

39. "... que omnia Dei naturae ascribere conveniet, si recipimus animam esse Dei essentia, vel arcanum divinitatis influxum. Quis ad hoc portentum non exhorreat? Vere quidem ex Arato Paulus nos dicit esse Dei progenium (Act. 17 f. 28): sed qualitate, non substantia, quatenus scilicet divinis nos dotibus ornavit" *ICR* I, 15, 5.

40. Calvin grapples with the old dilemma of a choice between Traducianism and Creationism. Talma, op. cit., draws attention to the fact that Calvin, in his doctrine of original sin, thinks in the traducianistic way (cf. foot-note 1, p. 51), but that he does not, in doing so, accept Traducianism (cf. p. 97). According to Talma, Calvin says in his commentary on Joh. 3:6 that his doctrine of the *peccatum originale* does not conflict with his Creationism (cr. p. 97). He also ascribes the fact that Calvin does not offer any rounded off doctrine on original sin to the fact that Calvin vacillated between Traducianism and Creationism (cf. p. 104). According to Den Hertog, however, Calvin is indeed a Creationist. Cf. De Anthropologie van Calvijn. *Vox Theologica*, 9:146 (foot-note 3), 1937.

the eternal life of the redeemed with God[41].

If Schroten's interpretation of Calvin is correct, then Calvin's thinking is decidedly more in accordance with Holy Scripture than it would seem at first glance, for Holy Scripture uses the conception "immortality" (except for God) in the case of the believer only of his state after resurrection[42]. The question of course still remains as to whether, according to Holy Scripture, man as such (set in dichotomistic terminology: body *and soul)* does not die and rises from death and that only then can mention be made of the immortality of *man* (as against the second death of the unbelievers).

Wendel maintains that the immortality of the soul, according to Calvin, is a gift of God which He can withdraw from man, so that it can cease to exist just like the body. In Calvin's viewpoint the soul does thus not possess a natural immortality. In this connection Wendel quotes from Calvin's *Treatise on freewill* against Pighius which he translates as follows: "For likewise we do not agree that the soul is immortal of itself. What is more, that is the teaching of St. Paul, who ascribes immortality to God alone. We do not therefore believe, however, that the soul is mortal by its nature, for we do not estimate the nature of the same by the primary faculty of the essence, but by the perpetual state, that God has put into his creatures"[43].

According to this statement of Calvin it thus seems that in using the expression "immortality" he wishes to express the Biblical idea that man as a result of God's mercy is an imperishable being, so that even the second death which the unbelievers die, does not entail the destruction of man. The question still remains, however, why Calvin speaks only of the immortality of the soul. In spite of all attempts to defend Calvin here, it is clear that certain effects of unscriptural thoughts can be discerned in him.

This becomes even more evident in Calvin's thoughts concerning man as the image of God, to which subsequent attention will be paid.

5. MAN AS THE IMAGE OF GOD

Calvin arrives at the idea of the image of God by introducing it as one of the proofs that the soul is an immortal being. To him it is a foregone conclu-

---

41. Schroten, op. cit., p. 61-2.

42. Cf. Snyman, Lewe, dood en onsterflikheid. *Koers,* 28(10):417-30, 1961.

43. Wendel, *Calvin, The origins and development of his religious thought,* p. 175.

sion that the actual seat of the image lies in the soul[44]. Arising from the fact that he employs the word seat *(sedes)*, it appears that he sees the state of being an image of God as there being something *in* man. That this "something" is considered to be divine or heavenly is also evident from his criticism of Osiander who applies the idea of the image of God without distinction to body and soul. Calvin's criticism is that heaven and earth get mixed up in this fashion[45]. (It is surely not necessary to draw attention once more to the dualistic background of these thoughts in the mind of Calvin. He wishes to make a distinction between heaven and earth, or the transcendent and the non-transcendent. The soul is clearly regarded by him as something transcendent. Compare the following paragraph as well where he maintains that man rises above other creatures or is separated from them as a result of being endowed with a transcendent soul.)

Calvin wishes to apply the idea of the image of God also to the body but not without reservations and differences: "And although the primary seat of the divine image *(divinae imaginis)* was in the mind and heart, or in the soul and its powers, yet there was no part of man, not even the body itself, in which some sparks *(scintillae)* did not glow. It is sure that even in several parts of the world some traces *(lineamenta)* of God's glory shine. From this we may gather that when his image is placed in man a tacit antithesis is introduced which raises man above all other creatures and, as it were, separates him from the common mass"[46].

The thoughts expressed here by Calvin are found in the writings of many early Christian and Medieval thinkers and are typical of a hierarchical structure of being. The human soul comes from heaven and therefore from God himself (the transcendent) and is thus the image *(imago)* of God. In the body, which is the lower (non-transcendent) part, only sparks *(scintillae)* of his divinity glow. In the different parts of the world some traits *(linea-*

---

44. Cf. *ICR*, I, 15, 3 in which he repeats it time and again. Cf. also *Ps.*, p. 12 and 13. (The body is fashioned out of the earth, but only after the breath of life was blown into it, is it said that man is the image of God.)

45. Cf. ibid.

46. "Ac quamvis primaria sedes Diviniae imaginis fuerit in mente et corde, vel in anima eiusque potentiis: nulla tamen pars fuit etiam usque ad corpus, in qua non scintillae aliquae micarent. Certum est in singulis etiam mundi partibus fulgere lineamenta quaedam gloriae Dei: unde colligere licet, ubi in homine locatur eius imago, tacitam subesse antithesin que hominem supra alias omnes creaturas extollat, et quasi separet a vulgo". *ICR* I, 15, 3.
It is interesting to note that Calvin in this statement apparently uses the concepts "mind", "heart" and "soul" as synonyms.

menta) of God glitter, too[47].

The fact that Calvin says that man is called the image of God because "he is equal to God"[48] or that God "made himself perceptible in the form of an image by means of engraved marks of likeness"[49] shows how literally Calvin regarded the idea of an image of God.

That this entire train of thought is intimately linked up with his philosophical view of law *(logoi spermatikoi)* as a divine seed implanted in creation is also apparent from the fact that he does not regard man alone as divine. He does not only regard nature as divine but "in pious sense" says that nature itself *is* God![50].

Calvin's doctrine of the *imago Dei* becomes even clearer when he asserts[51] that it is not necessary to go outside one's self to find God as man finds God within himself hundreds of times. The fact that some philosophers have designated man as a microcosm (the world on a small scale) meets with Calvin's approval in a context like this.

Calvin's ideas about man as microcosm in his *Institutes* is not very clear. It is possible that he used the concept more or less "innocently", to explain to his readers in an illustrative way something about the difficult problem how man could be the image of God. The other possibility is that Calvin was more "serious"; that his utilization of the idea of man as microcosm describes exactly his own viewpoint about the ontological (instead of, to my mind, religious) relationship between God and man. What is offered below is therefore merely a preliminary hypothesis.

It seems as if God is viewed as the macrocosmic world and man as the microcosmic world. In accordance with the classical macro-microcosmic theory the macro- and micro-cosmos were respectively the universal and the individual. The universal and the individual, according to this type of partial universalism, look exactly the same and differ only in size. Possibly owing

---

47. Torrance rightly avers that in Calvin a distinction should be made between *imago Dei* in its general meaning (God is reflected by the whole of creation as if in a mirror) and *imago Dei* in the narrower meaning in which it applies only to man (specifically his soul). Cf. *Calvin's Doctrine of Man,*, p. 35-42.

48. Cf. *ICR* I, 15, 3: "... deinde in re ipsa nulla est ambiguitas quin Dei imago nominetur homo, quia Deo similis est."

49. Cf. Ibid: "... in quo seipsum velut in imagine repraesentaret, propter insculptas similitudinis notas".

50. Cf. *ICR* I, 5, 5.

51. Cf. *ICR* I, 5, 3.

to ignorance of the classical theory of macro-microcosm, or because he wished to adapt the original theory to fit into his thinking, Calvin accepts partial universalism with a macro-micro-cosmic theme, whereby God is seen as the macro- and man as the micro-cosmos. The idea that the macrocosmos (the world on a great scale) and the microcosmos (world on a small scale) are identical, irrespective of size, is retained. Hence he could say that man on a small scale is divine or displays the image of God.

Although there is a difference between Calvin's view of man and what could generally be termed "the view of man in Medieval times" the similarities are evident[52]. Den Hertog is correct when he says the following about Calvin's anthropology: "Ofschoon Calvijn zich krachtig verzet heeft tegen Humanisme en Scholastiek en reformatories teruggegrepen heeft op het Schriftgetuigenis, bovenal op Paulus, is het hem toch niet gelukt met die beide sterke geestesrichtingen, geheel af te rekenen en ze restloos te doen verdwijnen. Reeds als reactie mag Calvijns leer niet los van haar historische omgeving beschouwd worden"[53].

Wolmarans affirms the following regarding Calvin's views of man as the image of God: "As in the case of Tertullian Calvin is prone to be inclined to attack philosophers sharply, but he is just as ready to accept much more from pagan philosophers than could be brought to tally with Holy Scripture. His anthropology is actually Hellenistic and reveals a great number of anti-Israelitic elements ... it must be concluded, in particular from his love of Plato, that humanism exerted great pressure on Calvin..."[54].

Irrespective of the question as to whether Plato should be branded as the culprit, Wolmarans is correct in his assessment. Calvin's idea that the soul alone constitutes the image of God tallies with his dichotomistic view of man in which the soul is regarded as the divine, godly or better part of man. As already stated, this form of dichotomy does not find any substantiation in Holy Scripture. Furthermore, Holy Scripture does not teach that *something in man,* viz. his soul, is the image of God, but that *man* is created in the image and likeness of God. The image and likeness of God is not *in* man but man *is* His image and likeness. (Hence it would also be wrong to

---

52. Something like "the current view of man in the Middle ages" of course does not exist, for every thinker's view of man is indeed different in details — even if the differences are minute.

53. Den Hertog, op. cit., p. 139.

54. Wolmarans. *Die mens naar die beeld van God,* p. 104. (English translations by B.J. van der Walt.) On p. 108 he even avers that Calvin's view of man inclined more to Plato than to the Bible.

speak of man as the image *bearer* of God, considering that it creates the impression that man, irrespective of his state of being man, yet has some additional attribute which renders him the image of God). Although it is to be appreciated that Calvin expresses no desire to call the soul "a shoot from divine being", it still remains an open question whether he has succeeded in his ideas concerning the image of God in maintaining the radical difference between God and man. In the writer's opinion the danger of a relativism of being is no longer imaginary when the image is seen as something divine in the human soul. (It is not a suitable occasion now to go into detail on how Calvin makes use of various sections of Holy Scripture to substantiate his dichotomic view of man).

The problems Calvin experiences by assimilating, in his view of man, data from Holy Scripture *and* pagan philosophy – which he takes over via early Christian and Medieval synthetic though – are clearly evident from his representation of the parlous state of man as the image of God after his fall into sin.

6. NATURE AND SUPERNATURE IN MAN

In Book I, chapter 15, paragraph 4 of his ICR Calvin says that merely by saying that the soul is the reflection of God's glory, one has not yet given any complete indication of the image of God. Calvin agrees with Paul who sees the image of God as knowledge, righteousness and holiness, from which Calvin deduces that in the beginning the image of God existed in the light of the intellect, uprightness of the heart and the soundness of all its parts.

Everything relating to the spiritual, eternal life is included in this idea of the image of God. The image of God is the undefiled, unscathed excellence of human nature.

A problem arises at this stage: On the one hand, in the writer's opinion, the *imago Dei* is correctly taken (according to Holy Scripture) as knowledge, righteousness and holiness. But on the other hand Calvin links it with human nature. ("Nature" understood here as the essence or soul of each human being.)

For the latter he appeals to Plato who, according to Calvin, finds the image of God in the soul[55]. The image of God is then connected with reason and with the seed of religion *(religionis semen)* which is engraved in **reason**. He accepts Plato's five senses and apparently the theory of know-

55. Cf. *ICR* I, 15, 6.

ledge which is concomitant[56]. Later he brings in Aristotle[57] and accepts that there are two parts in the human soul, viz. intelligence (*intellectus*) and will (*voluntas*).

Calvin's argument gives the impression of uncertainty. He says that he gladly leaves it to philosophers to deal with the faculties of the soul more soundly. He agrees with Plato's classification of the faculties of the soul or at least regards it as probable, and says that anyone who wishes to classify them in any other way, may do so, as far as he is concerned. On the one hand he condemns Aristotle for splitting hairs and on the other hand he admits that Aristotle spoke the truth[58]. Eventually the reformer of Geneva falls for the division of the soul into two faculties viz. mind (or reason) and will and he is able to embroider further on them both.

This uncertainty in Calvin is caused by his effort to combine different philosophical ideas about man into one conception. The question can be asked if Calvin was not aware of the fact that pagan philosophical ideas are irreconsilable with the Biblical revelation about man.

In our assessment of Calvin's ideas it should, however, be kept in mind that he stands in a long Christian tradition. During the previous more than a thousand years Christian thinkers assimilated data from Holy Scripture *and* pagan philosophy. Foreign philosophical ideas in the thought of Calvin may also be part of this heritage. Acknowledging this fact should, on the one hand, encourage a mildness in our judgement of Calvin. On the other

56. Cf. Ibid.: "Therefore I admit in the first place that there are five senses, which Plato preferred to call organs, by which all objects are presented to common sense, as in a sort of receptacle. There follows fantasy, which distinguishes these things which have been apprehended by common sense; then reason, which embraces universal judgement; finally understanding, which in intent and quiet study contemplates what reason discursively ponders..."

57. Cf. here as well *Ps.* p. 10: "Plato delivered outstanding work on the soul in various places, but the most sagacious of all was Aristotle. But what the soul is and whence it comes is sought in vain from them."
From the last sentence it is evident that Calvin did not uncritically accept everything offered by the past. It is a pity that he did not mention precisely in what respect he differs from, for instance, Plato. His own viewpoint then, would have been much clearer. Calvin's preference however, is evident, viz that the Word of God deserves the final authority.

58. Talma, op. cit., p. 43, also indicates the change that occurs when Calvin treats of the *animae facultates*: "De stijl verliest aan levendigheid, de gedachtengang aan regelmaat; en het geheel maakt den indruk, dat Calvijn zelf zich op dit gebied niet bijzonder thuis voelt. Het gevoelen van Plato en dat van Aristoteles worden eerste meegedeeld; zonder eenige nadere verklaring of protest; de meededeeling begint met een woord van goedkeuring".

hand it makes our research more difficult: it is possible that the Plato, for instance, which Calvin had in mind, was not the original Plato but a Christianized version of the Platonic philosophy.

Apart from this the question asked earlier, viz. how serious Calvin's statements should be taken, again arises here. Especially when he says, for instance, anyone who wants to classify the faculties of the soul in another way may — as far as he is concerned — do so.

In recapitulation it can, however, be said that Calvin's vision of the soul as the image of God consists of two components of which the one originates from Holy Scripture and the other from pagan philosophy.

From Book II, chapters 1 and 2 of the ICR, which treat of the fall of man, it appears that Calvin sets out the two parts as the natural, as opposed to, the supernatural. In Chapter 1 he had already contrasted the natural and supernatural[59]. In Chapter 2, however, he explicitly says: "And, indeed, that common opinion which they have taken from Augustine pleases me: that the natural gifts were corrupted in man through sin, but that his supernatural gifts were stripped from him"[60]. Augustine's distinction between natural and supernatural is thus adopted by Calvin. An important question is whether Calvin accepted the doctrine of the two realms which during the Middle Ages usually had specific anthropological links. According to Klapwijk Calvin usually makes use of the distinction between natural and supernatural only in the sense of natural life (birth from earthly parents) and spiritual rebirth[61]. Klapwijk says in this connection: "Calvijn was een kind van zijn tijd, ook van de denkwereld van zijn tijd. Het is derhalve begrijpelijk, dat hij veelszins nog gedacht en geschreven

---

59. Cf. *ICR* II, 1, 7 (end) and II, 1, 9 (middle).

60. "Ac illa quidem vulgaris sententia quam sumpserunt ex Augustino, mihi placet, naturalia dona fuisse corrupta in homine per peccatum, supernaturalibus autem exinanitum fuisse" III, 2, 12.
It is exceedingly interesting that Calvin bases his doctrine of a residue of the image of God in man on John 1:5 and thus lands in the age-old tradition of the logos-speculation. We encounter this theory already with the Christian Apologists to whom the prologue to the gospel of John also formed the favourite text. According to Calvin this text means that sparks still glitter in the depraved nature of man which shows that he is a being capable of reasoning and therefore differs from the animals. Cf. *ICR* II, 2, 12.
Talma, op. cit., p. 67, states correctly that John did not have in mind the remnants of the image of God in the first chapter of his Gospel, but gives a resumé of the course of God's revelation to Israel.

61. Cf. Klapwijk, Calvijn over de filosofie. *Correspondentiebladen van de Vereniging voor Calvinistische Wijsbegeerte*, 36:15, March 1972.

heeft in denkschemas en voorstellingen van zijn eeuw, zonder dat men deze nu direkt moet zien en beoordelen als tijpisch voor Calvijn. Met Kuyper ben ik van mening, dat het typische van Calvijn niet zozeer schuilt in wat hij gemeen heeft met zijn tijdgenote, maar in wat hem juist van zijn tijdgenoten onderscheidt en waarin hij iets nieuws naar voren heeft gebracht"[62].

What Klapwijk propounds here, is indeed true but in the writer's opinion Calvin, by distinguishing *naturalia-supernaturalia*, dit not have the difference between an unconverted and a converted person in mind. Calvin is in this respect decidedly influenced by the Scholastic doctrine of two realms and speculations closely related to the image of God.

Calvin hence divides the *dona* of the image of God into *naturalia* and *supernaturalia*. The *naturalia* consists of the qualities which make man man *(facultates animae)*, and the *supernaturalia* consist of those qualities that constitute a Christian (knowledge, righteousness, holiness)[63].

The supernatural image was lost with the fall of man, but the natural image was only corrupted. For if it was lost, man would cease to be man — man without mind and will does not exist[64].

This distinction explains why Calvin sometimes says that nothing good was left in man after the fall of man[65] and why on other occassions he apparently contradicts himself when he mentions so many good gifts in (sinful) man[66].

It is apparent how Calvin's Anthropology could impede him in seeing the

62. Ibid., p. 13, 14.

63. Later Calvinistic thinkers would appeal to this distinction for their own distinction between formal and material image, *imago essentialis et accidentalis* or image in wider and narrower sense.

64. Talma rightly shows that there is not a great difference between Calvin's vision and that of Roman Catholicism according to which the fall of man entails merely the loss of supernatural endowments without any considerable change in the nature of man.
Cf. op. cit., p. 64, 65 where Talma gives a clear exposition of Calvin's teachings on the *dona naturalia* and *dona supernaturalia*.

65. Cf. e.g. *ICR* II, 1, 9: "Unde sequitur partem illam, in qua refulget animae praestantia et nobilitas, non modo vulneratam esse, sed ita corruptam, ut non modo sanari, sed novam prope naturam induere opus habeat." Cf. also II, 3, 1.

66. According to *ICR,* II, 2, 16 these gifts must evidently not be seen as a proof that man did not fall in his entirety, but as gifts of the Holy Spirit which He bestows for general use on mankind, to whomsoever it pleases Him.

fall of man in all respects as radical[67]. The natural image in the soul (the mind and will) is in a certain sense unaffected by sin[68]. In this way, however, Calvin succeeds in preserving man from pride as well as passivity, for if anything is left of the image of God man still remains responsible. This also makes it possible for him to be able to justify a certain *semen religionis* in man after his fall from grace.

In ICR Book II, chapters 2 and 3 (in which Calvin deals with the fact that man is subjected to pitiful bondage and that from man's depraved nature nothing but the damnable comes forth) time and again the fact that something good remained in man comes to the fore. In paragraph 13 of chapter 2 he differentiates between earthly and heavenly affairs. In earthly affairs man is still capable of attaining something but not in heavenly affairs (the pure knowledge of God and the mysteries of the heavenly kingdom). Man's reason in spiritual matters is blinder than a bat[69].

---

67. Den Hertog op. cit., p. 145, states that Calvin is prevented by his acceptance of the Scholastic distinction in the image of God from reaching a correct viewpoint: "Teveel heeft hij zich hier aangesloten bij de gangbare anthropologie zijner dagen om werkelijk in alle onderdelen, reformatories en bijbels, radikaal met de oude brekend, de zuiver-theocentriese lijn zijner mensbeschouwing te kunnen doortrekken."
Battenhouse offers criticism (although possibly exaggerated) which confirms our idea that Calvin (as a result of the bipartition of the image) does not always regard the fall of man in a sufficiently radical way. He says: "... I think it may be remarked that the loss of this 'image' seems to be for Calvin... a more central concern than man's loss of God. That is, fallen man's formlessness rather than his loneliness receives chief attention: the corruption of his nature as man more than the disruption of fellowship with his Creator." Op. cit., p. 456, 457.

68. Den Hertog, op. cit., foot-note 5, p. 147, sees a close relationship between Calvin's ideas on a residue and immortality. On the one hand the residue is maintained and thus also the idea of immortality, and on the other hand immortality (which is an inherent quality of the image) necessitates the acceptance of a residue.
Torrance who devotes, in *Calvin's doctrine of man*, four chapters to Calvin's ideas concerning the image of God, also stresses his distinction between the spiritual (supernatural) and the natural image of God. The spiritual image is not a natural (but supernatural) property of the soul — although the soul is seat of the image! Cf. chapter 4, 5 and 6. In chapter 7, in which Torrance treats of Calvin's ideas about the fall of man, the distinction is again broached and he explicitly affirms that the fall of man deprived him of his spiritual (supernatural) gifts and corrupted his natural ones. The remains or residue of the image of God relate exclusively to the natural side of the image of God. Cf. p. 83, 84.

69. Cf. *ICR* II, 2, 18. Calvin says here that three things are of prime importance as far as spiritual matters in the kingdom of God is concerned: knowledge of God, his grace on which our salvation is based and the organisation of our lives according to the rule of law. In the first two, but particularly in the second he contemptuously compares man's reasoning ability to the blindness of bats.

To the first group (earthly matters) belong government, home life and the various arts and sciences. Man is capable of living in a state and in a family because "the seeds of law are implanted in all human beings"[70], "in all people a certain seed of civic order is strewn" and no man is deprived of "the light of reason".

Hence Calvin can also express appreciation for the works of pagan writers and the excellence of various sciences[71]. He is compelled to acknowledge the excellence of their works and the little drops of truth (*veritatis guttulae*). We are confronted here with the problem of the "elements of truth" in pagan thought. Possibly the problem should not be seen as *whether* man after his fall into sin could exercise arts and sciences but *how* he did so, what direction he took (e.g. to the glory of God or with the aim of self-glorification.) Because Calvin sees the fall as a loss of supernatural gifts, it is a problem as to how man still has all kinds of abilities at his disposal, and Calvin could only explain these as residues of the (natural) image.

7. SYNTHESIS OF CALVIN'S ANTHROPOLOGICAL VIEW

Keeping the above-mentioned in mind, the Anthropology of Calvin could preliminarily be characterised as follows according to the consistent problem-historical method. It is a dichotomic view of man rooted in a dualistic Ontology. In dualistic ontologies two types of anthropologies can be differentiated. According to some, man has an entirely non-transcendent nature. Such views are indicated as dualism without an anthropological dichotomy. Others — and of these Calvin's Anthropology is a clear example — believe that man is not purely of a non-transcendent nature, but in his "composition" also contains something transcendent (usually the soul or a part of it). Man thus consists of two different parts. Hence the term dichotomy for this type of anthropology over against the first mentioned

---

70. Calvin stresses natural law (*lex naturalis*) in particular. In *ICR* II, 2,22 he links it to conscience (*conscientia*) which acts with the force of law as it distinguishes between good and evil. Conscience is therefore evidently something unscathed in man, a part of the residual, natural part of the image of God. (In *ICR* II, 2, 24 he speaks of the testimony of conscience which persuades man.)

In *ICR* II, 3,3 Calvin explicitly draws the conclusion that human nature cannot be entirely sinful. He relates it to the grace of God — not to purify depravity but to keep sin under control. Also in II, 2, 17, he speaks of God's (general and particular) grace in this connection.

71. Cf. *ICR* II, 2, 15.

type which does not see two different "parts" in man, because man is in that case wholly of a non-transcendent character. Calvin acknowledges the existence of a spiritual sphere above the material. Besides the lower body he also accepts a higher soul. Taking into account that the soul is regarded by him as spirit *(spiritus)*, it seems if his Anthropology can be classified as spiritualistic: the spirit, as soul, originating from the transcendent God which is also Spirit, returns after the death of the material body to its transcendent Origin.

8. BALANCE

What has been said thus far about Calvin's view of man may seem — especially to some Calvinists — rather hyper-critical.

Calvin has, however, been quoted from his own works and as far as possible not been judged by any contemporary philosophical anthropology. (In any case it would be unfair to condemn anyone in such a way 450 years after his lifetime!) An attempt based on Holy Scripture — which Calvin also regarded as the final authority — has been made to show that a large part of his Anthropology cannot stand the test. (We should of course consider to what extent our understanding of Holy Scripture is also influenced by philosophical presuppositions of our own times!)

The sense of writing an article like this can also be queried. Would it not be much better to concentrate on the positive aspects by bringing out what is unique in Calvin's view of man? There were surely facets in his view of man in which he broke with tradition! (For instance: After Augustine he is the first again to realize the importance of the Biblical concept of the heart — compare his idea of the offering of the heart to God. We mentioned at the beginning the deep religious character of his anthropology: man cannot be understood apart from his Creator.)

To my mind Calvin's own particular contribution in this respect cannot be shown unless one assesses the extent to which he was tied down to earlier and contemporary anthropological ideas. In this article an attempt has been made to show how Calvin still adhered to traditional views — often unbiblical ones. (Of course this cannot be taken amiss: posterity will possibly say the same of us!) However, with these facts at our disposal the way is paved for a more positive appreciation of the Reformer of Geneva's view of man.

14 NATURAL THEOLOGY WITH SPECIAL REFERENCE TO THE VIEWPOINTS OF THOMAS AQUINAS, JOHN CALVIN AND THE *SYNOPSIS PURIORIS THEOLOGIAE* *

CHAPTER 1

Chapter 1 is an introduction in which the problem is stated first; attention is drawn to its relevance; the defects in the present state of research are indicated; the structure of the study is explained; the character of the investigation is determined; the method of investigation and the author's own philosophical presuppositions are briefly stated.

The study intends being an investigation into the philosophical *presupposita* of Natural Theology amongst Christian thinkers (up to about 1800). The research in order to uncover the philosophical roots of this discipline will at the same time be systematic, historical and critical in character.

It intends being systematic in the sense that it aims to discover certain underlying philosophical problems closely connected with the issue of Natural or Philosophical Theology. The following basic problems, closely connected with the central issue of Natural Theology, are important: a specific view about the relation between God, law and cosmos; the acceptance of a sphere of nature and super-nature (grace); a specific idea about the relationship between God and man in which the interpretation of man as the image of God plays an important rôle as a point of contact; a certain point of view with regard to the relation between the revelation in the Word of God and in nature; some presuppositions about the relation between reason and faith and in accordance with that, between Philosophy and Theology, as well as a certain apologetic tendency.

The purpose is to trace these themes in their relation to *theologia naturalis* in the course of history, i.e. to show why and how they originated and developed.

The description of philosophical conceptions accomplished in this way according to the Consistent Problem Historic Method at the same time implies criticism. This critique is not immanent nor transcendent or transcendental, but a radical root-criticism in the light of the Word of God.

---

* Summary of my D. Phil. dissertation, Potchefstroom University for Christian Higher Education, 1974 (2 Volumes, 917 pages, summaries in Afrikaans, English, German and French). Original Afrikaans title: *Die Natuurlike Teologie met besondere aandag aan die visie daarop by Thomas van Aquino, Johannes Calvyn en die "Synopsis Purioris Theologiae" — 'n Wysgerige ondersoek.*

In order to make our interpretation of the different works to be analysed in this study comprehensible, the last part of the first chapter is devoted to an exposition of the writer's own philosophical presuppositions. The second part of the last chapter (VI) offers an extensive elaboration of the cursory, preliminary treatment of the various issues dealt with in this latter part of the first chapter.

The outline then of the whole study is the following. At the beginning (Chapter I) the writer's own viewpoint regarding Natural Theology is briefly stated. This is followed by the history of this discipline with the intention of discovering its philosophical roots (Chapter II to V). Enriched with this systematic-historical insight into the problem, the study is concluded (in Chapter VI) when the whole issue is discussed in detail in the light of a radical biblically-obedient philosophy.

Chapter I states *why* the phenomenon of Natural Theology is a problematic one worthy of closer examination; Chapters II-V show *how* this problem appeared in the course of the history of Christian thought; Chapter VI contains a final consideration of *what* the solution of this problem might be.

CHAPTER II

The roots of Philosophical Theology in Greek philosophy are traced in the conceptions of the following: the Pre-Platonic thinkers (c. 600 – c. 400 B.C.), Plato (427 – 347 B.C.), Aristotle (384 – 322 B.C.) and the Stoic philosophers (c. 300 B.C. – c. 200 A.D.).

The birth of Natural Theology amongst the early Christian thinkers is discussed with reference to Philo of Alexandria (c. 25 B.C. – c. 40 A.D.), Justin Martyr (c. 110 – 165 A.D.), Clement of Alexandria (died 212 A.D.), Origen (182 – 233 A.D.), Tertullian (C. 150 – 223 A.D.), Augustine (345 – 430 A.D.) and Dionysios the Pseudo-Areopagite (c. 500 A.D.).

Further developments during the Middle Ages is traced in the systems of John Scotus Eriugena (c. 810 – c. 877), Anselm of Canterbury (1033 – 1109) and Peter Abelard (1079 – 1142).

In this historical survey different themes closely related to *theologia naturalis*, forming the basis of its existence, are studied.

In Greek and Roman thought the distinction between a *triplex theologiae* originated. Of the three theologies, the *theologia civilis* or *politica*, *mythica* or *fabulosa* and *physica* or *naturalis*, the latter was the ancient predecessor of *theologia naturalis* amongst Christians. A second important result of research into ancient philosophy was that it became evident that certain ideas about the law were an important constituent. Furthermore allegorical exegesis and an apologetic tendency accompanies this kind of science right from its start: the Greeks were already defending them-selves against atheism with the help of Philosophical Theology.

Early Christian thought is characterized by the struggle to attain a com-promise between pagan Greek and Roman philosophies on the one hand and Biblical revelation on the other. The different attitudes and solutions of Apologists and Church Fathers are discussed. The dilemma in which these people found themselves gave birth to the theory of nature and superna-ture — a most important prerequisite for the distinction later on between *theologia naturalis* and *theologia supernaturalis*. Pagan philosophies also penetrated into their conception of the law with the result that the Apolo-gists and *patres ecclesiae* could not maintain — as the Bible does — the radi-cal distinction between God and his creation. Their idea of the law as *logoi spermatikoi* relativised the difference between God and His creatures and paved the way for a kind of *theologia* of which the aim was to prove the existence of God in a rational way from the visible world.

During the period of Medieval Thought three problems of vital impor-tance are investigated in terms of their origin and consequences for our sub-ject. First the problem of the relation between faith and reason. Different points of view on this problem imply different attitudes towards Natural Theology. This is illustrated in the case of different Medieval thinkers. Secondly it is indicated how the distinction between sacred and profane al-ready existed in primitive Greek thought, how it was accepted by the early Christians and modified to the two-realm theory of nature and grace and what its significance is for our subject. Thirdly the complex problem of *universalia* is unravelled and the implications of the different points of view regarding this problem for Natural Theology are indicated. The various con-ceptions of law in so-called realism, moderate realism and nominalism make the existence of Natural Theology either possible or impossible.

In a retrospect on the results of this chapter the following were the most relevant to the problem of Natural Theology: the synthetic mind of the early Christians especially acquired by way of allegorical exegesis of the Bi-ble; conceptions of the law which served as a "bridge" between God and creation; the nature-grace theme; the reason-faith dilemma and the relation-ship conceived between philosophy and theology.

CHAPTER III

Chapters III, IV and V give a detailed analysis of three different works of which we tried first to ascertain the basic framework or philosophical groundwork in order to decide, in the second place, what the influence of these philosophical presuppositions on the different authors' attitudes to-wards Natural Theology was.

In Chapter III *theologia naturalis* in the *Summa Contra Gentiles* (1258/ 1259 – 1263/1264) of Thomas Aquinas, the real architect of Natural Theology, is discussed. His philosophical conception in this book is described according to the Consistent Problem-Historic Method as purely cosmological, dualistic, partially universalistic without macro-microcosmos theory (hulemorphism).

He accepts the existence of the law *ante rem* (in God's mind), *in rebus* (in the created universe) and *post rem* (in the human mind). He adheres to a dichotomistic anthropology to be qualified as a Platonizing form of the subsistence theory. These ontological and anthropological *presupposita* determine his idea of man as *imago Dei*. Furthermore Aquinas is a proponent of the two-realm theory of nature and grace. In his theory of knowledge he held an inconsistent empiricism: apart from knowledge of visible reality (nature) attained by reason through the senses, faith acquires knowledge of the supernatural (grace). The knowledge reason has of the cosmos is called Philosophy and the knowledge faith obtains through revelation is called Supernatural Theology. Natural Theology has a position in between Philosophy and Supernatural Theology. It also operates through reason directed at the visible cosmos but its aim is not knowledge of the cosmos as such, but rather to obtain knowledge of God and prove his existence *via* his creatures. This is possible because of Aquinas' idea of law: God implanted his essences also in the created beings and from these traces one can reason back to the existence of the Creator.

Knowledge of the philosophical presuppositions of the *doctor angelicus' Contra Gentiles* facilitates our exposition of his attitude towards Natural Theology which is given in the second part of this chapter. Critical remarks are not withheld.

CHAPTER IV

The introductory part of this Chapter is devoted to a background sketch comprising the following: the place of the Reformation in Western thought; the most important philosophical currents during this period; the motivation for concentrating on Calvin's *Institutio Christianae Religionis*, and a brief exposition of Luther's and Zwingli's points of view regarding natural knowledge of God.

In the first section dealing with Calvin the philosophical presuppositions of his thought in the *Institutes* are distilled from their more or less theological context with the following result. Calvin's Biblical insight of the absolute sovereignty of God was a really brilliant start. Also, the fact that he did not think purely cosmologically opened the way to beginning directly with knowledge of God. It was not necessary for him to introduce God through the back-door with the help of some or other kind of Natural Theology.

These Biblical insights are, however, darkened because of his dualistic ontology; his dichotomistic (spiritualistic, semi-materialistic) anthropology; his acceptance of a partial universalism with a modified type of macro-microcosmos theory; his application (though not consistently) of the two-realm theory and his conception of the law. His idea of *lex naturalis* in particular betrays the definite influence of both Stoicism and Neo-Platonism. Furthermore Calvin, to a certain extent, still operates with the Augustinian *credo ut intelligam* and the traces of a Platonic theory of knowledge are clearly detectable.

In spite of the evidence of all these non-Biblical effects on his thought which could open the way toward a Natural Theology, the conclusion of the second part of this chapter is that Calvin's *cognitio Dei Creatoris* does not imply a Natural Theology. It is explained why Calvin was held back from a *theologia naturalis* in the Thomistic sense.

CHAPTER V

This Chapter deals with Natural Theology in the *Synopsis Purioris Theologiae* (1624) written by J. Polyander, A. Rivetus, A. Walaeus and A. Thysius, professors at the University of Leyden. The introductory section of this chapter provides firstly some information about P. Melanchton and T. Beza, transitory figures between Reformation and Post-Reformation, and secondly gives a brief characterization of Protestant Orthodoxy during the seventeenth century.

As in the case of the *Summa Contra Gentiles* and the *Institutio Christianae Religionis* the philosophical basis of the *Synopsis* is traced first, followed by an exposition of its attitude towards Natural Theology.

The philosophical position of the *Synopsis* can be summarized as follows: purely cosmological, dualistic, partial universalistic without macro-microcosmos theory (hulemorphism). The law exists *ante, in* and *post rem* resulting in similarity in essence as well as in being (*analogia entis*) between God and creatures, providing in this way a philosophical basis to Natural Theology. The anthropology of the *Synopsis* is dichotomistic, its theory of knowledge closely resembles that of Aquinas but also reveals kinship with that of the *Institutes*.

Regarding its attitude towards Natural Theology there is a greater congeniality between the *Synopsis* and the *Contra Gentiles* than between the *Synopsis* and the *Institutes*.

CHAPTER VI

The final Chapter first gives a recapitulation by way of comparison of the philosophical presuppositions of the *Contra Gentiles, Institutes* and *Synopsis*. Attention is drawn to both similarities and differences, revealing a remarkable affinity between the *Contra Gentiles* and the *Synopsis*. In spite of some striking points of agreement the *Institutes* reveals a different philosophical approach.

The second part of this chapter contains a final critical confrontation with the different ontological, anthropological and gnoseological problems which, when solved incorrectly, may necessitate a Natural Theology. This concluding perspective comprises an effort towards a more radical Biblical philosophy. The following problems are dealt with: the relationship between God, law and cosmos; man as the image of God; Theory of Knowledge; Philosophy of Science with special attention to the relationship between Philosophy and Theology. In each of these instances my own point of view is contrasted with that of the *Contra Gentiles, Institutes* and *Synopsis*. It becomes evident that consistent radical Biblical philosophizing is not only capable of solving many age-old problems, but it also offers illuminating new perspectives.

The conclusion regarding Natural Theology is that it was the result of a synthetic mind and consequently unbiblical Ontology, Anthropology, Theory of Knowledge and Philosophy of Science amongst Christians. Apart from the fact that the history of Western thought has already proved its failure, such a discipline is not required or welcome in a truly scripturally directed scientific endeavour. Natural Theology is not only haunted with many dilemmas but it can be a very dangerous enterprise to the Biblically-obedient Christian.

15 THEOLOGIA NATURALIS REDIVIVUS. SOME CRITICAL REMARKS ON THE RESURGENCE OF NATURAL THEOLOGY AND THEODICY*

Natural Theology aims at proving the existence of God (or a god) from the cosmos or created reality. It is designated as *Theology* because it has to do with God (or a god), and more specifically as *Natural* Theology because it does not obtain its knowledge of God from his Word-revelation (as ordinary Theology, also called Supernatural Theology, does) but instead draws it from creation, with the aid of human reason. Unlike the so-called Supernatural Theology, the existence of God is not *accepted* in faith as a fact. His existence has to be *proved* by reason. The methods of Natural Theology are thus closer to those of Philosophy (in its traditional sense) and consequently one can often speak of the results of Natural Theology as proving the "god of the philosophers".

1. A REMARKABLE REVIVAL

We exist in a spiritual climate with no room anymore for God and faith in Him, still less for a scholarship which attempts to demonstrate the existence of God. "God is dead" — the slogan even of today's theology — implies that there is no more place for God even as a Filler of empty space ("Lückenbüszer") or as a Hypothesis to fill the voids in our view of the universe. In proportion as human knowledge expanded, so was God — as many believe — forced to retreat, until the vacuums are today more or less filled and an idea of god has become quite superfluous. The "god of the philosophers" is dead!

On the surface it might thus appear as if the chance of existence for a Natural Theology is extremely limited — which is not at all the case. In fact the climate is highly favourable now that the so-called "problem of god" has landed theological and philosophical thought in a crisis which has no equal in history. It is most remarkable that just at this time, when God (and gods) threaten to sink below the human horizon, the problem of god excites an interest stronger than ever. Books about God (gods) written from theological and philosophical points of view have begun to swamp the market in the

* Originally published in *Bulletin van die Suid-Afrikaanse Vereniging vir die Bevordering van Christelike Wetenskap*, no. 45, July 1975, p. 42-57 under the title *"Theologia Naturalis Redivivus. Enkele immanent-kritiese opmerkings oor die herlewende Natuurlike Teologie en Theodisee"*.

past few years. Even toughened atheists like the followers of Karl Marx are taking part in the discussion and maintaining that God (god?) is still not dead!

It seems as if man cannot live without God, or without idols in the place of God. And for this reason the modern person without God, in a godless world, longs for a god once again, and a good many gods who had emigrated are coming back.

Just over a decade ago scholars — probably still remembering the radical "Nein!" of K. Barth — could declare that the stocks of Natural Theology had sunk very low and that it could no longer be counted among the topical questions of the day.

But before the seventies had arrived this situation had completely altered and a particular interest in Natural Theology was pointed out as one of *the* features of contemporary theological thought.

The present actuality of the matter is apparent from a special edition of the *Gereformeerd Theologisch Tijdschrift* (February 1974) which was completely devoted to the modern renaissance in Natural Theology. In the preface the writers speak of Natural Theology as a wide-ranging problem with many facets and the right to demand everyone's attention.

Within the space of more or less a single decade, then, the Cinderella of Natural Theology has been restored to favour. At the moment this appears to be only a partial restoration without all the erstwhile glory. Without donning the prophetic mantle, there is in these words nevertheless an important element of the task of the philosopher: "De wijsgeer staat op een vooruitgeschoven post: hij observeert, signaleert, combineert, systematiseert. Hij gaat voorop en moet een sterke intuitie hebben om te weten en te voelen wat er leeft". If, like a seismograph, we pick up the delicate "vibrations" of the "spirit" of the age, the signs seem to be very favourable that Natural Theology — even if in a totally new guise — is on the point of entering a completely new era of great blossoming and of being (rightly or wrongly) fully restored to favour.

Of the many areas of thought in which Natural Theology is today once again topical, we can only mention a couple.

1.1 Roman Catholicism

Within Roman Catholicism (Thomism in particular) Natural Theology has undoubtedly suffered the fewest major crises since the Middle Ages. Since the end of the previous century in particular there has been a new awakening. The immense interest shown by Roman Catholic thinkers in Natural Theology is perfectly understandable, seeing that the First Vatican Council (1870) had confirmed Thomas of Aquinas' views in this regard.

Although the Second Vatican Council was more cautious, it once again confirmed the pronouncements of the First Council as well as the Anti-Modernist Oath of 1910.

Even in spite of the often powerful influence of modern philosophical currents on contemporary Roman Catholic thinkers, they generally remain more or less faithful to the conception of a Natural Theology as the preliminary to a Supernatural Theology.

1.2 Protestantism

In his book *The future of Theology. A philosophical basis for contemporary protestant theology* (1969) F. Sontag makes the observation that the most urgent task of Protestant theology today is the development of a new conception concerning God, for without this, he maintains, "... Protestant theology does not seem to be able to keep its God alive". This urgent task of developing a new (Natural) doctrine of God cannot be executed by Theology without the aid of Philosophy.

Others argue that the proofs of God are not completely valueless and engage with Roman Catholics in discussion about them.

Within Protestant thought in North America several persons (Ch. Hartshorne, D.W. Sherburne, W.A. Christian, D.D. Williams, S.M. Ogden and J.B. Cobb among others) have begun to develop a new Natural Theology within the framework of the metaphysical thought-patterns of A.N. Whitehead.

1.3 Logical Positivism and Linguistic Analysis

Advocates of these systems, who mostly stamp religious language and thus concepts such as "god" as without significance, also have some colleagues who show a new interest in Natural Theology and related problems.

In the "century of nihilism" Natural Theology — even though it be in new forms — has still not perished. A last, especially striking example is

1.4 In the area of the natural sciences

In certain present-day scientific reflections — not necessarily those of a more Christian colour — something of a trend towards a Natural Theology is beginning to glimmer through. According to some Christian researchers the Christian nature of their scientific endeavours inheres in the fact that from their studies of the creation they can conclude that an all-wise and almighty being exists. Someone in referring to this observed that the God whom theology had declared to be dead, comes to life today in the natural sciences!

2. MORE CLOSELY EXAMINED

In the light of the remarkable revival of this discipline, which is as old as early Christendom and has roots going deep into ancient Greek and Roman thought[1], we are compelled to examine it anew. This article is limited to immanent criticism of a few points. But it is important to bear in mind that so-called immanent criticism is not really sufficient[2].

2.1 Is the "that-what" question separable into component parts?

Most advocates of Natural Theology declare that its goal is not primarily to say *what* God is, but simply *that* He is. Here the first problem comes to surface. Can one consider the existence of God without giving a certain content to that concept, or without expressing oneself on the "how?" of God's existence? One must after all first have an idea of what one is getting at before trying to prove the existence of this something.

2.2 "Petitio principii"?

And this gives rise to another problem. If one already has a certain idea of that God whose existence he wants to prove, is that proof still quite as objective and neutral? Put differently: is it not true that the investigator was already convinced about his idea of God before he provided the proof that God existed? In which case it is not the proofs which brought about the conviction, but rather the opposite. This would mean that the natural theologian had previously believed in the existence of God and because of this his proof *that* God exists is actually no longer necessary.

Is Natural Theology not guilty here of the fallacy known as *petitio principii* wherein that which is to be proved is already inconspicuously present in the proof as a premiss? Doesn't this argument expose a circular reasoning? "All too often in the past the Christian apologist has put himself into the position of the schoolboy who knows how the theorem should come out, but, through not following the proper proof, has found himself obliged to "cook" it. Just as the shrewd eye of the maths. master soon spots the cooking, so the modern secular philosopher refuses to be taken by

---

1. Cf. Chapter II in my thesis: *Die Natuurlike Teologie met besondere aandag aan d` visie daarop by Thomas van Aquino, Johannes Calvyn en die "Synopsis Purioris Theologiae" — 'n Wysgerige ondersoek* (1974).

2. In the above thesis I go further and attempt to offer more radical criticism of the foundations of *theologia naturalis*.

the lame arguments of natural theology"[3].

Possibly this touches upon an even deeper-rooted problem, namely that of the relationship between scientific and pre-scientific knowledge. Since scientific knowledge is in my opinion determined and directed by pre-scientific knowledge, arguments for the existence of God (or a god) are not *grounds for* but rather the *product of* (a certain) faith.

2.3 Aimed at believer or unbeliever?

And this brings the investigator face to face with another query: What might the motives of the natural theologian who wants to prove the existence of God be? Does he want to convince himself or others of God's existence? Such a proof cannot be of any significance for him since — as just pointed out — he already believes in the reality of God.

A motivation of the natural theologian is mostly, then, apologetic in nature: the unbeliever must be brought to a belief in God via a refuting of his objections. Before the unbeliever can believe, however, he has to be persuaded on the rational level. The authority which is believed in must first be legitimized according to the demands of reason. And this legitimization must take place on grounds which are evident to all. The rational persuasion (the so-called *preambula fidei*) usually takes place in two stages. In the first place it is inferred, from premises which should be clear to everyone, that God exists. Then, by means of an appeal to signs and wonders, it is demonstrated that the church and God's Word possess divine authority, and that for this reason the doctrine of the church concerning that God whose existence has just been proved, is derived from this authority. The natural theologian thus reasons more or less as follows: to believe is after all the accepting of statements, the truth of which is not evident to everybody. Believing is not however unreasonable, since the authority on which the belief is grounded can itself be justified on rational grounds acceptable to all.

---

3. Brown: *Philosophy and Christian Faith*, p. 276. Swagerman gives a similar criticism in the form of an equally striking image: "De conclusie is onontkoombaar, dat de auteurs als kenners van de bijzondere openbaring hier bewust naar Bijbelse noties of posita uit de christelijke dogmatiek toewerken en met alle reverentie voor de goede bedoelingen van hun opzet worden we gedrongen hen, mede door de zelfverzekerdheid van hun betoogtrant en door de indruk, die zij (willen) wekken, dat hun conclusies met een vanzelfsprekende 'gladheid' getrokken worden, te vergelijken met goochelaars, die met een zekere triomfantelijkheid een konijn uit een hoge hoed toveren, waarvan zij weten, dat ze het er eerst ingestopt hebben". *Ratio en revelatio. Een theologisch onderzoek naar het Godsbewijs en de Godsleer uit de menselijk ratio en de verhouding van de natuurlijke tot de geopenbaarde theologie bij enige Nederlandsche hoogleraren in de theologie of in de filosofie van 1650 tot 1750*, p. 180.

The problem is thus shifted from belief to reasonable grounds for it. But it has already been shown that these rational grounds are based precisely on that faith to which they are intended to bring the unbeliever. The conclusion that God exists only follows from the premises when the premisses are interpreted from a belief in the existence of God. Such existence is only evident to those who are already convinced of it. The same also holds for the miraculous nature of God's Word and the church: only someone who has already accepted it as authoritative will really see the miracle.

The problem with Natural Theology is thus that it is doomed in advance to failure, since it appears to have no value whatsoever either for the believer or for the unbeliever.

2.4 "Provisional" doubt?

The question has to be asked as to whether Natural Theology is not an extremely dangerous occupation for the believer. A person who wants to prove the existence of God has to query that existence in some or other degree — even if it is just for appearance' sake, as far as the unbeliever who is to be won over is concerned.

2.5 "Whether" or "how" — which is primary?

For the believer (who already knows God) the question of *whether* He exists is not primary, what is essential, is *how* God exists in relation to his creation in general and man in particular. However, one has to be careful not to put such an emphasis on *how* God exists, that the problem *that* God exists is put in the shade. Since the *that* and the *how* cannot be separated (as we have shown above), the one may not be played off against the other. It is just as important for the human being to know that God is there. Especially in today's world, even believing Christians doubt sometimes whether God really exists.

2.6 A proper occupation?

One might also ask whether it is entirely proper for man to prove the existence of God. According to S. Kierkegaard God is made laughable every time someone attempts to prove his existence. Either He exists, in which case man cannot prove it, or He does not, and then man cannot do so either.

2.7 What does the Bible say?

It is most important for a Scripturally obedient Philosophy to listen to the Word in this connexion. In his Word God indeed reveals Himself to man.

But it is remarkable that there are no attempts to prove the existence of God in the Bible. Instead of giving a rational proof, the Bible usually proceeds from the fact of God's existence.

2.8 A merely logical construction?

When God is a sort of conclusion to a logical process, the question arises as to whether He — who is, according to Scripture, different from that which He has created — is not forced into the mould of a merely human proof. Would this not imply the most appalling presumption on the part of man? Or to be somewhat paradoxical: if the radical difference between man and God announced in the Bible is maintained, then the failure of all attempts at proof would be a "proof" that He really exists!

2.9 Can human proofs transcend creation?

Moreover it could be maintained that the so-called proofs of god eventually end up referring to something *within* created reality without ever reaching the true God. The proofs of god begin with the limited cosmic reality and cannot transcend it — unless an inadmissible leap is made. One can for instance reason from the causal coherence of the cosmos to a first cause, but to conclude that this first cause is identical to God, i.e. something which transcends the universe, implies an unjustifiable leap. F. van Steenberghen rightly observes, "you can never obtain an absolute being from the multiplication of completely relative beings, any more than you can set a chariot in motion by harnessing it to wooden horses. Keep for every multiplying beings that are dependent in their very being and you multiply imperfection infinitely"[4].

To try and meet this problem by appealing to "general revelation" is useless as well, since there first has to be a *belief* in the reality of God's revelation in nature.

2.10 Two sets of gods?

The question thus is really, in the words of Pascal, whether the "god of

---

4. F. van Steenberghen: *The hidden God. How do we know that God exists?* p. 186 Christian Natural Theology actually makes two leaps: the first from the relative (cosmos) to the absolute and the second from the absolute (god) to the God of Holy Scripture.

the philosophers" is the same as the God of Abraham, Isaac and Jacob[5]. For the natural theologian who is firmly established as an apologete or missionary it ought to be the same God. He cannot first try to win the unbeliever over on rational grounds, demonstrating that a god exists, and only then producing a new idea of God. (It has already been shown that the question of the *that* is not possible without some comprehension of the question of the *how*).

2.11 Intellectual idolatry?

Even if the natural theologian were to succeed in proving the existence of a god, it would be in my opinion merely an abstract god and not the God of the Christian faith to Whom one can pray and with Whom one can daily walk. A god who is proved cannot be anything else than an idol which is a projection of man. One can certainly come to an idol which one has thought out by oneself, without being changed one little bit, without being converted. Or, to be even more precise, is this not the direct result of a state of unregeneration? Is it not very probable that Natural Theology is not only a useless intellectual sport, but also a dangerous form of intellectual idolatry? Is speculation about God not also a sin against the second commandment? Doesn't Scripture indicates that one can only come to the true God if God Himself alters something in man, if God brings him to conversion and faith. The path to knowledge of God does not run from man to God, but takes the opposite direction!

2.12 Argument from motion as an illustration

The following criticism of this proof is valid, with the necessary modification, for most of the other proofs of God as well. The argument from motion proceeds from the fact that everything in the universe which moves is moved by something else, which brings one eventually to God (as the Unmoved Mover). But in this connection the following critical questions are immediately raised:

This argument proceeds from the unproved presupposition that there has to be an end to the series of movements and does not take account of the fact that movement might continue *ad infinitum*.

---

5. This does not imply that the Christian philosopher may have no "idea of God" referring to that which God has revealed about Himself in His Word. On the contrary, we deal with the concept of "the god of the philosophers" in order to criticize the natural theologians, who go to work without the light of God's Word.

The fact of motion does not imply that *one* unmoved mover must exist. There could be various series of movements and they do not necessarily have to be moved by something else.

The end of the series must, according to the proof, be situated not inside, but outside the chain of motion, and be of an utterly different nature, viz. be divine. And this cannot be proved but only accepted by leaping from the relative to the absolute. Consequently an immovable mover does not necessarily have to be divine at all: this still has to be proved!

In addition it is accepted — without proof — that the final stage in the line of movement is identical to the God of the Scriptures. And this too is an unproved acceptance or presupposition of *faith*.

A decision as to the concrete, actual existence of an Unmoved Mover is made on the basis of an abstract, theoretical concept.

3. THEODICY AS A SISTER DISCIPLINE OF NATURAL THEOLOGY

In all the aforegoing points of criticism we have not even touched on the problem as to whether discord, evil, misery and so forth in creation do not prove exactly the opposite, namely that God does *not* exist. This problem has given rise to the fact that many of the advocates of a Natural Theology have also developed a matching Theodicy, either together with their Theology, or as an inherent part of it.

We have to do with similar problems in Theodicy as in Natural Theology, and deal with practically identical critical queries to those already posed.

3.1 A long history

Theodicy is quite as ancient as Natural Theology itself. We meet it in the Stoa, where Natural Theology had already played such an important part; the early Christians occupied themselves with it; in the eighteenth century massive volumes on the subject saw the light — although criticism was not wanting — and even in the twentieth century it remains a topical matter even amongst reformed thinkers. A good many varieties of Theodicy have consequently already made their appearance in the history of Western thought.

3.2 Purpose

Whereas Natural Theology especially wants to prove the existence of God, Theodicy does not aim to demonstrate the existence of God (or a god), but rather to prove certain attributes, viz. his justice and goodness, among others, and especially the correctness of his actions in history. The basis of it is closely linked to that of Natural Theology, since (as just noted) a criticism can be raised against all the so-called proofs of God, enquiring whether all the misery, evil, discord, injustice, sickness, death and so on in the world do not prove precisely the opposite, namely that God does not exist, or, if He does, that He is not a just and righteous God. Theodicy (from the Greek *theos* = god + *dike* = just, i.e. "justification of God") thus endeavours to defend the governance of God against the evil in the world, or tries to reconcile the misery of the world with the perfect goodness of God.

3.3 Correct name?

Many place a question mark against the name "theodicy". Is it man's task to defend God? Should not an *Anthropo*dicy rather be devised? Luther turned the tables in this connection: God has no need to defend Himself before the court of human understanding, but man has to be defended by God. Does the great God need to be defended by a nonentity, whose knowledge of God's anger and man's guilt is but partial? May He be summoned before the feeble, limited human reason?

This might be possible in the case of the heathen gods who stand on the same level as men, but is it not the most excessive presumption on man's part when it is a question of the only true God? Scripture reveals clearly that He is impenetrable. Do simplistic human answers still apply?

3.4 God's goodness doubted

The matter becomes even more dubious when one recalls that the Bible clearly states that God is just and good. Man has to begin with this certainty, this must be the start of all considerations of this matter. But in current Theodicy there is a certain surrendering to the doubt that God might perhaps not be just and good, and a long detour is made in order to try and conclude with the help of rational arguments that God *nevertheless* is a good God. The method is thus more or less the same as that sketched above for Natural Theology: it begins from the unbeliever's presupposition that God does not exist in order to arrive at the acknowledgement of his existence — via its denial!

Some advocates of Theodicy may possibly maintain that they begin not with a search for God's goodness but with a certainty that He exists. The question however then arises as to why they do not convey this certainty *directly* to the seekers, instead of travelling along the detour of doubt.

3.5 Is it of any use to the believer?

The investigator is brought to face the same problem as in the case of Natural Theology, viz. whether it has any persuasion-value for the unbeliver. Dialectically stated: it is not necessary to prove God's goodness to those who already believe, and those who do not believe are not going to accept this as proof — precisely because they do not believe. Conviction as to the existence and goodness of God lies at a far deeper level than that of rational analysis, argument and demonstration.

Just as God's existence in Natural Theology is the conclusion of human thought, so is His goodness in Theodicy the end result of human intellectual labour. Man is not dependent upon God, but God's existence and goodness are made dependent on man!

3.6 Not simply speculation?

The same question posed of Natural Theology earlier can thus be put here too, viz. whether it is the *true* God Whose goodness is being confirmed in this way, or whether it is not perhaps a speculative "god of the philosophers". The final result might perhaps be a picture of God which is rescued and defended before the court of the human intellect, but it is pale and without substance because human standards are made applicable to God.

Just as Natural Theology desires to prove the existence of God with the aid of autonomous reason, divorced from the Word-revelation of God, so does Theodicy try to prove his goodness. G.C. Berkouwer rightly remarks: "Niemand zal ooit *uit* de werkelijkheid kunnen opklimmen tot de rechtvaardigheid Gods, omdat de werkelijkheid alleen gekend kan worden door het verklarend spreken Gods... Dáárin ligt het principieel onaanvaarbare van alle theodicee"[6].

3.7 Leap from that which is creaturely and negative to the divine and the positive

As with Natural Theology Theodicy climbs up to God from created reality. It was clear from the previous critical questions put to Natural Theology that this appeared to be impossible, because no matter how far one gets with cause and effect, for instance, one remains within creation and can only escape from it by means of a leap (which is no longer answerable to

6. Berkouwer: *De voorzienigheid Gods*, p. 299.

reason) in order to "prove" the existence of God in an irrational manner. And this is even more impossible in the case of Theodicy which reasons from the evil (negative) in the world to its goodness (positive) – and not that only, but to the goodness of *God* as well.

3.8 Circular reasoning

Furthermore Theodicy is caught up in a vicious circle. It wants to climb out of reality, up to God, using the ladder of human thoughts, in order to prove that He is just. On the contrary, however, the evil in the world is explained in an ingenious manner from the existence of God which (teleologically) directs the evil towards the good!

3.9 Hidden self-justification

G.C. Berkouwer focusses attention upon another error of Theodicy which is not so immediately apparent, viz. that man can try to excuse himself from his sins and the judgement of God. This can occur in many divergent ways, depending on the type of Theodicy: "De dualistische theodicee roept een eeuwige strijd uit tussen twee oerbeginselen: het licht en de duisternis, het goed en het kwaad en heft daarmee de verantwoordelijkheid en de schuld op. De teleologische theodicee vliegt over de realiteit van zonde, leed en dood heen en meent in haar denken te kunnen doen, wat alleen Góddelijk privilege is: het *kwade* nog *ten goede* schikken en zo Zijn doel bereiken. De harmonistische theodicee neemt het kwaad in al z'n vormen in de schepping op en ontwijkt daardoor de concrete oordeel Gods, terwijl tenslotte Monod de Almacht Gods ook in Zijn gericht in de katastrofes dezer wereld uitschakelt en het pluralisme eindigt met de spanningen uit deze wereld in te dragen in God".

"In al deze variaties is één ding gemeenschappelijk: de grens der *schuld*, zoals ze door de Schrift wordt aangegeven, word gepasseerd met het gevolg, dat zo een theodicee 'mogelijk' wordt geacht..."[7]).

3.10 Newer fashions are just as unsatisfactory

After the catastrophic happenings, which the twentieth century has already experienced, there has, remarkably, not been an upsurging interest in but rather a strong aversion to Theodicy. Anyone who still uses it does so in a very circumspect and cautious manner. Actually it must be said that a revulsion against a rationalistic form of Theodicy has come into being. The same

---

7. Berkouwer: op. cit., p. 316.

phenomenon made its appearance after the Second World War in irrationalistic and even atheistic forms.

Not only rationalistic Theodicy (which arraigns God before the court of human reason) but also the irrationalistic form (which attempts to find peace in the arbitrary action of a hidden God) and the atheistic variation (which converts the charges against God into a judgement on man himself) give no satisfaction at all. So even the irrationalistic form does not offer the "peace that passes all understanding".

4. CONCLUSION

It is apprent from the aforegoing that Theodicy and Natural Theology are historically and systematically very closely related: Natural Theology "proves" the existence of God from certain events in creation, whereas Theodicy again tries to prove that less fortunate things do not prove the contrary, viz. that God does not exist as a good and just God. As a result of their relationship our criticism of both was more or less the same.

One should not conclude from the critical questions put to Natural Theology (as well as to Theodicy which often accompanies it or is a part of it) and to the proofs of God in particular that there is any doubt as to the existence of God himself (or his goodness) or that these are in any way denied. Our criticism was aimed at the human *proofs* of God and not at God Himself!

16 ACTS 17:15-34 AND ROMANS 1:18-25: EVIDENCES OF CONTACT-POINTS IN MISSION WORK, OR PROOFS FOR A NATURAL THEOLOGY*

1. ECUMENICAL AND HEATHEN RELIGION

In today's ecumenically-inclined world it has become fashionable for many Christians to look with a very sympathetic eye at the pagan religions. All kinds of hidden truths and positive elements are sought in the traditional religion of the Bantu, Muslim, Buddhist and Hindu. Every religion possesses certain so-called "moments of truth" which can be seized and built upon. So the Gospel is actually viewed merely as a keystone which can be added to round off the edifice.

But it is forgotten that (heathen) religions are primarily the result of man's foolishness and blindness, of his flight from the true God instead of his search for Him. "There is no one who does seek God" (Rom. 3:11). Modern man has a respect for "religions without God" which the Word of God clearly lacks. In not a few places in Scripture idols are mocked! Coversely "natural" man finds the Gospel repulsive, incomprehensible, ununderstandable, strange, offensive, unacceptable.

A.J. van Rooy (in his contribution to the collection *Kontak en Kommunikasie*, chapter V): justly remarks, "It is undoubtedly to be expected that differing peoples which have received various gifts from God in his goodness will unearth varying treasures from their contact with the Gospel which have remained hidden from other peoples, in order to mine those riches and to purify them, and one day to carry them into the New Jerusalem as the glory of the nations (Rev. 21:24-27). But I do not believe we have any reason to expect that this glory will have any traces of the heathen religions."

* Originally published in *In die Skriflig*, 10(38):47-51, 1976 under the title: "Handelinge 17:15-34 en Romeine 1:18-25: Bewyse vir aansluitingspunte in die sending of vir 'n Natuurlike Teologie?"

2. ACTS 17 AND "THEOLOGY OF CONTACT"

This article briefly examines Acts 17[1] in particular to see whether it gives us any right to develop a "theology of contact", or provides any grounds for a Natural Theology.

Those who want Acts 17:15-34 to speak in favour of Natural Theology lay a great deal of stress on the mildness of Paul's judgment of heathen thought. All sorts of words and expressions in his speech on the Areopagus in Athens betray, according to them, the strong influence of Hellenistic and particularly Stoic thought on the apostle. It is for this reason that he could have such a deep appreciation for the heathen thinkers and poets. Paul would then have noticed an "inner coherence" between heathen wisdom and the Gospel. The beliefs of the heathens would already have contained the message of the Gospel in germ. Hence Paul could make positive contact with their ideas of a natural knowledge of God and find a handy point of contact in their idea of the unknown god especially. The apostle would have advocated a Natural Theology on the lines of the Stoic philosophers (of which there were many that day in his audience) in accord with which man would be in a position to reach to knowledge of God with his own reason.

But this exegesis really distorts the actual state of affairs during this famous evangelistic sermon of Paul. In Acts 17 we actually have a confrontation of   Scriptural thought with the pagan natural theological speculations of his time!

3. ACTS 17 AS MISSIONARY MESSAGE

Paul's so-called generosity in this speech must not be interpreted incorrectly. It must be remembered that it was a missionary speech and that much more could be achieved by proceeding cautiously and courteously than by acting ill-manneredly and slating the heathen thinkers for all that was bad. Paul did not wish to put them off unnecessarily, for he very much desired to convert them. But if he had flattered them (by glossing over their own concepts) he would not have attained his goal, namely their conversion, either. His courteous behaviour in no way implies that he was linking up with the pagan thought-world in the sense that he would have taken

---

1. See in this regard J.H. Bavinck: *Alzo wies het Woord,* p. 99-104, 110-139; J. Blaauw: *Goden en mensen,* p. 133-7; B. Gärtner: *The Areopagus speech and natural relevation;* K.J. Popma: *Evangelie contra evangelie,* p. 43-58 and *Eerst de Jood maar ook de Griek,* p. 74-93.

responsibility for it. In this sense he only joins his audience by trying to use a familiar language, without thereby approving the pronouncements of their poets (e.g. Aratus) amongst others. In this way he tries to touch them with the Gospel in the depths of their being.

4. ACTS 17 AGAINST HEATHENDOM

It is abundantly clear from the following factors that Paul's polite and civil appearance before the elite of the contemporary philosophical world was simultaneously sharply scathing and laid the tragedy of heathendom open to the very bone.

In the first place Paul speaks of his hearers as unwitting or ignorant (v. 30). He could hardly have said anything more unpleasing to the Epicurean and Stoic philosophers, who occupied themselves daily with the search for truth. The edge on these words cut deeply in a city which regarded itself as the keystone of all human wisdom. Nor could his hearers misunderstand him. If Paul had immediately begun with their unrighteousness and the wrath of God, they might perhaps have understood wrongly.

When Paul went on to demonstrate that this ignorance was guilty ignorance, they were forced to make a choice: Either continuing to believe in their own "wisdom", or rejecting it as stupidity and accepting the Gospel. According to Paul God had spoken unambiguously to them through his revelation in creation, but they had rejected Him in their folly by distorting his revelation.

Paul also tried to show in his speech (and this is in agreement with the teaching of Romans 1) that the heathens may push the truth of God onto one side but are in no condition to destroy it utterly. How this is possible is very apparent from the character of the lie, viz. that it can have no independent existence of itself, but only through the tolerance of the truth it tries to deny. It is continually bound, though negatively, to the truth. The lie has no inherent right of existence, but is something which is parasitic upon truth and can only exist in its reversal. The inherent poverty of the lie is equally apparent from the fact that it tries to set itself up as the truth. On a closer examination there is no stronger proof for the truth than the very fact that the lie exists[2].

The severity of Paul's speech is evident too from the fact that, apart from speaking of ignorance in the city of wisdom, he also talks of Godlessness in the city of many gods. We are told that Paul's spirit became angry when he

---

2. Cf. K.J. Popma: *Eerst de Jood maar ook de Griek*, p. 87.

saw how full of idols the city was (v. 16). He was not pleasantly struck by this "religiosity" because it gave him the opportunity to latch onto their natural knowledge of God, but rather troubled thereby. When he later (cf. v. 22) adds that he perceives that the Athenians are in every respect most religious, he does not intend a compliment either. The word "religious" could just as well be translated as "superstitious" which is hardly praise. The polytheistic Athenians suffered to such a degree from a religious hoarding mania that they had even erected an altar to the unknown god in order to make quite sure that they had not perhaps left one out! Paul wants to put an end to this very polytheism by proclaiming the only true God to them. As with the accusation of ignorance, the fact that Paul had no appreciation for their hyper-religiousness must have hit the audience hard, so that they eventually chose to take refuge in one of the loser's strongest weapons, viz. mockery.

5. NO COMPROMISE WITH NATURAL THEOLOGY

Paul certainly does not link up with the idea of an unknown god because he agrees with it. He does not accept a Natural Theology (which tries to prove *that* there must be a god, but leaves man in the dark because it cannot say *what* nor *who* this god is) in order to use it as a basis to bring the Athenians the Gospel, which gives them more information about the unknown God. The very altar of the *unknown* god is a proof that the Athenians had already admitted their ignorance of religion! By erecting this altar with its striking name they admit that their polytheism does not really offer a solution — it ends in an unknown god!

Paul does not therefore make approving use of this unknown god, but rather a disapproving one. The learned Athenian philosphers are made ridiculous in that they honour a god of whom they have no knowledge! The words of Paul, "Him then whom ye honour without knowing Him", are admittedly applied by him to the true God in the next verse, but here possess a powerful irony which unmasks the heathen wisdom as stupidity. And this too can hardly have been a compliment to the Greek scholars.

In the light of these few remarks it appears highly unlikely that Paul would have advocated a Stoic Natural Theology of the "unknown god" from where he would have lifted the heathen to the higher level of the "known God"[3]. Owing to their polytheism the Athenians did not just believe in the existence of one god, but in that of many gods. It would thus

3. Cf. B. Gärtner: op. cit., p. 82, 90, 146, 167 and 169.

have envinced an untactful and completely incorrect approach on the part of Paul had he tried to approach his hearers on the natural-theological level: their problem certainly was not that they were sceptical about the existence of some god or other.

Nor may Romans 1:20 (provided it is taken correctly, i.e. in the context of this verse) be advanced as evidence for a Natural Theology[4]. It deals with the revelation of God in his creation. This so-called general revelation of God finds no point of support or contact in man himself (his reason, understanding or religious belief). There is no continuity between something like a *semen religionis* and the Gospel, but only between God's revelation in creation and His Gospel or word-revelation.

6. NATURAL THEOLOGY AND THE REVELATION IN CREATION

Since the Fall resulted in a massive gap between the clarity of God's revelation in creation on the one hand and man's reaction on the other, the acceptance of the reality of this revelation need not necessarily lead to a Natural Theology.

It is a faulty interpretation of this revelation, and not the fact of the revelation in creation as such, which makes a Natural Theology possible. Only in the light of the Word and with the help of a Scriptural Philosophy can this revelation of God in creation be rightly read.

Calvin and others correctly emphasize that although one cannot speak of a positive knowledge of God on the grounds of the "general revelation" alone, the clarity of God's revelation in creation removes all excuse from man. Ignorance in this connection remains guilty ignorance, for man is responsible for his fall into sin.

7. CONCLUSION

In conclusion, therefore, I advance the following reasons as to why Acts 17:15-34 and Rom. 1:18-25 do not proclaim (the possibility of) a Natural Theology.

Paul may be polite in Acts 17, but simultaneously exposes the pagans' ignorance and foolishness with respect to matters of religion. He definitely

---

4. In this connexion see J.H. Bavinck: *Religieus besef en Christelijk geloof*, p. 171-80 and 187-91; G.C. Berkouwer: *De algemene openbaring*, p. 118-24; J. Blaauw: op. cit., p. 138-49 and K.J. Popma: op. cit., p. 107-9.

does not make positive use of their "natural knowledge of god" (in the idea of the "unknown god", inter alia) in the sense that he approves of it and intends to transport them from their "germ of truth" to knowledge of the true God.

Romans 1 teaches that God's revelation in his creation is undoubtedly clear, but that as the result of man's sin it cannot lead to true knowledge of God, since it is supplanted, replaced and distorted. And this revelation does not declare the *existence* of God either, since his existence needs no demonstration. Merely His *power and divinity* are revealed therein, in the fact that He is strong and mighty in comparison with the lifeless gods. His might and omnipotence are evident in all that happens to men and creatures. Not only does He perform miracles in nature, but He also guides and determines the entire history of mankind. It is indeed true that He reveals His will in the laws for his creatures, but here too they are not concerned with his *existence* as such (which is self-evident) but with his *will* — which is only knowable via the laws in the things. And besides, God's revelation in creation can only be rightly understood in the light of the revelation of his Word.

17 THE RELAPSE INTO SCHOLASTICISM DURING THE FURTHER REFORMATION. A PRELIMINARY SURVEY*

A preliminary survey

After the reformatorial labours of Luther and Calvin there was a rapid relapse into synthetic thought similar to that previous to the Reformation. C. van der Woude remarks, "De Reformatie ligt beklemd tussen twee perioden van scholastisch denken. De Reformatoren zelf, Luther en Calvijn, hebben zich min of meer ontworsteld aan de invloed der scholastiek, maar bij hun directe navolgers, Melanchton en Beza, duiken de scholastieke denkmethoden weer op, om zich vervolgens bij de latere epigonen, Sadeel en Ursinus, Keckerman, Lubbertus en Maccovius, met kracht door te zetten"[1].

The era following the great reformers is generally known as that of post-Reformation Orthodoxy or Protestant Scholasticism (from the end of the sixteenth century and during the seventeenth). As an introduction, it is necessary to try to define the concept "Orthodoxy" as well as that of "Scholasticism" more closely. Many people simply employ these terms today — without further analysis — as pejorative terms implying that the past is done with.

1. THE CONCEPTS "ORTHODOXY" AND "SCHOLASTICISM"

1.1 Orthodoxy

The concept "orthodox" (From the Greek *orthos* = right + *doxa* = opinion) which is usually used as the opposite of "heterodox" is not at all

---

* Originally published in *Tydskrif vir Christelike Wetenskap*, 11:117-133, 1975 under the title: "Die terugval in die Skolastiek ten tye van die Nadere Reformasie".

1. Van der Woude. *Op de grens van Reformatie en Scholastiek*, p. 5. Cf. also Cramer, *De Protestantsche Orthodoxie en het Protestantisme*, p. 3 where he states of Reformed and Lutheran orthodoxy that it "... maar al te zeer van den katholieke zuurdesem was doortrokken". See also Malan, Die Skolastiek in die Protestantisme. *Tydskrif vir Christelike Wetenskap*,4 (1st and 2nd quarter):26, 1968: "After Calvin a relapse quickly took place in reformational theology into an adaptation of the Scholastic, alternatively humanistic philosophy". (Translated by B.J. van der Walt). Cf. Further Rückert, The reformation — Medieval or Modern? *Journal for theology and church*, 2:10, 1965 and for Lutheran Orthodoxy cf. Kooiman: Luther *In:* Cultuurgeschiedenis van het Christendom II, p. 1129-30.

specifically Christian (Aristotle already used it), nor is it a very precise concept to describe a certain (religious) tendency. Of it Cramer observes: "Nu kan natuurlijk, als er in de kerkleer verschil is, orthodox zijn in de ééne kerk, wat heterodox is in de andere. Ook kunnen er in dezelfde Kerk graden zijn in de orthodoxie. Ja, den eenen tijd kan voor orthodox doorgaan, wat den anderen tijd niet zoo genoemd wordt. Grotendeels hangt dit van de vraag af, wat op een gegeven oogenblik door de openbare meening tot het kenmerkende in de kerkleer gerekend wordt. Maar altijd moet er eene kerkleer zijn, die als maatstaf werd gebruikt. Naar mate de strijd der geesten op dogmatisch gebied grootere afmetingen aannam, en niet alleen wat de groote Kerken der Hervorming verdeelde, maar ook wat haar tegenover Rome vereenigde, heftiger werd bestreden, begon men ook te spreken van eene protestantsche Orthodoxie. Men verstond er dan onder een vasthouden aan de zoogenaamde protestantsche centraaldogmen, vooral de christologische en soteriologische, zooals die in de verschillende Belijdenisschriften waren geformuleerd"[2].

1.2 Scholasticism

As far as the term "scholasticism" is concerned, is it merely a certain method, or an entire system of thought, or something even more profound, such as an attitude of life which governs the system of ideas?

The word "Scholasticism"[3] is derived from *scholasticus,* which means a teacher or pupil of a certain school. For instance, the teachers of the cathedral and monastic schools founded by Charlemagne were called *scholastici* and their knowledge scholastics. Since scholarship during the Middle Ages was practised almost exclusively at these schools and at the universities which came into being after them, the (theological and philosophical) sciences which were born during this period (and especially during the 12th to 14th centuries) are called Scholasticism, i.e. school-philosophy (or theology). Philosophy and Theology are practised according to a method used in the schools, which had developed from the *lectio* and *disputatio* to the weighty *summae* of which the *Summa Contra Gentiles* of Thomas, and above all his *Summa Theologiae,* are striking examples.

Even if the concept "Scholasticism" were to be limited to the thought of the 12th to 14th centuries (and to those who followed it as neo-scholas-

---

2. Cramer, op. cit., p. 4.

3. Cf. for this, inter alia, Ueberweg, *Die patristische und schlastische Philosophie* (elfte Auflage), p. 143-4.

tics), it would remain vague, as this period yielded a highly coloured spectrum of philosophical systems. For this reason one usually looks for definite general, characteristic traits in the theories of the differing thinkers from the 12th to 14th centuries which might justify the common name of "Scholastic thinkers".

The following could be highlighted as outstanding features of Scholasticism. In the first place it is synthetic thought. Although a synthesis between different sorts of thought is possible (so that one can speak of an Arabic and a Jewish Scholasticism as well as of a Christian), synthetic thought here specifically means the compromise between Scripture and Greek Philosophy (that of Aristotle in particular). To distinguish it from other sorts of Christian synthetic thought, we shall in the second place understand by "Scholasticism" only that synthesis which operates with the method of nature and grace. In the third place Scholasticism, as here intended, is recognizable by the typical distinction which it makes between faith and knowledge and consequently between Theology and Philosophy, but above all by the definite relationship between them, viz. that Theology (belonging to the realm of the supernatural) employs Philosophy (belonging to the realm of nature) as a subordinate servant.

2. THE IMMENSE DIFFERENCE BETWEEN CALVIN AND CALVINISM

Calvin succeeded in a really miraculous way in escaping to a very great extent from the magnetic pull of Scholasticism. But such was not the case with many of his Protestant contemporaries and especially his successors. Instead of there being a self-critical, progressive reformation aiming at continually more Scriptural thinking, relapses soon began to occur. D. Nauta describes what happened as follows: "In veel opzichten heeft men niet de moeite genomen eigen standpunt door te denken en in praktijk tot uitvoering te brengen.

"Men heeft de gemakelijker weg gekozen en zich gewoonweg aangepast aan de opvatting van anderen, die vreemd stonden tegenover het religieuze standpunt der reformatie.

Een valse synthesedrang kreeg op meer dan één terrein de overhand... Het kwam niet tot de opbouw van een eigen wetenschap, beheerst door de reformatorische beginselen... Op deze wijze kwam het geloof los te staan naast de wetenschap. Deze werd door het geloof niet doordrongen als door een zuurdeeg..."[4].

---

4. Nauta. Standpunt van Luther en Calvijn tegenover het Humanisme. (In: Cultuurgeschiedenis van het Christendom II, p. 1092).

There was consequently a wide gap between the views of Calvin and those of post-Reformation Calvinism[5] similar to the distinction between the ideas of Luther and those of post-Reformation Lutheranism. Post-Reformational thought wanted to theorize in an orthodox, i.e. rightly-inclined manner by holding fast to the Protestant faith. In reality it largely relapsed into Scholasticism.

3. P. MELANCHTON AND T. BEZA AS HEIRS OF THE REFORMATION AND BEQUEATHERS OF SCHOLASTICISM

Before we examine Protestant Orthodoxy more closely, we shall first give some attention to the two thinkers who could be regarded as transitional figures between Reformational and post-Reformational thought. Melanchton is important for Lutheran Orthodoxy while Beza exercised much influence on Reformed or Calvinistic Orthodoxy.

3.1 P. Melanchton (1497-1560)

Melanchton was born fourteen years after Luther and twelve years before Calvin. In a certain sense, therefore, he can be regarded as a contemporary of both great reformers. His ideas had a massive influence upon Protestant educational systems, and his fatherland acknowledged this by honouring him with the title *praeceptor Germaniae.*

3.1.1 Course of development

It is generally accepted that there are three major stages to be discerned

5. Hall rightly inquires: "To what extent was Calvin himself a Calvinist?" Calvin against the Calvinists. (*In* Duffield, ed.: John Calvin, p. 19) and he states in *John Calvin. Humanist and Theologian,* p. 6: "... what passes for 'Calvinism' is one thing, and Calvin's 'Calvinism' is often very much another thing". Torrance makes the same point when he says: "Calvin made such a forward advance in theological thinking that he outstripped his contemporaries (and his successors — B.J. van der Walt) by centuries, with the result that they tended to fall back upon the old Aristotelian framework, modified by Renaissance humanism, in order to interpret him. Thus there was produced what history has called 'Calvinism', the rigid straitjacket within which Calvin's teaching has been presented regularly to succeeding generations". Knowledge of God and speech about Him according to John Calvin. *Revue d'histoire et de philosophie religieuses,* 44:402, 1964.

in the development of Melanchton's thought[6]. In the first period (c. 1512-1518), before he met Luther and was won for the Reformation, he was a Humanist. In the second phase (c. 1519-1521) he became a champion of the Reformation. During the third stage (from 1522 onwards) he returned very largely to his Humanistic ideals and developed a very definite synthesis between the Reformational heritage and his love for the classics[7].

3.1.2 Synthesis

Our interest here is focussed especially on the final phase of Melanchton's thought, when he reveals himself as a synthetic thinker. H. Maier concisely categorizes this phase as follows: "Melanchton lebt in der Vergangenheit, im Altertum und im Mittelalter, und er lebt in der Bibel"[8]. Just as the bee flies from flower to flower, siphoning out the nectar and instinctively avoiding the poison, so does Melanchton also assemble his truth eclectically out of various systems.

Different scholars have drawn attention on his great respect for Aristo-

6. See for this, among others, Neuzer, *Der Ansatz der Theologie Philipp Melanchtons*, chapter I. Also Maier, *An der Grenze der Philosophie. Melanchton — Lavater — David Friederich Strauss*, p. 29-54. Sperl, too, in his work *Melanchton zwischen Humanismus und Reformation*, refers to the clear shift which took place between 1521 and 1522 in the thought of Melanchton.

7. Of Melanchton Ueberweg comments: "Sein oberste Ziel war, durch die Alten und das Evangelium das Leben zu versittlichen". *Grundriss der Geschichte der Philosophie* III, p. 101. Further down the same page he states that Melanchton endeavoured to reconcile both of the great forces of his time, viz. the newly-discovered Antiquity and the newly-understood Holy Scripture.
For the motives of this change in Melanchton, see Neuzer, op. cit., p. 34.

8. Maier, op. cit., p. 91. On pages v and vi he speaks of "... Melanchton, der Philosoph und Apologet der Reformation, der, zum Heil und Unheil seiner Kirche und ihrer Theologie, den neuen Glauben durch Anlehnung an einen humanistische scholastische Aristotelismus zu stützen sucht, der Begründer der protestantischen Schulphilosophie, der aber in und mit dieser der Neuzeit doch auch das rationale Erbe des Altertums und des Mittelalters übermittelt".

9. Apart from most of the works already mentioned, see also Geyer, *Welt und Mensch. Zur Frage des Aristotelismus bei Melanchton* and especially Petersen, *Geschichte der aristotelische Philosophie im protestantischen Deutschland*, who on p. 17-108 treats Melanchton as the founder of Aristotelianizing thought.
For the revival of Aristotelianism in general and its assimilation into Lutheran thought, c.f. Troeltsch, *Vernunft und Offenbarung bei Johann Gerhard und Melanchton. Untersuchung zur Geschichte der altprotestantischen Theologie*, p. 107-117.
For Melanchton's affiliations with Patristic thought see Fraenkel, *Testimonium Patrum. The function of the Patristic Argument in the Theology of Philip Melanchton*.

tle[9]. C. van der Woude provides examples of this[10]. G.P. Hartveld shows how in this fashion Melanchton influenced the Theology of the sixteenth century and thereafter in a most far-reaching way[11].

However, Melanchton's thought can not be described adequately as pure Aristotelianism, but should rather be seen as an interpretation of Aristotle. He reads Aristotle with coloured spectacles, tinted by Medieval Scholasticism. H. Maier comments on this: "Melanchtons Denken ist seinem innersten Wesen nach nüchtern konservativ. Er knüpft an das Alten an. Er achtet wissenschaftliche Uberzeugungen, die sich im Laufe von Jahrhunderten bewährt haben. Er scheut jede revolutionäre Regung. Luthers rücksichtlos vorwärtsdrägendende Kraft, die das Alte, wo es im Wege steht, pietätlos niedertritt, ist ihm unheimlich. Auch im wissenschaftlichen Leben ist ihm jede Störung zuwider, welche die Kontinuität der geschichtlichen Entwicklung zu sprengen droht. Sein Ideal ist die reformatorische Weiterbildung des Bestehenden. Seine Reorganisation des Universitätswesens nimmt die alten Formen und den alten Studiengang wieder auf, wenn auch der Betrieb selbst wesentlich umgestaltet wird. Und seine Philosophie selbst ist im Grunde nichts anderes als erneuter Aristotelismus, dem scholastischen Aristoteles erheblich näher stehend als dem wirklichen. Ein bahnbrechender, schöpferischer Denker ist Melanchton gewiss nicht gewesen"[12].

According to H. Dooyeweerd the *praeceptor germaniae* also failed in his task of radically reforming university studies from the roots up. "When he undertook the gigantic task of establishing a relation between the Reformation and modern science, he fell back upon the scholastic standpoint of accommodation"[13].

10. Cf. Van der Woude, op. cit., p. 13. Cf. also Kuyper, *Encyclopaedie der Heilige Godgeleerdheid*, I, p. 146.

11. Melanchton has "... door zijn aristotelisme de s.g. natuur van de theologie in de 16e eeuw en later beslissend bepaald. Begonnen als anti-aristotelicus heeft hij toch Aristoteles aan de toenmalige Europa overhandigd". Hartveld, Over de methode der dogmatiek in de eeuw der Reformatie. *Gereformeerde Theologisch Tijdschrift*, 62: 110-111, 1962.

12. Maier, op. cit., p. 4. Cf. also p. 67.

13. Dooyeweerd, *A new critique of theoretical thought* I, p. 513.

3.1.3 Doctrine of the two kingdoms (influenced by that of the two realms)

Melanchton's thought is tinged with the theory of the two realms. He here latches on to Luther's[14] doctrine of the two kingdoms and his distinction between law and Gospel[15]. Melanchton maintains that all one's troubles stem precisely from this, that the sacred and the profane are intermingled. The true merit of Luther lies in his separation of the two. According to R. Stupperich, Melanchton lays even greater stress than Luther on the opposition between the two realms[16]. He thus embraces a more antithetical attitude towards the *duplex regimen*. Even so, the *regimen corporale* is the preamble on the way to the *regimen spirituale*.

3.1.4 Faith and knowledge, Theology and Philosophy

Since Luther and Calvin occupied themselves initially with the proclamation of the newly-discovered Gospel, the scholarly systematization of the Protestant faith is not a primary concern of theirs. In Germany it was not Luther but Melanchton, and in Switzerland not Zwingli and Calvin but Bullinger and Beza, who busied themselves with the Theological Encyclopedia and Methodology. But intellectual formulations of the content of faith bring new problems to the fore or accentuate others. E. Troeltsch shows how the problem of the relationship between faith and knowledge, which for Luther was not acute, became a serious problem the moment Melanchton began to reconstruct Luther's opinions into a systematic Theology, or began attempting to provide a scholarly foundation for the new Reformational belief: "Eine Fixierung des Verhältnisses von Vernunft und Offenbarung war auch ganz überflüssig, so lange die religiöse Reform noch eine allgemeine, inner-katholische Bewegung war. Für diese Periode lag das ganze Gewicht auf den durchschlagenden grossen Grundgedanken Luthers vom

---

14. An interesting study of the relationship between Melanchton and Luther is that of Neuzer, *Luther und Melanchton — Einheit im Gegensatz. Theologische Existenz Heute* (Neue Folge), 91:1-41, 1961.

15. Neuzer says of Melanchton's distinction between *res sacrae* and *res humanae,* "Wichtig ist die Zueinanderordnung der res humanae und res sacrae: die res sacra ist die höhre und wichtigere; aber sie baut auf der res humana auf... Es gibt ein stufenweisen Aufstieg von der Vernunft zur Offenbarung... Es ist das Schema von Gesetz und Evangelium." Op. cit., p. 39.

16. Cf. Stupperich, *Melanchton*, p. 37. Cf. also his other work on Melanchton *Der unbekannte Melanchton. Wirken und Denken des Praeceptor Germaniae in Neuer Sicht.*

Glauben und von der Freiheit des Christenmenschen. Erst nachdem sich bei Niederwerfung der Revolution aus der grossen nationalreligiösen Bewegung bestimmt begrenzte fürstliche Territorialkirchen ausgeschieden hatten, erwuchs, wie bei jeder Umbildung von Ideen zu Institutionen, die Notwendigkeit einer genauen, vollständigen Festlegung des Bestandes. Diese hat nun aber nicht Luther vorgenommen, sondern Melanchton, der als der Unterrichtsleiter, der wissenschaftliche Publizist und der theologische Diplomat der sächsischen Kirche Luthers Ideen immer erst durch seine Formulierungen hindurch gehen liess. Erst in diesen Formulierungen sind die wunderbar reichen und bunt bewegten Ideen Luthers zur Theologie geworden und haben feste Prägung angenommen"[17].

Melanchton had to consolidate, shape, think through and methodically and systematically arrange, on the theological level, everything that Luther had given prominence to in a much more impartial and prescientific fashion. Unfortunately this formulation was done in the models and categories of thought associated with Aristotelian-Scholastic patterns, and Melanchton did not realize that they were in tension with the heritage of the Reformation nor that they would eventually negate the intentions of the Reformation. H. Maier correctly observes that by relapsing into the two-realm theory Melanchton surrendered the most important discovery of the Reformation, viz. that service of God cannot be limited to a certain area of life[18].

According to W. Kickel the relationship between reason and belief in Melanchton can be described by the word "co-ordination", although this co-ordination often becomes a relation of a subordination of reason to faith[19]. Q. Breen even holds the opinion that Melanchton's view of the faith-knowledge problem "was ... tarred with the stick of the *duplex veritas*"[20].

The relationship between Philosophy and Theology is determined in Melanchton by his two-realm doctrine, which goes hand in hand with the distinction between Law and Gospel[21]. Theology, then, is also the queen of the sciences, as is apparent from the following summary which Hübner

17. Troeltsch, op. cit., p. 58.

18. Cf. Maier, op. cit., p. 134-5.

19. Cf. Kickel, *Vernunft und Offenbarung bei Theodor Beza. Zum Problem des Verhältnisses von Theologie, Philosophie und Staat*, p. 60.

20. Breen, The twofold truth theory in Melanchton. (*In* Christianity and Humanism, p. 90. Cf. also footnote 65 on p. 92).

21. Cf. Hübner, *Natürliche Theologie und theokratische Schwärmerei bei Melanchton*, p. 130.

gives of Melanchton's theory of science: "Grammatik, Rhetorik und Dialektik als alles übrige tragende Basis. Darüber die verschiedenen Stockwerke der *philosophia naturalis* und *moralis* mit ihrer Einzelzweigen. Dann Jurisprudenz und Medizin als selbständige Fachwissenschaften. Und schliesslich die *theologia sacra* als Krone und organisierendes Prinzip aller Wissenschaft. Dieser imposante Bau ruht auf dem Fundamente von Gesetz und Evangelium. Er ermöglichte die Einbeziehung und Unterordnung aller übrigen Wissenschaften unter die Theologie. Sie halten sich als zum Gesetz Gehörig im Raum des Gesetzes zu bewegen, genossen als solche eingehende Pflege, aber waren als solche auch unschädlich gemacht und ungefährlich für die Theologie, die sich auf die Offenbarung gründete. Die Philosophie war im wahren Sinne die Magd der Theologie"[22].

As the maidservant, Scholastic Philosophy has to provide the material which makes the Christian faith into a scholarly system. A. Kuyper did not perceive that the *praeceptor Germaniae's* attempt at an exclusively "formal" use of Aristotelian-Scholastic Philosophy was self-deceit[23]. H. Maier rather more clearly notices the dangers inherent in such an attempt when he observes that Melanchton's theology becomes every more and more philosophized[24]. G.P. Hartvelt remarks accurately that even if Melanchton had only wanted to use the Aristotelian-Scholastic method in order to expand the reformational heritage into intellectual Theology, the Philosophy (behind the method) would nevertheless have had a decisive influence on his Theology, for: "In de methode gaat 't toch tenslotte om iets meer dan het 'op-een-rij-zetten-van-de-gegevens' van de Schrift. In de methode speelt een visie mee op de werkelijkheid tussen God en mensen. Men kan *in* de keuze van de methode de dogmatiek iets laten zèggen, — of iets laten *verzwijgen*... Methode betekent zorgvuldigheid, plan, tactiek, maar ook: ergens willen komen, de gegevens iets laten zèggen, afzonderlijk, loci-gewijs, maar ook in hun totaliteit"[25].

3.2 T. Beza (1519-1605)

Just as Melanchton followed Luther and consolidated his work, so did

---

22. Ibid., p. 138-9. Cf. also p. 120 as well as Kickel, op. cit., p. 57-9.

23. Cf. Kuyper, *Encyclopaedie der Heilige Godgeleerdheid* I, 146-7.

24. Cf. Maier, op. cit., p. 129. On p. 131 he even says: "... in Melanchtons Gedankenkreis hat die Philosophie die Theologie bewältigt und die Religion getötet".

25. Hartvelt, op. cit., p. 139.

Beza succeed Calvin in 1564 at the Academy of Geneva and exercised immense influence upon Reformed Protestant thought. As with Melanchton Beza was also a transitional figure between the sixteenth century Reformation and the Orthodoxy of the seventeenth.[25a] W. Kickel even says that "... die Theologie Bezas in direkter Weise in den Strom der Orthodoxie einmündet"[26].

3.2.1 Over-emphasis on Theology at the expense of faith

As in Melanchton's case the stress in Beza is not laid primarily on (pre-scientific) faith but on the discipline of Theology. While Calvin deals with the certainty of faith, Beza aims at a rational defence of Reformational Theology. The intimate, direct connection of faith with Scripture disappears — faith is systematized in an intellectually-written textbook. "Calvins Denken kreist um das Problem der Schrift und Glaubensgewissheit, Bezas Denken um das Problem der Gewissheit der Theologie als Wissenschaft, d.h. um das der Sicherheit ihrer Methode, die Schriftgewissheit schon voraussetzt und aus der die Glaubensgewissheit erst sekundär folgt. Bilden bei Calvin Wort und Glaube noch eine Einheit, die zwar schon als Subjekt und Objekt unterscheiden, aber doch durch das Geistwirken zusammengehalten werden, und wurde die Vernunft daneben in einem lockeren Subordinations- und Koordinationsverhältnis als nicht wertlose, aber prinzipiell doch überflüssige Grösse geduldet, so treten nun bei Beza zwischen die Schriftoffenbarung und den Glauben die vernünftigen überlegungen und Beweis-

25a. This *preliminary* survey of Reformed Orthodoxy (not only the section on Beza) is merely the result of my personal study of secondary sources on this era. One of the main problems still open for consideration is whether the relapse into Scholasticism was as serious as indicated in most of the studies on this period. Recent discussions I had with Beza-students at the Institut d'Histoire de la Reformation (Geneva) revealed that much more "Kleinforschung" need to be done to answer this question properly. Some scholars at this institute for Reformation History seriously doubt the idea that Beza may be regarded as the father of post-Reformation Scholasticism. Beza, in his controversy with Roman Catholicism, tried to systematize and explain his predecessor Calvin, in the first place. It is, therefore a serious oversimplification of the actual situation to believe — as many still do – that Calvin was a purely Biblical theologian and his successors (i.c. Beza) scholastic theologians. It is utterly wrong to consider on the one hand everything Calvin produced as without spot or blemish and on the other hand to regard the work of his followers with suspicion.

26. Kickel, op. cit., p. 252. Cf. also p. 10 and Graafland *De zekerheid van het geloof. Een onderzoek naar de geloofsbeschouwing van enige vertegenwoordigers van reformatie en nadere reformatie*, p. 74 and Hall, Calvin against Calvinists. (*In* Duffield, ed, John Calvin, p. 25-7).

gänge der theologischen Wissenschaft, von deren Sicherheit die Glaubensgewissheit schliesslich abhängig wird. Von da aus muss die Gewissheitsbegründung der Theologie als Wissenschaft zu einer Hauptfrage werden"[27].

3.2.2 Aristotelian, scholastic thought

Beza employed an Aristotelian, scholastic philosophy for the intellectual elaboration of the Reformed confession[28]. Most recent researchers point out this strong Aristotelian influence in Beza[29]. Beza maintained that there were three reasons why Aristotelianism was more acceptable than any other philosophical system: It makes a definite philosophical preparation for Theology possible; Aristotle's Ethics, Psychology and Politics are not seriously opposed to those of Christianity, and the Aristotelian views of the world and of nature can be reconciled with the Bible.

We share the amazement of W. Kickel: "Selbst wenn mann die Metaphysik des Aristoteles ausklammert... so ist doch nicht zu verkennen, dass auch die aristotelische Logik und Methodik nicht rein formal sind und ebenso wie die Physik und Psychologie durchgehend metaphysische Voraussetzungen haben"[30].

A significant factor explaining this easy absorption of Aristotelianism by Melanchton and Beza is undoubtedly the fact that this was no longer a pure brand. The preceding Scholastic synthetic thought had already divested the philosophy of Aristotle of all the sharpest edges which conflicted with Scripture.

27. Kickel, op. cit., p. 45.

28. Cf. A. Kuyper, op. cit., p. 137; Hartvelt, *Gereformeerd Theologisch Tijdschrift*, 62:149, 1962; Van der Woude, op. cit., p. 13 and Graafland, op. cit., p. 76. Dooyeweerd says that "... de gereformeerde Theologie, die sins BEZA weer de studie van de aristotelische logica en metaphysica als noodzakelijken grondslag voor de universitaire theologische opleiding wist in te voeren, geleidelijk in de banen van het scholastisch denken werd teruggevoerd, waaruit Calvijn de gereformeerde theologie grootendeels had bevrijd". *Philosophia Reformata*, 11:51, 1946.

29. Cf. ibid., p. 10. According to him one should distinguish between the Melanchtonian Aristotelism of the sixteenth century (which Beza also accepted) and the Aristotelianism of the Spanish Jesuits during the 17th century which was popular amongst the Orthodox.

30. Kickel, op. cit., p. 62.

3.2.3 Belief and knowledge, Theology and Philosophy

Beza tried to solve the dilemma of faith and knowledge by distinguishing natural reason *(ratio)* from Christian reason *(intelligentiae* or *fides generalis)*.[31]. It is the latter which acquires knowledge of the truths of Revelation, something which the former is not able to do. Christian reason *(fides generalis)* is distinguished from faith, since it implies not personal *appropriation* of salvation but only *knowledge* of salvation[32]. General faith however, is not elevated by particular faith but rather surpassed. General (Christian) faith apparently functions as a link between rational knowledge and belief.

Beza perceives a relationship of subordination between knowledge and faith, reason and Revelation. The subordination of reason to Revelation does not mean that there is a contradiction between the two but rather that, should a descrepancy arise, reason will have to yield[33].

And as with this relationship of faith and knowledge, so with that between Theology and Philosophy. Philosophy and all the other sciences are servants of Theology[34]. Such service incorporates three facets[35]. Firstly Philosophy provides Theology with its *method*. Secondly philosophical arguments can be used for *apologetic ends,* and in the third place one can (in emergencies) even use new *philosophical concepts*. According to Kickel[35a] all Beza's works are of a polemic and apologetic nature and it is to be expected that the influence of Philosophy on his thought will not be trivial.

In the third main section of his study[36] Kickel undertakes an investiga-

31. Cf. id., p. 27-8.

32. It appears as though Beza's twofold belief (general and particular) corresponds with twofold revelation. The *fides generalis* acknowledges the *revelatio generalis,* i.c. the *historia Christi,* as true, and the *fides pecularis* applies generally acknowledged truths to the individual person, i.e. personally appropriates the *revelatio pecularis.* Cf. id., op. cit., p. 52.

33. Cf. id., p. 37, 60.

34. According to Kickel, op. cit., p. 46, the *Leges Academiae* of the Academy of Geneva (of which Beza was the co-founder) determine the relation of Theology and Philosophy exactly as Melanchton had seen it.

35. Cf. id., p. 33 and 38.

35a. Cf. id., p. 8.

36. Cf. id., p. 98-282.

tion into the influence of the (Aristotelian-Scholastic) Philosophy on certain key themes in Beza's Theology (among others his theory of predestination, of justification, of the Trinity, of the two Natures of Christ, of his view of the Lord's Supper and his conception of the relation between church and state), and concludes: "Bei jedem der behandelten Lehrstücke konnten wir am Schluss feststellen, dass die Vernunft zwar offiziell in den Dienst der Theologie gestellt, also der Offenbarung untergeordnet waʳ, dass aber diese Indienststellung unbemerkt in eine geheime Herrscherstellung überging. Uberall war es die ungebrochene Durchführung meist aristotelischer Begriff und Denkschemata, die diese geheime Herrscherstellung bewirkte und die Offenbarung aus dem Zentrum der Theologie verdrängte"[37].

Having given attention to the two most important transitional figures between Reformation and Orthodoxy, we can turn briefly to some features of seventeenth-century Protestant Orthodoxy.

4. PROTESTANT ORTHODOXY OF THE SEVENTEENTH CENTURY[37a]

Of necessity what follows is a very broad categorization, which does not for instance make a distinction between Lutheran and Reformed Orthodoxy. To make this still little-studied facet of Western thought better known, the following will be discussed: The most notable representatives of this period, reasons for their unfamiliarity, the importance of the period and the causes of this relapse into scholasticism.

37. Id., p. 280, 281. On the following page (282) he remarks: "Über die Offenbarung wird so das Strukturkreuz philosophischen Denkens gelegt, welches die Offenbarungswahrheit rational schematisiert und nicht mehr in ihrer ganzen Fülle zu Geltung kommen lässt".

37a. Apart from the secondary literature on this period mentioned in the references below, I have given a brief bibliography in my dissertation *Die Natuurlike Teologie met besondere aandag aan die visie daarop by Thomas van Aquino, Johannes Calvyn en die "Synopsis Purioris Theologiae". 'n Wysgerige Ondersoek* (1974), Vol. II, p. 616-618. I would like to add to it the following works: Armstrong, B.G.: *Calvinism and the Amyraut Heresy. Protestant Scholasticism and Humanism in Seventeenth-century France* (Madison, The University of Wisconsin Press, 1969); Bray, J.S.: *Theodore Beza's doctrine of predestination* (Nieuwkoop, B. de Graaf, 1975); Fatio, O.: *Méthode et Théologie Lambert Daneau et les débuts de la scolastique réformée* (Geneve, Librairie Droz, 1976) and Leube, H.: *Kalvinismus und Lutherthum in Zeitalter des Orthodoxie* (Aalen, Scientia Verlag, 1966).

4.1 Most important representatives of Reformed and Lutheran Orthodoxy

Only the names of some representative figures are mentioned. Some of the most familiar[38] are these: J.H. Alsted (1588-1638), W. Ames (1576-1633), G. Amesius (1576-1633), J. Arminius (1560-1609), G. Calixtus (1586-1656), J. Coccejus (1603-1669), E. Coles (about 1608-1688), J. Gerhard (1582-1637), F. Gomarus (1563-1641), J. Howe (born 1630), A. Hyperius (1511-1564), F. Junius (1545-1602), B. Keckermann (1571-1609), J. Maccovius (1588-1644), S. Maresius (1599-1673), W. Perkins (1558-1602), P. Ramus (1515-1572), T. Shephard (1605-1649), Z. Ursinus (1534-1583), G. Voetius (1589-1676), C. Vorstius (1569-1622) and G. Zanchius (1516-1590)[39].

4.2 Reasons for the unfamiliarity of this era

From a philosophical point of view in particular, this aspect of seventeenth-century Western thought is in great measure still terra incognita. Older standard works like Ueberweg's *Grundriss der Geschichte der Philosophie*[40] say very little. From about the beginning of the century various

---

38. Wundt (in his *Die deutsche Schulmetaphysik des 17. Jahrhunderts,* p. xxvi) mentions not only most of these figures but also a good many more unfamiliar names, as well as the most important works of all these thinkers with the places, dates of publication and the libraries in Germany where each work is to be found.
Figures of the Anglo-American world such as Ames, Coles, Howe, Perkins and Shephard are discussed in the thesis of Chalker, *Calvin and some seventeenth century Calvinists.*

39. A proof of the relapse into Scholasticism with one of the thinkers of this period, is provided by the thesis of O. Gründler, *Thomism and Calvinism in the theology of Girolamo Zanchi 1516-1590.* He demonstrates how Zanchius' theories with respect to central dogmas show a modified but definite connection with Thomism, and demonstrates how this was a deliberate and uncritical return from reformed theology to Medieval tradition. He concludes with respect to Zanchius, "... we have, indeed, encountered a striking congruity between his views and those of Thomas Aquinas on almost every point. This congruity is not merely one of form and method, but rather the result of common ontological and epistemological presuppositions provided by the philosophy of Aristotle in its modified Thomistic form...
In the theology of Zanchi, at the very point of transition from Reformation to Orthodoxy, the spirit of medieval Scholasticism had thus begun to replace that of the Reformers at a point where it counted most".

40. In volume III of *Die Philosophie der Neuzeit bis zum Ende des XVII. Jahrhunderts* attention is admittedly given to Luther, Melanchton and Zwingli under the heading "Humanismus und Protestantismus in Deutschland" (p. 88-118) but only the names of a few figures in Protestant Orthodoxy (such as B. Keckermann and J.H. Alsted) are given (on p. 110, 111).

persons have explored different areas of this long-forgotten country.

Several factors were responsible for the long philosophical neglect of this fallow land, which still exists in some measure today. One reason might be[41] that historians of Philosophy mostly had individual (great) philosophers in mind rather than philosophical schools. And we are busy precisely with such a school-philosophy attached to various universities. Another significant reason is the (to my mind groundless) prejudice that this period is of lesser importance to the history of Western thought[42]. This phase would not be of intellectual importance because it merely leans on the previous stage and offers no independent thought. Related to this is the idea that making a closer acquaintance with the philosophy of this period is just not worth the trouble, since independent research had not at the time been primary, but a faithful relaying of that which was received. Consequently (it was felt) knowledge of one work or figure from this school actually gave sufficient knowledge of all. A third argument as to the philosophical irrelevance of this period, is that Philosophy groaned under the yoke of Theology and could only teach that which was permitted by Theology[43]. A final reason (related to the other) for the 'unimportance' of this age is the supposed fact that this period is merely an echo of Medieval thought. Admittedly there is truth in this (as in all the other arguments) but it is exaggerated and furthermore it is forgotten that this time did act as a transition to the new age[44].

4.3 Its importance as a phase in Western cultural history

It is a great pity that this period has lacked serious philosophical attention, since it is by no means a trivial phase of Western cultural history. Orthodoxy was in fact the most general trend within Protestant thought of the seventeenth century. For instance, Wundt comments: "Es ist die philosophische Scholastik 'Schulweisheit' mit Recht so geheissen, weil sie auf allen Schulen, schon in den Gymnasien und dann in den philosophischen

41. Cf. Lewalter, *Spanisch-jesuitische und deutsch-lutherische Metaphysik des 17. Jahrhunderts*, p. 5.

42. Cf. Wundt, *Die deutsche Schulmethaphysik des 17. Jahrhunderts*, p. 5-11.

43. Wundt quite rightly remarks, op. cit., p. 10: "... man kann daher sehr wohl fragen, ob nicht vielmehr die Philosophie die Theologie beherrscht habe als umgekehrt".

44. Lewalter comments with good reason: "Ehe man Descartes, Leibniz, Spinoza, 'und ihre Zeit' verstehen kann, muss man in den breiten Strom der 'Scholastik' jener Jahrzehnte hinabgestiegen sein". Op. cit., p. 5.

Fakultäten der Universitäten gelehrt wurde, durch die bekanntlich jeder Student hindurchgehen musste... Sie beherrschte deshalb aber auch als das allein und allgemein anerkannte Verfahren sämtliche Wissenschaften der oberen Fakultäten, insbesondere auch die für die Geisteshaltung der Zeit massgebliche, die Theologie. Auf diesen Wege drängte sie sozusagen in alle Poren des Zeitalters und bestimmte dessen Aussehen und Haltung. Wenn also eine Philosophie den Anspruch erheben kann, als kennzeichnend für das 17. Jahrhundert und als die eigenliche, 'Barock Philosophie' zu gelten, so ist est diese...

"Sie war über ganz Europa verbreitet und beherrschte überall den Schulunterricht; beinahe kann man sagen, es war die letzte wirklich ganz gemeinsame Bildung der europaïschen Völker, die dann eben unter die Wirkung der sogenannten neueren Philosophie auseinanderbrach."[45]

As already pointed out, seventeenth-century Scholasticism also serves as an important link between Medieval and Modern thought. It is also exceedingly important as one of the key sources for the Dutch Reformed theologians who wrote at the end of the previous century and the beginning of the twentieth – such as H. Bavinck and A. Kuyper[46].

In addition, seventeent-century Orthodoxy is characterized by an Aristotelianizing Scholasticism: "Die neuprotestantische Scholastik ist wie die alte im wesentlichen aristotelisch ... Aristoteles ist *der* Philosoph. Man wird nicht müde, sein Lob zu singen"[47].

Aristotle, avers Scaliger, is "divinus praeceptor incomparabilis", "de universa humana sapientia praetor supraque caeteros omnes mortales bene meritus". Pacius adds of Aritstotle, "omnius quos ab urbe conditio novimus scriptorum (sacris exceptis) praestantissimum". Keckermann and Goclenius call him a wonder of nature, his "ingenium" is "omnium ingeniorum mundi clarissimum exemplar atque idea". Meisner calls Aristotle the "dictator in

---

45. Wundt, op. cit., p. 3. For the spreading of Protestant Orthodoxy in England and from there (by the Puritans) to America and elsewhere, cf. the thesis of Chalker, *Calvin and some seventeenth century English Calvinists.*

46. For example, in 1881, H. Bavinck saw an edition of the *Synopsis Purioris Theologiae* (which had not appeared since 1658) through the press, and it is quite clear from Bavinck's *Gereformeerde Dogmatiek* how great the influence of this work on him was.
A. Kuyper rescues two other Orthodox theologians from oblivion in his work. *D. Francisci Iunii opuscula theologica selecta* (1882) and by putting out a new edition of G. Voetius' *Cathecisatie over den Heidelbergschen Catechismus* (in 1891).

47. Weber. *Die philosophische Scholastik des deutschen Protestantismus in Zeitalter der Orthodoxie,* p. 35.

philosophia summus", Calixtus the "princeps philosophorum" and Futke does not hesitate for a moment to declare "Aristotelis logica ipsius Dei logica est"[48].

It would be very valuable if the reason(s) for the relapse into Scholasticism during the seventeenth century, immediately after the pioneering work of Calvin in particular, could be tracked down — even if they only had the negative result of preventing similar mistakes in the search for a Scriptural scholarship today.

4.4 Causes of the relapse into Scholasticism

While the era of Renaissance and Reformation might create the impression that, as a result of the growth of Nominalism as well as the criticism of Humanism and all the other new intellectual currents, Scholastic thought lost its meaning, further developments demonstrate quite clearly that Scholasticism had by no means lost its force. A good many universities (of which the most important were Paris, Oxford, Cologne and Padua) acted as stout bulwarks: The Counter-Reformation saw a strong resurgence, most particularly as far as Spain was concerned.

Spain experienced no real Renaissance. Attempts at independent thought were smothered by the Inquisition, so that Spain was spared any serious break with the Middle Ages. As a result Spain became the centre of the Counter-Reformation, which aimed at restoring Thomistic Scholasticism. There Catholicism could blossom in the time of transition between Medieval and Modern thought as in no other land[49]. The proponents of this restoration were the Dominicans and Jesuits in particular. Their labours led to a new resurgence of Thomism.

Among neo-Scholastic Spanish thinkers it was largely the Jesuit Franz Suarez (1548-1617) who had the greatest influence, not just on Roman Catholics, but also on Protestant thinkers[50]. F. Sassen, who made a comprehensive study of the earliest philosophical training at the University of Leiden (between 1575 and 1611), comes to the following conclusion:

---

48. Cf. ibid.

49. Cf. Ueberweg, *Grundriss der Geschichte der Philosophie*, III, p. 206.

50. Cf. id., p. 210-215 for an exposition of Suarez. Also of interest for Suarez are Conze, *Der Begriff der Metaphysik bei Franciscus Suárez;* Ehrle, P. *Franz Suárez S.J. Gedenkblätter zu seinem 300. Todestag;* Schneider, Der angebliche Essentialismus des Suárez. *Wissenschaft und Weisheit,* 24:40-68, 1961; Werner, *Franz Suárez und die Scholastik der letzten Jahrhunderte* and Copleston, *A history of Philosophy.* Vol. III: *Occam to Suarez,* p. 353-405.

"Zoo is vooral Suarez in de metaphysica de leermeester geworden van de Leidsche Scholastiek"[51].

Suarez' massive influence is also apparent from this statement by Ueberweg: "Die spanische Neuscholastik, insbesondere die Lehre des Suarez, fand weite Verbreitung sowohl auf katholischen wie auf protestantischen Universitäten... Hereboord nennt den Suarez geradezu omnium metaphysicorum papa atque princeps und meint, alle kürzeren und geordneter geschrieben Metaphysiken der damaligen Zeit seien aus ihm genommen... Das Ende des Jahrhunderts scheint sich Suarez auf manchen deutschen Universitäten desselben Ansehens erfreut zu haben, das früher Melanchton genoss..."[52].

Sassen's conclusion in this regard is "... dat het leerplan van het oudste wijsgerige onderwijs te Leiden geheel aansloot bij dat van de laatste periode der Middeleeuwen en het tijdvak van het Humanisme. *De Hervorming heeft in deze niets veranderd.* (Italics by — B.J. v.d.W.) ... Van overheidswege wordt het volgen van Aristoteles en de cursorische interpretatie van diens werken bij herhaling voorgeschreven ... Een directe invloed van Melanchton valt niet waar te nemen... Als tegen de begin der 17de eeuw de belangstelling in de metaphysiek ontwaakt, blijkt men meer geneigd, de leiding van de Spaansche Jesuïetenschool te volgen dan die van de Luthersche Scholastiek in Duitsland. Van een eigen Nederlandsch karakter van het oudste Leidsche Scholastiek kan men niet spreken"[53].

The most urgent question is, how was it possible for the Reformation to be of such short duration and for the Scholasticism of Spain to have such a powerful influence on Protestant universities in Germany and Holland? Although the fact that during the time of Melanchton and Beza a return to Aristotelian Scholasticism had already occurred, partly explains this, it does not clear matters up completely. It is indeed true that Scholasticism was "in the air"[54]. Other explanations, which have their moments of truth, are

51. Sassen. Het oudste wijsgerig onderwijs te Leiden. *Mededelingen der Nederlandsche Akademie van wetenschappen, Afd. Letterkunde (Nieuwe reeks):* 4(1), p. 40.
De Geschiedenis van de Letterkunde der Nederlande (edited by F. Baur), IV deals with the Calvinistic thinker J. Revius on p. 165-210 (by G.A. van Es) and on p. 168 mentions the following: "De *Disputationes Metaphysicae* van Franciscus Suárez, den beroemde Spaanschen Jezuiet, maakte Revius door een critische bewerking geschikt voor leerboek op de Protestantsche scholen".

52. Ueberweg, op. cit., p. 42.

53. Sassen, op. cit., p. 42.

54. Cf. Eschweiler, *Die Philosophie des spanischen Spätscholastik auf den deutschen Universitäten des siebzehnten Jahrhunderts,* p. 289.

that Protestant thinkers wanted to turn their own weapons against the Roman Catholics, that there was an intellectual affinity between Protestant Orthodoxy and the neo-Scholasticism of the Jesuits, and that Scholasticism's methods could be used for the expression of the Protestant doctrinal system and scholarship[55].

Possibly the puzzle is easiest solved by concentrating on the task which Orthodoxy had to perform. For Luther and Calvin the stimulating rediscovery of the Gospel was primary. With their followers such creative originality had to make place for a more slavish revision and defence of this heritage. The generation after the Reformers, the Orthodox in particular, made it their task to consolidate, shape and scientifically formulate the Reformational heritage.

"... Calvinistic theology became rigid or hardened in the centuries following Calvin's death... whereas Calvin himself wrote with the exuberance and enthusiasm of one who had made a new discovery, his followers were left the less exciting task of filling in the gaps left by Calvin and explaining his doctrines so that the common man could understand them"[56].

The reformed heritage did not only have to be popularized for the "ordinary" believer, but had also (especially at the theological schools) to be thought through and intellectually systematized. A shift occurred from (pre-intellectual) belief towards (intellectual) Theology[57] in which everything was systematically and methodically studied. Epistemological and methodological problems became of importance. The accent shifted (speaking theologically) from Exegesis to Dogmatics and in the latter (which examines the creed of the church) it was especially the *prolegomena* which were important, for they dealt with the philosophical foundations of (Reformational) Theology. The philosophical presuppositions of Theology as well as the relationship between Theology and Philosophy[58], faith and knowledge, came up for discussion. Reformational *faith* now became a *science* — Theology.

55. Cf. for a summary and discussion of the various attempts to solve the problem, Lewalter, op. cit., p. 7-20 and Robbers, *Bijdragen. Tijdschrift voor Filosofie en Theologie*, 17:44 ff., 1956.

56. Chalker. *Calvin and some seventeenth century English Calvinists*, p. iii.

57. There is nothing wrong with this as such as long as it does not end in a theoretical, orthodox dogmatism and lose its living contact with Scripture.

58. Cf. Rossouw, *Klaarheid en interpretasie*, p. 272: "the controlling viewpoint from which the problem of the orthodox formulation is approached, has become the relationship between Revelation and reason, between theology and philosophy". (Translated by B.J. van der Walt).

The tragedy is that during the Reformation no radically Christian Philosophy was developed. Actually it is obvious that post-Reformation thinkers (who were not very original but more or less slavishly adapted the Reformational legacy) would take refuge in Scholastic synthesis. Rossouw points out, "The plans of post-reformational orthodoxy aimed at the preservation and maintenance of a reformed witness by means of a precise formulation, which took place in the categories and paradigms of the scholarly mode of thought at the time, viz. the aristotelian-scholastic"[59].

This relapse into Scholasticism is understandable, since Scholasticism was the result of centuries of struggle with the problem of faith and knowledge, Theology and Philosophy. Scholasticism succeeded by its scheme of nature and grace in so demarcating the areas of the two disciplines that the (mostly Aristotelian) Philosophy could still serve by helping to expand Christian dogmas into scholarly Theology.

The reason for this retreat into scholastic thought can be summarized thus[60]: Post-reformation scholars wanted to base their heritage on an intellectual (Theological) foundation but lacked the necessary philosophical apparatus. They found that Scholastic philosophy served this purpose, and the way to using it had already been smoothed by the relapse of Melanchton and Beza (among others) into synthesis. One of the motives behind this endeavour was also apologetic in nature. The Reformed heritage had to be defended — first against Catholicism and later against the growth of Rationalism. This apologetic defence had to be effective.

No wonder that Natural Theology during the seventeenth century was a key discipline. Rossouw elucidates: "As soon as the various articles of theo-

---

59. Rossouw, op. cit., p. 282 (Translated by B.J. van der Walt): Kooiman says precisely the same of the Lutheran Orthodoxy: "De lutherse orthodoxie had tot taak de theologische erfenis van de reformator in systeem te brengen, maar heeft in de hiermee gepaard gaande worsteling menige aan hem vreemde gedachte laten meespelen. Enerzijds dreigde ze in een nieuwe scholastiek te verstarren, anderzijds werd ze, in aansluiting aan Melanchtons leer der natuurlijke Godskennis, in de richting van een, meer aan de Stoa dan aan het Evangelie ontleend, pedagogisch georiënteerd humanisme gedreven..." Luther. (In Cultuurgeschiedenis van het Christendom, II, p. 1129, 1130).

60. J.H. Robbers (a Roman Catholic) gives the following summary of the reasons for the powerful influence of Spanish Scholastic philosophy upon Protestant thought in Germany and (from there) in Holland: "This revival of scholastic philosophy at the protestant universities cannot be explained by the supposition that the Protestants cultivated Scholasticism merely to prepare themselves for the controversy with Catholics, nor because Suarez has produced such a handy pattern for schemes. There were many who felt the need for a rational elaboration of the dogmatic truths; a natural theology was wanted too. In humanistic circles they wished to go back to the sources and strove for wideranging erudition. Therefore they returned to Aristotle". *Bijdragen. Tijdschrift voor Filosofie en Theologie*, 17:55, 1956.

logical knowledge come up for discussion, the quantitative query about the *number* of divine and eternal things which the autonomous reason can know on the grounds of its own principle, rears its head as a legitimate problem. For this reason the question of the *theologia naturalis* and its relationship to Scriptural theology is no incidental question for orthodox scholasticism, but a query which *must* be put with intrinsic urgency on the basis of the underlying premisses of orthodox theology"[61].

The true degree to which the various Protestant, Orthodox thinkers were influenced by Scholastic Philosophy can only be determined by a really thorough study of their works. It is here necessary to warn against exaggeration just as much as against underestimation. I feel that someone like H. Rückert exaggerates when he declares, "... Protestant theology in the period of Orthodoxy is a purely medieval phenomenon and shares certain essential characteristics with Scholasticism: the re-acceptance of Aristotelianism; the distinction, of such enormous consequence for theology, between natural and revealed theology; and the strong tendency towards system-building"[62]. On the other hand someone like S. van der Linde has a tendency to underestimate the Scholastic influence on the Orthodox thinkers when he avers: "In het algemeen heeft de Nadere Reformatie evenmin als de theologie van Calvijn, een wijsgerig karakter"[63].

61. Rossouw, op. cit., p. 315. (Translated by B.J. van der Walt). The familiar terminological distinction between *articuli puri* (questions purely of a supernatural, theological nature) and *articuli mixti* (questions of mixed nature, i.e. belonging to the area of Natural Theology) saw the light in this era.

62. H. Rückert. "The reformation — Medieval or Modern?" *Journal for theology and church*, 2:5, 10, 1965.

63. Van der Linde. De betekenis van de Nadere Reformatie voor kerk en theologie. *Kerk en Theologie*, 5:221, 1954. See also his essay De Anthropologie der Nadere Reformatie. (*In* Waarheid, wysheid en leven, p. 65.)

18 HOW DO WE KNOW THAT THE BIBLE IS THE WORD OF GOD? A FEW REMARKS ON GENERAL CANONICS AND APOLOGETICS*

In my study for my doctor's degree I frequently came across the age-old problem of faith and knowledge[1]. This provoked further thought about another problem which is just as old: viz. the problem of how we can know that the Bible is the Word of God? What is presented here is purely intended to provoke exchange of ideas and must thus not be taken too "seriously"! Criticism would be welcomed. The philosopher is forever questioning. Even if he does not find answers to many of his questions his work is not in vain.

1. TWO ILLUSTRATIONS FROM HISTORY: THOMAS AQUINAS AND JOHN CALVIN

We begin by looking at the great master of the Middle Ages, Thomas Aquinas[2]. Even in his time we find the problem with which General Canonics (the study of the Canon) still grapples today, viz. how do we know that the Bible really is the Word of God?

According to Aquinas *rationes demonstrativae, manifesta indicia* or *evidentia signorum* can be presented for the truth of divine Revelation. He accepted a clear distinction between the natural and supernatural, and accordingly believed that to prove the truth of the supernatural (in casu Holy Scripture) only supernatural proofs are acceptable[3]. Therefore the *doctor*

---

* Originally published in *Bulletin van die Suid-Afrikaanse Vereniging vir die Bevordering van Christelike Wetenskap*, no. 15:215-224, Sept. 1968 under the title: "Hoe weet ons dat die Bybel die Woord van God is?"

1. Cf. my dissertation: *Die Natuurlike Teologie met besondere aandag aan die visie daarop by Thomas van Aquino, Johannes Calvyn en die "Synopsis Purioris Theologiae" — 'n Wysgerige ondersoek* (1974).

2. Some of the viewpoints of the early church fathers on this subject are given by A. Waibel: *Die natürliche Gotteserkenntnis in der apologetische Literatur der zweiten Jahrhundert*, (1916), For the viewpoints of the Medieval thinkers cf. A. Lang: *Die Entfaltung des apologetischen Problem in der Scholastik des Mittelalters* (1962), chapter 7, p. 129 and *Die Wege des Glaubensbegründung bei den Scholastikern des 14. Jahrhunderts* (1931).

3. Cf. his *Summa Contra Gentiles*, Book III, chapter 154.

angelicus accepted as the only valid proof for the divine inspiration of Scripture the miracle as supernatural activity of God. He distinguished quite a number of different types of wonders which could serve as *motiva credibilitates*[4].

P.H. Lang, in his work *Die Lehre des hl Thomas von Aquin von der Gewissheit des übernatürlichen Glaubens* has, inter alia, made an investigation into the role that the *motiva credibilitates* plays in Thomas' approach as evidence or ground for his supernatural faith. (As wel shall see, F.W. Grosheide uses the same term, namely *motiva credibilitates* for our faith that the Bible is God's Word.) This questioning into the *motiva credibilitates* goes, according to Lang, together with Thomas' specific view of the faith - knowledge problem, namely that knowledge can give the *praeambula fidei*, the reasonable grounds for faith[5].

Our second example from history is John Calvin[6]. As could be expected, he discusses this problem very early in his *Institutio Christianae Religionis*. Already in chapter 7 of Book I he rejects the idea of the suspension or proof of the authority of Scripture on the judgement of the church. He cannot accept the idea of some people that the Scriptures have only so much weight as is conceded to them by the sanction of the church — as though the eternal and inviolable truth of God depends on the arbitrary will of men. "We do not seek arguments or probabilities to support our judgement, but submit our judgements and understandings to a thing concerning which it is impossible for us to judge..."

The principal proof, according to him, of the authority of the Scriptures is derived from the Writer itself. The Holy Spirit who inspired the human writers of the Bible at the same time also assures us that the Bible really is the Word of God. Calvin, therefore, strongly emphasized the self-evidence of the Bible — a problem to which we will return further on in this essay.

However, a clear proof that Calvin himself is still grappling with the problem of faith and reason is found subsequently in chapter 8 of his *Institutes* which discusses the rational proofs for establishing belief in Scripture. Space does not permit me to enumerate all the proofs Calvin discusses in this chapter. He maintains his viewpoint that the certainty of the Scriptures can only be founded on the internal persuasion of the Holy Spirit. Human testimonies may, however, serve as secondary aids to contribute towards its confirmation (Calvin uses the words *adminicula, probationes* and *indicia*).

---

4. Cf. ibid, Book I, chapter 6.

5. Cf. Van der Walt, op. cit., 274-279.

6. Cf. Van der Walt, op. cit., 434-439.

An important difference between the viewpoints of Calvin and Aquinas is that whereas Aquinas tries to prove from the outset that the Bible is God's Word in order to be able to believe, Calvin contends that rational proof is only possible subsequent to our belief in Scripture. (Aquinas: *intelligo ut credam;* Calvin: *credo ut intelligam).* His viewpoint in this regard is more Augustinian (cf. end of chapter 8 of the *Institutes).*

We conclude this brief review of Calvin with an evaluation of his proofs by E.A. Dowey who says: "These arguments are of uneven value, and some of them have become quite useless, at least in the form Calvin gave them... For example, in the argument from antiquity Calvin asserts that the Scripture is the oldest of all books and jokes about the Egyptians whose false chronicles extend their own antiquity to a point beyond the creation of the world. Correspondingly, the mere survival of the books is not so impressive today as it was to Calvin. The arguments from predictive prophecy are mechanical and go rather too heavy on the traditional dating of the Penteteuch, Deutero Isaiah, and Daniel, to serve us now without refurbishing, and the chronicles of patriarchal disgrace might well be construed as examples of human honesty rather than proof of divine inspiration. Others, such as the sublimity of the matter when contrasted with even the greatest non-Biblical writers, the consent of the church, and the price willingly paid by the martyrs cannot fail to impress a reader, although none of them leads necessarily to conclusions about the divine origin of Scripture"[7].

2. SOME CRITICAL REMARKS

The question arises as to whether the problem, of how we can know that the Bible is God's Word, actually fits Scriptural thinking; and whether it possibly only has a right of existence within synthetic thinking, where the false problem of faith and knowledge plays an important rôle.

It is not in principle wrong to search for so-called *notae cannonicitatis* because man may not determine what is canonical and the canonicity cannot be made dependent upon the changing result of fallible theological research? Further, is this possible in practice? In the search for a canon of the canon (which therefore questions the canonicity of the canon!) one never finds satisfaction. Once the search for *notae* had begun, it had to increase constantly. It becomes a *regressus ad infinitum*. A proof that no single *nota* will suffice!

---

7. *The knowledge of God in Calvin's Theology* (1952), p. 113-114.

3. EFFORTS OF CONTEMPORARY REFORMED THEOLOGIANS

In spite of this, most Reformed theologians have not broken radically with the attempt in one way or another to give in General Canonics proof(s) of the reliability (trustworthiness or inspiration) of scripture.

F.W. Grosheide (in his *Algemene Canoniek van het Nieuwe Testament*) sees as the task of this subject the investigation of the question as to whether the twenty-seven books of the New Testament are really canonical. Or: General Canonics is the science whereby we will ascertain that precisely these twenty-seven books and only these books are the Word of God.

He prefers to speak of *motiva credibilitatis* in place of *notae cannonicitatis*. In fact it boils down to the same thing. The question is again asked whether the Bible is the Word of God and it is made dependent on the science of Theology which should assure us that this is really the case.

In fact, whether the Bible really is the Word of God is placed in doubt, and this is followed by an attempt to disprove this doubt by way of science (Theology).

The same thing strikes us in H.N. Ridderbos' *Heilsgeschiedenis en Heilige Schrift van het Nieuwe Testament*. Like Grosheide he does not want to speak of *notae canonicitatis*. In its place he uses, not *motiva credibilitatis* (like Grosheide) but *principia cannonicitatis* which in fact is synonymous with it. According to him General Canonics must investigate with what right the church accepts the collection of books we have in the Bible as the canon. Or, it must ask on what ground it stands firm that the canon of the church is also the canon of Christ. He therefore also asks about the ground or proof for our faith that the Bible is the Word of God.

W.J. Snyman is much more careful in this regard, but (if I interpret him correctly) something of a similar vein strikes us here (in his *Diktate Tekskritiek en Algemene Kanoniek van die Nuwe Testament*).

He sharply and principially criticizes the idea of the so-called *notae cannonicitatis* but his definition of the task of General Canonics does not seem satisfactory either. It is very similar to the description given by F.W. Grosheide which we have already discussed[8].

For instance, he describes General Canonics as "... the science which assures us that the Word of God as it lies before us written, truly is the Word of God and which ensures us that exactly these books, and these alone, are the Word of God"[9].

General Canonics, according to him, does not give the ground (proof)

8. Cf. Snyman, op. cit., p. 6.

9. Ibid., p. 6, 7.

for our faith but assures us and demonstrates that our faith is not peculiar[10]. General Canonics seeks, in the New Testament and in history, to
make credible the fact that the books, these books alone, and no other, together form the Canon of the New Testament[11].

We find it difficult to agree with this assertion that Canonics should
assure us, or that it must *make it credible* for us that the Bible is God's
Word, or must demonstrate that our faith is *not so queer*.

Often it is argued that General Canonics can show the *wonderful*[12] origin of the canon. For example, no specific factor can be named which
caused the church to decide to accept precisely these books as the canon.
God led in such a way that many factors (which the secular historian might
describe as being purely chance) worked together for the recognition of the
canon. There is a special providence of God (*providentia specialissima*)
spoken of in this regard. Scripture had a unique origin. The church did not
canonise Scripture, but only recognised and later acknowledged it as God's
Word.

This is true, but now it is asserted that the wonder of the origin of the
Scriptures can be used to convince unbelievers that their holy writings
(which do not have such a wonderful origin) are not true and that the
Scriptures alone are the true Word of God. It is forgotten that science may
well indicate the wonder, but can not make faith more "acceptable".

4. SIMILAR PROBLEMS IN REFORMED APOLOGETICS

This brings us from the territory of General Canonics to that of Apologetics where there is the same grappling with the faith - and - knowledge problem.

The view still exists today that Apologetics is the scientific defence of
the Christian faith.

Just as in the case of General Canonics the Apologetic approach begins in
doubt (in this case, that of the unbeliever) and attempts to arrive at faith
from doubt (by means of science or reason). If doubt, however, is once

10. Ibid., p. 7.

11. Ibid.

12. I recently read with much interest — but in total disagreement with his viewpoint —
the article of R.L. Purtill: "Proofs of miracles and miracles as proofs". *Christian Scholars Review*, 6(1):39-51, 1976.
Why I personally cannot agree with him will be clear from my essay: "Thomas Aquinas' idea about wonders: a critical appraisal". (Essay no. 9 in this volume)

allowed faith will never be attained — faith completely excludes all doubt!

According to S.P. van der Walt it is not the task of Christian Apologetics to prove Christian truths to the opponent, but to unmask the unfounded nature of his attacks[13]. The question is *for whom* the unfounded nature of the attacks of the opponent must be unmasked: for the opponent himself or for the believing Christian? To expose it for the believing Christian has no sense because his faith has no need for this. To expose the unfounded nature of the attacks of opponents of Christian truth for the opponents themselves gains nothing if they are not convinced of the truth of Christendom!

It will not help to prove the untenable nature of their own point of view to the opponents of Christian faith on the intellectual plain by, for example, paying attention to the antinomies and the impracticalities of their viewpoints. The reason for this is that the contest for the Truth does not take place on the intellectual level. It concerns the opposition and unbelief of the heart. The intellectual objections of the unbeliever often only camouflage the deep and profound offence to the Truth. Therefore no-one will be able to persuade a person who rejects the Word by means of rational arguments. (Only the Holy Spirit, who changes the *heart*, is capable of this task.)

The danger here is also that an attempt is made to support the Word of God with weak human arguments. If these arguments totter (because the unbeliever lays bare the believer's arguments with stronger counter-arguments) then the invincible Word is also believed to totter!

This has led some to think that Apologetics can prove in a scientific way to the believing Christian, the unfounded nature of the unbeliever's attacks on the Christian faith. The basic fault remains just the same and similar to the fault of those who contend that the task of General Canonics is not to prove from the *outset* that the Bible is God's Word in order that we can believe in it but rather to prove *subsequently* that the Bible is God's Word; that is to say, *after* we have already believed in it.

5. A RATIONALLY PROVED FAITH?

Really the question now is whether the science of General Canonics is not a meaningless activity. Certainly it is clear that there is not much difference in an attempt to find *a priori* (prior) or *aposteriori* (subsequent) scientific proofs for faith. In fact it remains the old faith-knowledge dilemma, which also shows this characteristic throughout history that the empha-

---

13. Cf. Van der Walt, S.P.: "Apologetiek — 'n spraakverwarring?" *Perspektief*, 3(2/3): 33, 1964.

sis is shifted from faith to reason. Sometimes the primacy of faith is stressed and then again reason is emphasized[14]. Here we have a case where the emphasis is placed on faith first and reason is required afterwards.

Whether faith comes first, and is then followed by reason, or vice versa, it remains a false problem. If faith must afterwards be rationally or scientifically proved, it means after all a disqualification of faith. Faith alone *(sola gratia)* is regarded as incomplete and is placed in doubt when without reason.

It makes one think of the tendency in some books about Biblical Archaeology to conclude that the Bible is true because of the results of diggings![15].

6. OTHER CRITERIA?

It is not necessary to discuss further arguments such as, for example, the one that our faith really is not a blind faith, or that we must examine with open eyes. (Belief without reason is regarded as blindness.)

The Christian faith really is not blind or uncertain and no proof (reason) is necessary: "Now faith is the substance of things hoped for, the *evidence* of things not seen". (Heb. 11:1).

We do not mean hereby that *faith* (in place of *reason)* now becomes a criterion for the reliability of Scripture! The criterion for the truth of God's Word is neither human faith nor fallible human knowledge. In both cases the Word of God would be subjected to the yardstick of man!

If the canon (Scripture) is judged, it is no longer the canon! Then man himself, or his science, becomes the canon or yardstick. The canon demands unmitigated subjection. When God speaks I keep quiet and I do not ask if He really has spoken. If the question is brought up by a person: "How do I know that the Bible is God's Word?" then the question itself contains its own condemnation.

First obedience, absolute subjection and then you know by faith that the Bible is God's Word. (Not that obedience is now taken to be "proof"!)

7. SELF-EVIDENCE?

In closing we must show that General Canonics is also at fault if it asserts

14. Cf. my above-mentioned dissertation where the problem of reason and faith is discussed at various places.

15. Cf. the title of W. Keller's book: *Und die Bibel had doch Recht!*

that the Bible is God's Word because it *bears witness to itself*. It is especially S. Grijdanus who in his *Schriftgeloof en Kanoniek* approached this problem from the side of the autopistic character (reliability based on its own evidence) of Scripture. Scripture is like a diamond: it sparkles so that a person cannot doubt that it really is a diamond!

J.D. du Toit says, inter alia: Our point of departure is the self-witness of Holy Scripture. The proper witness for the divine inspiration of Scripture is the testimony that the *Scripture itself gives*, namely, that it is God's Word. It *is* and *remains* the Word of God even if not a single person accepts this testimony. A diamond *is*, due to its internal structure, a diamond, and it remains a diamond even if it lies in the earth for thousands of years[16].

Other images are also used: We recognise the Bible as God's Word because of the light that shines out of it. How does the lamb know from its first day that its mother is its mother? Simply because it is its mother!

How do I know that the voice of my father, which comes hundreds and thousands of miles over telephone or radio, is my father speaking? I do not need proof. I also cannot check it at that precise moment because I cannot be here and there at the same time[17].

Initially it looks as though this approach provides a solution. But, because it arises from a false problem, it also seeks, in the final analysis, for a guarantee for the truth of the Truth — although it is then within the Truth itself! The "truth of the Truth" in this case is also dependent on the *human* proofs of the Word of God.

Behind the search for the criterion lies the search for the law or norm. And therefore the search for the law of the Word of God lies in the problem of General Canonics as described above. Whether this law is sought in something outside the Word of God or in the Word itself, it remains equally wrong. The Word of God is, like God Himself, exalted above every law. God cannot be His own law and His Word also cannot be its own law.

We thus absolutely reject the idea of the self-evidence of Scripture because behind it lies a false criterion-search. Here the Word of God is subjected to a law and as a result the Speaker of the Word (God Himself) is also made submissive to the law!

The basic fault is that God is first separated from His Word and that science or reason must subsequently prove it nonetheless to be the Word of

---

16. Du Toit: *Die Bybel is die Woord van God,* p. 14.

17. Ibid., p. 18. Cf. in this connection Calvin's ideas in Chapter 7 of his *Institutes:* "For the Scripture exhibits as clear evidence of its truth, as white and black things do of their colour, or sweet and bitter things of their taste." In Chapter 8 he repeats that Scripture is self-authenticated, carrying its own evidence and ought not to be made the subject of demonstration and arguments from reason.

God[18].

8. THE OTHER SIDE OF THE COIN

The argumentation of the preceding pages has emphasized only one side of the problem. It was done on purpose in order to make my point clear and to be able to indicate possible wrong tracks in the disciplines of Canonics and Apologetics. On second consideration the following should be conceded.

The question of General Canonics, viz. why exactly these books and these alone are the Word of God, can be a legitimate issue. The condition, however, is that this problem should not be approached in a rationalistic way. Human reason and theological science cannot give the final decision. Also the fact that Scripture itself testifies about its divine nature is important. (Many New Testament authors, e.g. Paul, show how the Old Testament prophecies have been fulfilled.) My critical remarks merely warned against possible pitfalls.

As far as Apologetics is concerned, rational arguments are not devoid of any value. Such arguments may, for instance, help to remove misapprehensions about Christian faith in general and the Bible in particular. In this sense it may help to pave the way towards belief.

We cannot and should not separate (rational) knowledge and faith. Belief also has a rational side. True faith is not only a firm confidence which the Holy Spirit works in the heart through the Gospel, but also a sure knowledge (*Heidelberg Catechism*, answer 21). The intention of this article was not to advocate an antithesis between faith and reason or to propagate over against a rationalistic a fideistic approach.

18. K.J. Popma correctly states in his article "Schriftbeschouwing en Schriftprobleem." *Correspondentiebladen van de Vereniging voor Calvinistische Wijsbegeerte,* 14(1):25, January 1951: "Ook de overweging: indien de Bijbel Gods Woord is, kan niemand mij dat met Goddelijk gezag verzekeren dan de Bijbel zelf, daar hij immers de enige instantie kan zijn waarmee God tot ons spreekt — ook die oorweging is, al bevat ze veel goeds, niet helemaal te vertrouwen. Want het begint met dat scholastieke 'indien'. En dat laat een achterdeur open, onverschillig of ik van die open deur gebruik wil maken om weg te komen of niet. Want 'indien de Bijbel Gods Woord is' stelt de zaak op hypothetisch plan. Het heeft geen waarborg voor het geval de Bijbel nu eens niet Gods Woord zou zijn. Ik kan in dat geval niet zeggen: en indien de Bijbel Gods Woord niet is, mag het er ook niet in staan dat hij dit wél is."
We should also pay attention to the other danger Popma signals: "... dat het niet redelijk zou zijn aan de Schrift zelf te vragen wat zij is. Want het getuigenis dat iemand omtrent zich zelf geeft, is niet geldig. De redenering: 'De Bijbel is Gods onfeilbaar Woord, want het staat er in' maakt op menigeen een komischen indruk. Terecht?"